# Administr

## NVQ Level 3

Second edition

Lynda Bourne and
Pamela Scott

RECOGNISED TRAINING ORGANISATION

28, Greencastle Street, Kilkeel
Tel. :- (06937) 64362

London · Hong Kong · Johannesburg · Melbourne
Singapore · Washington DC

PITMAN PUBLISHING
128 Long Acre, London WC2E 9AN
Telephone: +44 (0)171 447 2000
Facsimile: +44 (0)171 240 5771

A Division of Longman Group Limited

First published in Great Britain 1993
**Second edition published 1996**

© Pearson Professional Limited 1996

*British Library Cataloguing in Publication Data*
A CIP catalogue record for this book is available
on request from the British Library.

ISBN 0–273–60620–4

10  9  8  7  6  5  4  3  2  1

Typeset by ↗\ Tek-Art, Croydon, Surrey
Printed and bound in Great Britain by Bell and Bain Ltd, Glasgow


*The Publishers' policy is to use paper manufactured
from sustainable forests.*

# CONTENTS

# Contents

# INTRODUCTION

This book has been designed to help you collect the correct evidence in order to gain NVQ Level 3 Administration. The information contained in the book covers the knowledge and understanding required and provides **Do-It-Yourself** tasks which, when completed, generate evidence that can be used to claim credit against the performance criteria and range. Take your time to read through the book and use the information it contains to help you complete the relevant DIYs.

Administration NVQ Level 3 is divided into 15 different units. The units are divided into different elements: some units have 2 elements, others have 3. Units 1–8 are core units and must be completed. Units 9–15 are optional units. To gain a full NVQ you must gain all 8 core units and one optional unit of your choice.

You do not have to work through the units in any particular order, but it is advised that Unit 1 is completed as early on as possible as it contains record sheets and advice that will help in the completion of further units. Unit 8 contains information on setting up systems and procedures and therefore should also be started as soon as possible. If you are unable to complete all units a unit certificate can be claimed for the units in which you have proven competence by providing all the necessary evidence.

The award of an NVQ is dependent upon your assessor being satisfied that you have provided sufficient evidence of competence across all the performance criteria and range. Evidence is sufficient when the assessor feels able to judge your competence against the national standard beyond reasonable doubt.

Evidence drawn from your day-to-day work is crucial and your assessor(s) should make maximum use of opportunities to make themselves aware of your performance. Evidence needs to be recorded, referenced and assessed against individual elements/outcomes, but remember that one piece of evidence will often cover several elements/outcomes.

In some cases questioning in the workplace will be an effective and appropriate way of assessing your knowledge and understanding; in other cases oral or written tests and examinations provide a suitable means. However, it must be remembered at all times that work-based evidence is the primary source of evidence and should be used wherever possible.

### Introduction

If you have already gained knowledge through experience an APL (Accreditation of Prior Learning) approach may be suitable. You and your assessor will need to judge the best mix of knowledge and understanding evidence according to your own personal circumstances.

# ■ Accreditation of prior learning

APL allows you to use your past experience to show that you are competent. Things that you have done in the past can be used as evidence against a particular element to show that you have met a competence standard. However, you must still prove that your competence is 'current' and that you are able to repeat today a competence demonstrated months or years ago.

Your APL assessor will discuss with you the means by which you are to prove that you are still competent. This may involve a one-off assessment, question and answer session and/or a written testimonial from you and/or employers, customers, suppliers and other people in authority who will testify your level of competence. Your APL assessor should possess a D36 assessor's award.

APL recognises that you have learnt through previous experience and does not expect you to be part of a formal training programme in order to prove competence. The APL process accepts that people learn through experience in the same way as they acquire ability through a traditional learning programme. You are able to use APL for individual units and elements of the award, or as a means to a full award provided you have the required experience and can provide relevant evidence such as that already detailed above.

In order to gain credit using the APL process you must still complete personal action plans and an evidence portfolio. There must also be a personal summary statement stating what you have done to prove competence.

If you are in, or have recently left, work of a relevant nature it is likely that you will have already shown competence in some of the performance criteria and range for some or all of the units.

# ■ Sources of evidence

Your evidence can come directly from your own work performance or indirectly from other people who have observed your performance.

Direct evidence is the best as it is evidence of what you have done and helps assessors to judge your outcomes against performance criteria – it demonstrates that a certain level of performance has been achieved. Performance evidence can be achieved through direct observation by an assessor. This assessor must be trained and hold a D32 Assessor's Award.

The assessor should work to an assessment plan that allows them to monitor your actions against the performance criteria and range statements. The assessment plan is essential as the performance evidence must be documented if it is to be placed in your portfolio. Supplementary evidence such as questioning and testing may also be used to support observation of work.

Work examples such as letters, memos, log books, computer/financial data, reports, documents, etc, can be used to demonstrate clearly the results from your actions. Direct observation of a piece of work or general observation over a period of time can also be used. However, this must be supported by a testimonial from the observer stating that you have achieved the standard of performance required.

Simulation can be used to fill in the gaps. This means that you must use actual work-based evidence whenever possible, but as it will not always be possible to do this, it is acceptable to carry out a simulation that shows you can perform to the required standard. Work such as assignments, case studies, projects, exercises, activity tasks and skills tests can be used for this, but always remember that work-based evidence is classed as a primary source and should be used wherever possible.

# ■ Portfolio development

As you progress through your qualification you will see that you can help your assessor by presenting clear, organised, documented evidence. Your portfolio should be organised in unit and element order (dividers are good for this), with the use of clear, descriptive statements that explain what you have done and which put the work completed into its proper context.

Cross-referencing should be used when evidence in one unit or element is relevant to another, but make sure this is logically sequenced so as not to cause confusion. The evidence may be presented in a separate folder suitably referenced. Always be on the look-out for evidence that can be cross-referenced as this will help you to reduce your workload and makes efficient use of evidence.

Your claim to competence must be completed with your own account of what you have done to prove that you are competent: there is one record for each element of the award. These records must be completed by you with a personal summary statement stating what you have done: this must be supported by relevant evidence. You will find a sample statement at the end of each element, but do not be tempted to merely copy this; use it only as an example and produce your own personal account of what you have done.

You should also include in your portfolio an up-to-date curriculum vitae that summarises your personal background – this is particularly useful to the external verifier who knows nothing about you. You should also ensure that your portfolio contains sections that describe your organisation and personal responsibilities. Remember to include certificates that are relevant to the award and for which you may have claimed APL.

Perhaps the most important thing to remember is that you have produced your portfolio in order to gain a Level 3 award in Administration. This qualification consists of units that assess your ability as an 'administrator' which should be reflected by the quality of your evidence portfolio. Above all, your ability to present organised, well written, error-free evidence will be at a premium.

# ■ Recording your progress

The following Progress Chart shown in Fig 1 can be used to map your progress as you work through your Level 3 Administration Award.

The Progress Chart can be placed at the front of your evidence portfolio and can be used to record your progress. It is completed by you and signed when you have checked through your evidence and confirms that you wish to claim that you are competent in all the units that you have ticked. This will be checked by your assessor and signed to confirm that they agree with you.

Finally, the evidence must be checked by a person in the organisation acting as an Internal Verifier, and then signed. Your completed evidence portfolio is then checked by the awarding body's External Verifier who may ask you a number of questions to confirm your knowledge and understanding of certain units.

## NVQ LEVEL 3 ADMINISTRATION PROGRESS CHART

Name  . . . . . . . . . . . . . . . . . . . . . . . . . . . . . . . . . . . . . . . . . . . . . . . . . . . . .

(Tick + date in box = completion)

| Unit 1 | | Unit 2 | |
|---|---|---|---|
| 1.1 | 1.2 | 2.1 | 2.2 |
| | | | |

| Unit 3 | | | Unit 4 | |
|---|---|---|---|---|
| 3.1 | 3.2 | 3.3 | 4.1 | 4.2 |
| | | | | |

| Unit 5 | | Unit 6 | | |
|---|---|---|---|---|
| 5.1 | 5.2 | 6.1 | 6.2 | 6.3 |
| | | | | |

| Unit 7 | | Unit 8 | |
|---|---|---|---|
| 7.1 | 7.2 | 8.1 | 8.2 |
| | | | |

**Optional Units 9 – 15**

| Unit 9 | | Unit 10 | | |
|---|---|---|---|---|
| 9.1 | 9.2 | 10.1 | 10.2 | 10.3 |
| | | | | |

| Unit 11 | | | Unit 12 | |
|---|---|---|---|---|
| 11.1 | 11.2 | 11.3 | 12.1 | 12.2 |
| | | | | |

| Unit 13 | | Unit 14 | | Unit 15 | |
|---|---|---|---|---|---|
| 13.1 | 13.2 | 14.1 | 14.2 | 15.1 | 15.2 |
| | | | | | |

Final completion date  . . . . . . . . . . . . . Trainee's signature  . . . . . . . . . . . . . . .

Assessor's signature  . . . . . . . . . . . . . Internal Verifier's signature  . . . . . . . . . .

**Fig 1 Progress chart**

# ■ Element completion checklist

Use the Element completion checklist in Fig 2 to ensure that all performance criteria and range statements have been covered by your evidence. The completed form will help you to write a descriptive account of what you have done to prove that you are competent. It may also be used to complete the awarding body documentation. You do not have to tick every box 1–10 for either performance criteria or range, but remember that the majority of your evidence must be work-based.

Produce a copy of the form for each element, inserting the relevant number of sections for each of the performance criteria. Complete the form yourself by inserting the performance criteria and range statements. This will help you to understand what is required from you and to identify work that you have completed which is relevant to the element. Remember to look for opportunities to cross-reference your work within the element or across other units.

**NVQ LEVEL 3 ADMINISTRATION**
**Element completion checklist**

| Unit number: Element number: | | | | | | | | | | |
|---|---|---|---|---|---|---|---|---|---|---|
| | Types of evidence submitted for verification | | | | | | | | | |
| Performance criteria and range statements | 1 | 2 | 3 | 4 | 5 | 6 | 7 | 8 | 9 | 10 |
| 1 | | | | | | | | | | |
| 2 | | | | | | | | | | |
| 3 | | | | | | | | | | |
| 4 | | | | | | | | | | |
| 5 (insert more sections for elements with more than 5 performance criteria) | | | | | | | | | | |
| Range – When completing the above criteria, how have you covered them? | | | | | | | | | | |

**Evidence key:**
**1** Assessor's observation of performance. **2** Action plans. **3** Records or log book (eg visitors/telephone). **4** Work examples, documentation (eg memos, letters). **5** Testimony from line manager or clients. **6** Testimony from colleagues or other staff. **7** Personal report of actions and circumstances. **8** Question and answer sessions (written or verbal). **9** APL/A evidence. **10** Work assignments or projects.

**Fig 2 Element completion checklist**

# ACKNOWLEDGEMENTS

During the writing of this book we have had the support of company representatives, colleagues at BPCFE and friends, and we thank them for their assistance.

We would especially like to thank Jerry, Pete, Kris, Carly, Natalie, Leila and Perri for their patience and assistance.

We should also like to thank the following for permission to reproduce forms and documents:

Acco-Rexel Limited
British Telecommunications plc
Canon (UK) Ltd
The Leisure and Community Services Department, London Borough of Bromley
The Controller of Her Majesty's Stationery Office
The Department for Education and Employment
M Flanagan
IBM United Kingdom Limited
R B Jackson
Kodak Ltd
Philips Dictation Systems, Philips Electronics UK Limited
The Royal Society for the Prevention of Accidents (RoSPA)
J Sierra
WordPerfect Corporation

# UNIT 1

# Contribute to the improvement of performance

■ ## Element 1.1
## DEVELOP SELF TO ENHANCE PERFORMANCE

### Performance criteria

**1** Own development needs are identified against current work activities and career potential

**2** Own development objectives are defined and, where necessary, agreed with appropriate persons

**3** Identified development opportunities are realistic and achievable in terms of resources and support from relevant persons

**4** Performance and progress are reviewed and evaluated appropriately

### Element introduction

This element is about helping you to recognise and plan your personal development. To make the most of yourself and your working life you must learn how to manage your own personal development; you must identify what you want to achieve and how to achieve it if you are to be successful. It is of no use waiting for others to help you achieve your personal and professional goals if you are unable to identify your own needs as a starting point.

You must plan, monitor and control your career path by constantly assessing, reviewing and recording your development. Remember that development is a life-long process that is important not only in work but also in life itself. If you become competent at managing your work, this will help you to identify and achieve what you want from life.

It is important for you to understand that you can learn something every day, and it is only through such learning that individuals and organisations prosper. Success depends on having the right people with the right skills doing the job most suited to them. This is why there must be a

1

commitment by you, the people that manage your progress and the government itself to ensure that training and development is a continuous process that is available throughout your working life.

## ▶ *Setting yourself goals*

Your career is based on how well you do a particular job and your ability to identify and prepare for future roles. In order to do this, you must continually review your development needs in light of new opportunities and personal goals.

Your goals will be related to your personal and professional life and can be measured as short-, medium- and long-term goals.

- Short-term goals are those that you wish to have accomplished within the next few weeks or months.
- Medium-term goals relate to things that you wish to have completed within a year.
- Long-term goals cover a period of one to five years.

Nothing in life stands still; you must constantly assess your achievements against the goals you have set yourself in order to decide upon your next set of goals.

## ▶ *Personal development needs*

Your personal development needs are governed by 3 factors as shown in Fig. 1.1:

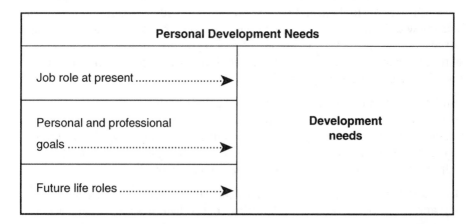

Fig 1.1 Personal development needs

# ■ DIY 1.1.1

Copy the development needs self-assessment sheet in Fig 1.2 and, in your own words, complete the empty boxes. You may wish to discuss each part with your line manager or a colleague. Try to insert as much information as possible, because this will help you to complete the last section of the sheet.

## ▶ *Personal development record keeping*

To complete the above activity you would have had to take into account your prior and/or current achievements.

Think about how you did this.

Did you use your Record of Achievement or Curriculum Vitae or did you rely on memory?

In order to identify your development needs you must have readily at hand all the relevant information. If you rely solely on remembering your achievements you will, without doubt, forget some of them. You should be building upon your life experiences and achievements and can only do this if you have recorded your progress in a logical and clear way.

Your prior and current achievements will reflect how you have responded to the need for change in both your personal and professional life. It is likely that you have set yourself goals, the success or failure of which has ultimately affected the next stage in your personal and career development. Once you have achieved a goal it is very easy to under-value or forget the process that you have been through in order to achieve that goal. This is why it is so very important to record your achievements in a logically sequenced, concise but descriptive manner. Using a Record of Achievement or Curriculum Vitae (CV) is a sure way of doing this. Figure 1.3 shows a good example of a CV.

# ■ DIY 1.1.2

Prepare a Curriculum Vitae for yourself that lists:

- personal details
- education/training
- qualifications
- work experience
- personal statement (this should be a positive statement about yourself that details your personal qualities, aptitudes and goals in life)
- references

| DEVELOPMENT NEEDS SELF-ASSESSMENT SHEET | | |
|---|---|---|
| My job/training role at present is: | My personal goals are:<br><br>Short-term<br><br><br><br><br>Medium-term<br><br><br><br>Long-term | My professional goals are:<br><br>Short-term<br><br><br><br><br>Medium-term<br><br><br><br>Long-term |
| My future life goals are: | | |
| My development needs at present are: | | |

**Fig 1.2 A development needs self-assessment sheet**

```
Curriculum Vitae

Name              Margaret Mary FUDGE
Address           88 Western Avenue, Dartford, Kent DA1 4JJ
Telephone         013344 6657
Date of birth     5 January 1968  Age    25 years
School            Ashurst High, Bromley Road, Sidcup
Qualifications    GCSE – Typewriting, Biology, Home Economics,
                  French, Mathematics, English – Grades B-D
                  RSA – Typewriting Stage 2, Shorthand 80 wpm
College           Henley College, Sidcup (day release)
Qualifications    RSA – Typewriting Stage 3, Shorthand 100 wpm
```

**WORK EXPERIENCE**

**De Verney Hotel, Lewisham** (1988–1994)
Secretary to General Manager, later promoted to Personnel
Officer. Dealing with staff training and recruitment.

**Carlton Cars, Blackheath** (1983–1987)
Office Administration dealing with sales and related
documentation. Duties included bookkeeping and banking
responsibilities.

**Hobbies**
Playing netball in local league. Fully qualified netball
umpire. Walking, reading and cinema. Secretary of Drama Club.

**Personal Statement**
I am a fit and healthy person who enjoys working with the
public. I have an outgoing personality and relate well to
others. I have gained secretarial qualifications at college and
I am currently attending word processing evening classes. I am
ambitious, hard-working and dependable. I would like to
broaden my career by taking on a more challenging position
where I can put my organisational and communication skills to
greater use.

**References**
Mr J B Peasbody, Carlton Cars, Manor Road, Blackheath
Telephone: 0181-778 8576

Mrs Bushard, De Verney Hotel, Trafford Way, Lewisham
Telephone: 0181-477 7380

**Fig 1.3 Example of a Curriculum Vitae**

Think about whether this activity has made you change your mind about your development needs detailed in DIY 1.1.1.

## ▶ *Records of achievement*

Records of achievement and profiling were mentioned earlier as a means by which a record of your achievements could be discussed and recorded. Part of your training at school or college will probably be recording your achievement. You will usually have a Record of Achievement issued by your trainer in which you write all the qualifications and experience you have gained while training. This should be the start of your record of self development which should be added to when you achieve further qualifications or carry out more training.

One of the first things to do will be to update your Record of Achievement. If you have gained a new qualification then the certificate, or a copy, should be placed in your record and your Curriculum Vitae updated. If you have attended a training course or learnt a new skill, a statement from you, signed by your trainer, line manager or assessor, would be a suitable document to put in your record. Always include the dates of training on your record, as this will ensure it is accurate and up to date. Later it may be difficult to remember exactly what you did and when.

Your Record of Achievement should not contain any spelling errors, as you may wish to use it at interviews. The way in which you organise your record will reflect the type of person you are: a record with documents and certificates falling out, or with dirty and torn statements, will not impress an employer. A Record of Achievement should be something you are proud to show and can be used by everyone regardless of age or level of award.

## ▶ *NVQ assessment*

The NVQ assessment system checks that you are able to meet the standards required by the Awarding Body and the National Council (NCVQ). To do this you will be required to present evidence based upon assessment carried out in the workplace or training centre. The assessment carried out by your assessor will verify that you are able to do a task in accordance with the performance criteria and range statements detailed in your NVQ folder or book. You must prove that you have met all criteria and covered the full range before you may be judged as competent.

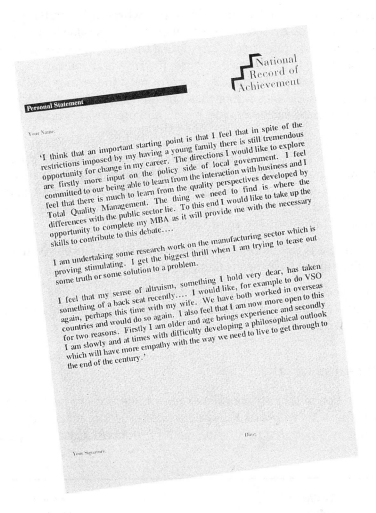

**Fig 1.4 A page from a National Record of Achievement**

The NRA was introduced in 1991 to be the single, national record for recording achievement and planning individual development throughout life. It has two purposes:

1 to act as a record of achievement for the individual. In this sense the NRA is a "presentational tool" for use in preparing applications for continuing education, work and training, and in selection and recruitment; and

2 through the processes of reviewing and recording achievement and action planning, to help the individual to gain the ability needed to determine and plan future development.

(Photograph courtesy of the Department for Education and Employment.)

NVQ assessment is based on what you know, what you do and how you do it. You must provide evidence that you have the knowledge and understanding required prior to attempting the task. The task itself must then be assessed, to a national standard, to prove that you can put into practice what you have learnt. The assessor must judge your ability to perform whole work roles rather than one-off tasks and this in itself leads to continuous assessment of achievement and progress towards a national qualification.

Assessment can be carried out in a number of different ways. Figure 1.5 shows how your autonomy is affected by the different methods that can be used. The word autonomy relates to your own independence; in your training environment it means that you take some, or all, of the responsibility for identifying your training needs.

Self-assessment is therefore often used as a method to involve you in actually identifying your own training needs.

Collaborative assessment should then be carried out so that an opportunity exists for you to discuss the needs you have identified with your line manager, trainer or assessor.

## ▶ Self-assessment

In order for you to identify your development needs you must be able to evaluate your achievements. You will use assessment to make judgements about your own performance. Assessment of your performance can be

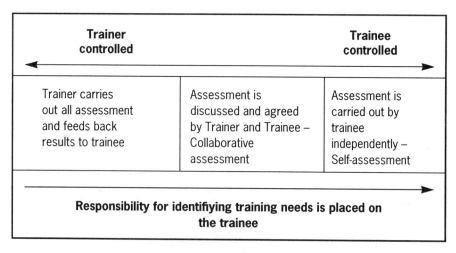

Fig 1.5 Responsibility for identifying training needs

undertaken using written, oral and competence-based assessment. Written and oral testing proves your academic ability, while competence-based assessment proves that you are able to do a particular task or job. A good CV or Record of Achievement will show a combination of both academic and practical ability.

It would be foolish to expect a trainee to progress through their NVQ without help and guidance. But it is important to remember that the trainee must be encouraged to take responsibility for their training. Self-assessment allows you, the trainee, to set your own goals, monitor your progress and judge the final outcome. It encourages a more active interest and helps you to understand reasons for your own training performance.

You will use your self-assessment skills to plan your development needs. The outcome of your self-assessment will indicate positive areas of your work or life together with the less positive areas for which you may need to seek advice, guidance and/or support. Areas of need, once identified, must be discussed with your line manager, trainer or assessor so that a training plan can be negotiated between you.

## ■ DIY 1.1.3

Self-assessment is often discussed as an aspect of Staff Appraisal, Records of Achievement or 'profiling'. It should be used: to help you reflect and evaluate your performance; to provide information to let others know your feelings and points of view about your training; and as a result of this to enhance your motivation, and support your self-development.

This is quite a tall order. But for the purpose of this activity:

Have a go at writing a statement about your training needs that gives details of the units and elements completed to date and how you feel you should progress in order to complete your final award successfully. There is no set format provided for this, but try to fill a sheet of A4 paper with your statement.

### ▶ *Action planning*

Many companies are taking training more seriously than in the past and are introducing action plans to their staff. Action planning and training has the advantage of ensuring that the employees cover everything they need and want to know. They are taught how to carry out tasks properly, and this usually means more efficiently, therefore saving time. Action planning has become widely used as a method of planning what you and your company need to do to ensure you receive the right kind of training.

An action plan may be short, medium or long term, or include all 3. A short-term plan may cover the areas of training needed in the next few weeks or months, medium-term up to 1 year and long-term 1–5 years. Once written the action plan may need to be reviewed to take into account changes in your circumstances. When writing your short-term action plan you will need to think about:

1 What you want to achieve in the next few weeks.
2 What you need to know and be able to do to achieve your aim.
3 Who you need to contact and what equipment and materials you will need.
4 What time you will have to commit to your plan and what arrangements need to be made.

Once you have a skeleton plan you can start to break it down into sections. For instance you may look through the units of the qualification and identify which ones you can carry out quite quickly, with only a little training – because you are already doing those particular jobs at work. You will also be able to identify those units and elements which are best covered at work or in a training centre.

## ■ DIY 1.1.4

Complete a short-term action plan for one of the units or elements in Administration that you have not yet completed. List what you need to know, the equipment you need to use and who can help you achieve this. There is no set format for this; just use a piece of A4 paper.

Most action plans will need updating on a regular basis because you and your circumstances change. You may change your job at work, move from the area, have an upset at home – literally anything may affect your action plan. When these changes occur you should update your action plan to take account of the changes. Discuss any problems with your line manager, trainer or assessor and make sure they are aware of your new action plan – especially if you are expecting them to help you.

Taking control of your career is about planning what you wish to achieve, organising resources and others around you in order to achieve your plan, taking action and then monitoring your progress. If things do not go exactly to plan, and it is unlikely that they will, your next job will be to decide upon the corrective action to take in order to achieve the goals you have negotiated and agreed with your line manager, trainer or assessor.

There will be a number of unforeseen circumstances that will affect your action plan. Although these things should not be seen as a setback, remember that many things in life do not go exactly as planned.

## ▶ *Appraisals*

Some companies and organisations have appraisal or review systems in place. These provide a regular review (usually once a year) of your progress that helps you and the organisation to identify where your future development may be. It is at this time that you will have an opportunity to identify any opportunities or training that you wish to follow. Do not be afraid to discuss your ambitions at an appraisal interview.

An appraisal interview is also an opportunity to identify any training and development needs that you feel are required to help you in your work. The company will be unlikely to be able to help everyone do everything but there is usually a system to ensure that the assistance given by the organisation is fairly distributed around the staff.

## ■ DIY 1.1.5

Draw up a medium-term (up to 1 year) action plan for yourself. Identify what achievements you would like to make, who and what are needed to assist you to meet these achievements. Again, no set format has been given; just use a piece of A4 paper.

## ▶ *Reviewing progress*

Your success will be based upon your ability to continually assess your progress, identify and resolve problem areas and make corrections that will get you back on course. This is why it is so important to work according to a negotiated action plan that is reviewed at regular intervals to assess your progress. Regular reviews provide an opportunity for you to discuss your plans with somebody who is interested in your progress. Your line manager, trainer or assessor is there to help you work through any obstacles you have encountered and identify possible solutions. Likewise, remember that other people such as your family, friends, work colleagues and other trainees can play a part in helping you to plan ahead for your future.

When reviewing progress the first step in the cycle is to complete an action plan that sets down the progress and achievement you wish to accomplish within a set period of time. The plan is not rigid, it is as flexible as you and your line manager, trainer or assessor wish it to be –

you are the people doing the negotiations and agreeing on the plan.

If you are being over-ambitious others are there to slow you down, and if you are being lazy they are there to help you speed up. The action plan should be signed by both of you to prove that it has been discussed and agreed by both parties.

It is normal practice for one formal review to be carried out each month, although this may vary from place to place. Your aims and objectives will be discussed and your progress compared against your long-term aim – in other words, the qualification(s) you wish to achieve at the end of your training plan. The outcome of each review will form the basis of your next action plan and will be written in terms of units and elements that have been completed.

## ▶ *Documenting your personal action planning*

A Personal Action Plan is a useful way of documenting decisions concerning your personal development. Look at the example in Fig 1.6. If you have already identified your own development needs, the negotiating procedure will be a two-way process with your line manager, trainer or assessor that takes into account your own personal feelings, achievements and aspirations. Remember that we have already said that it is of no use waiting for others to help you achieve your personal and professional goals if you are unable to identify your own needs as a starting point.

You must also remember that the development opportunities you identify must be realistic and achievable in terms of the resources and support available from other relevant people. Your line manager, trainer or assessor is unlikely to drop everything at short notice just because you wish to be assessed for a certain element; forward planning is therefore a must. Likewise, the organisation you work for is unlikely to invest in expensive, unnecessary equipment for assessment purposes and arrangements will have to be made for your assessment to take place elsewhere.

Perhaps the most important thing we can say about using resources efficiently is to remind you once again that one piece of evidence can be cross-referenced to cover a number of performance criteria, in the same or different units – always look for opportunities to use the same piece of evidence more than once.

The organisation that you work for may have an appraisal system in operation that allows you to carry out your own self-assessment prior to an appraisal interview with your line manager. A similar system may also be in operation within your training centre, where you are given the

| PERSONAL ACTION PLAN |
| --- |

Name ..................*Sally Simmons*.................Work Role ...*Supervisor*................

Period of training...*Feb '96 – Apr '96*.......................................................

### Part A – Self-assessment

| NVQ Elements/Units | Name of Unit | Completion date |
| --- | --- | --- |
| NVQ 3 – Units 1<br>2<br>3<br>4 | Improvement of perf.<br>H&S<br>Planning. org. etc.<br>Working rels. | |

Other goals I wish to achieve  *Complete CLAIT course and attend shorthand lessons so that NVQ 3 Unit 14 can be completed.*

### Part B – Action required

| By me | By my Assessor/Manager | By the organisation |
| --- | --- | --- |
| Complete skillscan for Units 1, 2, 3 & 4. Collect relevant evidence | Assess skillscan and advise re: APL. | Arrange day-release for CLAIT and shorthand lessons. |

### Part C – Agreement made
*Forms provided for U1 and H&S. Induction arranged to help with U2. Shorthand lessons not available until Jan. Start CLAIT now. See line manager re U1 & 2.*

Assessor's/Manager's signature....*P Scott*............. Date ...*1/2/96*...........

Trainee's signature.....*S Simmons*............................ Date ...*1/2/96*...........

Date and place of next review....*1/3/96   Rm 165*.................................

### Part D – Review

Trainee's review of progress  *Started to complete forms for U1. 1.1 OK. but 1.2 needs me to work with colleague, which has still not been arranged. U2 complete. U3 and U4 nearly done.*

Assessor's/Manager's review of progress  *All work checked. U2 signed off (U3 & 4 next week). Arrangements in hand for Level 1 trainee in same office. Start U5, 6 & 7.*

Assessor's/Manager's signature *P Scott*..................... Date........*1/3/96*...........

**Fig 1.6 An example of a completed Personal Action Plan**

opportunity to identify your own training needs prior to discussion with your trainer or assessor. This is often referred to as 'profiling' and should form an integral part of your training programme.

In either situation you must realise that this procedure has been set up to give you an opportunity to have an influence on your own work role and future – make sure you use it!

In order for your organisation to support your training and development needs, it is important for them and for you to ensure that your own needs match those of the organisation. Remember that training and development costs money and it is unlikely that an organisation will support your development plan if you have identified areas that do not complement your work role. Look for relevant methods of development that will enhance your own work role and will also make you a more valuable asset to the organisation. A Personal Action Plan will help you to do this.

The Personal Action Plan specifies the training, development and assessment that your organisation has agreed you follow as part of your work or training role. The plan must detail the programme of activities, training, work experience, projects, assignments and simulations necessary for you to fulfil the performance standards set by the organisation.

Your Personal Action Plan is used to detail 4 major areas:

- Your **development needs** based on your own self-assessment and the outcome of your previous plan.

- **Comments** made by your line manager, trainer or assessor during a two-way discussion.

- The **agreement** you have reached regarding your future development needs and how these will be implemented.

- Self-assessment and **review** at a set future date, discussed with your line manager, trainer or assessor, resulting in an agreed review of progress and assessment of performance.

Your NVQ is broken down into units and elements that cover a discrete part of your work activities and it is your responsibility to identify the units and elements that can be carried out in the workplace. Use your Personal Action Plan to detail the unit and element numbers for which you wish to prove competence during the period of time covered by the plan. You should also include details of other goals you wish to achieve. This information can then be used as a base upon which a formal interview can be carried out and your development needs discussed and agreed with a person in authority.

# ■ DIY 1.1.6

Use the following guidelines to help you fill in our example (Fig. 1.7) of a Personal Action Plan (or use an existing form if you have one). Ask your line manager, trainer or assessor if they will complete the bottom section of the plan after they have discussed it with you.

## ▶ *Guidelines*

### Part A – Self-assessment

- Insert your name, work role and the period of training to which your plan relates.
- Insert the unit or element numbers you wish to achieve during this period of time. Also include other details of goals you wish to achieve during this time.
- Leave the date column blank as this will be completed when each area of development has been achieved.

### Part B – Action required

- List the actions that you, your trainer, line manager or assessor and your organisation will have to take to ensure your action plan is achieved. This may include work activities, projects, assignments, training, discussions, self-study, simulations, etc, as well as named personnel, dates, resources and equipment needed.

### Part C – Agreement made

- You must now discuss your entries with your trainer, line manager or assessor and they must complete the next section of your plan. This will provide an opportunity for you to discuss your needs and agree a plan of action that is acceptable to you and the organisation.
- You must both sign the plan to confirm that it has been agreed and that both you and your trainer, line manager or assessor will work towards your success.
- You should also agree a date and place for your next review and put details of this on the plan. However, intermittent reviews should be arranged to check progress and identify any problems.

### Part D – Review

- The last part of the plan is left to the end of the training period when you can self-assess your progress. Complete this section before attending your review. Discuss your progress with your line manager,

**PERSONAL ACTION PLAN**

Name ...............................................Work role .................................................

Period of training ...................................................................................

**Part A – Self-assessment**

| NVQ Elements/Units | Name of Unit | Completion date |
|---|---|---|
| | | |

Other goals I wish to achieve

**Part B – Action required by**

| Me | Assessor/Manager | The organisation |
|---|---|---|
| | | |

**Part C – Agreement made**

Assessor's/Manager's signature ................................... Date ...................

Trainee's signature ...................................................... Date ...................

Date and place of next review...........................................................................

**Part D – Review**

Trainee's review of progress

Assessor's/Manager's review of progress

Assessor's/Manager's signature ................................... Date ...................

**Fig 1.7 A blank Personal Action Plan form, for use in DIY 1.1.6.**

trainer or assessor, who will in turn write an account of your progress to date. This information forms the basis of your next Personal Action Plan.

You must now be aware that there is no one with more interest in your career than you. If you wish to succeed, you must treat the learning process as your own responsibility and seek out the opportunities and people who can help you. Your line manager, trainer and assessor are all people who are employed to assist you in your role as worker, trainee or both.

## Knowledge and understanding question bank

1 Describe your own work role and responsibilities.
2 How do you go about identifying your own development needs?
3 How do you set self-development objectives?
4 How do you use training, discussions and self-study of relevant materials in your development?
5 What resource implications need to be taken into account when identifying your development opportunities?
6 How do you go about implementing your development activities?
7 How do you assess your performance and progress?
8 How do you evaluate and review your progress by yourself?
9 How do you evaluate and review your progress in conjunction with others?
10 How do you record your achievements?

## Claiming credit

For Element 1.1 records must prove that you have sought development through training, discussions and self-study of relevant material. You must show that you have reviewed and evaluated your own performance and progress through self-assessment and in conjunction with others such as your line manager. The following work products are potential sources of evidence:

- self-assessment notes
- records of discussions
- development objectives statements
- listing of development activities
- records of achievement
- notes relating to evaluation of your progress.

Once you have completed your final assessment, you will need to write in your record book or folder how, when and what you have done to prove that you are competent.

The following statement is an example of how one trainee completed this claim:

*As part of my training programme at Coopers & Co I have attended monthly reviews with my line manager. Prior to my review I complete a self-assessment plan where I detail all of my achievements compared against the action plan from the last review. I used my CV and Record of Achievement to provide me with the information I needed to start my first personal action plan. This helped my line manager and me to match my needs against those of the organisation. The action plan related to my current work activities and took into account my development needs and career potential. I have attended training sessions 1 day each week and take part in discussions with my line manager, assessor and tutor. I have also used open learning packs for 2 of the units.*

# ■ Element 1.2
# CONTRIBUTE TO IMPROVING THE PERFORMANCE OF COLLEAGUES

### Performance criteria

1 Own contribution to the development of colleagues accurately reflects their needs
2 Contributions to training and development activities for colleagues are in accordance with agreed methods and objectives, and take into account existing levels of competence of the individual
3 Agreed support is provided on time
4 Feedback on the progress of development activities is provided promptly and accurately to appropriate persons
5 Training and development activities comply with legal and regulatory requirements and organisational procedures

### Element introduction

This element is about helping others to prove competence in their work role. Your role is to contribute to their training and development according to agreed methods and the level of their competence. You must be able to provide support and feedback on progress to both your trainee and other appropriate persons such as their training co-ordinator or line manager. For the purpose of this element we have used the term trainee to describe the person undergoing assessment. Your role is described as the supervisor, although if you hold the D32 and D33 assessor's awards your real title would be that of assessor.

In order to complete this element you must show that you have contributed to your trainee's development through:

● identifying their training needs

- organising specific work assignments
- providing direct training activities
- advising
- coaching

This element has been based upon the delivery and assessment of NVQs (National Vocational Qualifications), although the actual development of the trainee may require some other form of training, development and/or qualification. NVQs are competence based and therefore rely heavily on observation in the workplace by qualified assessors. The NVQ itself is designed by members of a **Lead Body** who research and identify the needs of the relevant industry and design the NVQ performance criteria around their findings. The **Awarding Bodies** design their qualifications in accordance with the Lead Body's findings and submit their proposal for Lead Body approval.

These 2 bodies are explained further:

## Lead Bodies

NVQ awards are based on the requirements of industry. There are various Lead Bodies that have been set up for different sectors of employment and it is these bodies that decide upon the content of NVQ awards. The Qualifications and Standards Branch of the Employment Department keeps a list of all Lead Bodies together with a contact name.

The list can be obtained by writing to:

- Mr D Wright, Qualifications and Standards Branch, Room W736, Moorfoot, Sheffield, S1 4PQ. Telephone: 0174 259 4888.

The Administration Lead Body, which covers administration and secretarial awards, can be contacted through:

- Ms Imogen Hobbs, Secretary, Administration Lead Body, The Institute of Chartered Secretaries and Administrators, 16 Park Crescent, London, W1N 4AH. Telephone: 0171 580 4741.

Local government, office skills and post office counters also come under this body.

The Lead Bodies design national standards relevant to the requirements of industry. These national standards are produced as units and elements which are supported by the performance criteria and range statements that are found in the NVQ folder or book.

The actual qualification is designed by the Awarding Body and checked by the National Council for Vocational Qualifications before it is given its NCVQ stamp of approval.

## Awarding Bodies

The Awarding Body for each vocational area has the job of taking the standards laid down by the Lead Body and making them into a qualification. The Awarding Body will then advertise and co-ordinate each award, making sure that quality standards are followed. A document called the 'common accord' sets out the way that all Awarding Bodies should operate in terms of quality control, terminology and so on, to make sure that standardisation is maintained across the Awarding Bodies.

There are over 300 Awarding Bodies in England and Wales. Scotland has its own separate system and is monitored by SCOTVEC (Scottish Vocational Education Council). The Awarding Bodies that you are most likely to be interested in are:

- BTEC (Business and Technology Education Council), Central House, Upper Woburn Place, London, WC1H 0HH. Telephone: 0171 413 8400.
- City and Guilds of London Institute, 46 Britannia Street, London, WC1X 9RG. Telephone: 0171 278 2468.
- London Chamber of Commerce and Industry Examinations Board, Marlowe House, Station Road, Sidcup, DA15 7BJ. Telephone: 0181 302 0261.
- Pitman Qualifications, 1 Giltspur Street, London EC1A 9DD. Telephone: 0171 294 2471.
- Royal Society of Arts Examinations Board, Progress Way, Westwood Way, Coventry, CV5 8HS. Telephone: 0120 347 0033.

The Awarding Bodies design schemes of training and assessment according to the national standards laid down by the Lead Bodies. These schemes are accredited by the NCVQ or SCOTVEC who keep an up-to-date database of all Awarding Bodies and the awards they offer. The following addresses may be of interest to you:

- National Council for Vocational Qualifications, 222 Euston Road, London, NW1 2BZ. Telephone: 0171 387 9898.

- Education and NVQ Unit, Training and Enterprise Agency, Clarendon House, 9–21 Adelaide Street, Belfast, BT2 8DJ. Telephone: 0123 289 5668.

- Scottish Vocational Education Council, Hanover House, 24 Douglas Street, Glasgow, G2 7NQ. Telephone: 0141 248 7900.

**Fig 1.8 The NVQ symbol**

## ▶ *Delivering NVQs*

The purpose of competence-based qualifications is to prove that the trainee is 'able to do' a specific task according to the level of competence required by industry. This requires competence-based assessment to establish that a trainee can perform consistently to the required standard in a workplace role.

This is achieved by:

- **planning** and agreeing how competence is to be demonstrated
- **collecting evidence** which meets the specified standards
- **assessing** the evidence against the standards
- giving **feedback** to the candidate which enables them to plan the next stage

This procedure is called the assessment cycle, as illustrated in Fig 1.9.

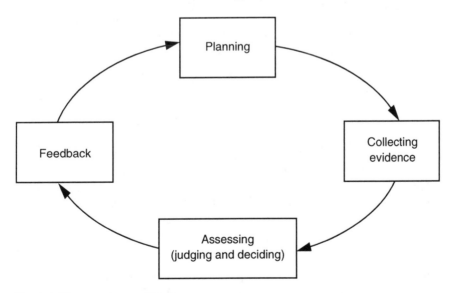

**Fig 1.9 The assessment cycle**

21

Before you can begin to agree an assessment plan you must familiarise yourself with the trainee's needs and training preferences. If the trainee wishes to complete an NVQ then it is vital that you have the relevant standards for your own use. You must pay particular attention to the evidence requirements stated in the standards.

Through discussion you and the trainee can consider the possible sources of evidence to be collected and whether evidence from past achievements is acceptable.

The next stage of the process is to meet with the trainee to agree:

- how and when **training** will take place
- the **evidence** to be presented for assessment
- the **method** of assessment
- **when** assessment will take place

However, before looking at NVQs more closely we need to spend some time considering the types and methods of training available. Not only is it important to discuss how and when training will take place; the actual training preferences of the trainee, related to opportunities available, need to be considered.

## ▶ Methods of delivering training

In order to deliver training successfully it is wise first to assess the training preferences of the person being trained. It is important that you recognise their preferred style of learning and that you understand the process and methods for the learning being used. We are all different and therefore it is obvious that different people will prefer different learning styles.

The 4 main styles are:

- **Experimental** – learning by experimenting, sampling and actually putting things into practice.
- **Reflective** – learning by listening and observing what is going on; thinking about what has been observed before making a decision.
- **Experiential** – learning as part of a group involved in a group exercise, where discussion and feedback from other members form part of the learning.
- **Theoretical** – learning through principles, models and theories using a scientific approach that analyses concepts.

The learning process must be supported by reviewing the outcome of the experience, learning from it and then applying it to new situations.

22

The process has 4 important aspects, as Fig 1.10 shows.

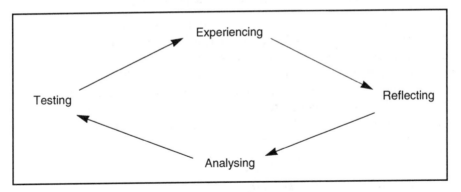

**Fig 1.10 The learning process**

The learning process is about:

- **experiencing** a situation by being involved
- **reflecting** and thinking about the experience and evaluating what has been learned
- **analysing** how the experience could be of use in other situations
- **testing** the learning in new situations and under various circumstances

Try to understand the way in which the trainee learns best and then seek out opportunities for training by discussing the trainee's needs with other colleagues and people in authority who may be able to help. This may be line managers, other supervisors, trainers or other colleagues. Seek out advice and information on the training and development offered by your own organisation or training centre first in order to link this with the training requirements and/or preferences of the trainee.

There should be many different methods of learning available that you can use to suit the trainee's preferred style:

- discussion
- self-study
- work experience
- projects
- simulations
- open learning packs
- audio/video programmes
- attending training courses
- reading
- observation
- lectures
- practical activities

Finding the right learning style depends on individual preference, but it is important for you to identify as quickly as possible the learning style that best suits the trainee's needs. With this in mind you can start to be more selective about the choice of available training opportunities so as to choose the one at which the trainee is most likely to succeed because it matches both their needs and the way in which they prefer to learn.

The learning process also takes into account assessment, review and evaluation. In terms of the NVQ award, the assessment is carried out to check competence. Competence is the ability to perform a task to the standards required. The standards are those required by a real working environment and include all the related pressures. The trainee must prove not only that they are competent in practice but that they also have the underpinning skills, knowledge and understanding to apply themselves in a real work situation.

## ▶ *Direct training activities*

Training completed by the trainee can either be on-the-job or off-the-job.

### Off-the-job training

Before starting work it is likely that the trainee will have carried out training, either at school or at a training centre or college. This training is called off-the-job as it is carried out away from any job of work. It will cover the basic skills required for a particular job. For administration awards this may include typewriting, basic computing, filing, answering and making telephone calls, dealing with the post, etc.

However, once in employment the trainee will need training on how to use their skills within the organisation they are working for. For example they may be capable of creating a database, but may not be familiar with the structure of the database used in the organisation or with system security, or they may not understand the importance of inputting correct information.

Most training centres have qualified, specialist staff to train and assess trainees in the required skills, knowledge and understanding. The equipment available is selected for training purposes and the trainee will have uninterrupted time to learn new skills and procedures. The training staff will also negotiate action plans with them and help to develop a programme to suit and enable them to acquire their qualifications.

If the trainee has special needs then these are usually catered for with special equipment or specially trained staff. Textbooks and special training manuals, in addition to resource centres containing books, computers, videos, tapes and other facilities should be readily available. The trainee will be able to mix with others who are learning the same procedures and skills. In addition, the skills gained are general and can be adapted to suit any organisation or company.

However, although the staff are qualified trainers and assessors they may not have up-to-date experience of working in an organisation or carrying out the procedures and skills that they are teaching. The equipment at the centre may become dated and faulty through over-use or by careless handling by inexperienced trainees. Individual attention may not be available in large groups of trainees. Some of the procedures and skills may be difficult to learn in a training room and it is difficult to learn how to become part of a team and how to deal with unexpected interruptions.

## On-the-job training

The training received while working in an organisation is called 'on-the-job' training. It makes sure that the trainee is totally familiar with the organisation's rules, regulations and procedures.

The procedures and skills are learnt by the trainee while carrying out the job. A line manager or supervisor will usually spend time with the trainee demonstrating how the job is done and then observe while the trainee completes the task. If the trainee makes mistakes in this situation they will be corrected and further training given. Once they are able to carry out the task without supervision they will be allowed to continue with the task unsupervised.

The trainee remains in the company of the people they work with and will be able to see how their part of the job fits into the section or department they are working in. They will be able to see the problems that occur in everyday work, the interruptions, such as constant telephone calls and visitors, and learn how to deal with them.

However, line managers and supervisors are not always qualified assessors. They may know how to do a job but may not necessarily have all the knowledge and understanding that surrounds the task. The information passed on may be relevant to the organisation but may not be useful when the trainee changes jobs. Interruptions, such as telephone calls, visitors, urgent work and the demands of other staff may cause the training to stop and start.

It can be difficult to provide a quiet period of time with the trainee to show them a new skill or procedure. In addition others may expect the trainer to get all their work finished as well as carry out the training. The duties carried out in one job are unlikely to cover all the areas the trainee wishes to develop and other opportunities will need to be identified so that all of the qualification can be completed. For instance, if the trainee wishes to acquire their Administration qualification, there may be some units that are not dealt with by the section in which both the trainee and trainer work.

From the above summary, you can see there are many advantages and disadvantages to on-the-job and off-the-job training and you can probably think of more. Some large companies have the advantage of having their own training section, where staff can be released from their normal place of work to attend on a day or half-day basis. The staff within these training centres should be qualified trainers and have up-to-date experience gained from working within the company.

# ■ DIY 1.2.1

If you are not already responsible for supervising and/or assessing training, make a list identifying where on-the-job and off-the-job training would be required for a trainee wishing to complete an NVQ Administration Level 1, 2 or 3.

## ▶ *Work shadowing*

At NVQ Level 3 you should be working closely with your line manager and may intend to take over such a role as part of your own future development. What better way to learn about your line manager's work than to spend time shadowing him/her to find out what they really do? A particularly useful way of showing a trainee how their own work role can develop is to have them observe your activities for a period of perhaps one day or a week.

Shadowing has become very popular in recent years as it gives a real insight into the actual daily tasks, problems, priorities, etc that a person has to deal with in a particular job. Work shadowing provides an opportunity for trainees to find out if this is really the job they think it is and whether it will fit into their career plans.

## ▶ *Coaching the trainee*

If the trainee requires assistance in learning how to perform a particular task this can be achieved by the use of coaching. The trainee may be following a formal training programme perhaps at a training centre or college or may require coaching for a particular task in the workplace. It is important that any coaching undertaken follows a set plan and covers all necessary stages.

The coaching session must be planned to ensure that all materials required are to hand and have been checked. The layout of the office or training area must be appropriate for the task being demonstrated. It is important to put the trainee at ease and to motivate them by clearly setting out what is expected from them and what they can gain from a competent performance. The competencies involved must be clearly stated with the standards explained in relation to the task.

When demonstrating a task you must position the trainee so that they can see your actions and hear your clear, complete, step-by-step instructions. Make sure your information is accurate and that you stress the key points. Always adhere to health and safety regulations (explain these as you carry out the demonstration) and encourage the trainee to ask questions if they are unclear about anything.

When monitoring the trainee's performance give appropriate guidance and supervision but try to encourage the trainee to learn by their own mistakes. If mistakes are made, these must be identified, corrected and explained. It is important to ask the trainee how they felt about the coaching session; it may be that the trainee is not comfortable with this type of training and an alternative should be found.

Constructive feedback must be given: always give positive feedback first to encourage and try to balance good with bad. Use questions when the observation is complete to check the trainee's knowledge and understanding of the task.

## Coaching plans

Prior to carrying out a coaching session you must break down the skill you wish to demonstrate so that you can demonstrate it in small parts. This is called a **task analysis** and allows you to deliver the coaching session using a step-by-step approach that provides a more logical sequence to the task.

It is important to plan training to allow time for preparation, training and supervision. The trainee will also need practice time built into this plan. The learning should be arranged in logical sequence so that one thing leads to another. The key learning points must be identified and pointed out to allow the trainee to concentrate on particular points and avoid overloading. This will help the trainee to progress successfully and this will in turn increase their confidence when carrying out the task.

A task analysis is a plan that details what is going to occur and how it will happen.

Figure 1.11, which provides an example of a completed task analysis, may be of help to you.

The task analysis should detail:

- **getting ready** – what needs to be done prior to carrying out the task

27

**Task analysis**
Task: Handle and record payments made by cheque and credit/debit cards.

| Skills | Standard | Knowledge/Understanding |
|---|---|---|
| Getting ready:<br>Identify fee payable/code | Correct fee identified | Operation of till |
| Enter into till | Till displays fee due | Company procedure for processing cheque/credit cards |
| State price due to customer | Price stated verbally | Responsibilities of people within organisation |
| Identify method of payment | Confirm method and check payment | Company procedures for processing payment |
| Get equipment and materials to hand | All appropriate materials and equipment at hand | Location of equipment and materials |
| Doing the task:<br>Check validity of cheque/ credit card | Cheque/credit card valid and authorised by appropriate authority | What action to take in event of an irregularity |
| Process card | Card and cheque processed according to company policy | What information to enter on payment voucher and why required |
| Complete payment order/ cheque endorsement | Equipment used according to manufacturer's instructions | What floor limit is and what to do if exceeded |
|  |  | How to use equipment |
| Monitoring/Checking:<br>Check all details are complete and legible | Information complete on all copies of documents, all details legible and accurate | Importance of checking |
| Check signatures match | Signature match confirmed | Action to take if signatures do not match |
| Finishing off:<br>Return card (and payment slip) to customer together with receipt | Customer received all necessary items connected with payment | What documents to be given to customer |
| Return equipment | Equipment returned to appropriate place | Recognise need for receipt Where to store materials and equipment |
|  | Transaction carried out politely and in optimum time | Importance of good customer service |

**Fig 1.11 A completed task analysis**

- **doing the task** – actually carrying out the task in light of the performance criteria being assessed
- **monitoring/checking** – making sure that all details/information is correct
- **finishing off** – completing the task and replacing equipment

If you prepare your own task analysis following this sequence it will help you to ensure that your own performance follows a logical sequence and so aid the successful performance of the trainee.

Use of the **coaching plan** set out in Fig 1.12 will help to ensure that the coaching follows a logical path and that the trainee receives the correct form of introduction, demonstration, monitoring and feedback.

The coaching plan can be used to identify the task and equipment required, as well as the name of the trainee and the date and time the coaching session will take place.

There are 4 main stages to be followed:

1 **Introduction**
   - State the task and standards to be covered (this will require the element and performance criteria from the NVQ).
   - Discuss the requirements with the trainee to help motivate them by explaining what they can achieve by performing the task successfully.
   - Check on the existing knowledge of the trainee as this will save time going over knowledge, understanding and skills that they already possess.
   - Discuss time available, content of the session and methods you are going to use.

2 **Demonstration**
   - Get ready by preparing yourself with relevant equipment and resources in order to demonstrate the task.
   - Carry out the demonstration explaining your actions as you progress.
   - Monitor and check that the trainee has understood everything that you have said and done by asking and inviting questions.
   - Complete the demonstration by returning equipment and so on to its correct place and asking the trainee if they wish to ask any further questions.

3 **Observation**
   - Observe the trainee carrying out the task; try not to interfere. Correct the trainee only if necessary and encourage questions if the trainee is unsure of the next stage or procedure.
   - Use questions to check on the trainee's knowledge and understanding. They may be able to do the task but do they

# COACHING PLAN

Date ............................ Time ................................ Unit/Element No ....................

Task ...................................................................................................................

Equipment required ..........................................................................................

Name of Trainee ................................................................................................

| Stages | Learning methods | Special requirements | Time allowance |
|---|---|---|---|
| **1 Introduction** <br> • Discuss task, relate to unit/ element and performance criteria <br> • Motivate and arouse interest by stating benefits of successful observation <br> • Check trainee's existing knowledge <br> • Discuss time, content and methods to be used <br><br> **2 Demonstration** <br> • Follow task analysis <br><br> **3 Observe trainee** <br> • Do not interrupt <br> • Correct only if necessary <br> • Encourage questions <br> • Check knowledge and understanding <br><br> **4 Conclusion** <br> • Summarise key points <br> • Agree future action plan <br> • Invite further questions and views on coaching <br> • Update records | | | |

**Fig 1.12 Example of a coaching plan**

understand why they have carried it out in such a way?

## 4 – Conclusion

- Summarise the key points of the task and the demonstration you have given; confirm trainee's achievement.
- Agree future action with the trainee. This could be the follow-on from the task if they have performed successfully, or a repeat demonstration if they did not prove competence.
- Encourage further questions regarding the trainee's views on learning and training.
- Update your records.

## ■ DIY 1.2.2

Carry out a coaching session with a trainee using the blank coaching plan provided in Fig 1.12, or a similar form used by your organisation. Prior to this you must complete a task analysis (see Fig 1.11) detailing how you are going to organise your own performance to aid the trainee's success.

## ▶ *Identifying training needs*

Ideally arrangements should be made for the trainee so that there are links between the different types of training he or she receives, depending on the opportunities available to them. As we have seen, some things are better learnt in a specialist training centre, others in the workplace. Quite often the trainee will be the only person who sees both places and will be in the best position to decide which things they learn in the training centre and which they learn at work. This will become an important part of their action planning.

If they have the opportunity of going to a training centre one day a week or during the evening, make sure they have an action plan. (These are explained in greater detail on page 32.) Only they will know what opportunities they have at work and what they need to have included in their off-the-job training. The trainee should complete a personal action plan and discuss it with their assessor to make sure that the training programme they are entering will fulfil their personal needs and the organisation's requirements.

## ■ DIY 1.2.3

Look through your own NVQ Administration Level 3 award and identify for yourself how and where you plan to cover each unit and element. Will you require coaching prior to assessment or will training be required off-the-job?

## ▶ *Self-assessment*

We have already mentioned action planning but prior to dealing with this in more detail we need to look first at the process of self-assessment.

In order to identify needs, monitor and review progress and document success it is wise to use an action plan. However, the action plan should be completed by the trainee who, after self-assessing their own training needs, should have identified the areas of work in which they already possess competent skills. This plan then forms the basis upon which further negotiation can be carried out between the trainee and trainer.

The development needs self-assessment sheet shown in Fig 1.13 may be useful if you wish to assist the trainee to identify what their present development needs are in light of their future life goals, personal goals and professional goals. It is likely that you have already used such a form yourself prior to completing your own action plan for the Level 3 award.

It is part of your role to talk through the trainee's comments with them and help to identify and prioritise their training needs. It is useful to advise them to refer to their CV or Record of Achievement prior to completing the self-assessment sheet as they must take into account their prior and/or current achievements. When a specific type and level of training has been selected and agreed with the relevant authority, you will need to help them identify how they are to achieve success.

This is when an action plan should be used, upon which further discussion can be based.

## ▶ *Action planning*

The action plan may be short, medium or long term, or cover all 3. Once written however the action plan must be flexible enough to take into account changes in the priorities or circumstances of the trainee. When advising how to complete the action plan, you will have to tell the trainee to think about:

- what they want to achieve in the next few weeks or months
- what they need to know and need to be able to do to achieve their aims
- whom they need to contact and what equipment and materials will be required
- the time limit they have to commit to their plan and what arrangements may need to be made

Once there is a skeleton plan it can be broken down into sections. For the purpose of an NVQ you and the trainee may look through the units and

| DEVELOPMENT NEEDS SELF-ASSESSMENT SHEET | | |
| --- | --- | --- |
| My job/training role at present is: | My personal goals are:<br><br>Short-term<br><br><br><br>Medium-term<br><br><br><br>Long-term | My professional goals are:<br><br>Short-term<br><br><br><br>Medium-term<br><br><br><br>Long-term |
| My future life goals are: | | |
| My development needs at present are: | | |

**Fig 1.13 A development needs self-assessment sheet**

33

elements to identify which can be achieved in the workplace, or which require training or coaching prior to assessment.

The action plan in Fig 1.14 will help you to break down the trainee's programme into manageable parts and prioritise training according to need and available resources.

The Personal Action Plan specifies the training, development and assessment that the organisation has agreed the trainee follow as part of their work or training. The plan must detail the programme of activities, training, work experience, projects, assignments and simulations necessary for them to fulfil the performance standards set by the organisation.

The Personal Action Plan is used to detail 4 major areas:

- The trainee's development needs based on their own self-assessment and the outcome of their previous plan.
- Comments made by their line manager, supervisor or assessor during a two-way discussion.
- The agreement reached regarding their future development needs and how these will be implemented.
- Self-assessment and review at a set future date, discussed with their line manager, supervisor or assessor, resulting in an agreed review of progress and assessment of performance.

The NVQ is broken down into units and elements that cover a discrete part of the trainee's work activities and it is the trainee's responsibility to identify the units and elements that can be carried out in the workplace.

Advise the trainee to use the self-assessment sheet to identify their needs and the Personal Action Plan to detail the unit and element numbers for which they wish to prove competence during the period of time covered by the plan. They should also include details of other goals they wish to achieve. This information can then be used as a base upon which a formal interview can be carried out and their development needs discussed and agreed with a person in authority.

### ■ DIY 1.2.4

If you have not already done so, use the following guidelines to help you advise a colleague or trainee on how to complete a Personal Action Plan like that in Fig 1.15 (or use an existing form if you have one). The trainee should of course complete a self-assessment prior to this.

| PERSONAL ACTION PLAN | | |
|---|---|---|
| Name .......... *Sally Simmons* .............. Work Role .. *Supervisor* ........... | | |
| Period of training .......... *Feb '96 - Apr '96* ........... | | |

**Part A – Self-assessment**

| NVQ Elements/Units | Name of Unit | Completion date |
|---|---|---|
| *NVQ 3 - Units 1* <br> *2* <br> *3* <br> *4* | *Improvement of perf.* <br> *H&S* <br> *Planning. org. etc.* <br> *Working rels.* | |

Other goals I wish to achieve   *Complete CLAIT course and attend* <br> *shorthand lessons so that NVQ 3 Unit 14 can be completed.*

**Part B – Action required**

| By me | By my Assessor/Manager | By the organisation |
|---|---|---|
| *Complete skillscan for Units 1, 2, 3 & 4. Collect relevant evidence* | *Assess skillscan and advise re: APL.* | *Arrange day-release for CLAIT and shorthand lessons.* |

**Part C – Agreement made**
*Forms provided for U1 and H&S. Induction arranged to help with U2.* <br> *Shorthand lessons not available until Jan. Start CLAIT now.* <br> *See line manager re U1 & 2.*

Assessor's/Manager's signature.......... *P Scott* .......... Date .. *1/2/96* ........

Trainee's signature.......... *S Simmons* .......... Date .. *1/2/96* ........

Date and place of next review..... *1/3/96   Rm 165* ........

**Part D – Review**

Trainee's review of progress   *Started to complete forms for U1. 1.1 OK.* <br> *but 1.2 needs me to work with colleague, which has still not been* <br> *arranged. U2 complete. U3 and U4 nearly done.*

Assessor's/Manager's review of progress   *All work checked. U2 signed off* <br> *(U3 & 4 next week). Arrangements in hand for Level 1 trainee in same office.* <br> *Start U5, 6 & 7.*

Assessor's/Manager's signature .......... *P Scott* .......... Date .. *1/3/96* ........

**Fig 1.14 An example of a completed Personal Action Plan**

| PERSONAL ACTION PLAN | | |
|---|---|---|

Name ................................................Work role ...........................................

Period of training .............................................................................................

**Part A – Self-assessment**

| NVQ Elements/Units | Name of Unit | Completion date |
|---|---|---|
| | | |

Other goals I wish to achieve

**Part B – Action required by**

| Me | Assessor/Manager | The organisation |
|---|---|---|
| | | |

**Part C – Agreement made**

Assessor's/Manager's signature ................................. Date ...................

Trainee's signature .................................................. Date ...................

Date and place of next review..............................................................................

**Part D – Review**

Trainee's review of progress

Assessor's/Manager's review of progress

Assessor's/Manager's signature ................................. Date ...................

**Fig 1.15 A blank Personal Action Plan form, for use in DIY 1.2.4**

## ▶ *Guidelines*

### Part A – Self-assessment – completed by trainee

- Trainee inserts name, work role and period of training to which the plan relates.
- Trainee inserts unit/element numbers they wish to achieve during this period of time, followed by details of other goals they wish to achieve.
- Leave the date column blank as this will be completed when each area of development has been achieved.

### Part B – Action required – completed by trainee

- Trainee lists the actions that they, their trainer, line manager or assessor and the organisation will have to take to ensure their training requirements are met. This may include work activities, projects, assignments, training, discussions, self-study, simulations, etc, as well as named personnel, dates, resources and equipment needed.

### Part C – Agreement made – completed by supervisor

- You must now discuss the entries with the trainee and complete the next section of the plan. This will provide an opportunity for you to discuss their needs and agree a plan of action that is acceptable to you, the trainee and the organisation.
- You should both sign the plan to confirm that it has been agreed and that both you and the trainee will work towards their success.
- You should also agree a date and place for your next review and put details of this on the plan. However, intermittent checks should be arranged with the trainee to ensure progress and identify any problems.

### Part D – Review

- The last part of the plan is left to the end of the training period when the trainee can self-assess their progress and complete the trainee's review of progress section prior to attending their review.
- Discuss their progress with them and write your own account of progress to date in the assessor's/manager's review of progress section.
- The information in the review section forms the basis of the next Personal Action Plan.

## ▶ *Role of the assessor*

An assessor should be able to motivate the trainee as well as give guidance and support. Trainees will generally respond well if given clear targets on their action plans, that are reasonably demanding and varied and which allow a sense of achievement and job satisfaction when completed. Encouragement and praise should always be given to the trainee even if the work carried out is not what was hoped for.

Safe working conditions must be provided for the trainee at all times. Training should be planned and negotiated to avoid overloading and to ensure that sufficient and appropriate resources are available. Once the unit or element to be attempted has been identified the tasks should be studied and the trainee coached on the assessment procedures.

The assessor should be friendly and sincere in order to make the trainee feel relaxed. If the trainee has any special needs these should be identified and support given. The trainee should always be aware of what is expected from them and should feel free to talk to the assessor about difficulties or lack of understanding.

## ▶ Assessment methods and quality control

It is preferable for a meeting to take place in private with an adequate amount of uninterrupted time being allocated. The trainee should be encouraged to take the lead in putting forward the proposals they have prepared using their self-assessment sheet and action plan.

When discussing possible evidence with the trainee you must take into account whether the evidence being suggested is appropriate in meeting the standards. Ask yourself whether the evidence will cover any of the performance criteria or range – if it does not then it is of no value to the award.

In order to assure quality standards the suggested evidence must be:

- **Valid** – does the evidence reflect the standards? A written report on how to produce photocopies would not be valid evidence if the standards have specified that the trainee must be observed in practice.

- **Authentic** – the evidence must be the trainee's own work. If in doubt, ask the trainee further questions to check their knowledge and understanding of the procedure they have followed.

- **Reliable** – assessment must not vary from one assessor to another. The only way to achieve this is to match evidence to the performance criteria and nothing else.

- **Current** – if the trainee is providing evidence completed previously, the assessor must ensure that they are still competent now. A keyboarding certificate from 10 years ago is not current evidence of competence and the trainee will need an up-to-date assessment to ensure currency.

- **Consistent** – the assessor needs to be sure that the trainee will consistently perform at the level at which they were assessed. Observation over a period of time or a supervisor's testimony are ways of achieving this.

- **Sufficient** – evidence must cover all performance criteria across the range and meet any specific evidence requirements given in the standards.

Perhaps the most important thing to remember is that **quality** of evidence is more important than quantity.

The following summary of the use of different assessment methods is intended as a guide only. Any method of assessment may be used as long as it is appropriate for the task being carried out.

| | |
|---|---|
| • Demonstration<br>• Observation<br>• Presentation of a work product | normally used to assess a skill |
| • Verbal questioning<br>• Interviewing<br>• Written test/short answers | normally used to assess knowledge and understanding |

It is crucial that the person carrying out the assessment has the relevant D32/D33 Assessor's Award or is working towards achieving the awards. This will have trained the assessor to use an appropriate assessment plan and to know what to look for when assessing the trainee against the performance criteria and range.

A good assessor will get to know the trainee and show interest by giving advice and time and by being approachable and patient. The trainee may not be familiar with the work environment or NVQ language and may therefore need to rely on the assessor who should use the most appropriate language to aid the trainee's understanding.

The assessor must listen to the trainee and give constructive feedback based on the trainee's performance. This should be given after the assessment, not during, and the trainee should only be interrupted if the assessor feels it would be dangerous or detrimental to the trainee to continue. Above all, the assessor should be setting an example to the trainee and provide encouragement and praise when it is needed.

## ▶ *Assessment in the workplace*

It is the responsibility of the trainee to decide when they are competent at carrying out a task. Competent means carrying out the task in work, consistently to the standards required in employment. The standards have been set nationally by the Lead Body and are listed under each unit as performance criteria.

Assessment should take place in the workplace after the trainee has completed the necessary training or coaching. The trainee must be assessed under normal working conditions with telephones ringing and general interruptions. However, no unnecessary pressure that may discourage or prevent the trainee from showing what they are able to do should be allowed to interfere with the assessment.

Each part of the task must be assessed to the criteria before competence can be claimed. The assessor must therefore be completely aware of what the trainee is trying to achieve; this should be detailed on the negotiated and agreed assessment plan.

The example of an assessment plan given in Fig 1.16 may be useful in helping you to understand how an assessment plan should be completed. This assessment plan layout, completed by you, can be used as evidence towards the D32 and/or D33 Assessor's Awards.

## ▶ *Completing assessment plans*

Although it is the trainee's responsibility to decide when they think they are competent, it will still be necessary to give guidance and support to help them identify the performance criteria they are being assessed against. The trainee will need help to identify their strengths and weaknesses. The task and the performance criteria need to be discussed before an assessment is arranged so that both parties know what is expected from them.

The trainee and the assessor should agree on what work is going to be carried out to achieve competence and the relevant accommodation, equipment, machinery, etc, arranged. Usually the work carried out will be of a practical nature and the assessor will observe the trainee and examine their final result. If this satisfies all performance criteria a series of questions may be needed to test the trainee's underpinning knowledge and understanding.

You may have already noticed that a question bank is provided at the end of each element in this book to ensure that you as the trainee have gained

**ASSESSMENT PLAN**

Trainee's name............ *Sally Simmons*

Assessor's name .......... *P Scott*

NVQ Level ....... *1* .............. Unit ... *6* .............. Elements ..... *1*

Does the trainee understand the performance criteria and range
statements?  (Y)N

Proposed evidence....... *Observation of storage in correct location,*

*undamaged, safe and secure. Correct classification used or query*

*referred. Completion of out card and cross ref. cards.*

Does the proposed evidence agree with the assessment guidelines?  (Y)N

Where is the evidence to be obtained?

(Workplace/training) room/simulation/other (give details)

Are difficulties anticipated in obtaining the evidence?  Y(N)

Are there any special needs to be met?..... *No*

Agreed date of assessment(s) ..... *11/1/96* ............. Time ....... *3.30 pm*

Assessor ..... *P Scott* ..................... Trainee..... *S Simmons*

Review(s) ............ *Performance criteria for U6 discussed together*

*with required outcome of assessment.*

Observation notes ....... *12 personnel records were correctly stored in*

*filing cabinets and out cards completed. 1 file req'd cross-ref action.*

*Query re unnamed file referred to supervisor. H & S maintained.*

**Fig 1.16 Example of an assessment plan**

Is knowledge evidence required? .................................................................... Ⓨ/N

List questions asked (or attach question bank)............*What other*

*classifications are used? Explain numerical filing. Why are out*

*cards & cross-ref used? How do you maintain security? Why is it*

*important for files to be stored in correct location?*

................................................................

Were suitable replies given?                                                    Ⓨ/N

Summary of replies attached:                                                Ⓨ/N

Has trainee achieved competence?                                      Ⓨ/N

Is any further evidence required for the units/elements being assessed?    Y/Ⓝ

If no, complete necessary recording documentation for assessor
and trainee.

If yes, is further coaching or training required?                     Y/Ⓝ

Identify and discuss areas requiring improvement and complete unit/element
assessment action plan:

**Unit/Element Assessment Action Plan**

*Element complete.*
....................................................................

*No further action req'd.*
....................................................................

....................................................................

....................................................................

....................................................................

....................................................................

....................................................................

....................................................................

....................................................................

Agreed:        Assessor....*P Scott*...........Trainee....*S Simmons*........

**Fig 1.16 continued**

the required knowledge and understanding. If you are unable to answer these questions correctly your own assessor will not be fully satisfied that you understand why you have carried out tasks following certain procedures. If this is the case, you will be required to carry out further training activities prior to another assessment.

If competence has not been achieved the trainee should not be made to feel that they have failed. The trainee must receive constructive feedback from the assessor which tells them where they went wrong and details of any weaknesses that have been identified. A brief action plan must be discussed with the trainee detailing what coaching, training and/or action needs to take place prior to their next assessment. The trainee must be given further opportunities to prove competence in light of further training, coaching and/or experience.

## ▶ *Giving constructive feedback*

Constructive feedback increases the trainee's self-awareness, offers options and encourages development. It is therefore important for the assessor to learn how to give feedback that is constructive and does not demoralise the trainee. Constructive feedback does not mean that only the positive outcomes are discussed. Negative outcomes, when discussed and fed back constructively, can be very important and useful.

Most people need to be told when they are doing or have done well. It is important to emphasise the trainee's strengths rather than their weaknesses. The positive should be discussed first before any negative remarks are made. The negative is more likely to be listened to and acted upon if it is based upon and related to positive feedback.

It is important to avoid general comments. Detail must be given if the trainee is to understand what they need to improve or put right. Giving specific feedback gives the trainee more opportunity for learning. Positive or negative comments must be based upon specific reasons and not generalisation.

Negative feedback should never be delivered as a criticism. The assessor must suggest ways in which the trainee could have performed more competently. Turn the negative into a positive suggestion by offering an alternative.

Rules to remember are:

- Start with the **positive**
- Be **specific**

- Do not **criticise**
- Offer **alternatives** and remedies

# ■ DIY 1.2.5

Complete the assessment plan given in Fig 1.17 when observing a trainee carrying out an activity for which they have received coaching or training. If the trainee is not successful, a brief action plan must also be prepared stating what the trainee must do in order to improve their performance.

## ▶ *Setting work assignments*

In order to gain an NVQ unit the trainee will need to have been assessed as competent by a qualified assessor. The unit or element being assessed may be covered by part of the trainee's normal working activities. However, these will still need to be checked to make sure all performance criteria are covered. If not, additional tasks may be required in order to cover the whole element or unit.

It may be the case that a series of tasks must be identified and set as a work assignment that will gain credit towards a number of performance criteria and even elements or units, particularly if cross-referencing of evidence is possible. Therefore, a series of work assignments can be set that involve the trainee being assessed carrying out tasks that they would complete in a normal working day.

Elements that require competence to be assessed using machinery, for example, would also provide evidence to be used against health and safety criteria in other units and elements. Therefore, when identifying specific work assignments for assessment it is wise to try to put together tasks that complement each other in terms of related performance but that also relate to a number of different performance criteria.

However, it is unlikely that the performance criteria in all units and elements will be covered by the trainee's normal working activities. In this situation it will be necessary to design simulated activities that may take 2 forms:

- Structured activity carried out in the **workplace** for the purpose of the assessment. Facilities, equipment and materials available in the workplace should be used and normal workplace conditions, for example relationships, constraints and pressures, introduced.
- Structured activity carried out in **realistic working conditions** outside the workplace. Working conditions should reflect those found

**ASSESSMENT PLAN**

Trainee's name..................................................................................................

Assessor's name ..............................................................................................

NVQ Level ......................... Unit ........................... Elements ..........................

Does the trainee understand the performance criteria and range
statements?                                                                                                     Y/N

Proposed evidence............................................................................................

...........................................................................................................................

...........................................................................................................................

...........................................................................................................................

Does the proposed evidence agree with the assessment guidelines?            Y/N

Where is the evidence to be obtained?

Workplace/training room/simulation/other (give details)

...........................................................................................................................

Are difficulties anticipated in obtaining the evidence?                                 Y/N

Are there any special needs to be met?..............................................................

...........................................................................................................................

Agreed date of assessment(s).........................................Time ..........................

Assessor..............................................Trainee ..............................................

Review(s) ...........................................................................................................

...........................................................................................................................

...........................................................................................................................

...........................................................................................................................

Observation notes .............................................................................................

...........................................................................................................................

...........................................................................................................................

...........................................................................................................................

**Fig 1.17 A blank assessment plan form, for use with DIY 1.2.5**

Is knowledge evidence required? ................................................................Y/N

List questions asked (or attach question bank)........................................

........................................................................................................................

........................................................................................................................

........................................................................................................................

........................................................................................................................

Were suitable replies given?                                                          Y/N

Summary of replies attached:                                                        Y/N

Has trainee achieved competence?                                              Y/N

Is any further evidence required for the units/elements being assessed?        Y/N

If no, complete necessary recording documentation for assessor
and trainee.

If yes, is further coaching or training required?                              Y/N

Identify and discuss areas requiring improvement and complete unit/element
assessment action plan:

**Unit/Element Assessment Action Plan**

........................................................................................................................

........................................................................................................................

........................................................................................................................

........................................................................................................................

........................................................................................................................

........................................................................................................................

........................................................................................................................

........................................................................................................................

........................................................................................................................

Agreed:    Assessor ...................................Trainee...........................

**Fig 1.17 continued**

46

in the workplace and include facilities, equipment and materials used in the workplace for the activities being assessed. This too should include relationships, constraints and pressures met in the workplace.

Naturally occurring evidence in the workplace is the first choice of assessment; simulated activity is a second choice mode of assessment which must be carefully designed and undertaken. Only high quality simulation which reflects the reality of a true work environment is acceptable.

If units and elements do require assessment of a simulated activity, the following guidelines should be observed:

1 Simulation must enable the trainee to carry out activities to the specified standard.
2 Activities must be those which would be carried out in the workplace.
3 Activities must provide a complete working situation.
4 Activities must reflect working practices such as constraints of time, work pressures/patterns, demands on personal responsibility and accountability in the job role.
5 Paper-based exercises, for example projects, assignments or case studies, may contribute towards evidence of competence but must not form the main evidence.

It is vital that work-based evidence is used whenever possible. If simulated activity such as in-tray exercises, projects, assignments, etc is used, it is very important that they cover the performance criteria and are completed in a workplace environment. Training centres designed as model offices and fully equipped assessment centres can be used for the assessment of simulated activities but it must be stressed that such activities must be carried out under normal workplace pressures.

There are a number of different textbooks, assignment packs and in-tray exercises written for the assessment of NVQs. It is vital that you understand that these can only be used as **part** of the evidence and that no unit or element can be assessed as complete if there is no evidence of practical activity. A trainee may be more than capable of writing a lengthy report about the use and comparison of different reprographic equipment, but this cannot be taken as evidence that they can actually operate the equipment competently!

When negotiating and planning a trainee's action plan you should always endeavour to use work-based evidence. If this is not available then opportunities must be identified for the trainee to complete the unit or element. This may require arrangements for the trainee to spend time in a different section or department, for example one day per week for 2 months spent in the mail room or reprographics department.

If no opportunity for assessment can be identified it is wise to use professionally written assignments that cover all of the performance criteria and lead the trainee toward using practical activity rather than methods such as report writing. Note that some of these packs can be bought with a licence to copy them, but that others have to be purchased individually because photocopying them is an infringement of the copyright law. You could write your own material, but if you do decide to do so, bear in mind that this takes much time and you must ensure that your assignment covers the appropriate performance criteria, range, knowledge and understanding and that it can be evaluated and assessed against the unit or element requirements.

## ■ DIY 1.2.6

Choose one element from an NVQ award and write an appropriate work assignment that covers all or some of the criteria. Indicate at the end of the assignment the criteria that will be covered by successful completion of the assignment.

### ▶ *Copyright law*

The copying of documents is controlled by the Copyright, Designs and Patents Act 1988. It is illegal to copy documents that are protected and in which the symbol © is printed, normally on the first page or on the back of the first page of the document. If you look at the front page of most books you will find the symbol as well as a statement that copying is not allowed. However, some documents may be copied for educational purposes and others may be copied if the author's permission is obtained first. You should always check before copying that the document you wish to copy is not protected. Obviously if the document has been written by someone in the office it will be all right to copy it. The Act also covers copyright in music and video tapes, CDs, records, TV and radio programmes and computer programs.

### ▶ *Health and safety laws*

Legislation under the Health and Safety at Work Act (HASAWA) ensures that we all work in a safe environment. When in an office or using any type of equipment health and safety laws must be adhered to. The Electricity at Work Regulations and Display Screen Equipment Regulations also exist to protect us. Electrical equipment must be checked regularly and maintained in a safe state. You will see that health and safety requirements are mentioned in most NVQ units and must be taken into account when assessing trainees.

**Fig 1.18 Check on the safety of your visitors . . .**

The temptation will always be there to cut corners in order to complete tasks quickly. This is quite in order provided the corners being cut will not affect safety in the office. Leaving the filing cabinet drawer open while you answer the telephone, putting boxes on the floor while you find the keys to open the stationery cupboard, or failing to contact the technician to report faulty wiring are all examples of potential hazards.

It is very easy to lapse when you are under pressure and if you have the added responsibility of supervising a trainee then they too have to be kept within the guidelines of company safety policy. Common sense is needed in most cases, together with an awareness that we are all responsible for each other's safety – if we choose to keep an untidy desk, block doors or overload electrical sockets then we risk not only our own safety but that of all other personnel in the office. Using the excuse that you were busy will not be sufficient when trying to explain why one of your colleagues has had an accident because of your unsafe practices or because a trainee was not fully advised of health and safety regulations!

## ▶ *Data protection legislation*

Data protection rules exist to protect computerised information on private individuals. If you use a database at work which stores personal information, your company must be registered with the Data Protection

49

Registrar; prosecution and heavy fines can result if they are not. Action plans, assessment plans and so on contain personal information about the trainee who is unlikely to want others having access to them. As a matter of courtesy such records should be protected and kept secure.

## ▶ *Security and confidentiality*

Information passing through an office will fall into one of the following categories:

1 **General or open** – can be seen by anyone.
2 **Restricted** – limited access to a certain department or group.
3 **Confidential** – seen only by the authorised person.

You will be expected to carry out the day's duties with the minimum of fuss, in an organised fashion that rises above the pressures of the day. In reality this does not always happen and there are bound to be some days that resemble organised chaos rather than a smooth-running office. The telephone continually ringing, other members of the company in and out of the office asking questions and making demands, the boss having a 'bad day', together with a host of other distractions will ultimately affect the smooth running of the office and your own strength of character.

The ability to cope with pressure comes with practice, but more importantly, the ability to ensure that security and confidentiality are maintained at all times will take precedence. You should not allow aspects of security and confidentiality to lapse so that tasks can be completed quickly. If you are to advise, coach, assess and be observed yourself, it is imperative that you set a good example.

When using a computer it would be normal practice to use passwords to access confidential information. Passwords should be changed regularly and words chosen that are easy to remember and that do not have to be written down. Some software packages prompt you to change the password on a monthly basis. You must keep a separate file for all confidential material that should not be seen by any unauthorised person, including any trainees, together with files for restricted information that may be accessed by a limited number of personnel and by others with discretion.

All back-up copies of confidential or restricted information should be kept under lock and key.

**Fig 1.19 Beware of giving visitors confidential information**

# ■ DIY 1.2.7

Look at the following list detailing the documents that might pass through your office. Rewrite the list in order of importance and indicate next to each document whether it should be treated in confidence.

1 Job application form
2 Trainees' assessment plans
3 Newsletter
4 Assistant's personal goals assessment
5 Company sales brochure
6 Colleagues' action plans
7 Trainees' self-assessment details

How would you ensure that confidential documents are seen only by authorised personnel?

## Knowledge and understanding question bank

1 How do you assess competence in others?
2 In what way do you identify another person's development needs?
3 What is on-the-job training?
4 What is off-the-job training?
5 How do you go about delivering a coaching session?
6 What is a task analysis?
7 How do you design work assignments for development purposes?
8 How do you evaluate work assignments?

**9** How do you provide feedback?

**10** What legal and regulatory requirements do you have to adhere to when providing training and development?

## Claiming credit

For Element 1.2 you must provide evidence that proves your contribution to the development of colleagues through identifying their training needs, selecting and implementing specific work assignments, delivering direct training activities, advising and coaching. You must also prove that you have taken into account statutory and non-statutory legal and regulatory requirements such as health and safety, equal opportunities, copyright and data protection requirements.

The following work products are potential sources of evidence:

- records of discussions
- training plans
- lists of development opportunities
- records of work assignments
- records of training/development activities
- records of progress
- notes relating to evaluation of progress.

Once you have completed your final assessment, you will need to write in your record book or folder how, when and what you have done to prove that you are competent.

The following statement is an example of how one trainee completed this claim:

*During the past 3 months I have been responsible for a level 1 student who has been at Coopers & Co on work placement. I have helped her to carry out a self-assessment based on information from her CV and Record of Achievement. I have identified the units that can be assessed in the workplace and those for which formal training is required at college. We meet each week to discuss progress and complete an action plan. I have provided some work assignments to cover 2 units that could not be covered at work or college. I took these assignments from the Pitman Publishing work packs and made sure that when the work was complete it covered all of the performance criteria and range. I provide feedback on progress during the action planning meetings and also to my own line manager. I am able to provide support and advice at all times and have completed coaching plans, based on task analysis, in order to demonstrate the use of equipment. I am currently working towards my D32 and D33 assessor's awards.*

# UNIT 2

# Contribute to the maintenance of a healthy, safe and effective working environment

■ **Element 2.1**
## MONITOR AND MAINTAIN A SAFE, HEALTHY AND SECURE WORKPLACE

### Performance criteria

1 Working conditions are monitored to ensure that legal and regulatory requirements and organisational procedures are satisfied
2 Working conditions which do not conform to requirements and procedures are promptly and accurately reported to the appropriate person
3 Actions taken in dealing with emergencies conform to organisational procedures and are within limits of own authority
4 Opportunities for improving the health, safety and security of the workplace are identified and recommended to the appropriate persons

### Element introduction

If people are to work efficiently in a working environment it is essential that they feel healthy, safe and secure. The maintenance of a healthy, safe and effective working environment is therefore taken very seriously by employers who through legislation can face prosecution if their safety standards are not maintained. The working environment requires the monitoring of working conditions to ensure that they comply with legal and regulatory requirements. Regulatory requirements can refer to the procedures set down by the organisation itself.

You need to consider ways of monitoring your working environment, taking into account legal and regulatory requirements, and the consequences of breaching these requirements. There are many potential emergencies just waiting to happen; illness, accident, fire, evacuation and breaches in security are but a few. Each organisation has its own procedures for dealing with emergencies, together with strict emergency reporting procedures that must be followed if they are to be used effectively.

In the event of an emergency it is imperative that you are fully versed in the organisation's emergency procedure; that you fully understand the use of emergency equipment, safety signs, notices and how the consequences of inappropriate use will affect you, others around you and the organisation itself. Your ability to identify security breaches from handbag thief to computer hacker are also a necessity if a secure working environment is to be maintained and organisational security procedures adhered to.

Employers have a duty to protect their employees and to keep them informed about health and safety, in the same way as the employees have a responsibility to look after themselves and others. If you identify a problem this should be discussed with the employer, or the safety representative if there is one. It is possible for you to contact the Health and Safety Executive, your Local Authority or perhaps the local fire brigade direct if you feel your employer is putting people's health or lives at risk.

## ▶ *Health and safety in the workplace*

All employers, employees and trainees in the workplace should know:

1 How to contact 'first-aiders'.
2 Where to locate the first-aid box.
3 What to do in the event of a fire.
4 Where to locate fire equipment.
5 How to select/operate fire equipment.
6 Where to locate the accident book.
7 To whom to report hazards.
8 How to lift/handle materials correctly.
9 When/where to use protective clothing.

This information should be covered in the safety policy, rules and emergency procedures of the organisation during induction training. If you do not know the answers to the 9 points above, now is a good time to ask your line manager for advice.

# ▶ *Possible hazards*

There is a wide range of possible hazards in an office and it is the responsibility of everyone to ensure that potential accidents are prevented before they happen. Examples are: drawers left open; cabinets placed in front of fire extinguishers; open scissors or sharp objects left on desk tops; chairs left in gangways; and overloaded electric sockets.

Are you guilty of throwing items such as sticky tape or correction fluid across the room to a colleague? Many people do this and it is only after an accident has occurred that they think twice before doing it again!

It is imperative that you appreciate the dangers that can occur from hazards such as:

- slippery or poorly maintained floors
- lifting heavy items without bending properly
- staircases and fire exits used as storage facilities
- poorly maintained or frayed carpets
- standing on chairs to reach high shelving

**Fig 2.1 Some safety hazards in the office**

- removing safety guards on machines
- trailing electric or telephone leads
- obstacles in gangways
- using faulty electrical equipment
- faulty storage/stacking of business items
- improper treatment of hazardous substances
- unsuitable positioning and use of furniture

The above list is by no means exhaustive, as the potential hazards are many and changeable. All you need to do at any one time is to look around your own working area and spot any potential hazards. Pay particular attention to the list above but always be on the lookout for other, less obvious, hazards. It is very important that we all understand and try to reduce risks by ensuring that we are fully aware of safe working practices.

## ■ DIY 2.1.1

Use the list in Fig 2.2 to carry out a safety check in your department or section. The checkist should cover equipment, fixtures and fittings not only in your own working area, but also in other areas within the organisation for which you are responsible. Make recommendations for improvement in the column provided if you think there are any.

### ▶ *Health and safety legislation*

There are legal minimum health and safety requirements that have to be followed in both the office and other working areas. Health and safety legislation covers lighting, heating, space, cleanliness, ventilation, and so on, to ensure people are offered a safe and comfortable place in which to work. It is in the company's interests that standards and procedures are followed in order to reduce absenteeism through poor working conditions, illness or accident.

Legal action against an employer who fails to provide a healthy and safe place of work includes fines, closure of premises and even imprisonment for persistent offenders. However, health and safety at work is such an important aspect of the welfare of employees that most employers do not need the threat of legal punishment to provide good working conditions.

There are about 30 Acts of Parliament governing the working environment; some of the more important ones are discussed in the following pages.

| HEALTH AND SAFETY CHECKLIST – LEVEL 3 | | | |
|---|---|---|---|
| **Question** | **Answer** | | **Comments** |
| | **Yes** | **No** | |
| **Filing cabinets:**<br>1 Are drawers left open?<br>2 Can more than one drawer be opened at once?<br>3 Are drawers overcrowded? | | | |
| **Telephones:**<br>1 Are they easy to reach?<br>2 Are wires kept out of the way?<br>3 Are mouthpiece/earpiece kept clean? | | | |
| **Computers:**<br>1 Is brightness correct?<br>2 Are screens and keyboards positioned correctly?<br>3 Is there enough light without glare? | | | |
| **Desks:**<br>1 Are they tidy?<br>2 Are any desks an obstruction?<br>3 Are desks the right height?<br>4 Is all equipment stored safely? | | | |
| **Chairs:**<br>1 Are they comfortable?<br>2 Do they support your back?<br>3 Are chairs left in gangways? | | | |
| **Electrical equipment:**<br>1 Are there trailing wires?<br>2 Do you know how to treat faulty equipment?<br>3 Do you know how to check the mains supply?<br>4 Do you know how to recognise faulty equipment? | | | |
| **Hazards:**<br>1 Do you know to whom you would report a hazard?<br>2 Do you know how you would report a hazard?<br>3 Do you know how to deal with the following emergencies?<br>(a) illness<br>(b) accident<br>(c) fire<br>(d) evacuation | | | |

**Fig 2.2 Health and safety checklist**

## ▶ Health and Safety at Work Act 1974 (HASAWA)

The **Health and Safety at Work Act 1974** is an enabling Act, which means that it is designed to bring together all the previous legislation and make sense of it. However, at the moment many of these earlier Acts exist side by side with the HASAWA. The basic idea of the Act is that there should be a joint effort by employers and employees to provide a safe and healthy working environment.

The employer has to provide safe:

- equipment and systems of work
- working conditions and adequate arrangements and facilities for welfare
- use, storage, transport and handling of substances and articles

**Fig 2.3 Employees are responsible for taking care of their own safety**

- means of access to and from work.

If an accident should occur the employer must investigate this fully and all staff should be fully informed, supervised and trained in accordance with their work role.

Employees are responsible for:

- taking care of their own safety
- the safety of other people affected by their actions
- co-operating with employers and any other persons involved in carrying out duties under this law.

The HASAWA includes the Electricity at Work Regulations 1989 and the Reporting of Injuries, Diseases and Dangerous Occurrences Regulations 1985 (RIDDOR).

**The Electricity at Work Regulations 1989** have been made under the Health and Safety at Work Act of 1974 and cover establishments such as colleges, hospitals and commercial premises. The purpose of these regulations is to require precautions to be taken against the risk of death or injury from electricity at work. Injury or death caused by electric shock, electric burn, fires of electrical origin, electric arcing or explosions initiated or caused by electricity are covered by these regulations.

There are maintenance guidelines for all electrical equipment: even the office kettle, word processor and electric fan have to be inspected and maintained on a regular basis. Employers are required to label their electrical equipment with details of when it was last checked and the date of the next inspection. Green labels are used for equipment that has passed its test and red labels used for equipment that is not satisfactory. If a piece of equipment is found to be dangerous it must be removed.

**The Reporting of Injuries, Diseases and Dangerous Occurrences Regulations 1985 (RIDDOR)** state that an accident book must be kept

**Fig 2.4 An example of a completed green label**

by anyone who employs workers. In the event of an accident the employer must make and keep a written account of what happened, which must be made available for inspection by the relevant authority. If an employee is off work, due to an accident, for more than 3 days the employer must inform the Local Authority Environmental Health Department or an Inspector from the Health and Safety Executive depending on who has legal responsibility for that particular premises. The relevant authority must be informed verbally within 24 hours of the accident occurring, and in writing using form F2508 within 7 days. This information is used to identify accident trends and unsafe working practices.

RIDDOR do not specify any particular form for an accident report. It is left to the responsible person to use a form or record that best suits the purpose. A photocopy of form F2508 kept in a file would be acceptable.

Section 2(3) of the Health and Safety at Work Act 1974 states that if 5 or more people are employed then, by law, the company has to have a written statement detailing its health and safety policy. The statement should be specific to the company and set out the general policy for protecting the health and safety of employees at work and the arrangements for putting that policy into practice. This statement must be brought to the attention of all employees and others who may be affected

| **Accident Report Form** (To be completed by Line Manager) | |
|---|---|
| Accident Details: | Location: |
| | Department: |
| | Date:<br>Time: |
| | Name & Address: |
| | Sex:<br>Age: |
| Details of Injuries: | Occupation: |
| Signature _____<br>(Line Manager) | Witnesses: |
| Distribution:  Copy 1 to Human Resources<br>Copy 2 to Facilities Manager<br>Copy 3 to Health & Safety Representative<br>Copy 4 to Facilities Manager Central Services<br><br>Notification of Unsafe/Unhealthy Conditions form completed.     YES/NO*<br>(Only complete where necessary)                                                       *Delete as applicable | |

Fig. 2.5 Accident report form

by the employer's business and it should be updated when working conditions change.

## Reporting accidents

If an accident has occurred it is important this is reported. An accident report form can be used to give details of the accident. It is vital that this form is completed after an accident, so that if the same accident occurs again and again the trend will be identified and can be put right. If, for example, a number of staff had all injured themselves falling over a broken drawer in the filing cabinet then it would be the employer's responsibility to have the drawer repaired before another accident occurred. An example of an accident report form appears in Fig 2.5.

All accidents at work should be reported to a line manager and recorded in writing using an accident report form. The reasons for this are:

1 The information can be used to investigate the cause of the accident and help to reduce hazards in the future.
2 A written record of the accident may be required by law.
3 The injury, no matter how small, should be given attention. What seems to be a small injury could possibly give rise to serious problems later.

## ■ DIY 2.1.2

Photocopy a page from your accident report book or photocopy the example in Fig 2.5. Insert the following information.

At 9.30 am today the Accounts Secretary, Shashi Doll, who was celebrating her 24th birthday, tripped over a filing cabinet drawer in the secretarial section of the Accounts Department. The drawer had been left open after a file was removed. Paul Varga was with her at the time and was able to administer first aid to Shashi's cut and bruised knee. Shashi was taken home to 22 Forest Gate, Kings Winford, Dartford and is expected to have the next 4–5 days off work.

## ▶ The Offices, Shops and Railway Premises Act 1963

The HASAWA has a general approach to health and safety in the workplace. The **Offices, Shops and Railway Premises Act 1963** is more specific, however, and stipulates working requirements and informs employees of their rights.

This Act states specific requirements, such as:

● adequate floor space for each employee
● temperature above 16°C and a thermometer displayed

61

- adequate ventilation without draughts
- adequate, separate toilets
- washing facilities with hot and cold water
- soap and clean drying facilities
- fresh drinking water
- facilities to hang and dry clothes
- isolation of noisy machinery
- safe and clear floors and stairways
- machinery or correct procedures to lift heavy weights
- chairs provided for employees who stand to do their work
- availability of trained first-aid staff
- adequately stocked first-aid boxes
- machine guards where necessary
- clear gangways and fire exits
- fire drills/assembly points brought to notice of all staff
- adequate fire extinguishers in working order.

Under this Act **The Information for Employees Regulations 1989** provide employers with a large poster that has to be displayed clearly in all offices. The poster informs employees of their rights and gives information detailing the employees' local enforcing authority and the address of the local employment medical service.

Other Acts in operation which relate to health and safety at work include:

- Fire Precautions Act 1971
- Employers' Liability (Compulsory Insurance) Act 1969
- Employers' Liability (Defective Equipment) Act 1969
- Occupiers' Liability Act 1957

## ▶ Control of Substances Hazardous to Health (COSHH)

A wide range of substances, from chemicals used in industrial processes to cleaning preparations or even natural substances like fungus, are capable of damaging health. In all types of business, factories, farms, leisure activities, offices, shops, to name but a few, workers' health can be at risk from the hazardous substances staff encounter from day to day if the right precautions are not taken. There are essential requirements for controlling exposure to hazardous substances and employers are responsible for protecting people who might be affected by these substances.

The basic principles of occupational hygiene are listed below. Employers must:

1 Assess both the risk to health arising from workplace exposure to hazardous substances and decide upon what precautions are needed.
2 Introduce appropriate, effective measures to prevent, or adequately control, the exposure.
3 Ensure that control measures are used, that equipment is properly maintained and procedures observed.
4 In some cases monitor workers' exposure and carry out appropriate health checks.
5 Inform, instruct and train employees about the risks and precautions to be taken.

Substances that are hazardous to health include substances labelled as dangerous, for example very toxic, toxic, harmful, irritant or corrosive substances. Agricultural pesticides and other chemicals used on farms and substances with occupational exposure limits are also classified as hazardous to health. These substances may also include harmful micro-organisms and substantial quantities of dust, indeed any material, mixture or compound used at work, or arising from work activities, which can harm people's health.

Here are some signs you may have already seen indicating a warning about hazardous substances:

Fig. 2.6 Hazardous substance signs

Employers have to ensure that the exposure of employees to hazardous substances is prevented or adequately controlled. The employer has to decide which control measures are required for the employees' workplace in order to deal effectively with any hazardous substances that may be present. This may mean preventing exposure by:

1 Removing the hazardous substance, by changing the process.
2 Substituting with a safe or safer substance, or using it in a safer form.

Where this is not possible then they must control exposure by, for example:

1 Totally enclosing the process.
2 Using partial enclosure and extraction equipment.
3 General ventilation.
4 Using safe systems of work and handling procedures.

It is the employer's responsibility to choose the method of controlling exposure. Personal protective equipment, for example respirators, dust masks, protective clothing, can be used as a means of protection only in those situations when other measures cannot control exposure.

The employer has an obligation to ensure that all control measures are kept in efficient working order and good repair. Controls should be examined and tested regularly and respirators and breathing apparatus also have to be examined frequently. The employer should monitor the exposure of workers in certain cases, for example:

1 Where there could be serious risks to health if control measures were to fail or deteriorate.
2 If they cannot be sure that exposure limits are not being exceeded.
3 Where they cannot be sure that particular control measures are working properly.

It may be necessary for medical examinations to be carried out. The services of a doctor or trained nurse could be used to check employees for effects such as severe dermatitis, or to ask questions about breathing difficulties if the work involves substances known to cause asthma. A simple record must be kept of any examinations carried out.

It is the employer's responsibility to keep their employees informed about:

1 The risks arising from their work.
2 The precautions to be taken.

and, if carried out:

3 The results of monitoring.
4 The results of health surveillance.

# ■ DIY 2.1.3

Take a photocopy of Fig 2.7 which shows types of protective clothing. On a separate sheet of paper write out why each of these items would be required and the type of hazard for which they are used as protection.

## ▶ *Protective clothing*

Depending upon the type of materials you, or other members of staff, deal with it may be a requirement to wear protective clothing. This may be a simple apron or overall to prevent you from getting dirty or it may be a hard helmet, protective footwear or perhaps goggles to prevent injury if an accident occurred. It is important that you know where protective clothing is kept and how to use it properly. The clothing must be maintained and cleaned according to instructions and always replaced in the correct location.

Eye protection must be worn    Wear hard hat    Wear ear protectors

Respirators must be worn in this area    Protective footwear must be worn    Hand protection must be worn

**Fig 2.7 Requirements for safety clothing**

It may be part of your job to give out protective clothing to members of staff or people visiting your company. This clothing may be issued on a booking in and out basis or the clothing may be available for them to help themselves. However, it is important that this clothing is worn at all times and that visitors are informed of the rules and regulations regarding protective clothing operated by your employer for the visitor's safety.

## ▶ *European health and safety law*

The European Union has introduced health and safety legislation which covers two main aspects – worker participation and the assessment and monitoring of risks. All member states must comply with EC directives and in the UK it is the responsibility of the Health and Safety Commission to ensure that this is done.

New regulations were introduced in the UK in 1993 and are commonly know as the '6-pack':

1 **The Management of Health and Safety at Work Regulations 1992.**   Under these regulations employers must carry out risk assessment and keep records of the assessments along with measures recognised as necessary to control the risk. Competent people must be appointed to help implement health and safety policy and make arrangements to plan, organise, control, maintain, monitor and review health and safety arrangements. Emergency procedures must be set up to deal with situations of serious or imminent danger. Lastly, they must provide full information and training to all employees with details of any risk they might incur.

2 **The Workplace (Health, Safety and Welfare) Regulations 1992.** These regulations state minimum legal standards covering health, safety and welfare. They cover such things as lighting, ventilation, temperature, space and room dimensions, workstations, seating, cleanliness as well as looking after the workplace and equipment in it. Welfare facilities such as toilets, washing facilities, rest rooms and eating accommodation are also covered.

3 **The Health and Safety (Display Screen Equipment) Regulations 1992.**   These regulations are applicable to all employees who regularly use display screen equipment. Employers must assess all workstations for health and safety risks and lower the risks if possible. Regular rest periods must be taken and eye tests, spectacles or lenses provided if advised by an optician. Training and information on use of equipment must also be provided.

4 **The Provision and Use of Work Equipment Regulations 1992.** These regulations relate to all machinery, appliances, apparatus or tools used at work. The employer must ensure that all equipment is suitable for the task and is well maintained. Training on how to use machinery must be given to staff.

5 **The Personal Protective Equipment (PPE) at Work Regulations 1992**. These relate to the provision of protective clothing and equipment when risks cannot be eliminated. Employers must make sure that protective equipment fits properly, is maintained in good condition and is provided free of charge.

**6 The Manual Handling Operations Regulations 1992.** Employers
must make sure that employees avoid handling and lifting activities that
may cause injury. The employer must assess and reduce the risk of
injury where possible and provide information to employees to help
them to avoid the risk.

## ▶ Lifting and handling heavy materials

Lifting and handling everyday working materials will cause no concern
and can be dealt with on an everyday basis. However, it is important that,
when dealing with materials that are heavy or awkward to move, you use
the correct procedure for this. First, you may need help and this may
come in the shape of a trolley or another person. If an item is far too heavy
to lift then it may be possible to make arrangements with the caretakers
for them to move the item for you. It may be necessary to make a written
request for this to be done.

When lifting heavy items yourself you must take care to follow the correct
procedures. These are listed below.

1 Bend your knees and take the strain on your legs, not your back.
2 Lift smoothly and do not jerk.
3 Keep the weight close to your body.
4 Stand upright and do not lean sideways.
5 Keep your spine straight.
6 Use trolleys and other aids if available.
7 If in doubt GET HELP, or use mechanical aid.
8 Realise your limitations and do not risk your health.

**Fig. 2.8 Correct method for lifting heavy items**

The majority of back injuries are caused when people lift heavy items incorrectly. Follow these procedures and you will use the strength of your legs to lift the item and not the weakness of your back.

## ▶ *Correct handling*

The type of handling and storage that items require will depend upon the kind of stock and the size of the business or training centre. Large organisations will have a stock room with specialist staff employed purely to take charge of the stock. A small organisation may only have a stock cupboard with one person in charge of the key.

Every item of stock must be stored neatly and be easily accessible when required. Shelves should be labelled so that it is easy to find what is needed, and the stock room or cupboard should always be locked. It is important that the storage area is kept dry at all times to prevent paper-based items from becoming damp and going mouldy. Large or heavy items should be kept low so that lifting is not required and when new stock arrives it should be placed at the back or at the bottom so that the older stock is used first.

It is important that you treat hazardous stock with care. Any liquids that are toxic, inflammable or give off fumes, for example thinners, glue or duplicating fluid, must be kept in a separate area and you must never smoke in this area or in the stock room itself. It is also very important that you are aware of the action to take to prevent accidents and that you are able to carry out remedial action if an accident does occur. If you identify any hazards, or problems arise with storing certain stock items, these should be reported to your line manager or the health and safety representative immediately. Likewise if damage occurs to any stock while it is being stored this should be reported. It may still be under guarantee and the supplier could arrange for exchange or repair or alternatively the business may be able to make an insurance claim.

## ■ DIY 2.1.4

You are responsible for a new office junior. Prepare guidance notes explaining general health and safety in the office, correct lifting techniques and the handling of substances hazardous to health.

## ▶ *Health and Safety Executive (HSE)*

The HSE was set up to work with local authority environmental health departments to make sure that legislation is enforced. Environmental health officers are responsible for offices and shops, whereas HSE inspectors are responsible for inspecting factories and industrial premises.

Inspectors have the authority to visit premises without notice and will often do this if they have received a complaint from a member of the public or an employee. Inspectors may carry out an inspection to check that appropriate legislation is adhered to or they may investigate a major accident or complaint. The inspector will advise the management on the necessary improvements required or where they have failed to meet legislation.

There are 2 notices that can be issued by inspectors:

- **Improvement Notice** which asks the employer to make suggested improvements within a given time period.
- **Prohibitions Notice** which forbids the employer continuing to operate a process which could endanger workers or the public. Before the business can operate again it must set up health and safety standards which conform to the regulations.

Fines or imprisonment can be a consequence of failure to comply with either of these notices.

## ▶ *Common forms of accident*

Common forms of accident or health emergency include fire, flood, risk of explosion, toxic fumes and accidents. In any of these events it is important that you know the correct procedure to follow to minimise the emergency and that you act efficiently. The procedures you may need to follow in any of these incidents include evacuation, activating alarms, detaching equipment from mains supplies and reporting accidents correctly. It is vital that you understand your own limitations when dealing with emergencies and that you know when and how to contact help if necessary.

## ▶ *Emergency procedures*

A busy organisation is likely to be crowded with staff, visitors and customers and it is important that in order to protect these people and the organisation's property much thought is given to fire and accident procedures. If the organisation stores inflammable, toxic or perhaps corrosive materials then even more attention should be paid to emergency procedures and every member of staff should know exactly what to do in the event of an emergency. Staff will be expected to escort visitors or customers who are unfamiliar with the evacuation procedure from the building.

When you join an organisation as a new member of staff you should undergo induction training which will show you what to do in the event of an emergency, how to recognise or sound the alarm and how to follow the evacuation procedure. It is important for you to know how to raise the alarm, whom to contact in the event of an emergency and how to evacuate yourself and possibly others from the building as quickly and safely as possible. You must know the quickest route to follow out of the building and at which point outside you should assemble for a name call.

## ■ DIY 2.1.5

On a piece of A3 paper draw a plan of the area in which you work. On your plan show the following:

- doors
- windows
- stairs
- fire extinguishers
- fire blankets
- furniture
- sand buckets
- water buckets
- fire escapes
- sprinklers
- fire alarms
- smoke detectors
- emergency notices
- fire exit location signs

What procedure do you think should be followed in the event of:

- illness
- accident
- fire
- evacuation
- breach of security

## ▶ *Fire precautions*

Fire precautions must always be strictly followed. There must be an effective means of giving a fire warning, for example a loud ringing bell or hooter that all staff recognise as being a fire alarm. Fire-fighting equipment must also be available and must be maintained properly so that it is always ready for use. Familiarise yourself with the type of fire-fighting equipment available, in particular the different coloured fire extinguishers that can be used for different types of fire.

All fire exits and fire doors must be marked. A fire door must never be left open, as the purpose of this door is to hold the fire back to give you more time to escape. It will be of little use if it is left open. Fire exits must be clearly marked as members of staff, visitors and customers will need to find them in order to get out of the building in an emergency. Fire exits must never be locked and must be kept clear at all times. They should never be blocked by items such as boxes or office equipment that is not in use.

All fire procedures should be displayed on a notice board and brought to the attention of all members of staff regularly. Most organisations have details of fire procedures in each separate room, giving details of the assembly point and the quickest route out of the building from that particular room. Remember that you should never smoke in a non-smoking area and you should never put lighted cigarette ends in to a waste paper basket. If you work in a non-smoking area it means just that; do not be tempted to smoke in toilets or quiet areas as this is likely to offend other members of staff and could be dangerous.

## Fire extinguishers

It is important that you understand the use of each type of fire extinguisher and the fires for which they are designed. There are six commonly used fire extinguishers.

| FIRE EXTINGUISHERS | | |
|---|---|---|
| **Colour** | **Contents** | **Use for fires** |
| GREEN | Halon, BCF | Paper, wood, fabric, liquids, fat, paint, spirits, oils, gases (such as oxygen, butane and propane), and electrical fires. |
| CHROME | Gas | As above. |
| CREAM | Foam | As above, but not electrical fires. |
| BLACK | CO2 | Liquids, fat, paint, spirits, oil, gases and electrical fires. |
| BLUE | Powder | Metals, such as magnesium, on fire. |
| RED | Water | Paper, wood and fabric fires. |

**Fig 2.9 Types of fire extinguisher**

Green fire extinguishers contain CFC gases, which affect the ozone layer, and as part of the Montreal Agreement it has been agreed that the use of these extinguishers will be phased out. However, they will still be in existence for a while yet and it is important to remember that, however much they affect the ozone layer, the fire itself is more harmful. When green fire extinguishers are no longer in existence, black or blue extinguishers can be used in their place.

There are other types of fire-fighting equipment that may be available for use in an emergency. Equipment such as fire blankets, sand buckets, sprinklers, smoke detectors, hosepipes and fire alarms are there to protect you in the event of a fire and to give you an opportunity to prevent a large fire breaking out. However, never under any circumstances risk your own life by trying to tackle a fire without giving the alarm signal first.

# ■ DIY 2.1.6

You have already drawn a plan of the area where you work. Check that you have included all the fire-fighting equipment, including sand buckets and so on. On your plan colour each extinguisher the correct colour. Add an A4 information sheet to your plan explaining each of the different coloured fire extinguishers and their uses. Describe what each extinguisher contains and for which fires it can be used.

You will also note that each extinguisher carries details on how to operate it in an emergency. Add these details to your A4 sheet including diagrams to clarify the information.

## ▶ *Evacuation procedures*

Remember that an organisation may have to be evacuated for reasons other than fire. These include an explosion, an accident, a flood, a bomb alert or perhaps a suspicious package has been found. Fire, police or ambulance may have to be called, but do not do this yourself unless you are the person who is responsible. It is likely to be your line manager's or the switchboard operator's responsibility to call the emergency services.

In the event of an evacuation customers, visitors and possibly other members of staff will need help in evacuating the building as quickly and safely as possible. It is important for you to act quickly, but to keep calm and never panic. There will be a set procedure to follow in order to evacuate each office, department, floor and so on, and this will include making sure that no one is left behind.

Every person in the work area should be encouraged to leave the building quickly but not to panic and run. In the event of a fire never use the lift when evacuating as heat, smoke and fire are likely to be sucked upwards through the lift shaft. Furthermore, the lift may break down and leave you stranded. It will be your line manager's responsibility to ensure that all members of staff have left the building and it is likely that they will do this by carrying out a name call. In order to help your line manager, make sure that you report to them as soon as you have left the building so that they know you are out of the building and safe. Never re-enter the building until you have been told it is safe to do so, and be on the lookout for other members of staff who have not reported in.

It is very important for you to understand that fire exits, fire doors and fire-fighting equipment are there to help you in the event of fire. They must never be hidden or obstructed in any way and if access is blocked this should be reported to your line manager immediately. It is too late once someone has been injured or possibly killed.

In the event of a fire it is useful for you to know how to use the fire-fighting equipment, but if it is a real emergency never risk your own life by trying to tackle the fire. It is more important that you sound the alarm and evacuate the building along with other members of staff and leave the fire-fighting to the experts.

## ▶ First aid

If a customer, visitor or another member of staff is injured or taken ill it is important to have access to a first-aid box so that treatment may be given, perhaps while waiting for an ambulance to arrive. If a first-aid box is not required it is still important to know how to make the person comfortable and safe while awaiting help.

There should be qualified first-aid staff available who will be able to use the contents of an adequately stocked first-aid box. In a large organisation it is likely that first-aid staff will carry pagers so that they may be contacted quickly and given details of the incident.

The first-aid box should contain:

1 Individually wrapped sterile dressings of assorted sizes.
2 Sterile eye pads with attachment.
3 Individually wrapped triangular bandages.
4 Safety pins.
5 Medium, large and extra-large size, sterile, individually wrapped, unmedicated wound dressings.

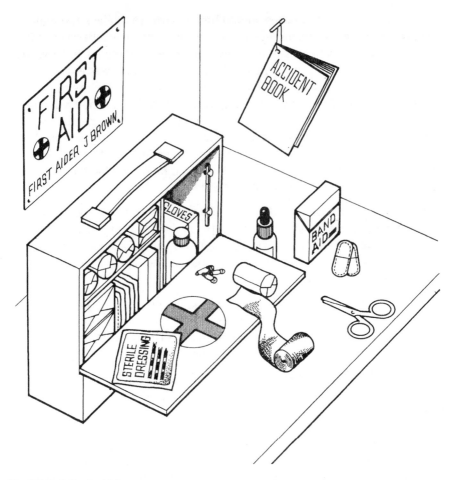

**Fig 2.10 A first-aid box**

6 Cleaning tissues, cotton wool, antiseptic, disposable gloves.
7 Disposable wipes.
8 Guidance notes on the use of the first-aid box.
9 Re-order forms.
10 List of contents.

The first-aid box should only contain items that a qualified first-aid person has been trained to use. It should not contain medication of any kind, for example, aspirin, as the first-aider is not a trained doctor. The first-aid box should be kept in a central place for all staff to use and it is reasonable to expect that at least one member of staff in your organisation will have first-aid training.

As an employee it is important that you follow safe working practices. If you see a potential hazard report it to your line manager immediately before somebody has an accident and make sure that you are aware of the following:

1 Who has had first-aid training in your office.
2 Where the first-aid box is kept.
3 Whom to contact in the event of an emergency.
4 How to record/report accidents.

Unless you have been trained to use the first-aid box yourself do not try to treat an injured person. Summon someone who is trained as quickly as possible. If the accident has been caused as a result of a broken fixture or fitting, or something which has been spilled on the floor, make sure that you clean up or clear up so that the accident spot is removed as soon as possible.

It is important that you do not panic. You must remain calm and keep a clear head. This will reassure anyone who has been injured and give them confidence that help is at hand and you know what you are doing.

## ▶ *Preventing machine accidents*

There are special rules for some machines used in offices. Some are classed as dangerous machines which people can use only after full instruction and sufficient training under close supervision. Examples include packaging equipment, guillotines and other cutting equipment.

Before you use such a machine make sure:

1 You know how to switch it off before you switch it on.
2 All guards are fitted and working.
3 All materials are clear of working parts of the machine.
4 Area around machine is clean, tidy and free from obstruction.
5 Your line manager is told at once if you think a machine is faulty.
6 You are wearing appropriate protective clothing.

Never:

1 Use a machine unless you are authorised and trained to do so.
2 Try to clean a machine when plugged in or switched on.
3 Use a machine with a danger sign or tag attached.
4 Wear dangling chains, loose clothing, gloves, rings or long hair that could get caught in moving parts.
5 Distract people who are using machines.

# ▶ *Using display screen equipment*

**The Health and Safety (Display Screen Equipment) Regulations 1992** affect workers who habitually use VDUs for a significant part of their normal work. There are also other workers who use VDUs, but who do not fit into this category. Employers have general obligations to protect them under health and safety legislation. The Regulations do not contain detailed technical information, but instead set more general objectives.

Employers have to:

● Analyse workstations of employees covered by the Regulations and assess and reduce risks.
● Ensure workstations meet minimum requirements.
● Plan work so there are breaks or changes of activity.
● On request arrange eye and eyesight tests, and provide spectacles if special ones are needed.
● Provide health and safety training.
● Provide information.

In order to reduce any possible negative effects on health through the use of VDU-based equipment for lengthy periods of time, the Health and Safety Executive has recommended a series of guidelines for ensuring that the office environment is compatible with the introduction of new technology. Leaflet IND(G) 36(L) *Working with VDUs*, published by the Health and Safety Executive, provides useful information regarding the use of VDUs in an office environment.

The guidelines recommend that in the operation of VDUs adjustable brightness and contrast controls are used to improve the displayed image, together with screen filters. The use of these will reduce eye strain. VDU keyboards should be detached from the screen so that the distance between the screen and operator can be adjusted according to personal preference, and the keys themselves should have a matt surround to minimise glare and have concave tops with adjustable slope to maximise operator comfort.

VDUs generate heat and this will have to be taken into account when heating an office environment to an acceptable temperature. Adequate ventilation and humidity also need to be maintained. Lighting has to be sufficient for the operator to read documents but neither too bright nor directed so that it glares on the screen and makes it difficult to read. Undue noise is also disruptive and therefore printers and other noisy office machinery should be sited away from operators or provided with acoustic covers.

Time spent at a VDU will depend upon the nature of the work being performed. Lengthy periods of keying in text may require rapid keyboarding but will not involve extensive concentration on the screen itself. However, if the work involves composition of text, work with spreadsheets, databases or desktop publishing this may require shorter work periods as far greater concentration on the screen is necessary.

# ■ DIY 2.1.7

If you do not already have a copy of the leaflet 'Working with VDUs' contact: HSE Information Centre, Broad Lane, Sheffield, S3 7HQ, or contact their free leaflet line on (Tel) 0114 289 2346; (Fax) 0114 289 2333 and ask for a copy.

## ▶ *Security in the workplace*

Whether you work for a large or small organisation, the way in which you deal with visitors is very important. A visitor is anyone who comes to see you or your colleagues and who does not work in your department or organisation on an everyday basis.

This could be:

- someone from another department or section
- someone from another branch
- someone from another company or other organisation
- a customer or client
- people attending a meeting
- people delivering or collecting items
- people attending an interview or asking about vacancies

Some of these visitors will be expected and others will be unexpected. The way in which these visitors are greeted and your attitude towards them are very important. However, while creating the correct company image you must be constantly aware of security and ensure that information is not given out to the wrong person in the name of politeness. Security relating to people, equipment and information should always be treated as a priority.

### Security when dealing with visitors

When receiving visitors you should always try to be:

- polite
- courteous
- positive
- friendly

- helpful
- patient

However, to protect the security of your organisation you must also be prepared to be:

- tactful
- diplomatic
- firm
- direct
- assertive

Above all, you should always be on the lookout for anything suspicious or out of place, and be prepared to act on your suspicions by reporting to an appropriate authority, such as your line manager, as quickly as possible.

Unless a caller is authorised, no confidential information should be given to them (in verbal or written form). Confidential information includes personal details of staff, their exact whereabouts and appointments schedule, financial details about the organisation and its customers, details of future projects or contracts etc. If you are unsure whether information may be passed on or not, always check with your line manager.

## ■ DIY 2.1.8

How should you ensure that security procedures are carried out correctly? Give full details of the action you should take if you become suspicious – what reporting procedures do you recommend for this?

Many companies now have strict rules about the security of the building. Callers and visitors may not be allowed to walk round the offices without a member of staff accompanying them. Usually a member of staff will collect the visitor from reception and accompany them to the meeting office. A receptionist should not leave reception unattended in case another visitor arrives and is left to wander round the building unsupervised.

In most organisations visitors are still allowed to find their own way to the office they require, but care must be taken to ensure that the visitor is given clear directions so that they do not get lost. When the business is complete and the visitor wishes to leave, the member of staff with them should make sure that they know how to get out of the building. There may be a quicker route from the building than the one by which they entered or the visitor may be required to leave the building through reception so that their name can be logged out of the visitors' register.

| VISITORS' REGISTER | | | | | | |
|---|---|---|---|---|---|---|
| DATE | | | | | | |
| Identity Badge No. | Time in | Time out | Name | Company | Appointment with | Action taken |
| | | | | | | |

**Fig 2.11 Visitors' register**

Some organisations rely solely on the visitors' register as a means to record visitors' details and the nature of their business. In some cases, such as government offices or high risk areas, the visitor may need to have their bag, briefcase or belongings searched before being allowed to enter the building. The visitor may even be required to leave items at reception, and these should be labelled with the visitor's name and kept in a safe and secure place until their return. In some extreme cases a body search may be carried out. Any company carrying out such procedures is likely to employ specialist staff such as security guards to attend to these duties.

Some organisations issue visitors with a badge or pass at reception to show that they have been authorised to visit the building. The badge or pass should be returned when the visitor leaves the building. Plastic badges bearing the name of the organisation and the word 'visitor' are often used, or badges with a blank space for the visitor's name to be inserted are popular and provide a more personal touch. Special reception registers can also be used that allow the visitor to enter details of their

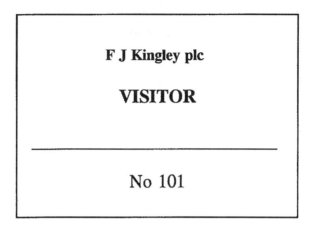

**Fig 2.12 Visitor's lapel badge**

business alongside their name. With these, a copy of the name portion of the register can be torn from the register and inserted into a small plastic holder which can be attached to the visitor's lapel as identification. In this way the visitor's entry and exit to and from the building is fully monitored.

## ■ DIY 2.1.9

If your organisation has no security procedures, now is a good time to introduce some. Write a memo to your line manager explaining the advantages of adopting security procedures and suggest the measures that could be taken in your own workplace to improve security.

### Security when dealing with equipment

A busy office is likely to be filled with expensive equipment such as computers, word processors, printers, photocopiers, fax machines, telephones, and so on. It is unlikely that a thief would try to steal large equipment such as photocopiers or main frame computers. However, smaller equipment such as word processors, that can be dismantled into a number of smaller, separate parts, may be targets for a thief.

It is usual practice to lock an office that is to be left unattended, to secure not only equipment but perhaps also personal items such as coats and handbags.

Equipment should be labelled with an indelible ink pen stating the name or initials of the organisation together with the post code. If the equipment is stolen but later found by police it can be easily traced back to its rightful owner by means of this information. Small, valuable equipment such as a desktop franking machine or a lap-top computer, must always be locked away in a secure place unless they are being used. Most office equipment will carry a serial number and this should be noted when the equipment is first installed. By doing this the equipment can be identified if it is stolen.

## Security when dealing with information

All company files could be classed as confidential. Personal information, company reports, financial accounts or minutes from a business meeting should never be discussed with people outside the company. It is important to recognise that information dealt with on a daily, routine basis may be of interest to a rival company. A member of staff may be interested in a colleague's salary or perhaps their home address and telephone number. Therefore, it is important that you do not leave paperwork lying round the office, however innocent you may think it is.

To secure paper-based information make sure all files are kept in one place under lock and key. Folders containing sensitive information should be marked 'CONFIDENTIAL' and must not be left on a desk or lent out to unauthorised personnel, however nice and friendly they may seem. Dead files should never be put in a bin or skip; they should be shredded or incinerated so they are unreadable.

Confidential information held in a computer must also be protected. Use passwords or keywords to restrict access and protect information. Only authorised staff should know the password or keyword and this should be changed regularly and never written down. Printouts should be kept in a folder marked 'Confidential' and disks should be kept locked away in a cupboard, not just locked in their disk box. Information stored on a computer database will be covered by the Data Protection Act.

## Data Protection Act

If you set up or use a database which has personal information on individuals then it must be registered with the Data Protection Registrar. The records should not be kept longer than is necessary and proper security procedures should be introduced to make sure only authorised staff have access to the information stored. The information should also be kept up to date and accurate and never be passed to anyone who may use it for other purposes, eg a list of doctors' patients being passed to a mail order firm to allow them to send sales material. Further information regarding registration can be obtained from the Post Office or direct from the Data Protection Registry who produce a very informative student information pack. Write to The Data Protection Registrar, Wycliffe House, Water Lane, Wilmslow, Cheshire SK9 5AF or telephone 0162 553 5711.

## ■ DIY 2.1.9

If there is no labelling and logging of equipment in progress in your organisation, you should write to your line manager explaining why and how this should be done. Explain the advantages of having such a secure system.

### Breaches in security

Situations such as a member of staff being threatened, equipment being stolen or information about the company being leaked would all be treated as a breach in security. In any of these cases it is important that you know the correct procedure to follow. You may need to get assistance quickly if you have an aggressive, suspicious or unauthorised visitor. In this case you may need to contact your line manager quickly, dial an internal emergency number to summon a security guard, or contact the police.

If you are suspicious of a person, even another member of staff, who you think is, or has been, stealing from the organisation you must report this to your line manager immediately. It is only by your quick action that further theft can be prevented. Also, remember that if you identify a potential security risk you must report this immediately so that something can be done about it. Make sure that you follow all security procedures properly and that potential security risks outside your own authority are reported to the appropriate person. Never under any circumstances risk injury to yourself, and recognise your own limitations for dealing with security risks.

## ■ DIY 2.1.10

You are an office supervisor at Coopers & Co Chartered Surveyors and just about to close the reception area at 5 pm. A member of staff runs back into the building and explains that they have left something in the office. They ask you if you can hang on for 5 minutes while they go and get it. You agree, but 20 minutes later you are still waiting to go home. You decide to go to the office to see if the member of staff has found what they are looking for. When you open the office door you see them coming out of the Managing Director's office with a computer disk in their hand. They look surprised to see you and explain that they had just popped into the office to close a window. It is now 5.30 pm and you finally see the member of staff out of the building and go home yourself. Some weeks later your line manager tells you that there have been problems with security and that details regarding the financial planning of the company have been leaked to a rival. Apparently they were copied from the Managing Director's database.

1 Write a memo to your line manager explaining the events of the evening when Mr Collins returned to the office. (Do you think this memo should be confidential?)

2 If you were to remain silent about this incident what might happen?

## Knowledge and understanding question bank

1 How do you monitor health, safety and security in your workplace?
2 What legal and regulatory requirements do you have to work to and what would be the consequences if these were breached?
3 What are the most common types of emergency and how do you go about reporting them?
4 What is your organisation's procedure for dealing with emergencies?
5 What emergency equipment do you have available to you and how do use it correctly?
6 What would be the consequence of inappropriate use of emergency equipment?
7 What safety signs, notices and equipment are you familiar with? Where should these be placed?
8 What are your organisation's security procedures and what types of security breach are you most vulnerable to?
9 What is the scope and limit of your own authority when dealing with emergencies and breaches in security?
10 What are your organisation's procedures for recommending improvements to your working environment conditions?

## Claiming credit

For Element 2.1 you must prove that working conditions are monitored to ensure that legal and regulatory requirements and organisational procedures are satisfied. If this is not the case, it must be reported promptly and accurately to the appropriate person. When dealing with emergencies, you must conform to organisational procedures and act within your limits of authority. Opportunities for improving the health, safety and security of the workplace should be identified and recommended to the appropriate persons. The following work products are potential sources of evidence:

- records relating to monitoring activities or actions taken
- reports relating to emergencies and actions taken
- reports of breaches in security and actions needed or taken

Once you have completed your final assessment, you will need to write in your record book or folder how, when and what you have done to prove that you are competent.

The following statement is an example of how one trainee completed this claim:

*At Coopers & Co it is my responsibility to ensure that the office is monitored to ensure that legal and regulatory requirements are satisfied. I use a Health and Safety checklist each month to ensure working conditions conform to the requirements of HASAWA, COSHH, Offices, Shops and Railway Premises Act, Electricity Regulations and Display Screen Equipment Regulations. I also encourage the junior office staff to complete their own checklist each week to ensure that their workstations are organised correctly in accordance with these regulations. Any irregularities that are identified are reported to the Health and Safety officer using a memo, a copy of which is sent to my line manager. I have attended induction training and regular health and safety up-date training where the requirements for emergencies such as illness, accident, fire, evacuation and breaches in security are discussed. I have recently completed a report on office security for my line manager where I have made recommendations on how to improve security in line with Data Protection Act requirements.*

# ■ Element 2.2
## MAINTAIN EFFECTIVE WORKING CONDITIONS

### Performance criteria

1  The workplace is organised to achieve agreed work objectives
2  The organisation of the workplace conforms to legal and regulatory requirements and organisational procedures
3  The use and maintenance of equipment are in accordance with requirements and procedures
4  Opportunities for improving workplace conditions to meet work objectives are identified and appropriate action taken

### Element introduction

Maintaining effective working conditions involves organising all work areas within your authority to suit work flow and the organisation's procedures for maintaining equipment. Positioning furniture, fittings and equipment to promote effective working conditions and the consequences of poor layout must be taken into account when recommending improvements to working conditions.

The term **ergonomics** is used to describe how the working environment can be organised to improve efficiency. This could include something as simple as positioning manuals for operating equipment next to the equipment to which they apply, or the purchase of specialist office furniture such as computer desks and typists' chairs to aid the comfort of the worker and thus improve their productivity.

When considering effective working conditions you must take into account work objectives set by yourself and those set by others. An efficient office is one where all staff work together as a team and by doing so improve not only their own efficiency but that of the office and ultimately the organisation itself. It is also wise to mention that again statutory and non-statutory legal and regulatory requirements must be adhered to. These include legislation such as the Health and Safety at Work Act 1974 and general organisational requirements which, although not legal requirements, are required by the organisation for a purpose.

## ▶ Legal and regulatory requirements

There are a number of legal and regulatory requirements that you must take into account when designing work areas or individual workstations. We have already covered the most important legislation in Element 2.1: HASAWA, the Offices, Shops and Railway Premises Act, and other amendments made to these Acts in recent years. Regulations contained in EC directives have also been discussed and their importance noted in the light of the modern working environment. However, it is wise at this stage to spend some time looking in further depth at the Display Screen Equipment Regulations that affect the workstations of all users of VDU equipment.

### Display screen equipment regulations

Many people believed that working at workstations which had VDUs could be a health hazard. Hazards such as radiation risks, eyesight problems, epilepsy, headaches, stress, skin problems and muscular-skeletal problems (known as Repetitive Strain Injury – RSI) were thought to be common among users. The Health and Safety Executive, after carrying out much research, maintained that none of these problems were the result of the display unit equipment itself but were caused by the effects of working long hours without sufficient breaks in poorly designed workstations.

The HSE published information leaflets, and regulations such as the Health and Safety (Display Screen Equipment) Regulations made it a requirement for employers to assess all workstations for health and safety risks and lower the risks if possible. Regulations stated that the employer must provide training and information on health and safety aspects and incorporate rest periods from the equipment at regular intervals. These regulations also stipulated that employers must pay for eye tests, spectacles or lenses if required by the employee when using a VDU.

The HSE recommended certain actions to be taken to avoid health risks when working with VDU equipment:

- Take regular breaks away from the equipment.
- Keep the display unit clean from dirt, dust and smears.
- Position the screen so that it does not reflect light.
- Use the brightness and contrast control to suit office lighting.
- Use an adjustable chair so that the correct height is maintained.
- Use a chair with a back rest that supports the small of your back when working.
- Use the correct posture by sitting upright.
- Keep your wrists straight when keying in.
- Place documents on a stand.
- Adjust the angle of the screen to suit your position.

The EC directive on workstations, listing the employer's responsibilities regarding the design and operation of the workstation, states that new workstations must comply with the regulations and existing workstations must be reorganised to comply by the end of 1996. This action must be supported by continuous monitoring of the workstation to assess any risk and the provision of adequate training, information and rest periods.

## ■ DIY 2.2.1

Complete the Display Screen Equipment Checklist in Fig 2.14 for one workstation, taking into account the regulations that must be followed. Make sure you make relevant comments as well as ticking yes/no.

### ▶ *Organising a workstation*

How you organise the workstation will influence the way you and others sit. The best arrangement will need to take into account the tasks involved with the job, the equipment that must be to hand and other staff whose job role and the work they produce affect you and vice versa. If your workstation is poorly designed so that you have to sit in bent or twisted positions, aches and pain in your back or neck are likely to result. Think carefully about the requirements of the job and arrange the workstation accordingly.

You will need to think how much time is spent reading from source documents, or looking at the screen. Many people assume that the screen should be placed directly in front of them. If you spend most of your time

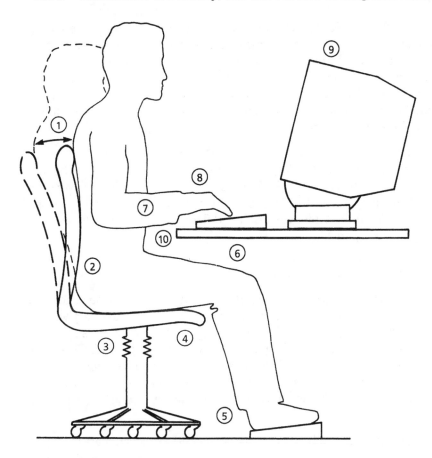

1  Seat back adjustability
2  Good lumbar support
3  Seat height adjustability
4  No excess pressure on underside of thighs and backs of knees
5  Foot support if needed
6  Space for postural change; no obstacles under desk
7  Forearms approximately horizontal
8  Minimal extension, flexion or deviation of wrists
9  Screen height and angle should allow comfortable head position
10  Space in front of keyboard to support hands/wrists during pauses in keying

**Fig 2.13 Seating and posture for typical office tasks.**
Crown copyright

reading from hard copy, the answer could be to move the screen to one side and use a copy holder to bring the documents up to a comfortable height. Position screen and source documents at a comfortable viewing distance depending on the size of the characters and eyesight capabilities. If they are too far away this will result in constant leaning forward, hunched and stooped positions which put a strain on the back and neck and often cause indigestion!

Equipment that is used frequently must be within easy reach. Items used less frequently should still be positioned nearby but should not be allowed to clutter the workstation. Make sure that the area under the workstation is free from obstacles to allow space for postural change and perhaps a footrest. An audio typist will also need floor space to place the audio machine foot pedal.

## ▶ *Organising workflow*

Sitting in the same place for a long period of time can cause aches and pains. The only remedy is to get up and walk around. An effective way to avoid aches and pains is to organise the workflow so that it is interspersed with other tasks such as filing, photocopying, going to the mail room, etc. A break does not necessarily mean sitting down and having a cup of tea! The regulations state that the break is 'away from the VDU equipment' and organising workflow efficiently means that this time is spent carrying out other tasks.

It is wise to organise breaks before aches and pains can start in order to prevent them in the first place. Taking a break once aches and pains have started means that the break is needed to recuperate rather than carry out other tasks. This means that the timing of breaks is more important than the length of the break. Frequent short breaks are much more beneficial than occasional longer breaks.

There is no legislation stating when and how long breaks should be. It is recognised that this depends on the individual and the type of work they are doing. Compare a touch typist who reads from hard copy and looks at the VDU infrequently with a desktop publisher whose full concentration is on the VDU. Both will need to take a break to relax tense muscles, but the desktop publisher will also need the break to give their eyes a rest from the screen. However, it is still true to say that a 5 to 10 minute break every hour is likely to be better than a 15 minute break every 2 hours.

The actual flow of work is best organised if it is first sorted into urgent/non-urgent tasks and important/not important tasks. The urgent tasks take priority over all others, followed by important tasks. Non-important tasks could be delegated to others, with a deadline making

| DISPLAY SCREEN EQUIPMENT CHECKLIST | | | |
|---|---|---|---|
| **Question** | **Answer** | | **Comments** |
| | **Yes** | **No** | |
| **Computer screen:**<br>Is brightness correct?<br>Is there enough light without glare?<br>Are screen and keyboard positioned correctly?<br>Is screen free from dust?<br>Are wires kept neatly?<br>Is contrast/colour correct? | | | |
| **Computer keyboard:**<br>Is keyboard free from dirt and dust?<br>Is keyboard positioned correctly for screen?<br>Are wires kept neatly?<br>Is keyboard easily adjustable to suit individuals? | | | |
| **Central Processing Unit (CPU):**<br>Is CPU kept out of the way?<br>Is CPU kept clean and free from dust?<br>Is hard disk backed-up regularly?<br>Are disks kept safely?<br>Are wires kept neatly? | | | |
| **Printer:**<br>Is printer noisy?<br>Does printer have acoustic hood and is it used?<br>Is toner/ribbon/ink jet checked regularly?<br>Is paper nearby and in regular supply?<br>Do users know how to amend paper jams?<br>Do users know how to refill paper tray? | | | |
| **Furniture/Resources:**<br>Is desk correct height?<br>Is chair adjustable?<br>Is there enough leg room?<br>Is area free from clutter?<br>Is there a document holder?<br>Are wires and electrical supply kept neatly?<br>Is electrical supply checked regularly?<br>Are operating manuals kept nearby?<br>Has user received correct training?<br>Is information on VDU regulations available? | | | |

**Fig 2.14 Display screen equipment checklist**

them a priority for someone else, and non-urgent tasks tackled when there is time but before they move up your list of priorities and become urgent. It is wise for all members of the department or section to use the same system so that, as a team, workflow can be shared out to improve efficiency.

The department head or section leader must monitor workflow to ensure that work objectives are achieved individually, as teams and departmentally. The most appropriate way to do this is to arrange team and departmental meetings where progress can be discussed and any problems resolved. It may be that a colleague has all the answers to your problems and vice versa. A team coming to the end of a project will have time and resources available to help others who in return will be more likely to reciprocate and return the help at a future date.

Work objectives may be those set by yourself, such as self-imposed deadlines to improve your efficiency, or those set by others who need work completed by a set time. It is always wise to set a timescale for tasks to ensure that nothing is forgotten.

## ■ DIY 2.2.2

Make several copies of the workflow plan in Fig 2.15 on A4 landscape paper. Complete one plan each week for the next month. Items brought forward from last week should be first on the plan, followed by new items for the week. Keep your plan up to date and ask your supervisor, line manager or assessor to sign it at the end of each week.

| WORKFLOW PLAN | | | |
|---|---|---|---|
| Name ................................................ Week commencing ................................. | | | |
| Item No | Action required | Problems encountered and resolved | Name of person or team work required for |
| | | | |
| | | | |
| | | | |
| | | | |

Fig 2.15 Workflow plan

# ▶ *Ergonomics*

One of the major factors in creating and maintaining efficiency in an office lies in the way in which the office is designed and laid out. Much research has been carried out on the creation of an office environment which will promote productivity and help to minimise staff turnover. Research has demonstrated the effects which colours and textures have on people's moods and attitudes. Strong colours have been proven to act as a visual distraction while pastel shades are easy to work near.

Equipment such as typists' chairs and computer keyboards are now designed to allow adjustment for different individual use. Wiring and cables are now being incorporated in walls, floors or furniture by modern designers in light of requirements laid down in the HASAWA. There is also legislation that affects the noise levels in the office and this has promoted the use of acoustic hoods to reduce the noise from printers and screens to divide open-plan offices.

The design and layout of the office is not therefore a matter of merely making it look attractive. There is much more to be taken into consideration.

Good design should take into account:

- Current legislation such as toilet and rest-room facilities, room space per person, heat and light.
- Workflow to avoid congestion and accidents and promote efficiency.
- The ability to reorganise the layout with movable furniture, equipment and room dividers.
- Allowing staff to personalise their work area with items such as pictures and plants.
- Privacy and the need for confidentiality by providing screened areas or interview rooms.
- Setting up teams of staff who work closely together.
- Use of standard equipment throughout the office and staff training in the use of that equipment.
- Correct use of colours, textures and even plants to create a pleasing working environment.
- Use of acoustic hoods, screens and covers to minimise noise levels.

The modern approach to these requirements is the open-plan layout which allows a large expanse of space to be divided, using acoustic screens and panels, into separate areas of work. Frequently used equipment, such as the photocopier, are placed centrally for all staff to use. Computer terminals can be networked so that fewer printers are

**Fig 2.16 An open-plan office**

required and information can be passed around the different sections quickly and efficiently.

The open-plan office can be made more attractive by the use of plants and modern office furniture that can be reorganised to suit changes in office requirements and workload. Communications are enhanced as there is less formality and there is also ease of contact with colleagues. However, there are disadvantages in that privacy, confidentiality and control over who takes up an individual's time may be reduced.

It is unlikely that all offices will conform to the vision of up-to-date, attractive, professionally designed working environments. Recent legislation has encouraged a drive towards the redesign of offices to ensure a healthy, secure and safe working environment that promotes efficiency and thus productivity. If your working area or section has been designed with recent legislation in mind it is unlikely that you will need to do anything more to it other than 'personalise' your space and maintain safe working habits.

However, it may be that your working surroundings are not what they should be! The onus is on the employer to provide and maintain a healthy, safe and secure working environment, although there are still actions you can take to improve your own efficiency and that of others. The first action you should take is to inform your line manager of your concerns and intentions. Secondly you can start to put together ideas on how the section or area for which you are responsible can be improved.

If you are concerned about anything to do with health and safety in the office this can be discussed with the health and safety representative if there is one. If there is not, and you feel that potential hazards are being ignored, you are quite within your rights to contact the Local Environmental Health Department or the Health and Safety Executive. However, it is more than likely that your employer would rather be informed of your concerns first and given an opportunity to investigate further.

# ■ DIY 2.2.3

Provide a plan of the area where you work. Carry out a survey that checks on the efficiency of the layout of the office and make recommendations as to how it could be improved. Take into account health and safety regulations.

## ▶ *Operating manuals*

When using a new piece of equipment you would expect to be given instructions on safe and efficient use of the equipment. You may even attend a training session or be visited by a technician who will explain and demonstrate to you how the equipment is to be operated. For most equipment helplines are provided so that if problems are encountered a simple telephone call is all that is required to find expert help. This is particularly so in the case of computing equipment and help is offered as part of the company's customer care service.

However, once the new piece of equipment is in place and training has been given, you may still need to refer to the operating manual on some occasions. You may encounter a problem that you are unsure of or you may wish to find out about a more sophisticated or difficult operation that the equipment is capable of performing. Operating manuals usually have a section on common faults and how to correct them. Electronic equipment often has a facility where a code number shows on the display panel to indicate what the problem is; if you look in the operating manual it will tell you what the problem is and how to correct it.

Operating manuals should always be kept close at hand, near to the equipment they refer to, so that they can be consulted easily. However, manuals can sometimes be long-winded and full of technical information which is of no use to the person trying to find out the remedy to a simple fault. Some manuals do however have a quick reference section that gives instructions without jargon which concentrate on the basic needs of the user.

If you are responsible for supervising or training other members of staff it is important that you have a good understanding of how to operate the equipment around you. Look through the operating manuals and decide for yourself whether it would be suitable to simply hand the manual to a trainee and tell them to read through it and then use the equipment. It is likely that this will not be the case!

You must be prepared to demonstrate the correct use of the equipment and then monitor the progress of the person using the equipment by observing them in practice. This procedure will be improved if you have a simplified set of instructions that can be referred to easily and which set out the main points of the operation. If the person learning how to use the equipment has a problem or a query they can refer to the instructions and try to work out the solution themselves rather than keep having to ask or refer to an operating manual that confuses them even further.

It is likely that you will have access to operating manuals for equipment such as the photocopier, computer, printer, fax, franking machine and most other types of office equipment. The equipment need not be electrical; guillotines, letter openers and basic office equipment such as calculators will all have been purchased with a set of instructions or operating manuals to ensure that you get the best out of the equipment. Refer to the manual yourself. Even if you are already familiar with the operation of the equipment, you may find that it is much cleverer than you thought and able to perform much more complicated and time-saving tasks.

## ■ DIY 2.2.4

Look around your immediate office area and make a list of the operating manuals or information sheets available to you. If there are not any, now is a good time to speak to your supervisor or line manager about this. It may be the case that information is available but you do not know where it is kept. Update your list when you have located this information and write a brief comment about the manuals and information sheets available to you – do they have a quick reference guide; are they jargon free; could you use them for training?

### ▶ *Maintaining equipment*

It is likely that the basic maintenance of office equipment will be carried out under a lease agreement or perhaps by a separate company. It is important for office staff not to get involved in the actual mechanics of the equipment as it is likely that they will cause even more damage.

However, maintenance of equipment does involve the general cleaning, care and attention needed to ensure that equipment works efficiently and effectively. The following examples will give you some ideas about how office equipment is maintained as part of a daily routine. However, it is important to stress that mechanical failure will always require an engineer or technician and electrical equipment must be checked by a trained person operating under the Electricity at Work Regulations.

## Photocopier

Toner cartridges need to be replaced when empty and any spilt toner wiped from the area. A soft cloth should be used to keep the top glass free from smears such as correcting fluid and care should be taken not to scratch the glass with jewellery such as diamond rings. The electrical

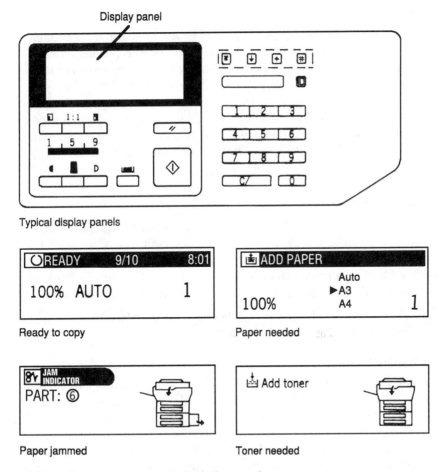

**Fig 2.17 Indicator panel on a typical photocopier**

supply must also be checked regularly and the machine must be switched off at the end of the day.

## Computer

The computer screen should be wiped regularly. Anti-static sprays reduce the build-up of static electricity which attracts dust. The computer casing can also be wiped over with a soft cloth and leads checked to ensure they are safe and firmly in place. The keyboard should also be kept clean and free from dust. Leads should be kept to the back of the workstation so that they do not interfere with or get in the way of other equipment. You should never eat or drink near a computer in case of spills. The central processing unit must be treated with care and maintained to ensure it does not overheat. The computer should be switched off at the end of the day.

## Printer

There are many different types of printer available that may use toner cartridges, ribbons or ink jets, all of which will need replacing when used or worn out. The printer can be placed away from the normal working area and may be used by a number of different people. The printer can also be wiped over with a soft cloth to remove dust and special brushes or vacuums are used on some printers to remove dust from the inside of the equipment. Care must be taken when loading paper into the paper tray and when removing paper jams. The printer should be switched off along with the computer at the end of the day.

## Franking machine

The ink on the roller will have to be replenished when the impression becomes faint. Also the feeder rollers must be kept free from obstacles such as ripped paper. Some machines also require water to be placed in a bottle so that envelopes can be sealed at the same time as the franking is carried out. The franking machine can be kept locked away securely until needed and replaced after use, although care must be taken when moving the machine around so that it is not knocked or dropped.

## Fax machine

The paper in the fax machine needs to be replaced regularly. When the paper roll is nearly finished, this is indicated, sometimes as an error code on the display. The paper roll must be inserted correctly into the machine or it is likely that the machine will jam. The fax must be kept plugged into a telephone socket and should be left switched on overnight to receive messages and to maintain information stored in the memory, such as the date and time. A check must be carried out regularly on the electrical supply to ensure there is no overheating.

## ■ DIY 2.2.5

A working office is likely to have equipment such as fax, photocopier and franking machines. Telephones, computers, printers and less bulky items such as guillotines, calculators and letter openers will also be used. Select 3 items of office equipment and explain how you would maintain them. Carry out research to find out what maintenance support would be provided when leasing a photocopier.

## ▶ *Recommending improvements to working conditions*

This element has concentrated on:

- legal and regulatory requirements
- organising workflow
- ergonomics
- office layout
- using operating manuals
- maintaining equipment

Your performance evidence for this element must show how you organise the workplace to optimise the flow of work and how you follow the organisation's procedures for improving conditions in the workplace. You need to prove that you know how the workplace should operate to improve productivity and safety.

The evidence you require to prove this can be supported by an observation record completed by your supervisor, line manager or assessor of you positioning furniture, fittings, materials and equipment to suit workflow; of you checking that the condition and positioning of furniture optimises the comfort and safety of the user; and of you checking that working conditions comply with organisational procedures and legal/regulatory requirements.

However, you must also prove that you know how to report any concerns you have about your working environment; how to identify and recommend improvements to workplace conditions and take remedial action when conditions do not comply with requirements.

## ■ DIY 2.2.6

Refer to DIY 2.2.1 where you completed a display screen equipment user's checklist. Look back at the information contained in this checklist and make recommendations for improvement. Include in your recommendations items such as emergency action, security and general health and safety.

## Knowledge and understanding question bank

1 What is the HASAWA 1974?
2 What do you understand by the Display Screen Equipment Regulations?
3 What is the 6-pack?
4 How do you organise your workplace to suit workflows?
5 How are your furniture, fittings and equipment positioned to promote effective working conditions?
6 How are productivity levels affected as a consequence of poor layout/furniture?
7 What does the term 'ergonomics' refer to when related to office furniture and equipment?
8 How and when do you use office manuals for equipment?
9 What are your organisation's procedures for maintaining equipment?
10 How do you make recommendations for improvements in working conditions following your organisation's procedures?

## Claiming credit

For Element 2.2 you must provide evidence that proves work areas within your own responsibility are organised to achieve objectives set by yourself and others. Again, you must ensure the organisation of the workplace conforms to legal and regulatory requirements and organisational procedures. The use and maintenance of equipment must be in accordance with requirements and procedures. Opportunities for improving workplace conditions to meet work objectives must be identified and appropriate action must be taken. The following work product is a potential source of evidence:

• Records relating to recommendations for improving workplace conditions

Once you have completed your final assessment, you will need to write in your record book or folder how, when and what you have done to prove that you are competent.

The following statement is an example of how one trainee completed this claim:

*My workstation at Coopers & Co is organised so that I can achieve my work objectives as efficiently as possible. The office is very modern and has been designed to ensure that everything is at hand. The positioning of furniture and fittings and equipment promotes an effective working environment and a pleasant atmosphere to work in. The weekly safety check carried out by the 2 office juniors and my monthly check ensure that the workplace conforms to legal and organisational requirements. We check our own equipment on a regular basis, but* electrical equipment is also checked by the office electrician who places a sticker on it stating that it is safe to use and the date of the last inspection. Equipment such as photocopiers and franking machines are maintained by the company from whom they are leased. If there are any difficulties with equipment I refer to the relevant manual to try to find out what the problem is before contacting the company to request a visit from their engineer. In the case of the new computing equipment I have a helpline number that can be used in the event of a query.

# UNIT 3

# Contribute to the planning, organising and monitoring of work

## ■ Element 3.1
## PLAN AND AGREE WORK

### Performance criteria

1 Tasks are identified and prioritised to meet organisational requirements
2 Resources are allocated to complete identified tasks in order of priority
3 Changes in priorities are recognised and resource allocations adapted accordingly
4 Relevant assistance is identified, negotiated and co-ordinated to meet specific demands and deadlines
5 Tasks are accurately defined and appropriate information provided
6 Work methods and activities are clearly defined and agreed with appropriate people
7 Work methods and activities conform to legal and regulatory requirements and organisational procedures

### Element introduction

This element is about your ability to plan, co-ordinate your own work and agree work with your colleagues. You must be able to demonstrate that you are able to organise your own resources, which include equipment, materials, your time and that of other people.

During your working day you are likely to encounter tasks which are routine: these may be daily, weekly or monthly tasks which are carried out either for your own purposes or for someone else. On top of this you are also likely to have tasks allocated to you from your line manager, on a regular basis or fairly infrequently. There will also be tasks that you offer to do for others, either because they are too busy or for an absent colleague.

Quite often the jobs that you do may be boring, routine and sometimes dirty. The more interesting jobs tend to be more complicated and take time to understand and complete.

At the beginning of each week and each day, you should have a clear plan of what you are going to try and achieve by the end of the day. The list of tasks that you want to get through should be written down and then prioritised. It is sometimes difficult to juggle all the work you may have to carry out in one day. All work usually needs to be completed within an agreed time-scale, but the various time-scales are unlikely to be the same. Some jobs can be left longer than others. How you organise your work will usually be up to you, but you should **prioritise** the work, that is, put it into an order where the most urgent jobs get done first. It is tempting to do the most interesting jobs first – don't be tempted to do this, prioritise sensibly. If you are really too busy to help others when they ask, explain politely and try to tell them when you think you will be free to assist. Do not carry out all of your routine work before you help your colleagues with their urgent work. Prioritising includes thinking whether your colleague's work is more important and urgent than the work you currently have to complete.

Time management is a skill that needs to be acquired, especially when you have a busy work load and frequent deadlines to meet. One of the popular methods of sorting work is by dividing it into 4 piles. Items are considered to be **urgent** if there is an impending deadline to meet: the nearer the deadline, the more urgent the job. Items are **important** if they can have a marked effect on your job or your career or on the organisation you work for.

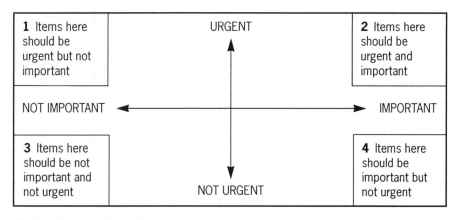

**Fig 3.1 Prioritising work**

**Remember:** Urgent is different from Important. Urgent items need to be dealt with in a short period of time. Important items may affect you, your colleagues or the organisation.

The first priority is to deal with all items falling into Box 2. These are important and urgent, usually those for which deadlines have been set. Due to the deadlines the work may be carried out in a hurry and consequently not to the best of your ability.

Those items falling into Box 1 are generally urgent but not very important. These are the tasks that you will waste quite a bit of time on. Generally these duties are quick and simple and should only have a minimum amount of time allocated to them, freeing up time for the items in Box 2.

Box 3 contains work that is neither important nor urgent. These tasks should be urgently reviewed as it is questionable whether you should be doing them at all – delegate where possible.

The work in Box 4 is important but not very urgent. These are likely to be the jobs that have a deadline but it is currently far off. The problem with these jobs is that they generally do not get done until they have moved to Box 2, as the deadline gets nearer.

# ■ DIY 3.1.1

Make a list of all the work you have currently outstanding at your training centre or at home. Sort it into the sections shown in Fig 3.1 and make out an Action Plan to complete the work.

| ACTION PLAN | | |
|---|---|---|
| **Date** | **Activity and resources needed** | **Date due** |
| | | |

**Note:** If possible this activity should be carried out each week. It will create evidence for Unit 3. In addition the action plan and analysis of work that you do can be cross-referenced and used as evidence for Unit 1 and Unit 4.

▶ *Organising your time, equipment, materials and other people's time*

Once you have organised the work, you may need to review your total organisation of time. Time should be allowed to complete the work you have identified for the day. This time should be uninterrupted by telephones and people – although this may be difficult to achieve. Quality time is important for carrying out your tasks, especially if you are to do them to the best of your ability. If people need to see you then a set time can be made for this, eg in the mornings. Leave sufficient time to travel to other venues; rushing is not good for the body or fellow travellers! Avoid taking work home: it is important for you to totally 'switch off' – it could be said that someone who takes work home is badly organised at work. Review how you use your time.

## ■ DIY 3.1.2

Keep a log of **all** activities carried out during a working week, in normal work hours. The log should show the time as well as the activity completed. Include everything, chats in the corridor, making the tea etc, as well as your actual work and assistance to others. It may seem time-consuming to compile this log, but it could save time in the future. At the end of the week total up the number of hours spent on the different activities and identify where time could be saved or where your routines and habits are wasting valuable time.

▶ *Delegation of duties*

You may be in a position where you can delegate some of the work for which you are responsible. As well as delegating the work you must be prepared to delegate the authority and responsibility to carry out the task. Overall you will still be responsible for the actions of junior staff carrying out your work, but without the necessary authority and responsibility it is unlikely that anyone will be able to complete the work successfully. Ensure you give full instructions and any information required to carry out the work. Make sure that your instructions are fully understood and the quality expected is also known. Avoid making regular checks but ensure that the person can approach you with any problems or difficulties encountered. It is important that your colleagues carrying out the work for you fully understand your requirements, ie that you have defined the tasks accurately, and that you have provided all the appropriate, relevant information necessary. The method of working should be agreed with the person(s) and the deadline for completion should be agreed.

▶ *Organising your work area*

Once you have identified all the tasks that need to be completed during the day, it is important to have a work area that is suited to the work that needs to be done. Your work area may include desk, chair(s), computer and printer, telephone, fax, reference books, directories, small consumables such as stapler, hole punch, paper, pens, pencils, erasers etc. How you arrange these items can have a marked effect on how you complete your work and the time taken to carry out tasks.

## ■ DIY 3.1.3

Make a list of the equipment and materials that you need for each timetabled task or subject. Identify which items are organised and supplied by you and which are supplied by your training centre or workplace.

For each of the tasks you have identified for the day, you will need to ensure you have the right equipment and materials to carry out the work required. It is a waste of time to get up constantly from your work area to fetch individual pieces of equipment or materials from stock. These items should be identified at the beginning of the week and a request put in for the supplies – before you run out.

No matter how well organised and planned your day is, there will always be the urgent item, the urgent phone call request, colleague off ill, etc. Something is likely to happen which will stop you carrying out your intended day. It is essential that when these deviations occur they are identified and the effects on your targets are identified. This may mean that you have to review your work, analyse what the effect is and evaluate the targets – ie are they now realistic or do they need moving? If necessary you should report the deviation to your line manager, especially if they are expecting the work to be completed soon.

## ■ DIY 3.1.4

Complete a work plan for one or more of the subjects for which you are currently completing work. This may include assignment work, where you need to identify resources, co-ordinate with others, consult with tutors, access specific resources etc.

| WORK PLAN | | | |
|---|---|---|---|
| Objective: .................................................................................................... | | | |
| Time allowed: ............................. Target completion date:............................... | | | |
| **Date** | **Task** | **Resources required (people and equipment)** | **Target date and time** |
| | | | |

Under the 'Task' column, list the tasks identified and being carried out but also identify any change of target or deviation in a different colour or highlighter. Include the reason for the change.

## ▶ Legal and regulatory requirements

While you are working it is important that you abide by the necessary legal requirements. There are about 30 Acts of Parliament governing the working environment. Some of the more important ones are:

### Health and Safety at Work Act 1974

The Health and Safety at Work Act (HASAWA) is an enabling Act, which means that it is designed to bring together all the previous legislation and make sense out of it. However, at the moment many of these earlier Acts exist side by side with the HASAWA. The basic idea of the Act is that there should be a joint effort by employers and employees to provide a safe and healthy working environment.

The employer has to provide safe equipment and systems of work, a safe working environment and adequate arrangements and facilities for welfare. It is also their duty to ensure safe use, storage, transport and handling of substances and articles, and if an accident should occur they must investigate this fully. There must be a safe means of access to and from work and all staff should be fully informed, supervised and trained in accordance with their work role.

Employees are responsible for taking care of their own safety as well as the safety of other people who may be affected by their actions. It is also stated that employees must co-operate with their employers and/or any other persons involved in carrying out duties under this Act.

**The Electricity at Work Regulations 1989** have been made under the Health and Safety at Work Act 1974 and cover establishments such as colleges, hospitals and commercial premises. The purpose of these regulations is to require precautions to be taken against the risk of death or injury from electricity at work. Injury or death caused by electric shock, electric burn, fires of electrical origin, electric arcing or explosions initiated or caused by electricity are covered by these regulations. There are maintenance guidelines for all electrical equipment. Even the office kettle, word processors and electric fans have to be inspected and maintained on a regular basis. Companies are advised to label their electrical equipment with details of when last checked and date of next inspection.

**Fig 3.2 An example of a completed electrical equipment label**

**The Reporting of Injuries, Diseases and Dangerous Occurrences Regulations 1985** (RIDDOR) state that an accident book must be kept by anyone who employs workers. In the event of an accident the employer must maintain a written account of what happened, which will be inspected periodically by the relevant authority. If an employee is off work, due to an accident, for more than 3 days the employer must inform the Local Authority Environmental Health Department or an Inspector from the Health and Safety Executive, depending on who has legal jurisdiction for that particular premises. The relevant authority must be informed *verbally* within 24 hours of the accident occurring, and *in writing* using form F2508 within 7 days. This information is used to identify accident trends and unsafe working practices.

The nature of the accident report is not stipulated by RIDDOR: it is left to the responsible person to use a form or record that best suits the purpose. A photocopy of form F2508 kept in a file would suffice, and so would an entry about an injury in a DSS Accident Book (B1 510) where kept by an employer for social security reasons. The Health and Safety Executive leaflet HSE 24 *Reporting under RIDDOR* provides details of these regulations.

Section 2(3) of the Health and Safety at Work Act 1974 states that if 5 or more people are employed then, by law, the company has to have a written statement detailing its health and safety policy. The statement should be specific to the company and set out the general policy for protecting the health and safety of employees at work and the arrangements for putting that policy into practice. This statement must be brought to the attention of all employees and others who may be affected by the employer's undertaking. Furthermore, it should be reviewed and amended, if necessary, periodically as and when working conditions change.

## Offices, Shops and Railway Premises Act 1963

The Offices, Shops and Railways Premises Act is much more specific than the HASAWA which has a general approach to health and safety in the workplace. This Act stipulates working requirements and informs employees of their rights.

This Act states specific requirements, for example, that premises must be kept clean and that adequate floor space must be provided for each worker and their equipment. The temperature must be kept above 16°C and a thermometer must be displayed at all times. Ventilation must be adequate, without draught, and there must be adequate, separate toilet facilities for both sexes. Washing facilities with hot and cold water, soap and clean towels must be available and fresh drinking water and a place to hang and dry clothes has to be provided.

This Act also states that excessive noise or vibration from machinery should be isolated, floors and stairways should be safe and kept clear, heavy weights should not be lifted, and chairs provided for employees who stand to do their work.

In accordance with safety provisions, personnel trained in first aid should be available at all times and adequately stocked first-aid boxes have to be provided. Office machines must be guarded where necessary. Gangways should be kept clear and fire exits together with fire drills and assembly points brought to the attention of staff. The provision of fire extinguishers that are regularly checked and kept in working order is also stipulated.

It is useful to note at this point that most local fire brigades are responsive to employers wishing to gain advice and receive demonstrations concerning the prevention of fire. It is a useful exercise for all personnel to have 'hands on' experience in the use of fire extinguishing equipment so that they know how to act in the event of a fire breaking out.

There are other Acts in operation which deal with different aspects of the working environment, such as:

- Fire Precautions Act 1971
- Employers' Liability (Compulsory Insurance) Act 1969
- Employers' Liability (Defective Equipment) Act 1969
- Occupiers' Liability Act 1957

There are also government regulations such as those for the Control of Substances Hazardous to Health (COSHH). The Health and Safety Executive leaflet IND(G)136(L) *COSHH – Brief guide for the employer* provides further information regarding COSHH regulations. There are also statutory requirements for specific areas such as construction, agriculture and the shop floor.

**The Information for Employees Regulations 1989** provide employers with a general document in the form of a poster that has to be displayed prominently in all offices (or in the form of a leaflet that is distributed to all peripatetic workers). The poster or leaflet also informs employees of their rights and should detail specific information regarding the employees' local enforcing authority and the address of the local employment medical service.

## ▶ *Your employer's legal responsibilities*

Employers have a duty to protect their employees and keep them informed about health and safety, in the same way as the employees have a responsibility to look after themselves and others. If there is a problem this should be discussed with the employer or safety representative if there is one. It is possible for you to contact the Health and Safety Executive, your Local Authority or perhaps the local fire brigade direct if you feel your employer is putting people's health or lives at risk. In very general terms all personnel in the work place or college should know:

1  how to contact first-aiders
2  what to do in the event of a fire
3  what to do if they discover a fire
4  how to operate equipment safely
5  where to locate a first-aid box
6  where the fire equipment is kept
7  where the accident book is kept

This information will be covered in the safety policy, rules and emergency procedures of the organisation which should be explained during induction training and followed as a matter of daily routine, with supervision, regular updating and adequate training.

## ▶ *Possible hazards*

There is a wide range of possible hazards in an office and it is the responsibility of everyone to ensure that potential accidents are prevented before they happen. It is imperative that staff appreciate the dangers that can occur from unsafe practices such as:

- slippery or poorly maintained floors
- lifting heavy items without bending properly
- staircases and fire exits used as storage facilities
- frayed carpets
- standing on chairs to reach high shelving
- removing safety guards on a machine
- trailing electric leads
- obstacles in gangways
- using faulty electrical equipment

The above list is by no means exhaustive as the potential hazards are many and changeable. All you need to do at any one time is to look around your immediate area and spot the potential hazards that we live with every day. It is critical that we all understand and endeavour to reduce risks by ensuring that we and our staff are fully aware of safe working practices.

Any organisation that employs staff is responsible for their welfare and must adhere to the legislation set down. Local Authority Health and Safety Officers are able to check any private company or organisation to inspect premises, accident report records and the provision of trained 'first-aiders' and adequate first-aid equipment. Colleges, however, are classified as government buildings and therefore come under the jurisdiction of the Health and Safety Executive.

Under **The Health and Safety (First-Aid) Regulations 1981**, workplaces must have first-aid provision. The form it should take depends on various factors, particularly the nature and degree of hazards at work, but also whether there is shift working, what medical services are available and the number of employees. The number of first-aiders you need depends primarily on the degree of hazards. If employees work in a low-hazard workplace (for example a bank or library) there should be at least one first-aider for every 50 workers employed. In a more hazardous workplace (for example a factory or quarry) a larger number would be required.

First-aiders must have undertaken training and obtain qualifications approved by the Health and Safety Executive. At present first-aid certificates are valid for 3 years. Refresher courses must be started before the certificate expires, otherwise a full course will need to be taken. A qualified first-aider will be trained to administer treatment using the contents of an adequately stocked first-aid box. First-aid boxes should only contain the items that a first-aider has been trained to use. They should not contain medication of any kind. They must always be kept adequately stocked and if antidotes or special equipment are needed to deal with a specific hazard these may be kept near the hazard area or in the first-aid box. Refer to leaflet IND(G)3(L) *First-aid in your workplace* for more information.

## ▶ *Ergonomics*

The word 'ergonomics' simply means the design of office equipment so that it is suited to its human operators, and will not cause them to waste energy. Chairs, desks and various other pieces of office furniture and equipment are designed to be comfortable and supportive. Desks and tables should be of a convenient height, and chairs in particular should be adjustable to give proper back support so that a relaxed, upright posture can be maintained easily.

Office furniture design is being taken very seriously, with increasing emphasis on the functional rather than the beautiful but impractical. Furniture is being designed with light, easy to move, linkable desks, cabinets, printer tables etc for total flexibility and use of available space. Easily cleaned surfaces and colour/style co-ordination are also taken into account.

Physical conditions and flow of work in the office environment have had to adapt over recent years to the technological explosion. For example:

- Heating, ventilation and 'clean', dry air are particularly important for the functioning of machines such as computers.
- Sufficient power and access to power points are essential.
- Dedicated circuits are necessary, to keep computers separate from the main power supply in case of electrical fault or power failure.
- Desks, chairs and office furniture are designed for wire management (keeping the many cables from telephones, computers, printers, etc, under control).

In order to reduce any possible negative effects on health through the use of VDU-based equipment for lengthy periods of time, the Health and Safety Executive has recommended a series of guidelines for ensuring that the office environment is compatible with the introduction of new technology. Leaflet IND(G) 36(L) *Working with VDUs* is published by the Health and Safety Executive and provides useful information regarding the use of VDUs in an office environment.

The guidelines recommend that the VDU's adjustable brightness and contrast controls are used to improve the displayed image. These, together with screen filters, will reduce eye strain. VDU keyboards should be detached from the screen so that the distance between the screen and the operator can be adjusted according to personal preference, and the keys themselves should have a matt surround to minimise glare and have concave tops with adjustable slope to maximise operator comfort.

VDUs generate heat and this will have to be taken into account when heating an office environment to an acceptable temperature. Adequate ventilation and humidity also need to be maintained. Lighting has to be adequate for the operator to read documents but not too bright or directed so that it glares on the screen and makes it difficult to read. Undue noise is also disruptive and therefore printers and other noisy office machinery should be sited away from operators, or provided with acoustic covers.

The time spent at a VDU will depend upon the nature of the work being performed. Lengthy periods of keying in text may require rapid keyboarding but will not involve extensive concentration on the screen itself. However, if the work involves composition of text, work with spreadsheets, databases or desktop publishing this may require shorter work periods as far greater concentration on the screen is necessary.

Our surroundings continually change and therefore the guidelines and legislation set out by the government, and more recently by the EU, will also be adapted to take into account the changes in our working environment. New regulations were introduced in the UK in 1993 and are commonly known as the '6-pack':

1 **The Management of Health and Safety at Work Regulations
1992** – Under these regulations employers must carry out risk
assessment and keep records of the assessments along with measures
recognised as necessary to control the risk. Competent people must be
appointed to help implement health and safety policy and make
arrangements to plan, organise, control, maintain, monitor and review
health and safety arrangements. Emergency procedures must be set up
to deal with situations of serious or imminent danger. Lastly, they must
provide full information and training to all employees with details of any
risk they might incur.

2 **The Workplace (Health, Safety and Welfare) Regulations 1992** –
These regulations state minimum legal standards covering health,
safety and welfare. They cover such things as lighting, ventilation,
temperature, space and room dimensions, workstations, seating,
cleanliness, as well as looking after the workplace and equipment in it.
Welfare facilities such as toilets, washing facilities, rest rooms and
eating accommodation are also covered.

3 **The Health and Safety (Display Screen Equipment) Regulations
1992** – These regulations are applicable to all employees who regularly
use display screen equipment. Employers must assess all workstations
for health and safety risks and lower the risks if possible. Regular rest
periods must be taken and eye tests, spectacles or lenses provided if
advised by an optician. Training and information on use of equipment
must also be provided.

4 **The Provision and Use of Work Equipment Regulations 1992** –
These regulations relate to all machinery, appliances, apparatus or tools
used at work. The employer must ensure that all equipment is suitable
for the task and is well maintained. Training on how to use machinery
must be given to staff.

5 **The Personal Protective Equipment at Work (PPE) Regulations
1992** – These relate to the provision of protective clothing and
equipment when risks cannot be eliminated. Employers must make
sure that protective equipment fits properly, is maintained in good
condition and is provided free of charge.

6 **The Manual Handling Operations Regulations 1992** – Employers
must make sure that employees avoid handling and lifting activities that
may cause injury. The employer must assess and reduce the risk of
injury where possible and provide information to employees to help
them to avoid the risk.

In addition to the legal requirements set down by the Government your
organisation may have its own requirements and procedures regarding
health and safety, security, confidentiality, etc.

# ■ DIY 3.1.5

Write a set of guidelines for students attending work placement, outlining the legal requirements they need to conform to while working with an organisation.

## Knowledge and understanding question bank

1  How are work roles and responsibilities identified and allocated within your organisation?
2  How do you identify and prioritise tasks on a daily basis?
3  What resources do you require for your tasks?
4  What targets do you usually set for completed work and how do you ensure they are met?
5  What method of time management do you use?
6  What co-ordination of tasks have you needed to carry out?
7  Which method of communication do you use when informing others of your work methods?
8  How do you negotiate the assistance of others?
9  How do you deal with changed priorities?
10  What legal requirements do you comply with while working?

## Claiming credit

For Element 3.1 you must prove that you have planned and agreed work of your own and tasks with others. The resources used must include equipment, materials, your own time and other people's time.

The following work products are potential sources of evidence:

● copies of correspondence
● initial and amended work plans
● records of discussions
● copies of information supplied

Once you have completed your final assessment, you will need to write in your record book or folder how, when and what you have done to prove that you are competent.

The following statement is an example of how one trainee completed this claim:

*During my work at D & G Scaffolding I completed work plans and set my own targets and deadlines. I made sure that I acquired all the resources necessary before starting a task, so that it could be completed in optimum time. If alternative tasks or urgent work interrupted me I returned to the original tasks as quickly as possible. If necessary I asked for assistance in order to complete both jobs. I made sure that I provided necessary information to my colleagues and agreed my work and the way in which I would complete it – prior to commencing. At all times I followed the legal requirements for working and followed D & G regulations regarding equipment storage and movement within the hardhat area.*

# ■ Element 3.2
# MONITOR AND CONTROL THE ACHIEVEMENT OF AGREED TARGETS

## Performance criteria

**1** Valid and accurate control mechanisms are maintained in accordance with organisational procedures

**2** Work outcomes are reviewed, analysed and evaluated against agreed targets

**3** Reasons for deviations from planned targets are identified and, where necessary, reported to appropriate persons

**4** Corrective actions are implemented, without delay, within limits of own authority, and relevant people informed

### Element introduction

In Element 3.1 we covered the requirement to identify and agree work for yourself and with others. Target times and dates were set and agreed, along with work methods and activities. This element is about your ability to monitor and control the targets and work agreed. It includes setting up your own procedures to monitor achievement of targets; checking actual targets against planned targets; reporting deviations and taking actions to correct activities.

### ▶ *Monitoring work progress*

Once a task has been agreed, either for yourself to complete or with others, it is important to regularly check and monitor the progress being made, to ensure that the work is completed by the agreed deadline. There are many dangers lying about, ready to interrupt and delay your work, ones that you should be aware of and on the lookout for.

### ▶ *Time-wasters*

Each person will have their own 'time-wasters' which may have become bad habits. To ensure that you cut down on wasting time and increase your productivity, you should try to identify where and when you are guilty of wasting time. Answer the following questions by ticking **Yes** or **No**.

| **Do you:** | **Yes** | **No** |
|---|:---:|:---:|
| • like and attend several meetings? | ☐ | ☐ |
| • accept too many jobs at the same time? | ☐ | ☐ |
| • have a disorganised, messy desk? | ☐ | ☐ |
| • spend too much time chasing papers and away from your desk? | ☐ | ☐ |
| • make too many non-productive telephone calls? | ☐ | ☐ |
| • go to work tired? | ☐ | ☐ |
| • read absolutely everything that comes to you, slowly and in depth? | ☐ | ☐ |
| • get several interruptions – telephone and visitors? | ☐ | ☐ |
| • plan and set yourself goals and targets every day? | ☐ | ☐ |
| • do other people's work? | ☐ | ☐ |
| • spend time on idle chit-chat? | ☐ | ☐ |
| • put off things that should be done today? | ☐ | ☐ |
| • have an active personal life? | ☐ | ☐ |
| • perform unnecessary work? | ☐ | ☐ |
| • have a good filing system that is up to date? | ☐ | ☐ |

This may help you to identify areas which have potential for improvement.
You should always write yourself a 'To Do' list or a list of tasks for the day,
and set targets for them. Identify those that you want to complete before
tea/coffee break, before lunch, before the meeting, etc. Where you are
fortunate to have secretarial support, make the best use of it. Secretaries
and administrative assistants are able to organise, exercise judgement,
obtain information and assume responsibility, screen mail and telephone
calls, to name but a few tasks. Organise your work area to facilitate the
workflow and eliminate unnecessary movement; ensure you have all the
consumables and equipment you need. Remove any unnecessary items
and make sufficient work space. Place the telephone on your left side if
you are right-handed, or on the right side if you are left-handed. This
leaves your writing hand free to take notes.

## ■ DIY 3.2.1

List your own personal 'time-wasters' and identify next to them the approximate
amount of time spent each day on them. Next prioritise them in order, the one
which wastes the most time first, down to the last one which wastes the least time

each day. Over the next week try to reduce the top three on your list: set yourself targets. At the end of the week, make a written report on how well you have done.

For each major task or project that you are responsible for, you should have a valid and accurate control mechanism, a procedure that will inform you of progress to date, if things are on target, or if there are problems. Your organisation may already have a system in place. Alternatively you may need to design something suitable for the work you carry out.

The frequency with which you need to check on progress will depend on the type of job, how many people are involved and the target date. The more people involved, the more co-ordination will be required to ensure that there are no hiccups. The type of problems that may occur could be: lack of understanding by an individual (or more) as to their role, lack of resources or information, individual(s) allocated work of higher priority, individual(s) off sick/on holiday, etc.

Projects should be broken down into smaller tasks with separate deadlines and targets set. Achievement of all the targets combines to become completion of the project. Planning will be necessary before allocating tasks and responsibilities or gathering required information and resources.

## ■ DIY 3.2.2

Identify a project/assignment or other piece of work that you need to complete within the next few weeks. Complete the plan shown in Fig 3.3 before commencing the work and review your targets regularly. Ensure you make a comment on each review. If problems occur, complete a problem sheet.

When problems occur that are outside your responsibility or authority you should discuss them with your line manager or the person requiring the tasks to be completed. This is particularly important when the problem is likely to affect the completion date.

### ▶ *Renegotiating deadlines*

If a difficulty or problem occurs that is likely to affect the completion date, then all those involved should be informed as quickly as possible. The person requiring the tasks completed should be informed first, and a new deadline renegotiated. It is important, at this stage, that you have all the necessary information to hand before proposing a new deadline date.

116

## WORK PLAN AND REVIEW

Description of task: ............................................................     Job No:............

Completion deadline: ............................................................

| Sub-tasks | Priority order | Time limit | Resources | Comment | Target met |
|---|---|---|---|---|---|
| List here the separate tasks required to carry out the project or activity | Number the tasks in order of priority | Estimate the time required | List here the resources needed, ie telephone calls to make, people to see, information sources, etc | Review comment and difficulties encountered | Tick if target met |
| | | | | | |

### Evaluation and review

At the end of the task, evaluate and review your actions, identify points that could be improved, changes you would make if repeating the task, etc.

Fig 3.3 Explanation of work plan, for use with DIY 3.2.2

**WORK PLAN AND REVIEW**

Description of task: .................................................................... Job No: ..........

Completion deadline: ....................................

| Sub-tasks | Priority order | Time limit | Resources | Comment | Target met |
|-----------|----------------|------------|-----------|---------|------------|
|           |                |            |           |         |            |
|           |                |            |           |         |            |

Evaluation and review

**Fig 3.4 Blank work plan, for use with DIY 3.2.2**

---

**PROBLEM SHEET**

Description of task: _____  Job No: _____

Cause of the problem: _____

_____

_____

Potential answers to the problem:

1 _____

_____

_____

2 _____

_____

_____

3 _____

_____

_____

Deadline: _____

Review dates and action: _____

_____

_____

_____

_____

_____

_____

_____

_____

**Fig 3.5 Problem sheet, for use with DIY 3.2.2**

Once a new date is agreed, you can then inform the rest of the team and others involved, and monitor progress once again to ensure that the new deadline is met without fail.

## ▶ *Maintaining quality*

Quality standards may already be part of your organisation, either in the form of your own agreed standards or your organisation may be approved to BS5750 or involved in Investors in People. All these schemes have particular standards that the employees and the organisation as a whole have achieved or are working towards. Part of the review and checks that you make should concern the quality and standards being achieved. Word processing should be 100 per cent accurate and follow the approved layout and format of the organisation (house style), customers' orders should be processed within an agreed period, eg 5 days, telephones should be answered within 3 rings, etc. Everyone involved in a project or joint task should be fully informed of the quality standards related to the task being undertaken.

## ■ DIY 3.2.3

Make enquiries as to the standards agreed within your training centre and in particular to your programme of study. State next to each standard the measure that is being used.

As well as checking quality you may also need to check on the **quantities** being produced. This is more likely to occur in a manufacturing industry. However, it is still relevant to service and other industries. Sales representatives may have set targets to achieve, eg 50 customers to see each month; accountants may have a set number of final accounts or audits to complete; you may have a set number of customers to write to per week/month. It is important to check that as the quantity of work increases, the quality still reaches the same standards. It is unfortunate that as people become more busy, the work they carry out may not be done to the same standard, ie corners tend to be cut. When monitoring and reviewing tasks involving quantities you should carry out a spot check regarding the quality as well as the progress towards deadline. A letter written to the last customer of the day should be of exactly the same standard as that sent to the first customer of the day. The first telephone enquiry of the day should be treated in exactly the same way as the last one – with the same politeness, courtesy and interest.

# ■ DIY 3.2.4

Produce a leaflet of guidance for junior staff relating to the meeting of deadlines, including quality and quantity targets. Before you start this task complete a work plan and review sheet and set your own standards for the task. Against each standard state how you will evaluate the standard, ie what evidence will be available. If problems occur, a problem sheet should be completed. Finally, after completing the task, produce an evaluation report of the standards you achieve .

## Knowledge and understanding question bank

1 What procedure for monitoring and checking targets and work in progress have you set up and used?
2 How and what corrective actions have you taken to ensure targets are met?
3 What is the scope and limit of your authority when taking corrective actions regarding deviations from targets?
4 What methods of evaluating work outcomes have you used?
5 What is your organisation's procedure for reporting issues and recommendations?
6 What is your organisation's procedure for amending work targets?
7 How do you collect information regarding progress towards the target?
8 What methods of evaluating quality targets have you used?
9 What methods of evaluating quantity targets have you used?
10 What methods of evaluating time targets have you used?

## Claiming credit

For Element 3.2 you must prove that you have monitored and controlled achievement of agreed targets by controlling information on the use of resources and progress towards meeting agreed targets. The targets should include quantity, time and quality.

The following work products are potential sources of evidence:

- records of work achieved
- records of discussions
- internal memos
- amended work targets

Once you have completed your final assessment, you will need to write in your record book or folder how, when and what you have done to prove that you are competent.

The following statement is an example of how one trainee completed this claim:

*Part of my work at D & G Scaffolding involved monitoring targets and deadlines of work. This was particularly important as customers expected scaffold to be erected*

121

at particular times. I kept a diary and work sheets for each of the jobs. I monitored the return of scaffold to the workshop and tracked it back out on to the next job. If the scaffold erectors were delayed for any reason I had to inform the office manager and the customer of the delay and of the new target times. I have also carried out special projects where I had to gain information and set up new control procedures. This evidence and the target information related to it is contained in Unit 8.

# ■ Element 3.3
# MANAGE APPOINTMENTS

## Performance criteria

**1** Appointments are managed to meet work objectives and the availability of the appropriate persons

**2** Appointments are negotiated with the appropriate persons and agreed within given time constraints

**3** Appointments are confirmed with the appropriate persons

**4** Essential information is recorded appropriately and is up to date, legible and accurate

**5** Reasons for non-attendance at appointments are promptly clarified and reported to the appropriate persons

**6** Security and confidentiality procedures conform to organisational requirements

## Element introduction

This element relates to your skills and ability in being able to negotiate and confirm appointments for yourself and on behalf of others. It includes the recording, scheduling and monitoring of appointments, dealing with changes in priority and emergencies and the consequent rescheduling of appointments. Documentation such as records of appointments, correspondence and notes of discussions relating to appointments will be essential evidence for this element.

## ▶ *Time allocation*

The smooth running of an office depends ultimately on the correct allocation of the time available during the working day. It may be part of your responsibility to ensure that your day and your line manager's day are organised effectively and efficiently so that meetings, conferences, interviews and so on are conducted with the minimum of fuss in an atmosphere that is free from worry about minor details.

There are a variety of aids available to help plan efficient allocation of time and scheduling so that time is used as effectively as possible. The choice of aid will depend upon both your line manager's and your needs and the type of appointments that need to be made – in other words it, or they, will be chosen to complement the daily activities of the office.

There are 3 main types of office scheduling aid in general use that are used to indicate, at a glance, time allocation. These aids may be used independently or in combination to provide a back-up and prevent double bookings being made.

1 **Desk diary** – This diary is normally A4 size and one page is used for each day of the week with the exception of Saturday and Sunday. The page may also be divided into hours or half-hours to assist in allocating time. The diary is kept to remind you and others of important dates and appointments in the future. It is also a record of the details of past appointments and notes taken.

2 **Visual planners** – These planners are often made of plastic for durability and also to allow information to be inserted and deleted by using non-permanent pens. It is usual for planners to be poster size and displayed on a wall so they can be viewed easily. Because of this they are often used for detailing holiday and closure dates. It is possible to

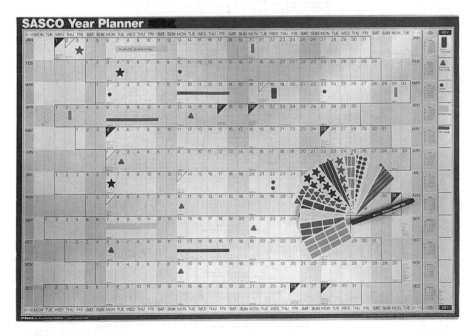

**Fig 3.6 Visual wall planner**

find A4 planners in diaries or personal organisers but these tend not to be so popular because of the lack of space available for insertions. Visual planners allow colour coding to be used to indicate particular or important dates/events but they are not appropriate for detailing confidential information.

3 **Microcomputer or electronic diary** – Details of names, addresses, telephone numbers and dates of appointments can be fed into the computer which can then be used as a diary, address book and appointments itinerary. Reminders of appointments are indicated on the display panel or can be printed out. When new appointments are fed into the program the user will be alerted if these overlap with previously made arrangements. The electronic diary is able to print appointment cards and can also be used as a reminder of past appointments and any decisions reached. It is possible to buy hand-held electronic diaries no larger than a pocket calculator. Alternatively software may be installed in a desktop computer networked to computers used by secretaries so that bookings can be made and confirmed at a glance throughout an entire company.

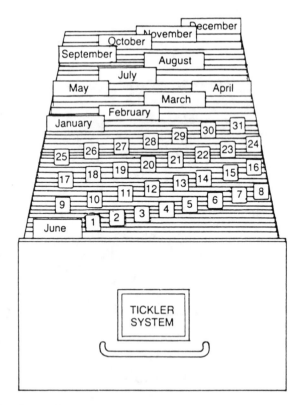

**Fig 3.7 A bring forward system**

There are also aids in use to ensure that our memory is jogged to perform certain tasks on a particular day or to remind us of appointments made for a particular date and time. A follow-up or bring-forward system can be made up using index cards or folders to indicate each day of the month. With this system every day a check is made to see what action is required to prepare for the following day or, in some cases, for some time in the future. (*See* Fig 3.7.)

## ▶ *Making appointments*

When organising time, correct diary management will ensure that the day runs as smoothly and productively as possible. The time available should be used to the full and regulated well. You may make decisions for yourself and on behalf of your manager and book appointments in accordance with your needs and priorities. To do so requires practical skills in organising and co-ordinating an effective working day.

Whether using a diary, planner or computer it is important that entries are:

1 Accurate – to avoid misunderstanding
2 Concise – to provide only relevant information
3 Up to date – to avoid double bookings
4 Confirmed – to ensure all parties have full details
5 Sequenced – to make the most of the working day

Always check to make sure there is not a clash and that enough time is allocated for the work that has to be carried out. It may also be necessary to allow travelling time between appointments and remember that lunch/dinner, coffee or tea breaks during the day will be appreciated.

It is usual to enter appointments into the desk diary in pencil so that corrections can be made easily, and always allow sufficient space between insertions for others to write in notes. Once an appointment has been made by telephone it is essential that this is confirmed in writing so all parties concerned are in possession of full details and any confusion can be clarified beforehand.

Appointments may be made in a personal desk diary or in a pocket diary when out of the office and it is essential that these are checked and confirmed immediately upon arrival back into the office in order to synchronise all scheduling aids and avoid double bookings.

Many people make a list of the appointments for the coming day on an appointments card so that it is easy to see at a glance who has to be seen and at what time. A special code against the appointment may be used to signify that papers are necessary. If the appointments are out of the office an appointments card will still be used, but this needs to be prepared in advance so that you have all the relevant paperwork in your possession the day before.

# ■ DIY 3.3.1

You work for Mrs Miller, Sales Manager, Coopers and Co Chartered Accountants, 4 The Broadway, Leeds. Using 10 sheets of A4 paper draw up two 5-day diaries (or photocopy 5 blank pages, twice, from a diary) for the following week – indicate date, time slots and allow enough space for notes to be added by your line manager. You and Mrs Miller are based in Room 4 and always keep Thursday 9.00–10.00 free to update your diaries and Friday mornings are kept free to allow time for administrative work. Appointments that have already been arranged are:

1  Monday (9.00–12.00) Monthly Sales Meeting – Rm 4
        (1.00–3.00) Marketing Committee Meeting – Rm 2
2  Tuesday (all day) Sales Presentation in Bristol
3  Wednesday (9.30–11.30) Interviewing (Joe Davis, internal applicant) – Rm 3
        (2.00 - 4.00) Interviewing (Lisa Sear, internal applicant) – Rm 3
4  Thursday (1.00–3.30) Annual Sales Review – Rm 7
5  Friday (12.00–2.00) Working lunch with MD – Rm 4

This information will be required by Mrs Miller but you will need to include more information in your own diary. Using the other 5 sheets of A4 paper draw up another diary for your own use detailing the information above but also including details of the paperwork you think you will have to prepare beforehand. Also, make a note of the meeting and interview rooms that need to be booked, tea/coffee to be arranged and when and where lunch will be served.

## ▶ *Booking and confirming appointments*

You may be called upon to book appointments directly with the person concerned, and this will be a simple task of discussing a mutually convenient time for all parties concerned and then writing to confirm the arrangements made. However, you may find yourself having to arrange a meeting for several people indirectly through their respective secretaries, and this will prove to be more involved.

The advantage of dealing with secretaries is that they too should be aware of their manager's priorities and working practices and will be in a position to make judgements, prioritise and discuss the most suitable arrangements. If you are dealing with a less experienced secretary you may need to take added precautions to ensure that all details are confirmed and accepted.

It is wise to remember that when arranging appointments out of the office you will need to request additional information to prevent you and others wasting time and ultimately running late for appointments. Points to remember are:

1 Full name, address and telephone number of contact
2 Travel arrangements
3 Car-parking facilities and security measures
4 Directions or identifiable landmarks
5 Lunch arrangements
6 Travelling time between appointments

## ■ DIY 3.3.2

Your manager has a working lunch arranged with the MD, Mrs Downes, on Friday. This appointment will have to be confirmed in writing and directions given as to the easiest route from her office at 126 Highbury Way, North London to Liverpool. You will also have to remind the MD that this letter will be needed to gain access to the company's car park and reception area and that a buffet lunch will be provided in Room 4.

### ▶ *Allocating time effectively*

The first point to remember in allocating time effectively is that you or your manager will require uninterrupted time for report writing, dealing with correspondence and making telephone calls. It will have to be agreed when this block of time will be – is your manager happy to arrange this time around appointments or should a regular block of time be allocated? If you are working for more than one person then this block will need to be allocated to different people at different times.

It is important to remember that ideas and problems do not happen according to a set timetable and therefore your skills of co-ordination will be tested when you need to schedule appointments. It is usual practice to discuss each week before it begins to ensure any changes have been noted and to discuss problems or emergencies that may have to be dealt with immediately.

When allocating time you will need to prioritise in order to schedule appointments appropriately. Ensure you are in possession of all the relevant information, together with a thorough knowledge of your manager's and the organisation's working practices, in order to make judgements.

Points to bear in mind when prioritising are:

1  Can you deal with the person yourself?
2  Is someone else better able to deal with the person?
3  How much time is required?
4  How urgent is the appointment?
5  Will additional information be required?
6  Whom are you dealing with?

The skill of prioritising will improve with experience and the longer you are involved with the same company or section the better your judgement will become. If you are ever in doubt your line manager should not begrudge you time to discuss matters and what they expect of you when it comes to arranging appointments.

## ■ DIY 3.3.3

You have just received a telephone call from the secretary of Mr Elliot explaining that he is unable to attend the working lunch arranged for Friday. The secretary has asked if this appointment could be rearranged for the same time earlier in the week, but you have confirmed all the other bookings and as they involve several people you are reluctant to have to reschedule. Your line manager has said that you really do have to fit it in somewhere – he is an important client! Once you have decided upon a suitable time and date, write a letter to Mr Elliot confirming the new arrangements. Remember to enter the details into both diaries.

### ▶ *Keeping on schedule*

There is nothing worse than spending time and effort planning your day only to find that the first appointment runs late and throws everything off schedule for the rest of the day. To avoid this situation, time should be rationed and allocated to each appointment according to its importance. This allocation of time should then be detailed in the written confirmation, thus preventing misunderstanding regarding the time you have available.

When booking appointments it is a useful ploy to use the natural breaks of the day to indicate the end of a meeting. Coffee and tea breaks, lunch-time and the end of the day can all be used to subtly indicate that the meeting has reached its close. It will be your responsibility to know whether people are happy to work through breaks, lunch and after work hours or whether they will be relying on you to come to the rescue, politely interrupt and signal the end of the meeting.

If an appointment is overrunning then discretion and tact should be used – you could arrange for a telephone call to be made, or pass a note to your manager or colleague as a reminder of the next appointment. It is important however that you are aware of others' feelings with regard to interruptions and whether these will be received gratefully or with anger. It is your responsibility to know under what circumstances it would be acceptable to interrupt a meeting and when to be prepared to reschedule the day at a minute's notice.

## ■ DIY 3.3.4

Mrs Miller is interviewing 2 members of staff on Wednesday for the position of Assistant Sales Executive. However, she has just received an application form from an outside candidate, called Penny Smith, whom she has decided should also be interviewed. The applicant lives in Manchester and has working commitments every day except Wednesday and will also require travelling time to get to Leeds. You will have to reschedule the appointments already made to enable you to fit in the additional applicant. To add to the confusion you have just received a memo informing you that the annual sales review booked for Thursday has now been moved to Friday.

If you have decided to reschedule one of the internal applicants you will need to write a memo explaining the situation and giving details of the new appointment. Also, have you remembered to enter amended details in both diaries and have you included additional arrangements to be made in your own diary?

### ▶ Refusing someone an appointment

The first question to ask when someone requests an appointment is whether you, your colleague or line manager is the most suitable person to be seen in the first place – if not, then it would be a simple exercise of referring the person elsewhere. If you are asked to make an appointment that conflicts with others then you will have to use your own initiative and decide whether the request is important enough to warrant rescheduling previously made appointments, or whether you will politely refuse and then use your negotiation skills to arrange another time that is mutually convenient.

The situation may arise when your tact and assertiveness skills are at a premium. It may be that you just do not want to see a particular person and it will be your job to explain the situation and firmly refuse the appointment. It is essential that you get the message across without being over-apologetic as this may indicate that a future appointment may be available. It is also important that you do not become over-aggressive, as your actions are a reflection on your company.

## ▶ Dealing with double-bookings

It is advisable that you and any others involved spend some time each day and certainly at least once a week to update each other on the arrangements that have been made during that day or week. You may discover that for one reason or another appointments have been made for the same time with different people. You will need to discuss how to go about rescheduling and identify which appointment(s) should be moved to another slot.

Rescheduling an appointment may be a simple matter of contacting the person in question and rearranging the time or date. The process of rescheduling becomes more complicated when dealing with several people, particularly if travel arrangements are also involved, and because of this the question of which appointment to rearrange may be answered purely by looking at how many people are involved. Another tactic used to avoid having to rearrange appointments is to find out if there is any one else who could attend the meeting in your place or whether your presence was essential in the first place.

Whatever solution is agreed upon, the most important point to remember is that sincere apologies should be given to those who, as a knock-on effect, may have to rearrange their own schedules to compensate for the double-booking.

## ■ DIY 3.3.5

While you were out of the office your assistant made a double-booking without referring to Mrs Miller's diary first. An appointment has been made for a Mr Jason Reeve on Friday afternoon, but this clashes with her rescheduled annual sales review. Mr Reeve is an accountant from an associate company called Booker & Co Ltd, 12 Parkview Road, Leeds, and had requested an hour to discuss a client's account with Mrs Miller.

You will have to write to Mr Reeve to apologise for the double-booking and offer an alternative time and date. However, after consultation with Mrs Miller you agree that this matter can be dealt with over the telephone and will therefore need to include in your letter an invitation for Mr Reeve to telephone Mrs Miller rather than attend in person.

## Knowledge and understanding question bank

1 How do you prioritise and organise your appointments?
2 How often do you update your appointment system and how is this done?
3 What non-routine or emergency situation have you had to deal with that altered your appointment arrangements and what action did you need to take regarding your appointment(s)?
4 What types of appointment system are you are aware of and what is the best use for each one?
5 What procedure do you use for recording appointments?
6 What information is generally recorded in your appointment system?
7 How do you report non-attendance at an appointment?
8 Apart from making your own appointments, who else have you arranged appointments for?
9 How do you deal with people who do not comply with arrangements you have made?
10 What security and confidentiality procedures do you carry out when dealing with appointments for yourself and others?

## Claiming credit

For Element 3.3 it is necessary for you to prove that you have managed appointments for yourself and others, for individuals and groups. The appointments should have been arranged by yourself and through organising others.

The following work products are potential sources of evidence:

- records of appointments
- records of discussions
- correspondence relating to arrangements

Once you have completed your final assessment, you will need to write in your record book or folder how, when and what you have done to prove that you are competent.

The following statement is an example of how one trainee completed this claim:

*During my work at D & G Scaffolding I managed the diary of appointments. This included the booking of scaffolding for customers, meetings with the directors and financial controller, meetings with customers and suppliers. All diary entries were made in pencil as they tended to be changed regularly. I confirmed the* appointments verbally (or in writing when someone was not available) and reminded them each morning of the commitments for the day. Prior to a meeting I would obtain the necessary information and file. If anyone was absent I would report this to the meeting when I attended or I would pass a note to the Director. My evidence includes pages from the diary and notes that I have made. This information is confidential to D & G and cannot be accessed by unauthorised personnel at the assessment centre.

# UNIT 4

# Create, develop and maintain effective working relationships

■ **Element 4.1**
## CREATE, DEVELOP AND MAINTAIN EFFECTIVE WORKING RELATIONSHIPS WITH COLLEAGUES

### Performance criteria

1 Constructive relationships with colleagues are established and maintained

2 Commitments to colleagues are met within agreed timescales

3 Where colleagues cannot meet timescales, assistance is offered, within own work constraints

4 Colleagues are provided with information and support to meet identified needs

5 Any concerns over quality of work are promptly raised and discussed with the appropriate person

6 Methods of communication and support are appropriate to the needs of colleagues

7 Working relationships with colleagues, which meet with difficulty and are beyond own authority to resolve, are promptly referred to the appropriate person

8 Confidentiality of information relating to colleagues is maintained

### Element introduction

Creating effective working relationships starts with defining your own work role and responsibilities in relation to your colleagues' work roles and responsibilities. In any organisation it is important for the staff to be able to work together harmoniously and productively. Awkward atmospheres and animosity should be avoided at all times. Managers may seek to identify potential conflict and deal with issues before they become a problem. You should be able to reduce conflict and identify potential difficulties if your awareness and perception of others are developed so that you are constantly trying to establish a constructive relationship with the people you work with, one that is conducive to harmonious working.

## ▶ *Establishing and maintaining effective working relationships with other members of staff*

An effective association or relationship with other staff means that you are efficient, reliable, trustworthy, honest, competent and friendly. There are probably many more words you can think of to describe the things that make up a professional relationship.

In business it is important to get on with the people that you work with. This may mean that sometimes you have to be amicable to people you do not like, or put up with annoying habits of others. Any business which is successful usually has an excellent working atmosphere and good teamwork. Working in a team is part of most businesses and how you fit in to the team will have a great effect on the business carried out. How you behave and work will depend on your attitude.

## ▶ *Attitudes and their effect on others*

Your attitude includes how you feel and act towards others – your interpersonal skills. Someone who has a 'good' attitude may be someone who

- always helps others willingly, even when doing jobs they do not like;
- is always cheerful, never seems unhappy or depressed;
- has a good opinion of others;
- does not gossip about others;
- does not snoop on others;
- has good presentation – clothes and hair;
- shows interest when being spoken to.

Part of being reliable means that you can be trusted to do something when you have agreed to do so. Once you have told your colleague at work that you will do a job, make sure you do. If you receive information from other departments or customers that your colleagues need, make sure you pass it on quickly. Any information you receive that needs to be passed on to someone else should be presented in a way that they can understand.

**Fig 4.1 Which is the right attitude to work?**

## ▶ *Methods of passing on information*

You may pass on information verbally, that is by speaking to the person. If this is the case make sure that the information you are passing on is absolutely correct: check with the person providing the information that you have it right before they leave. If the information includes figures or a lot of information is needed, it would be better to write it down.

Written information, to be passed to your colleagues, may be in the form of a memo or a note. The written information may be handwritten by you; if so make sure it is readable. Quite often when you are writing down information from a customer in front of you or on the telephone, the notes you make are messy and out of order. It would be better to rewrite the information into a form which can be easily understood by your colleagues.

Any information for colleagues must be passed to them as quickly as possible and without any errors. If your colleague is absent make sure that any urgent information is passed to someone else. Messages – especially urgent ones – should not be left on anyone's desk unless you know they will be returning shortly. You may need to telephone your colleague to pass on the information. Therefore you need to be able to use the telephone system properly, find telephone numbers easily and relay the information correctly. Planning and presenting information can sometimes be difficult.

**Fig 4.2 The case of the urgent memo**

## ▶ *Providing information to colleagues*

The way in which you choose to pass on information to your colleagues may depend on the needs of your colleague. For example, if your colleague is continually busy and you need to pass on some detailed figures, it would be better to write them down, rather than verbally pass on the information. This is because if your colleague is busy, they will be less likely to remember figures as their mind will be on other things, or if they jot them down on a scrap of paper this may become lost in the rest of the work being carried out.

You may work with colleagues who have special needs, not only those with physical and mental disabilities, but also those who lack confidence, feel inadequate – people that need more support and understanding from you than colleagues who are fully able, competent and confident. When passing on information to these colleagues try to select the method that will best suit their needs.

## ■ DIY 4.1.1

There is a meeting scheduled for 4.00 today in Room 27. All staff are expected to attend promptly. You have been asked to pass on this information to your colleagues who have the following special needs:

- One is deaf
- One is blind

136

- One is in a panic as they are behind with their work
- One is busy at other meetings all day in the building
- One is out of the office visiting a customer and cannot be contacted, expected back at 4.00

State how you will pass on the relevant information to each of the individuals.

## ▶ Responding to requests for assistance

If your colleagues ask you to help, what is your answer? No doubt it may depend on:

- who asked
- what they want you to do
- whether you are busy
- how you feel

If your manager asked you to do something, no doubt you would do it. If you did not the result could be losing your job, or losing some of the good working relationship you have been trying to improve. Assistance should be given willingly: show that you want to be helpful. When you receive the request make sure you understand exactly what you have to do. If the request is unclear or puzzling, ask for an explanation. Quite often things can be ambiguous, that is, they can be understood in different ways. Do not put your own interpretation into the request; always check that you have understood correctly, otherwise you will waste your time, your colleague's time and the company's time. Time costs money. In the same way, if you receive a written request, make sure that you can read and understand what it is asking. If you can't – ask.

If you are asked by a colleague, then you may not respond in the same way as you do to a manager. You may argue with your colleague that you have more work than they do; that their work is boring; that they should work harder – as you do! How you respond to requests from your colleagues is just as important as your response to your manager. A helpful, willing response will strengthen your working relationship and make the office mood better. You should split work and responsibilities between you and your colleagues in the most practical and useful way. It should benefit the business and all of the workers equally; that is, one person should not have to do a great deal more than the others, or be left with all the jobs no one else wants. Make sure that you treat any staff, especially office juniors, in a way that you would like to be treated.

Quite often the jobs that you get asked to do may be boring, routine and sometimes messy. It is important to respond to these jobs as willingly as you would a more attractive job. It is usually easier to ask someone to help with a routine job as it needs little or no explanation. The more interesting jobs tend to be more complicated and take time to explain and understand. However, if you offer to help when your colleagues are not so busy, they will have time to explain some of the more interesting jobs and later, when they are busy, you may be able to assist with them.

# ■ DIY 4.1.2

Make a list of 20 jobs you think you may be asked to carry out by a manager or colleagues in an office. The type of job you can do will depend on the skills you have or are presently learning. Use the 2 headings to make your list.

**Type of job**                                  **Skill needed**

## ▶ *Meeting deadlines*

It is sometimes difficult to juggle all the work you may have to carry out in one day. All work usually needs to be completed within an agreed time-scale, but the time-scales are unlikely to be the same. Some jobs can be left longer than others. How you organise your work will usually be up to you, but you should prioritise the work, that is, put it in an order where the most urgent jobs get done first. It is tempting to do the most interesting jobs first. Don't be tempted, prioritise sensibly. If you are really too busy to help others when they ask, explain politely and try to tell your colleague when you think you will be free to assist. Do not carry out all of your routine work before you help your colleagues with their urgent work. Prioritising includes thinking whether your colleague's work is more important and urgent than the work you currently have to complete.

Time management is a skill that needs to be acquired, especially when you have a busy work-load and frequent deadlines to meet. One of the popular methods of sorting work is by dividing it into 4 piles. Items are considered to be **urgent** if there is an impending deadline to meet: the nearer the deadline, the more urgent the job. Items are **important** if they can have a marked effect on your job, on your career or on the organisation you work for.

**Remember:** *Urgent* is different from *Important*. Urgent items need to be

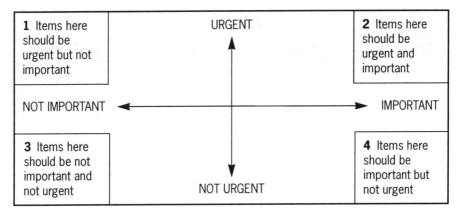

**Fig 4.3 Prioritising work**

dealt with in a short period of time, whereas Important items may affect you, your colleagues or the organisation.

The first priority is to deal with all items falling into Box 2. These are important and urgent, usually those for which deadlines have been set. Due to the deadlines the work may be carried out in a hurry and consequently not to the best of your ability.

Those items falling into Box 1 are generally urgent but not very important. These are the tasks that you will waste quite a bit of time on. Generally these duties are quick and simple and should only have a minimum amount of time allocated to them, freeing up time for those items in Box 2.

Box 3 contains work that is neither important nor urgent. These tasks should be urgently reviewed as it is questionable whether you should be doing them at all – delegate where possible.

The work in Box 4 is important but not very urgent. These are likely to be the jobs that have a deadline but it is currently far off. The problem with these jobs is that they generally do not get done until they have moved to Box 2, as the deadline gets nearer.

# ■ DIY 4.1.3

Make a list of all the work you have currently outstanding at your training centre or at home. Sort it into the sections above and make out an Action Plan (see Fig 4.4) to complete the work.

| ACTION PLAN | | |
|---|---|---|
| Date | Activity and resources needed | Date due |
| | | |

Fig 4.4  An action plan, for use with DIY 4.1.3

▶ *Organising your time*

Once you have organised the work, you may need to review your total organisation of time. Time should be allowed to complete the work you have identified for the day. This time should be uninterrupted by telephones and people, although this may be difficult to achieve. Quality time is important for carrying out your tasks, especially if you are to do them to the best of your ability. If people need to see you then a set time can be made for this, eg in the mornings. Leave sufficient time to travel to other venues; rushing is not good for the body or fellow travellers! Avoid taking work home; it is important for you to totally 'switch off'. It could be said that someone who takes work home is badly organised at work. Review how you use your time.

# ■ DIY 4.1.4

Keep a log of **all** activities carried out during a working week, during normal work hours. The log should show the time as well as the activity completed. Include everything, chats in the corridor, making the tea etc, as well as your actual work and assistance to others. It may seem time consuming to compile this log, but it could well save time in the future. At the end of the week total up the number of hours spent on the different activities. Identify where time could be saved or where your routines and habits are wasting valuable time.

## ▶ *Delegation of duties*

You may be in a position where you can delegate some of the work for which you are responsible. As well as delegating the work you must be prepared to delegate the authority and responsibility to carry out the task. Overall you will still be responsible for the actions of junior staff carrying out your work, but without the necessary authority and responsibility it is unlikely that anyone will be able to complete the work successfully. Ensure you give full instructions and any information required to carry out the work. Make sure that your instructions are fully understood and the quality expected is also known. Avoid making regular checks but ensure that the person can approach you with any problems or difficulties encountered.

## ▶ *Quality control*

Quality management is an enormous area which can only be touched on here. Quality control and standards may be in operation at your organisation, in which case you will know how they operate and how quality should be measured in your area of work. Quality management should be continuous, constantly improving the methods and procedures carried out in an organisation. Many organisations start with customer requirements when looking at quality standards. The aspects considered may include response time, delivery time and prices, as well as the quality of produce or service offered. Continuous improvement is necessary to meet the demands of the customer and other changing forces, such as price.

You may be able to set your own quality standards in your area of work, but ensure that you can measure the standard, otherwise you will not know whether it is effective or meeting the target or not.

Quality circles are another way of setting quality standards. In these, a section or group of people who have a common theme or aim will meet and set standards for the group to achieve. Again, the standards should be measurable. Quality programmes involve some risks. These include:

- they are too complicated
- they may have communication difficulties
- the onus lies with individuals instead of teams, therefore they lack cohesion

141

To set up a good quality management process there should be a strong committee, meeting regularly to approve, monitor and review action and report directly to the senior member in the organisation. Teams should be trained and briefed before starting the programme. Do not rush into the programme as it needs to be built specifically to meet your needs and your organisation's needs. As an individual, however, you can:

- Set your own goals.
- Get feedback from others on your performance.
- Check your work carefully and avoid errors.
- Treat everyone to whom you provide information as your customer and those that provide information to you as your supplier. Demand quality from others.
- Ensure you have the right equipment and resources to do the job.
- Recognise stress in others and control your own.
- Fulfil your promises and finish what you start.
- Raise any concerns over quality of work with the appropriate person.

# ■ DIY 4.1.5

You work in an office with 2 other colleagues and you all have your own work-loads. At the end of the afternoon on Friday you and another colleague have finished, but the other member of staff still has several letters to post, some phone calls to return and a parcel to wrap. One of the reasons why the work is not finished is that this person had a 2-hour lunch. You do not really get on well with this colleague and would prefer to go home. What will you do and why?

## ▶ *The importance of feeling well and rested*

If you go to work feeling tired, irritated, annoyed or sick you may not feel like helping others. Sometimes you may genuinely feel ill, but feelings of tiredness may be the result of too many late nights. Keep your late nights out for the week-ends, make sure you get into a good routine of getting up in plenty of time for work. You should avoid going to work feeling miserable or depressed: try to leave your problems and feelings at home. Sometimes it cannot be helped but you should remember to treat your colleagues courteously and not be rude. If you are ill, you should decide whether it is serious enough to go home. If so, explain to your manager. Do not make a habit of taking time off for trivial illnesses; a few aches and pains should not stop you from working. On the other hand, if you have flu it would be unwise to work and pass your germs round the office. If you have a constant illness or one that keeps recurring you should see your doctor for advice. An employee with a poor attendance record is unlikely to be considered for promotion and may be the first to be considered for redundancy. You will need to recognise when self-motivation is needed or when you can help others through motivating them.

## ▶ *Motivation*

Motivation is generally broken down into 2 separate types, extrinsic and intrinsic. Extrinsic motivators include pay, working conditions and benefits, job security and promotion prospects, environment and relationships with colleagues and others. Intrinsic motivators come from within a person. They differ between people so that what may motivate one person may have no effect on another. Motivators include the achievement of completing a job, being given responsibility or recognition for a job or achievement. One thing that you can do to motivate others is to take time to say 'Thank you'.

## ▶ *Dealing with personal problems*

Everyone sweats or perspires. Your personal hygiene should not be a problem. If you wash daily and use deodorants, your hygiene should be all right. On the other hand, if you rely on having a shower once a week, there could be a problem. You do not need to use expensive perfumes or colognes to hide smells. Any cologne or perfume used should have a light aroma, not one that is too strong. It is important to wash your clothes frequently as deodorants, perfumes and body smells will enter your clothes and they will become foul. If you smoke the smell will stay in your clothes – no matter how much you try to blow the smoke away. The result will be an offensive smell which your colleagues should not have to put up with. Even if you wash yourself regularly, if you have unclean clothes the smell will be disgusting. Be aware of your smell, other people are.

Cleaning your teeth is as important as frequently washing. If you eat spicy foods or drink alcohol or smoke make sure that your breath is fresh; use some breath fresheners or gum if necessary. Avoid strong-smelling food and drink if you know you will be dealing with special customers or have an important meeting.

Jewellery worn should be reasonable; anything large may be unsafe. Bracelets, chains and pendants may be caught in machinery or drawers. Large rings may catch in equipment or damage the glass of a photocopier. Any scratch on the glass of a photocopier will result in marks on the copies made.

People who do not pay enough attention to their personal presentation

143

can often cause conflict in an office situation. It may be one of your responsibilities to speak to someone about personal hygiene or presentation. This should be done as tactfully as possible, obviously out of earshot of others, and with positive recommendations to assist the person to improve their situation.

Remember, though, that all information relating to colleagues should be kept confidential – use your integrity.

## ▶ *Health and safety at work*

You should be aware of your duties under the Health and Safety at Work Act as well as the legal responsibilities your colleagues and employer have. When carrying out tasks for others you should take care not to break any of the rules of the Act and report any faulty equipment or hazards found.

### Health and Safety at Work Act 1974 (HASAWA)

This Act brings together many of the previous health and safety laws. The basic idea of the Act is that there should be a joint effort by employers and employees to provide a safe and healthy working environment.

The employer has to provide safe:

- equipment and systems of work
- working conditions and adequate arrangements and facilities for welfare
- use, storage, transport and handling of substances and articles
- means of access to and from work.

If an accident occurs the employer must investigate this fully and all staff should be fully informed, supervised and trained in accordance with their work role.

Employees have a responsibility for:

- taking care of their own safety
- safety of other people affected by their actions
- co-operating with employers and any other people involved in carrying out duties under this law.

When working in a company or training centre you should know:

- the names and location of trained first-aid staff
- the location of the accident report form, record or book
- the location of the first-aid box
- what to do if you discover a fire

- where fire-fighting equipment is kept
- how to select and operate the correct equipment

This information should be included in any training or induction you receive when starting work.

Other legislation that you should be aware of is that covering **equal opportunities**. Many employers have equal opportunity statements and guidelines for their staff to follow. This legislation makes it unlawful for anyone to treat a person less favourably than they would otherwise simply because of their race (nationality), sex, age, religious belief, or marital status. Equal opportunities are covered by several Acts, which include the Race Relations Act, Equal Pay Act, and Sex Discrimination Act.

## ▶ *Dealing with difficulties and conflict at work*

What you do about difficulties at work will depend on the type of difficulties that occur. Some you will be able to deal with yourself, others you may discuss with a colleague or with your line manager.

If you find that a difficulty arises at work which you cannot discuss with your colleague, manager or personnel department staff, try to find someone that you can confide in outside work. You may have someone in your family that will listen and make some suggestions for solving your problem, or you could talk to someone at an Advice Bureau. Quite often someone who is distant from the problem can see the solutions or possible answers.

If you decide to discuss a problem with a colleague or supervisor it is important not to exaggerate any of the difficulties. Report the matter exactly as it is. If you invent or make up details it is likely to create further difficulties and other people involved may not trust or rely on you in the future. You should also ensure that any information relating to colleagues is kept confidential.

Your ability to anticipate difficulties or conflict will also help to reduce the likelihood that these will occur. Being able to defuse a potential problem can save much time and potential distress.

## ▶ *Confidentiality*

Once you are established and have a good working relationship with others in the organisation you may find that you become a 'confidant' to some. It is important that you do not abuse this trust by divulging information to others. Some aspects of your work may give you access to personal files such as those dealing with recruitment, reference or appraisal information. This information should be kept strictly confidential and not discussed outside the work environment with anyone. This means you should not discuss it at home or with friends outside the organisation: you can never be sure 'who knows who' and things can have a nasty way of getting back round very quickly – especially if it is considered by some to be 'gossip' worth passing on. Breaking confidence may have an adverse effect on you, your colleagues and the organisation you work for and the benefits are usually very few.

## Confidentiality and legal requirements for databases

If you set up a database which has personal information on individuals then it must be registered with the Data Protection Registrar. The records should not be kept longer than is necessary and proper security procedures should be introduced to make sure only authorised staff have access to the information stored. The information should also be kept up to date and accurate and never be passed to anyone who may use it for other purposes, eg a list of doctor's patients being passed to a mail order firm to allow them to send sales materials. Further information regarding registration can be obtained from your local or training centre library, the Post Office or direct from the Data Protection Registrar (Springfield House, Water Lane, Wilmslow, Cheshire, SK9 5AX).

## Knowledge and understanding question bank

1  In which ways have you established constructive relationships?
2  What methods have you used to seek and exchange information? Give examples.
3  How do you deal with confidential information?
4  What disagreements or conflict have you needed to deal with and how did you deal with them?
5  How do you motivate colleagues?
6  What is your organisation's reporting procedure for difficulties or problems you cannot resolve?
7  What methods of communication do you use and how do you select the best method to suit the needs of colleagues?
8  How does your style of approach differ from that of the colleagues you work with?
9  What are your organisation's procedures for dealing with intimidation and harassment?
10  What is the relevant legislation for equal opportunities?

## Claiming credit

For Element 4.1 you must prove that needs are identified for yourself and others while you are working with colleagues within your organisation. The following work products are potential sources of evidence:

- internal memoranda
- work plans
- records of discussions
- records of meetings

In order to support this evidence you will need to supply your own personal account of competence, linked to the performance criteria and range, and authenticated testimonies from relevant witnesses. Your assessor may also wish to observe your performance and may carry out a question and answer session to ensure that all the performance criteria and range have been addressed and evidence provided.

Once you have completed your final assessment, you will need to write in your record book or folder how, when and what you have done to prove that you are competent.

The following is an example of how one trainee completed this claim:

*During my period of assessment I have been working as an Administrative Assistant to the Finance Manager in Abeco Limited. We have a weekly team meeting when we discuss the arrangements for the week. We agree who will carry out the relevant tasks and in particular who has a heavy work commitment for the week and may need assistance (see Evidence 1). I write memos and send e-mail to my colleagues to inform them of things I have completed or carried out on their behalf (see Evidence 2). If I have a query regarding quality I check this with the person concerned; most of the time this is related to the quality of the printouts I am able to obtain (see Evidence 3). I always try to communicate with my colleagues at a suitable pace and level. I tend to change the way in which I speak to different people automatically, but completing this unit has made me far more aware of the need to meet different needs. To date I have not had a difficulty with anyone working in the organisation, but if it occurred I would try to resolve the problem with the person concerned or discuss it with the Finance Manager. I keep all information (written and verbal) regarding colleagues and work confidential and do not discuss it out of work.*

# ■ Element 4.2
# CREATE, DEVELOP AND MAINTAIN EFFECTIVE WORKING RELATIONSHIPS WITH EXTERNAL CONTACTS

### Performance criteria

**1** Methods of working with external contacts are established accurately, agreed and recorded

**2** Positive working relationships are developed and maintained with external contacts to enable working arrangements to be fulfilled

**3** Requests for information are responded to promptly, courteously and accurately, within limits of own authority

**4** Confidentiality is maintained in accordance with organisational requirements

**5** Working relationships with external contacts, which encounter difficulties and are beyond own authority to resolve, are promptly referred to the appropriate person

### Element introduction

Creating and developing effective working relationships with external contacts is one of the most important skills. External contacts may be customers or suppliers; both are important to the continuity of business. Maintaining good relationships ensures that business continues, that you retain your customers and carry on getting good service from your suppliers.

## ▶ *Working with external contacts*

As you have seen in Element 4.1, it is important to be able to get on well with the people with whom you work to ensure good productivity and an effective working environment. Just as important is the need to get on well with any external contacts. They may be people who supply services such as cleaning and maintenance, or those who supply goods for your organisation to resell or use as consumables. Good listening is an important part of the process. Many people are too busy thinking of what they will say next, so that they do not listen effectively to what the other person is saying. This may lead to a misunderstanding of requirements or of the facts involved.

When greeting contacts, **smile** – this will make them feel welcome. Allow them to tell you what they need or whom they wish to see. If you are not familiar with them and they do not introduce themselves, ask for their

148

name and which organisation they represent. Always make sure that you know exactly what the requirements are before you contact anyone else or deal with the request yourself. Use appropriate body language.

## ▶ Body language

Your body language should be open and not closed. Make sure that your gestures are positive and link with the words you are saying. Smile and do not 'crowd' your contact – keep your own space. If you are in a noisy or crowded area try to take your contact to another part of the building. Body language is not just the way in which you move and control your body; it also includes your eye movements and facial expressions. It is important to maintain eye contact at all times, and your face should show appropriate expressions, such as concern, eagerness, enthusiasm, excitement, pleasure, thanks; not boredom, confusion, disinterest or indifference. Watch your contacts' body language as well as your own. You should be able to determine their mood and temperament. In this way you will increase your own awareness.

Your organisation may require you to record each meeting with external contacts. If you are dealing with suppliers you may have separate files or index cards to record your contact and the reason for their visit. These records must be accurate, legible and up to date.

## ■ DIY 4.2.1

Design a record system that would be suitable for recording contacts with suppliers and customers. Create instructions and guidelines for use of the system by other staff and include at least one completed record as an example.

## ▶ Motivation

Motivation is about getting the best out of people – people you work for and with. As we saw in Element 4.1 motivation may be intrinsic or extrinsic. To motivate your external contacts you will need to identify what is important to them. Motivators for yourself when dealing with external contacts include the satisfaction of a job well done, being given the responsibility to carry out the job, being recognised for your achievements and being given the opportunity to advance. You can use these motivators with your external contacts. Your requests will be demands on them, their requests are demands on you.

Achievement is usually seen as a job well done and one to be pleased with. By co-operating with your customers and meeting their demands as quickly and efficiently as you can you will be able to raise your motivation and achievement. Conversely, your demands on your suppliers and the agreements made will motivate your supplier if you enable them to get the job done. Praise for success should be given and recognition of effort should always be acknowledged.

## ▶ *Record keeping*

If your organisation keeps personal computerised records it will be necessary to ensure that you do not contravene any of the requirements of the Data Protection Act 1984. First, it will be necessary to register details of the information kept and its users. The information stored should only be that necessary to carry out business. It should be accurate and up to date. Information should be deleted when no longer required. Your organisation should have a policy which ensures that the information stored can only be accessed, altered, disclosed or destroyed by authorised people. Authorised people are those that need to access the information to carry out their duties and responsibilities. Such people should only act within the scope of their authority and, should data be lost or destroyed, it should be recoverable so as to prevent any damage, or distress to the data subjects. Remember that data subjects may obtain a copy of their record from you. Further information on the Data Protection Act may be obtained from the Office of the Data Protection Registrar, Springfield House, Water Lane, Wilmslow, Cheshire, SK9 5AX (Tel 0162 553 5777).

## ▶ *Making contact*

The methods you use to reach your external contacts are also important. These will probably include face-to-face conversations, telephone conversations and written means – memo, letter or fax etc. Preparation is required for all methods: collect all the information you need before you start.

Body language is not as important when you are not face to face with your contact, but it will still have an effect on how your contact perceives your actions. When answering the telephone, smile and be enthusiastic, make the caller feel welcome – even if they are interrupting something important. On the telephone your breathing is important as it affects your voice. Practise breathing from the diaphragm instead of from the throat which may cause distortion in your voice. Speak evenly and at the right pace and volume and check your understanding by asking the other person questions. In conversation and in writing, leave out jargon – it only confuses.

When writing, make sure that the tone and content are right. Open your written communication with an introduction, then state the facts and action required and finish with a conclusion. Use concise sentences of about 15 words. Give assurances when they are needed and be positive. If you promise or undertake to do something, make sure it is done. Follow up your own and others' actions. Always check your spelling and grammar by reading the document; do not rely on computerised spell checkers. Reliability and good service will make people want to come back to you and your organisation and not go to one of your competitors.

# ■ DIY 4.2.2

Complete the table shown in Fig 4.5, listing people who you contact during the next 2–3 weeks. You may include communications at your training centre or at home. If you are working part-time, your contacts at work may be included.

| Method of communication | Strengths | Weaknesses |
|---|---|---|
| Telephone | | |
| Face to face | | |
| Written | | |

**Fig 4.5 Record of contacts, for use with DIY 4.2.2**

You now need to build on your strengths and reduce your weaknesses. Identify your weaknesses and what action you can take to overcome them. To do this, complete the table shown in Fig 4.6.

| Weakness | Action required |
|----------|-----------------|
|          |                 |

**Fig 4.6 Record of weaknesses and action plan, for use with DIY 4.2.2**

## ▶ Positive working relationships

Positive working relationships are built and earned; they do not just happen. It is important that your contacts trust you. Trust is created through reliability and honesty. If you state that something will happen, ensure that it does, or get back to your contact and explain why there will be a different outcome. The satisfaction and goodwill of contacts are important to the organisation. If you constantly provide inadequate or insufficient information your organisation's reputation will suffer.

If you are requested to supply information you should do this promptly, courteously and accurately. Write down any figures or dates and use proper message pads when taking down information for others. Always check the information you are going to give, especially if it includes figures. Check the terms under which you are quoting any prices and confirm them in writing when necessary. The contact may ask you for something which you do not deal with. For instance in a company providing goods you may deal with only part of the range. You would have to call in a colleague or manager to help the contact with other items that are required. If the contact wishes to negotiate new terms for payment or obtain better discounts from your organisation you may have to refer them to another person. Do not make a decision if the responsibility is not yours. You must realise when the matter is outside your own job responsibility and direct the contact promptly and courteously to someone who can deal with it. The same applies if the contact asks you for confidential information that is outside your area of responsibility.

It is important that the contact comes back to you for their normal requirements and you should reassure them that you are always there to help. At the same time the customer must not think that your organisation does not trust its staff to deal with all problems. You should explain that everyone has particular duties, to ensure they serve the contact properly.

## ■ DIY 4.2.3

You have received the following letter of complaint. Draft a suitable reply. What assurances may you be authorised to give?

*Dear Sirs*

*Your engineers called to carry out the annual maintenance on our system last Tuesday. It appeared to be one qualified engineer and a trainee. They arrived at 10.00 when expected at 9.00, demanded tea from the receptionist before they started and spent much of the time chatting to staff instead of getting on with work down in the pump room. The whole procedure was completed in less than an hour.*

*We have been customers for the last 5 years and are currently paying over £200 for annual maintenance and would expect a better standard than we have currently received. Surely there is a set procedure for carrying out maintenance and certain components that need to be checked and/or replaced?*

*I would be interested to receive your observations and comments.*

*Yours faithfully*

*Mr D R Roys*
*Service Manager*

# ▶ *Legislation covering dealings with customers*

There are several laws that you should be aware of when dealing with customers requiring services. The following deal with your responsibility towards the customer.

## Sale of Goods Act 1979

This Act sets out terms about the **quality** and **fitness** of goods. There are three terms that have the same effect as a promise made by the supplier to the customer.

1 The goods are fit **for their usual purpose**. This means that the customer must be able to use the goods for the purpose intended, eg a can opener must be able to open cans.
2 The goods are of **proper quality**. If the customer pays full price for goods, they should be of a proper quality, eg a shirt should have all its buttons, a microwave should not be scratched. However, if the seller drew the customer's attention to the fault before selling the item, the customer cannot then complain.
3 The goods are **as described**. This means that the seller must describe the goods accurately. There is a further Act which protects the customer: the Misrepresentation Act 1967 states that the seller must not misdescribe the goods when selling, eg a tin of beans should not contain peas. Those in contact with customers should make sure that when they describe the goods or service they are correct in what they say.

## Trade Descriptions Acts 1968 and 1972

These Acts make it illegal for sellers to describe goods and services incorrectly. These laws are enforced by the Trading Standards Department, which has officers who visit premises to follow up any complaints by customers that they have been misled. Any false description could amount to a criminal offence. The Acts state that the description of goods must be correct in respect of:

- content or size, eg 1 litre, 1 ream
- method of production, eg handpainted
- manufacture and date, eg Made in Taiwan
- previous history of the goods, eg only one owner
- accuracy of pictures on the wrappers

There are strict rules regarding the pricing of goods that have been reduced or are in a sale.

## Weights and Measures Acts 1963 to 1979

These laws make it an offence to give a short weight or measure (even by accident). Local authorities employ trading standards officers to enforce these Acts and as part of their work they will visit premises and check that the measures are correct, eg the scales in a shop, the pumps and optics in a pub and the pumps in a petrol garage.

Other laws that are also important are:

## Compulsory Insurance Act 1969 (employers' liability)

Employers must, by law, take out insurance to cover their employees for any injury or disease which they may sustain while carrying out their normal duties. Employers who do not have the insurance may be fined up to £500. A copy of the insurance certificate must be displayed where all the employees can see it. If a copy is not displayed the employer may be fined £200. This type of insurance is called **employers' liability insurance**.

Employers may also wish to take out insurance for the visitors to the premises. This would cover any visitors such as drivers, delivery people, customers, children etc. If, for instance, a visitor came into the premises and tripped on a worn carpet and injured their head, they could claim compensation from the employer. If insured, the employer would get the insurance company to pay any compensation; if not they would have to settle the matter themselves. This insurance is not necessary but is recommended if the business has visitors or customers on the premises. This type of insurance is called **public liability insurance** and is covered in the Occupiers' Liability Act 1957.

## Financial Services Act 1986

This Act regulates investment business in respect of insurance business and business carried on in organisations such as building societies and banks. It is related to business in stocks and shares, government securities, life assurance policies and personal pensions, and in particular relates to people managing investments, introducing clients to investment business or buying, advising and selling investments. There are a number of penalties that can be imposed, including fines and imprisonment, for engaging in investment activity without being authorised and/or intentionally giving misleading information to customers to benefit self or organisation. Further information may be obtained by writing to HMSO Publications (PO Box 276, London SW8 5DT) for a copy of the Act or by purchasing the Act from HMSO Bookshops.

## ▶ *Dealing with confidentiality*

There will be many areas and topics of work that you come across which should be treated as confidential. Some of them you may not consider as very important, but in the wrong hands they may be very damaging to your organisation. Among the obvious things not to disclose to external contacts are the whereabouts of your organisation's staff on a day-to-day basis, home addresses and telephone numbers, details of customers and suppliers, account details and individual credit arrangements. Quite a bit of this information may be easily obtainable and may not be treated as confidential within your organisation. Therefore it is important to remember that when you receive an external contact face to face, information should not be accessible on your desk or screen.

In addition other staff within your organisation may be interested in information accessible by you, for example a colleague's salary. Confidential information should only be kept for as long as necessary; once obsolete it should be shredded or incinerated so it is unreadable. Any confidential information kept on the computer should be protected by a password or keyword. Printouts should be kept in a folder marked 'Confidential' and disks kept locked away in a cupboard. Your organisation may have further rules and procedures for maintaining confidentiality of information and restricting access.

## ■ DIY 4.2.4

Draw up guidelines for staff outlining the areas of confidentiality likely to occur in an office and how they should react to requests for confidential information.

Unfortunately, no matter how reasonable and amicable you are towards your external contacts, occasions are likely to occur where you will disagree and encounter difficulties. It is important that you are able to identify a confrontation and know what action to take.

## ▶ *Dealing with difficulties*

There may be occasions when you encounter clients or visitors who have a grievance or a disagreement or who are in conflict with your organisation. This can be difficult to deal with, especially when the person is actually present rather than on the telephone, but it is important first to listen carefully to what is being said to you. When complaining, people do not want to have to repeat themselves. It is frustrating for them and does not reduce the problem. Keep eye contact as much as possible and do not be distracted from what the person is saying. Take notes and ensure you get the facts – be patient and reassuring. If you cannot deal with the situation yourself or need to gather further information from within your organisation, keep the client informed at all times of what you are doing. Make sure that you fully brief anyone you contact, to prevent the caller having to state their grievance or difficulty again. If you are dealing with a written complaint it is slightly easier, as you do not have the added pressure of being watched by the complainant. However, when you reply to a written complaint the facts must be correct, and there should be no typing or grammatical errors in your reply. You should not promise anything to your contacts that cannot be delivered: work within your area of responsibility only. If you encounter any extraordinary difficulties or you are unsure, check with your line manager before deciding on your remedy for the situation. You will need to use tact and diplomacy at all times to ensure that you retain goodwill and continued business.

# ■ DIY 4.2.5

Design a leaflet which will help those starting their first job to deal with difficult external contacts. This should include suppliers and customers. Try to identify the different situations they may encounter, and include the different ways of dealing with disagreements and conflicts. Try to give examples of situations they may be able to deal with themselves and those that should be referred to another appropriate person.

## Knowledge and understanding question bank

1  How do you actively seek to establish a constructive relationship with external contacts?
2  What experience have you had of dealing with disagreements with external contacts and how did you handle them?
3  What methods do you have for dealing with confidential information as far as external contacts are concerned?
4  What method of consultation do you use when informing others of problems?
5  What different styles of approach do you use with external contacts?
6  What methods of communication do you use and how do you ensure it meets the needs of your external contacts?
7  How do you motivate individuals and how does this help maintain effective relationships?
8  Which legal requirements affect you in your work with external contacts?
9  What is your reporting procedure for difficulties beyond your authority to resolve?
10  How would you define 'active listening'?

## Claiming credit

For Element 4.2 you must prove that you have created, developed and maintained effective working relationships with external contacts supplying and requiring services. Observation by your assessor is particularly recommended as a form of evidence for this unit and the following work products are additional potential sources of evidence:

- copies of correspondence
- copies of agreements
- internal memoranda
- work plans
- records of meetings
- records of discussions

Once you have completed your final assessment, you will need to write in your record book or folder how, when and what you have done to prove that you are competent.

The following statement is an example of how one trainee completed this claim:

*As an Administrative Assistant in Abeco Limited I am responsible for dealing with callers delivering orders and requesting payment, as well as with customers wanting information regarding our equipment. Suppliers come to the main office where I check the items received and sign the delivery notes. I greet them cheerfully and by name when I know who they are. The customers usually call in without an appointment and request information or catalogues. I make sure that I am friendly and answer their questions whenever possible. Any confidential information is only passed on to those that require it. On occasions I have had to deal with difficult customers who have not received the service intended. I gain all the facts and pass the information to someone who can constructively help. At all times I keep the customer informed of the action I am taking, so they do not become further frustrated by lack of action. My evidence includes observation by my assessor, testimonies from a supplier and a customer, copies of notes made by me when dealing with difficulties and a personal statement.*

# UNIT 5

# Research, prepare and supply information

## ■ Element 5.1
## RESEARCH, LOCATE AND SELECT INFORMATION TO MEET SPECIFIED NEEDS

### Performance criteria

1 Specified needs are accurately defined

2 Appropriate sources are identified for meeting specific information needs

3 Information searches are accurately recorded

4 Selected information is accurate and relevant to the specified need

5 Working practices conform to relevant legal and regulatory requirements and organisational procedures

6 Required information is obtained within agreed timescales

### Element introduction

No day will go by without you being asked for some kind of information. You may immediately know the answer to the question being asked, or you may have to refer to reference material as a source of information. Sources of information include other people, computers and paper-based records.

### ▶ *Sources of information*

Your first problem may be finding the correct reference material for the information required. The following list gives details of common reference books and the information they provide.

| *Book* | *Information* |
|---|---|
| ● *Telephone directory* | Local telephone numbers and addresses |
| ● *Yellow Pages* | Local business telephone numbers and addresses |

- *Business Pages*      Local business telephone numbers and addresses (excluding retail outlets)
- *Thomson's Directory*      Local business telephone numbers, addresses and post codes
- *Mail Guide*      Information on all Post Office services
- Dictionary      Spelling and meaning of words and abbreviations
- Thesaurus      Different words with the same meaning
- British Rail timetables      Train times and destinations
- *ABC Guide*      Information on air travel, shipping and coaches
- *AA* and *RAC Guides*      Details of roads, towns, routes, hotels, garages, etc.
- *Whitaker's Almanack*      Information on world affairs, calendar year, statistics, prizewinning authors, plays, films, music, details about United Kingdom and a wide range of other topics
- *Who's Who*      Biographical details of famous people
- *Debrett's Peerage*      Details of correct forms of address
- *Good Food Guide*      Information on places to eat

Other sources of information that you may also need to use are:

- BT's Directory Enquiries
- Newspapers
- Road maps
- A–Z street guides
- Internal telephone directories
- Company organisation chart
- Company computer files
- Company paper-based files
- Company database
- Prestel, Teletext, Ceefax
- Library or company microfiche

People and organisations who are there to help you are:

- AA or RAC
- Local Authority
- Chamber of Commerce
- Citizens Advice Bureau
- British Telecommunications plc
- Post Office Customer Service
- English Tourist Board
- Inland Revenue

- The Department of Trade and Industry
- The Consumers' Association

Locating information may be a simple process of knowing 'who' to ask – your supervisor, boss, colleague or library staff may know the answer to your question, or they may be able to tell you from where you can get the information.

During the course of a day you may be called upon to access information either:

- orally over the telephone or face to face
- using a computer, eg Internet, Prestel or database
- using a paper-based source, eg files or reference books.

If you do need to ask for information make sure you are polite and know exactly what information you require – remember, you are asking someone to spend their time helping you! If you use the telephone to contact a person or organisation, be prepared with notes of the information you require and use the correct telephone manner.

It is important that when you are asked to find information you are aware of when the information is required. If the request is urgent you must prioritise it accordingly and fit it in with your daily tasks as quickly as possible. If the request is not urgent, wait until you have time to spare. All staff have to work to deadlines: remember that if you are late in obtaining information for a colleague you affect their deadline as well as your own.

# ■ DIY 5.1.1

| Element 5.1 – Research, locate and select information to meet specified needs. | | |
|---|---|---|
| Date | Information | Source |
| | | |
| | | |
| | | |
| | | |
| | | |
| | | |

**Fig 5.1 Information search record for DIY 5.1.1**

Find out the following information using people, computers and paper-based sources of information. Also prepare a table like the one in Fig 5.1 on the previous page and enter details of the information you have found for this task. Continue to complete the table each time you are asked for information.

(a) The value of the £ against the US $
(b) The member countries of the EU
(c) The time difference between Britain and Abu Dhabi
(d) The name of your local Member of Parliament
(e) The name of the person in charge of your department
(f) The name of their deputy (if there is one).

---

In an office environment you will also find information from paper-based files, microfiche or files held on a computer database. Some organisations provide computer and/or television access to information. This is called viewdata. You may have already used Internet, Prestel, Teletext and Ceefax.

### Prestel

Prestel links television screens or personal computers to large computers via BT lines. Information is updated every 24 hours and includes:

- company information
- directories
- market research
- business news/services
- share prices
- government statistics

- travel information
- weather information
- sport and entertainment
- banking and investment
- mailbox
- customer guide

Among the features of this service is that it allows the user to actually make bookings using their keyboard, for example to buy theatre tickets and air tickets. The user is charged according to how long they have used the line, in the same way as with a telephone.

Teletext and Ceefax give similar information to Prestel. This information is often available at no additional cost on television screens, but does not allow users to make bookings.

Information services such as the speaking clock are also provided by BT, and 0891 numbers, advertised in newspapers, can be used for information such as weather reports and traffic news.

### Microfilm and microfiche

Microfilm is used to store reduced size, photographic copies of documents. Each document is photographed on to strips of 16 mm film, to nearly a twentieth of the original size. A special reader is used which enlarges the document on screen back to its original size. Some readers will allow a copy of the document to be printed out.

Microfiche works on the same principle but documents are photographed on to single sheets of microfilm measuring 150 mm x 100 mm. Each sheet can be labelled with details of its contents and is placed on a reader when information is required. This system is most commonly used in libraries. If you look up an author's name or book title on the microfiche you are able to see if the library has the book and, if so, where it is located.

# ■ DIY 5.1.2

Sources of information we have spoken about include:

- People
- Computers
- Paper-based

Write an information sheet giving examples and details of the advantages and disadvantages of using each of these sources of information.

## ▶ *Extracting information*

When you are first asked to find information, write down the details of what is required. Use questions to make sure you are clear in your own mind exactly what you are looking for. When you have found the information it is likely that your source will give more than is required. It is your responsibility to go through all the information and pick out only the relevant points.

If, for example, you were asked to find the train times for London to Dover, your first question should be 'What day and between what times?' It is unlikely that you will need the time of every train for that day, only a train to get to/from an appointment or meeting. This means that you will only select the relevant information according to the request and not provide the whole timetable. You may be able to photocopy information directly from the source you have found, but take care that the information is not protected by copyright.

It is useful to underline or highlight information to pick out the important points. Make notes as you read through information and always remember to say from where the information was taken. You may be asked to get further details from the same source or you may be asked to find the same or similar information again. If you have kept a note of your source this will be an easy process. You may also be able to photocopy information from the source, but again make sure that you are not in breach of copyright law.

## Copyright law

The copying of documents is controlled by the **Copyright, Designs and Patents Act 1988**. It is illegal to copy documents that are protected and in which the symbol © is printed, normally on the first page or on the back of the first page of the document. If you look at the front pages of this book you will find the symbol as well as a statement that copying is not allowed. However, some documents may be copied if it is done for educational purposes and others may be copied if the author's permission is obtained first. You should always check before copying that the document you wish to copy is not protected. Obviously if the document has been written by someone in the office it will be all right to copy it. The Act also covers copyright in music and video tapes, records, TV and radio programmes and computer programs.

## Making notes

You should make notes of the information you find as you go along. Always use a note pad, never scraps of paper that can be easily lost. Leave plenty of room between notes so that additional information can be slotted in if necessary. A wide margin will also allow space for insertions or markers for important facts. Try to number the information so that it can be read back in a logical sequence. Leave out unnecessary words and use abbreviations to cut down on time. If you are unsure of standard abbreviations you can find these listed in your dictionary.

Write up notes as you find each piece of information and, when your research is complete, transfer the notes to your chosen form of presentation as soon as possible. It is better to present your information while it is still fresh in your mind. When taking notes from speech, edit any irrelevant information and listen for key words. Factual information such as times, dates, etc, should be noted in full.

## ■ DIY 5.1.3

You work in the Travel Department and have been given the following statistics (see page 165) regarding newly appointed couriers.

The Travel Manager has asked you to provide the information in (a)–(g) on page 165, using a memo. You must also indicate the source used. As you research the information required make sure that you keep details in a note book and remember to fill in details of this information search on the table you prepared in DIY 5.1.1.

| First name | Surname | Passport? | Languages spoken | Age |
|---|---|---|---|---|
| Amanda | Blacker | Y | German | 19 |
| Sally | Sager | Y | French | 20 |
| David | Presley | Y | French | 24 |
| Mark | Harrison | N | Italian | 18 |
| Rachael | Miller | N | Spanish | 19 |
| Jade | Chandris | Y | German | 28 |
| Perri | Scott | N | French | 29 |
| Leila | Scott | Y | Hindustani | 19 |
| Crystal | Harper | Y | French | 18 |
| John | Emrie | Y | Hindustani | 23 |
| Lynne | Patience | N | Greek | 19 |
| Shervin | Patel | N | Spanish | 28 |

(a) How many couriers have passports?

(b) What is the current cost of a 10-year passport?

(c) What is the average age of the couriers?

(d) How many couriers speak French?

(e) What are the couriers' dates of birth?

(f) What size shoes and uniform will each courier need?

(g) Have all the couriers completed application forms?

## ▶ *Finding the right information*

If you cannot find the information make sure you have looked everywhere you can think of. Others will not be pleased if you are constantly asking for help instead of looking for yourself. People around you may be able to point you in the right direction, or they may not know either! Once you have tried everyone and everything you can think of report back to the person who requested the information and explain your actions to date. This is particularly important if the person needs the information for a specific time or date.

In your search for the information you should identify other options and alternatives that may be of help. For example, you may be asked for the name and number of a local stationery supplier. It is sensible for you to supply 2 or 3 alternatives in case the first one cannot be contacted. Likewise, alternative hotels, venues, restaurants, travel times and so on will provide a wider selection to choose from.

If you have asked someone else to find the information for you, remember that you are still responsible for checking that the information they have found is correct. When delegating tasks to others it is important for you to remember that you still retain the responsibility for getting it right. If you have given a colleague the wrong flight times and they miss the plane it is no use blaming this on the office junior. You must always double-check to ensure the information is correct. It is therefore wise for you to ask others always to detail the source of information. It is then a much easier process for you to check rather than having to go through a number of different sources yourself until you find the right one.

# ■ DIY 5.1.4

You work for Coopers & Co, Chartered Surveyors, Plymouth. The Sales Executive, Mike Sears, has been invited to visit the London Branch based in Piccadilly. He will be travelling from the office and wishes to stay overnight in a 4-star hotel.

1 Look through the extract from his diary for the week and decide what day he should attend the meeting.
2 Check railway timetables and find the best times for him to travel by train to/from London.

| FEBRUARY DIARY | |
|---|---|
| **Monday**<br>**9** | *Meeting with Sales Director (Graham Green)*<br>*12.00-3.00 pm*<br>*Golf 4.00 pm* |
| **Tuesday**<br>**10** | *Sales Meeting - Room 66*<br>*9.30am-3.30 pm (working lunch)*<br>*Need sales figures for 1994/95* |
| **Thursday**<br>**12** | *Presentation at the CITB, Cannon Street, London*<br>*10.30 am-2.30 pm*<br>*Dinner with Debbie - La Jardin (pick me up at station 9 pm)* |
| **Friday**<br>**13** | *Lunch with Purchasing Manager*<br>*12.00-about 2.00 pm*<br>*Badminton 6.00 pm* |
| **Saturday**<br>**14** | *Write up Sales Meeting report* |

**Fig 5.2 Diary extract**

3 What underground tube(s) will get him from the railway station to Leicester Square?

4 Select a 4-star hotel within walking distance of Piccadilly Circus.

5 Write a memo to Mike giving full details of the arrangements you have made.

6 Remember to enter details of your search in your note book and complete the table you prepared in DIY 5.1.1.

## ▶ *Recording information searches*

Whichever type of work you do, you will at some time be asked for information. It is unlikely that you will be able to remember everything and it is important that you know where to find the information required. You may be asked 'What is Joanne's room number?' or 'What is the phone number for directory enquiries international?'

The type of question will vary. Some will be easy to answer and others may take some time to research. The answers may need to be written down in a letter or memorandum, or you may write down the information in note form and report it back verbally.

There are hundreds of sources of information to choose from, but the knack is remembering from where you got the information last time. Generally, the sources most often used include:

- people, including friends and work colleagues
- newspapers and magazines
- telephone directories – internal (lists all the people in the company along with their room number, location and extension number), and external (such as local directories, *Yellow Pages*, Thomson directories)
- fax and telex directories
- filing systems – paper-based, computerised, microfiche
- reference books and libraries
- organisations, eg AA, RAC, BT, Tourist Information Office, Local Council
- specialist organisations connected with your business
- company literature, eg organisation chart, price lists, sales leaflets, stock lists, staff handbooks
- viewdata, eg Teletext, Prestel and Ceefax
- dictionary, thesaurus and glossary

The type of work that you do and the work that the organisation for which you work undertakes will affect greatly the sources of information you will come into contact with. As said earlier, the knack is remembering where you found the information last time and making a note of it so that time is not lost trying to remember or using sources that are of no use.

When looking for new information you should carry out a systematic search. Make a list of the possible sources you plan to use and then cross them off if they are not of any use. Reference material that is used often should be kept nearby, or at least a record kept of where to find the information for the future. Always check to ensure that reference material is kept up to date: it is no use giving train times from a timetable that has now expired! You may keep a mental note of useful sources, although this is not recommended as it is so easy to forget.

A useful method is to keep a list of the information sources that you use together with details of what each source is used for. An information file can be used where copies of memos, letters, etc that contain information can be stored, together with old, dated, note books that record information searches which may need to be undertaken again. If you have kept your note book with the information it will be a simple process of finding the relevant, dated note book and looking up the information again.

## ■ DIY 5.1.5

Select 5 sources of information from the list on page 167 and find out exactly what information is supplied by each source.

List the types of information in the form of a chart, using the headings given in Fig 5.3. One example has been completed for you.

| Information source | Information available | How it is accessed | How it is presented |
|---|---|---|---|
| 1 Dictionary | • Spellings and meanings of words and abbreviations<br>• Weights and measurements<br>• Countries of the world etc. | Visual, reading | Written in a book |
| 2 | | | |
| 3 | | | |
| 4 | | | |
| 5 | | | |

Fig 5.3 Record of information sources

## ▶ *Organising information*

It pays to give careful thought to the most effective way of organising information sources. This could mean simply keeping all relevant sources nearby. If your work is more varied and you use a variety of sources this may not be possible and your only alternative will be to keep copies of information you have found on previous occasions or a note telling you where to find such information again.

There are several ways in which you can store the results from information searches. The most systematic method is to index and file the information so that it can be easily found at a future date. One simple method to adopt is to store your index in a card index filing system under different subject headings. The index card will give details of file names and/or numbers where this information has been researched before, or give names of suitable reference material or information sources where the information can be located again.

**Fig 5.4 Card index**

## ▶ *Determining information needs*

When information is requested it is likely to be done either in writing or verbally. In order to ensure that you are aware of the specific needs of the person making the request use your communication skills to clarify the request.

**1 Listening skills** – it is important to listen carefully to other people when they are passing information to you or making a request. The person may be speaking to you face to face, over the telephone (directly or from a recorded message), or over an intercom or loudspeaker. Always have a pen and notepad ready in case you need to jot down information or make notes. Do not rely on remembering it correctly – especially if numbers are involved. If you are unsure of anything, and you are in direct contact with the other person, ask for it to be repeated and you may be able to ask further questions in order to get more explanation. Read back to the other person the notes you have made, to check that you have the correct information, especially if numbers are involved. (These could be telephone numbers, prices, quantities, measurements, code numbers etc.)

If the person has requested information from you make sure you fully understand what is needed before you answer. Do not give out false information or information you are unsure of – check it first.

## ■ DIY 5.1.6

Your manager, Mr Vincent, has asked you to plan a route for him to travel by car from North London to Carlisle. List the roads you would expect him to use and work out the mileage. Supply him with the information in the form of a memo and include the name(s) of the information sources you have used. Remember to use your note book and enter details of your search on to the table you prepared in DIY 5.1.1.

**2 Verbal** – how you request or pass on information is extremely important. If you are asking someone to help, or you are dealing with a customer or colleague, you should do this politely. Speak slowly so that the person can understand exactly what you are saying and to avoid confusion. If you have unusual words or names to pass on, spell them out, using a telephone alphabet (see below) if necessary. Some letters and numbers sound similar over the telephone, such as t, b, p, e, g and 5 and 9. If there is a lot of information you should confirm it in writing later.

| | | |
|---|---|---|
| A – Alfred | J – Jack | S – Samuel |
| B – Benjamin | K – King | T – Tommy |
| C – Charlie | L – Lucy | U – Uncle |
| D – David | M – Mary | V – Victor |
| E – Edward | N – Nellie | W – William |
| F – Frederick | O – Oliver | X – X-ray |
| G – George | P – Peter | Y – Yellow |
| H – Harry | Q – Queen | Z – Zebra |
| I – Isaac | R – Robert | |

**3 Visual** – you should try to be observant and notice things, as well as being able to find things. It can be embarrassing if someone asks you to find an item or information from a particular place and you cannot see it! It may be that the item or information is not exactly where the person said it would be, but on the next shelf, next drawer or next page. Look carefully and make sure you do not miss anything. If you are able to notice things that need to be done, you may be able to predict some of the requests from your customers or colleagues. This will make you a more efficient and valuable employee, and people will appreciate the work that you do, especially if it saves them time.

# ■ DIY 5.1.7

Look around your office or training centre and identify visual information. This could be in the form of written instructions, advertisements and diagrams. List 5 pieces of visual information in the table below and write next to each one the type of information being supplied.

| Visual information | Information being supplied |
|---|---|
| 1 | |
| 2 | |
| 3 | |
| 4 | |
| 5 | |

Fig 5.5 Types of visual information

## ▶ *Confidentiality and security*

You must be sure that the information you are supplying is not confidential or, if it is, that you are supplying it to someone who is allowed to have it. You should check if you are unsure about a person's authority. For example, if you are requested by a telephone caller to supply the home address and telephone number of the sales manager, you should politely refuse.

Confidential information may also include the financial and accounts details of the organisation, staff location and detailed timetables, security arrangements, customers' records and requirements. In every situation you need to find out who is requesting the information and whether they are entitled to have it. NEVER disclose to competitors information about your organisation which can be used to benefit them or be used against your organisation. This could include customer details, financial position or future plans.

When dealing with confidential information it is vital that you do not leave papers lying around on desk tops or leave information on the computer screen for all to see. The use of passwords will help protect the information held on databases or other computerised information sources. This is seen as good practice and if you are in charge of other members of staff such as office juniors it is important that they too are aware of the procedures to use to protect information.

## Data Protection Act

If you set up or use a database which has personal information on individuals then it must be registered with the Data Protection Registrar. The records should not be kept longer than is necessary and proper security procedures should be introduced to make sure only authorised staff have access to the information stored.

The information should also be kept up to date, be accurate and never be passed to anyone who may use it for other purposes, eg a list of hospital patients being passed to a medical supplies distributor to allow them to send sales material on treatments for their condition.

Further information regarding registration can be obtained from the Post Office or direct from the Data Protection Registry who can supply you with an information pack (Telephone 0162 553 5777). The Data Protection Act protects people from having personal information about themselves passed to others. When you carry out an information search it is very important that you check the authority of the person requesting the information prior to passing it on. This would most certainly be the case if the request was made over the telephone.

## Knowledge and understanding question bank

1  How do you go about determining information needs?
2  What paper-based sources of information do you use?
3  What methods do you use to research information?
4  Explain the Copyright Act and Data Protection Act.
5  What people do you use as sources of information?
6  How do you ensure confidentiality and security?
7  How do you go about locating and selecting information?
8  How do you plan and organise research?
9  How do you record your information searches?
10  What computerised sources of information do you use?

## Claiming credit

For Element 5.1 you must provide records of discussions and searches, lists of sources of information, notes and copies of information and documentation relevant to copyright. Sources of information must include paper-based, computerised and people. Information sources must be searched to satisfy the needs of both yourself and others. Information must be that selected by both yourself and others and must comply with statutory and non-statutory legal requirements. The following work products are potential sources of evidence:

- records of discussions
- records of searches
- lists of sources of information
- notes of information
- copies of information
- documentation relevant to copyright

Once you have completed your final assessment, you will need to write in your record book or folder how, when and what you have done to prove that you are competent.

The following statement is an example of how one trainee completed this claim:

*In my work at Coopers and Co I am responsible for the administrative work of 3 accountants. I research, locate and select information from our departmental client database, paper-based files and from other partners or administrative assistants. I am able to use the database to sort and select information to meet specific information needs and to carry out information searches. At the end of each month it is my responsibility to collect the accounts spreadsheet for my department and check through any outstanding amounts. This information is produced as a memo to all 3 accountants. It is important that any information used in the office is not passed on to unauthorised people as it is very confidential. The computer database and spreadsheet programs are protected by passwords which are changed regularly. I recently completed a report for one of the partners regarding the possibility of installing an e-mail network. In order to carry out the research I spoke to the manager of our computing department, read through computing magazines and articles and contacted a local company to find out how much the software would cost. I included this information in the appendices of the report to ensure I did not break copyright law.*

# ■ Element 5.2
# PREPARE AND SUPPLY INFORMATION TO MEET SPECIFIED NEEDS

## Performance criteria

1 Information from a variety of sources is integrated and arranged to meet specified needs

2 The chosen format and presentation are appropriate to the specified purpose

3 Sources of information are acknowledged when appropriate

4 Working practices conform to legal and regulatory requirements and organisational procedures

5 Security and confidentiality of information are maintained

6 Where work is not achievable within specified deadlines reasons are promptly and accurately reported

7 Required information is supplied within agreed deadlines

## Element introduction

This element is about your ability to present the information that you have found in the most appropriate format. It is of no use being competent at researching and abstracting information if you do not have the necessary skills to present the information using the most suitable method. If you have been asked to locate and abstract information you will find a variety of sources that may be of help to you. These have already been discussed in the previous element.

However, when you discover the information needed you will be required to present your findings using one of a variety of methods. For the purpose of this unit you will need to format and present narrative, statistical, graphical and tabular information.

It is wise to remind you at this stage that if at any time you are tempted to merely copy the relevant information you must be sure that you are within the copyright laws or you will be committing an unlawful offence.

## ▶ *Copyright law – a reminder!*

Copyright is designed to protect the livelihood of the creators and producers of literary, dramatic, artistic and musical works. For example, it covers photographs and other illustrations in a book. Following an EC Directive, copyright now in most cases lasts for 70 years from the death of an author.

175

Single copies of copyright material may be made for private study, provided no more than a 'reasonable proportion' is copied.

All copyright material is denoted by the symbol © followed by the date, and this can be found on video, tapes, magazines, computer programs, etc, as well as on books. Multiple copies of this material may not be made without prior permission and payment may have to be made to the publishers for a licence to copy their material. It is normal practice for officers representing the British Copyright Council to visit organisations and ensure that the copyright law is not being broken.

## ▶ *Data protection law – a reminder*

If you set up or use a database which contains personal information on individuals then it must be registered with the Data Protection Registrar. The records should not be kept longer than is necessary and proper security procedures should be introduced to make sure only authorised staff have access to the information stored. The information should also be kept up to date, be accurate and never be passed to anyone who may use it for other purposes. This also applies to your responsibilities when researching and supplying information. If the information you are using is covered by the Data Protection Act make sure you adhere to the requirements. This information is confidential and should be kept secure at all times.

## ▶ *Confidentiality*

You must be sure that the information you are supplying is not confidential or, if it is, that you are supplying it to someone who is allowed to have it. You should check if you are unsure about a person's authority. As stated above, data held on computers about individuals is covered by the Data Protection Act and must be treated as confidential; would you like others to have access to your bank or medical records? Confidential information may also include the financial and accounts details of the organisation, staff location and detailed timetables, security arrangements, customers' records and requirements. In every situation you need to find out who is requesting the information and whether they are entitled to have it.

**Fig 5.6 Is the information confidential?**

## ▶ *Presenting information*

There are many different methods you can choose to present the information you have researched. It may be a simple task of telling someone the information they requested, for example a telephone number. More complicated information will, however, need to be presented in a more formal manner. For example, a weekly timetable will be presented in a tabular form. Imagine explaining the details verbally and expecting the other person to remember them!

The first thing you must always do is look at the information you have and decide the best method to use to make it as easy as possible to understand. Quite complicated material such as statistics can be simplified purely by presenting the information in an illustrated form. Graphics can also be used to illustrate complicated diagrams or to clarify a process by using a flow chart.

It is important for you to be aware of the methods available to you, although this can often depend upon the type of equipment and/or computer software you have available. Remember that this can mean combining a number of different methods in order to integrate a variety of sources of information. The following methods are those that you are most likely to use.

### Composing letters

Letters are received and despatched on a daily basis from most companies. Letters may request information, supply information or make arrangements; the aims are to get the information to the addressee, for it to be understood and acted upon.

You may be responsible for composing your own letters or letters for others. It is wise to draft your letter first so that you can read through it and check your spelling, grammar, content and detail. Your opening paragraph should put the letter into context by:

- giving the reason for the letter being written
- giving details of names, dates, locations or other information to set the scene
- acknowledging date, receipt and subject of received correspondence

The middle paragraph(s) give further information in a logical, brief and clear manner – for example, the nature of a complaint, details of payments made, information about goods. Some information may be displayed as a table, particularly if it is numerical.

The closing paragraph is used to clarify the main points and state the action requested by the writer from the recipient – for example, action to put right a complaint, payment of a bill, placing an order for goods. This paragraph states the reason for the letter and should be followed by a courteous closing statement.

When using a letter to provide information you must ensure that the information you are passing on is correct; check it first. Also make sure that details such as reference, name, address, post code and designation are correct if you want to make a good impression. Obviously, spelling and grammatical mistakes will not make you or the company you work for look professional!

## ■ DIY 5.2.1

Type a letter to the following customers, inviting them to the launch of our new Technoffice Furniture Exhibition. The Exhibition will be held on the 7th of next month. I've booked the local Civic Centre Hall (you'll have to look up the address and enclose a map of the local area with the centre marked so they know where it is). They should arrive at 11.00 hrs for the official welcome and opening addresses, after which a buffet lunch will be available at 12.45. Please ask them to let you know if they will be attending, as I shall need a list of guests for security. Use my official title of Company Secretary on the letter. Thank you. Maria Morgan.

(Use A4 paper with a space of 4" at the top for the letterhead.)

**128 Long Acre, London WC2E 9AN**

Tel: 0171 379 7383  Fax: 0171 240 5771

24 October 19--

Carly-Jo Born
Top Go Salon
224 Lyndsey Road
Branksome
POOLE
BH30 6DB

Dear Carly-Jo

I have been requested by the French authorities
to send you copies of a work placement agreement,
and I am enclosing three copies, one copy to be
retained by you, one copy for the students and
one to be returned to me in the envelope provided.

The document is required in France by all
students carrying out work placement.  Although
the document is not necessary under British law,
the French students are concerned that they will
not fulfil the requirements of their qualification
if this document is not part of their portfolio.

If you wish to delete any part of the document
please do so, or if there are any queries please
contact me.

Thank you for your co-operation.

Yours sincerely

*L Blakemore*

Leila Blakemore
Co-ordinator

Encs

**Fig 5.7 Blocked letter style**

Messrs R J Hoskins & Sons, 35 High Street, New Malpton, ESSEX ST35 5SK

Mr and Mrs J R Thees, 356 Justige Way, Upton, POOLE, BH23 5KS

Trumps, Kite, Froom & Strain Solicitors, The Chambers, 25 Straightway, CROMPTON, CR35 9LJ Attention Mr K Kite

Miss Jenny Stiger, Ceiling Prompts, 694 The Old Oak Way, OAKEN OA5 9JK (I'll do the salutation and comp close.)

---

## Composing memoranda

The memorandum (usually abbreviated as memo) is used to communicate information internally throughout an organisation. It can be used to pass on short, one-point messages or may run to a number of continuous A4 pages. It is usual practice to condense the content of information so that only essentials and matters requiring action are communicated to the recipient. The content of a standard memo is as follows:

---

**MEMORANDUM**

| | |
|---|---|
| **To** | Carol Baker |
| **From** | Lara Smith |
| **Date** | 5 October 199– |
| **Ref** | LS/EF |

MEDICAL CONFERENCE

Would you please arrange with the conference centre for a slide projector and screen to be available for Professor James's lecture on 15 October.

This will be required in addition to the OHP and flipchart.

*LS*

---

**Fig 5.8 Memo in fully blocked style**

- Heading (MEMORANDUM)
- Name of recipient (TO)
- Name of sender (FROM)
- DATE
- SUBJECT HEADING

The paragraph content should be kept brief; a salutation and complimentary close are not required. Although all communication should be polite, a memo is often used purely to provide a written record for future reference of perhaps a telephone conversation, meeting, or a chat in the corridor. Therefore, it is usual to keep content to a minimum and state only the important facts. It is normal practice in some companies for the person requesting the memo to read it through when complete and initial it at the bottom. This shows that it has been checked and its content authorised.

## ■ DIY 5.2.2

You are the Sports Secretary for a Sports Association. Draft a suitable letter to a local politician asking him or her to present the prizes at your annual presentation evening on 20 May. The heading for the letter should be Presentation Evening. Ask if he/she will be able to present the prizes this year and make a short speech. The evening is due to begin at 7.30 pm and you would like him/her to arrive at 7.00 pm if that is convenient. Use the designation of Sports Secretary.

Can you also draft a memo addressed to 'All Committee Members' giving them details of your letter and asking them for any other ideas just in case the politician is not available.

### Designing a notice

Most organisations use a staff notice board as a means to communicate with their members of staff. Provided the board is kept tidy, up to date, attractive and informative it can play a very important part in staff communication. The staff notice board can provide an inexpensive and quick way of getting certain types of information to the right people. Information which affects large proportions of staff that is not confidential and that does not have to be read by everyone as a matter of importance can be communicated well using a notice.

When designing notices make sure that:

- The size of the notice is large enough for the message but not so large that it will not fit on the board or overlap other notices.
- Your headings are clear and attract the people to whom you wish to get

181

the message.
- You keep the message short and to the point by giving only the important information.
- You tell the interested people what to do next to gain more information.
- You add a date by which time the notice can be removed from the board.
- The notice is attractive and eye-catching by adding illustrations and graphics relating to the message to attract attention.

*Staff Party*

*Civic Centre, West Quay Road, Poole*
*Friday 7th January 1996*

*Those interested please contact Sally in*
*Personnel, Extension 7585*

*Limited number of tickets – only*
*£5.00 per person including buffet*

**Fig 5.9 Example of a notice**

## ■ DIY 5.2.3

Produce a draft notice and ticket for the Sports Association Presentation Evening. Send a copy of each to the Entertainments Manager with a memo asking for his approval prior to sending them to the Reprographics Department.

### Producing reports

In order to make decisions, research is often carried out first to ensure that when decisions are made they are based upon informed, impartial and considered information. Reports play a great part in achieving a company's objectives and play a vital role in important decision-making.

There are 3 main types of report that you may be called upon to prepare and supply.

| | |
|---|---|
| **1** Routine reports – | safety inspection report |
| | progress report |
| | sales report |
| **2** Occasional report – | accident report |
| | disciplinary report |
| | work review report |
| **3** Commissioned report – | market research report |
| | sales forecasting report |
| | health and safety report |

However, the report may already have been prepared and it is your job to present it clearly to meet specified needs. Whether you are preparing or presenting a report it is important for you to understand the methods of preparing and presenting both formal and informal reports.

There are a number of different report styles which vary considerably. Some may run into hundreds of pages whilst others will simply fill one page of A4, possibly on a memorandum sheet. More formal reports tend to have headings and sub-headings with each paragraph numbered for easy reference. In some cases the report may be delivered orally to a number of people, perhaps in a meeting, where the information can be questioned, confirmed and discussed.

## Extended formal report

Normally this type of report is used by large companies, government or by commissioned writers.

The principal parts of this report are:

- Title page
- Contents with page numbers
- Synopsis of findings
- Terms of reference
- Procedure
- Findings (each paragraph numbered)
- Conclusions
- Recommendations
- Appendices
- Bibliography

## Short formal report

This sort of report is often used by management to investigate and research information prior to reporting to higher levels of management. This report is most often used internally and only when the situation requires a formal presentation of information.

- Title page or heading
- Terms of reference
- Procedure
- Findings
- Conclusions
- Recommendations
- Appendices

## Short informal report

This sort of report is used when the information needs to be documented but does not require the complicated content or layout of a formal report. This type of report is often required by department heads who need to gain information about their department prior to writing their own formal report.

- Background
- Introduction
- Situation
- Information
- Findings
- Conclusions
- Recommendations (if there are any)
- Action required

When a report is being prepared for internal use throughout the company it can often take the form of an internal memo. This is especially true when communicating within a department. The title information is contained within the memo heading and sub-headings are used to structure the information according to specified needs. Figure 5.10 presents an example of a report in this form.

---

**M E M O R A N D U M**

C O N F I D E N T I A L

TO:        J L Protheroe, Head of Department

FROM:      L Farrar, Personnel Officer

REF:       jlp/GH

DATE:      30 December 1995

SUBJECT:
Appointment of Office Assistant for Business Studies and Computing
Department. Applicant's profile.

NAME:   Mrs Margaret Mary Fudge

PERSONAL DETAILS:
AGE: 35 years        DOB: 26.5.60        STATUS: Married
ADDRESS: 21 Oxendon Way, Coventry, CV3 2HR

ATTAINMENTS:
School:             Binley Park Comprehensive, Coventry.
                    A level - English Lit, History, Sociology
University:         Greenwich University, London
                    B.Ed (2:1) Hons

PERSONAL STATEMENT:
Mrs Fudge's academic record shows her ability to work hard and
discipline herself. Reports from Greenwich University have
substantiated this and confirm her initiative and resourcefulness.

APTITUDES
During her course at university she attended evening classes to
improve her administrative and secretarial skills. Although no
examinations were taken she has tutors' references to confirm that
she has intermediate word processing and shorthand skills up to 80
wpm. She has experience of using Word Perfect 5.1, Microsoft Works
and Microsoft Office.

INTERESTS
Mrs Fudge is the Treasurer of the local drama group and has been
extensively involved with the group for the past 5 years. The group
provide entertainment for the local old people's home and junior
school.

DISPOSITION
Reports provide a variety of comments on the suitability of the
candidate. Personal references concentrate on her integrity and
loyalty whereas professional references have a suggestion of
impatience and intolerant nature. However, upon interview Mrs Fudge
did bring this to the fore and admitted that she did not get on
favourably with her last head of department due to a clash of
personality.

FURTHER INFORMATION
Mrs Fudge is available for employment immediately if her application
is successful. She has suggested that a trial period be arranged.
She is happy to attend another interview if we require to ask
further questions.

---

**Fig 5.10 A report in the form of a confidential memorandum**

## Appendices

The appendix, placed near the end of a formal report, is used as an additional source of information. It acts as a location point in the report for particular information which has relevance to all or part of the report's content. The appendix could comprise of a list of useful names and addresses or extracts from another useful source, anything that will provide additional information to the reader of the report.

## Bibliography

This word means 'a list of books' and is used by the report writer to detail any books or references used in the compilation of the report. The list is arranged in alphabetical order of author's surname, followed by the title of the book and its reference or ISBN number. The bibliography provides useful information to the reader of the report by giving details of useful books that provide further information for use either now or if they need to do further research.

## ▶ *Summarising techniques*

When preparing and summarising information to meet specified needs your summarising skills are at a premium. When asked to supply information you will not always be expected to supply all the information you can find, but a succinct presentation of that relative to the request being made. Time is a precious asset and you will no doubt be called upon to research information prior to presentation to your line manager. This means that you will have to read through the information, summarise it and then present only the core parts.

Your job may be to relay the essence of the message by using your comprehension, classification, analysing, evaluating and selection skills. You probably already do this, but did you realise exactly what you were doing? The steps you will be taking are:

1 Read and understand the information
2 Identify key points
3 Analyse and evaluate the essential parts
4 Select and present effectively to meet needs

How would you show an office junior how to maintain and use the photocopier? Do you think you would simply hand them the instruction manual or would you put the skills 1–4 above into practice?

The example above looks at using your summarising skills in the practical sense. It is likely that you would use demonstration and observation to

186

show how the photocopier works, supported by a summary of the key points either verbally or as a written or typed guide. However, there are a number of documents regularly used in an office that require specific summarising techniques. Do you use some of the following?

- Précis       a true but selective and reduced reproduction
- Summary     brief account giving key points
- Abstract      selective information from a long article or paper
- Conclusion/synopsis   outline of the main points.

The **précis** is used to reduce information by about a third but aims to keep its key points and views in a true reproduction.

The **summary** selects key points for a specific need, being much more selective than a précis and extracting only those points which are relevant.

The **abstract** also selects key points and is used to reduce a much longer article or paper according to specified needs.

The **conclusion/synopsis** identifies the main points made in the report.

# DIY 5.2.4

Write a short informal report regarding the suitability of equipment in your immediate office area. Comment on the age and condition of equipment and make recommendations as to new equipment that you feel should be bought. Provide up-to-date costs for the new equipment from an office supplies catalogue and include this in your appendix.

▶ *Presenting information pictorially, graphically and in text*

There are a number of ways in which information can be presented. If you have spent time searching for information it is important that when passing on your findings you do not confuse the person who asked for the information. You should choose a method of presentation that displays the information in an easy to understand format.

You must always remember to give a **heading** to your information and if necessary provide a key. A **key** is used to explain colour codes or small indicators on a plan or graph. Look at the key used for the London Underground: this identifies each line by using different colours, shading and patterns.

Methods of presenting information that you may choose are:

- diagrams
- graphs
- tables
- pie charts
- pictograms
- flow charts

There are many other methods, but the skill is to choose the method or methods that best suit the information you are trying to illustrate. Remember you are not trying to confuse others but to pass on information in an easy to understand manner.

## Diagrams

Diagrams are useful for showing a layout or how something works. You could use a diagram to show the directions of how to get from A to B, or

**Fig 5.11 An example of a diagram**

to show what something, such as a piece of equipment, looks like. A map is an example of a diagram.

## Graphs

Line graphs are used to show a set of figures. Different lines indicate different figures that can be compared against each other if plotted on the same graph. A line could be used to show sales figures and another to show staff wages in comparison.

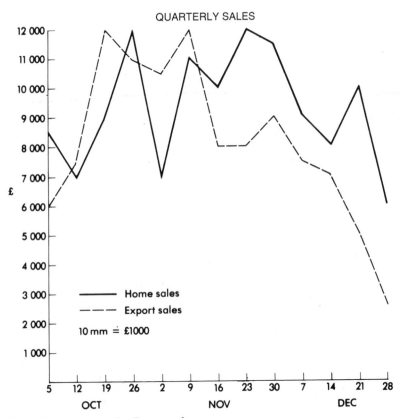

**Fig 5.12 An example of a line graph**

## Tables

A table can be used to present information in a logical sequence by using appropriate headings, columns and lines. The information can be boxed in so that separate pieces of information can be picked out easily. Information that seems complicated when written as text can be presented in a simple format by transferring it to a tabulated form. Examples such as train and bus timetables and mileage tables show how much easier the information is to understand if set out as a table.

189

| First name | Surname | Passport? | Languages spoken | Age |
|---|---|---|---|---|
| Amanda | White | Y | German | 19 |
| Sally | Gower | N | French | 20 |
| David | Talbot | N | French | 24 |
| Mark | Harris | Y | Italian | 23 |
| Rachel | Markham | Y | Spanish | 19 |
| Jade | Hamell | Y | German | 28 |
| Perri | Franc | Y | French | 24 |
| Leila | Scott | N | Hindustani | 19 |
| Crystal | Maze | Y | French | 30 |
| John | Patel | N | Hindustani | 23 |
| Lynne | Christanou | Y | Greek | 19 |
| Shervin | Sepanje | N | Spanish | 18 |

Fig 5.13 An example of a table

# ■ DIY 5.2.5

Look at the following information. Read it through and then present it using both a line graph and a table. You can do this either by hand or using a computer.

The amount of A4 paper being used in the training centre is getting out of hand: in 1993 we only used 35 reams in each of the first 2 months of the year, 43 in March, 35 again in April and down to 33 in each of the last 2 months of the half year. In 1994 the first month was totally over the top with 55 reams used, although the following 3 months dropped to 49, 45 and 40 respectively. The last 2 months remained at 41 reams each. Last year the college introduced a new method of ordering stationery and this seems to have solved the problem. The first 3 months of the half year saw further decreases from 36, 34 and 32 reams respectively and the last 3 months levelled out at 33 reams each. The figures for 1996 are not yet available.

## Pie charts

Pie charts are used to show figures as a percentage of the whole. The circle (pie) measures 360 degrees and is divided up into segments to show the different percentages, like the slices of a pie. The larger the slice, the larger the percentage in relation to the whole.

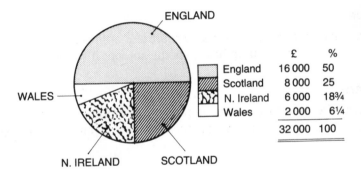

**Fig 5.14 An example of a pie chart for sales figures**

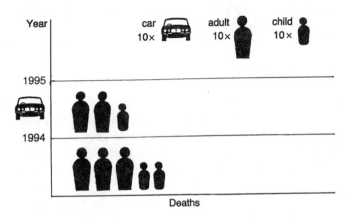

**Fig 5.15 An example of a pictogram**

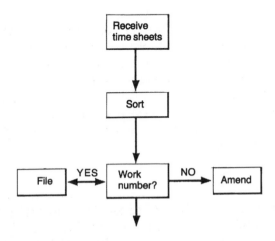

**Fig 5.16 An example of a flow chart**

### Pictogram

Pictograms use symbols or pictures to represent approximate figures. If the symbol or picture is cut in half, so is the amount it represents.

### Flow charts

Flow charts are used to show the steps through a process in the order they occur. By answering yes/no questions you are given the next stage in the process.

# ■ DIY 5.2.6

Look at the pie chart, pictogram and flow chart diagrams in Figs 5.14, 5.15 and 5.16. In your own words summarise the information that each diagram is giving. Also comment on whether you feel your written explanation is more easily or less easily understood when compared with the diagram.

## ▶ *Deadlines and prioritising*

When supplying information, apart from deciding on the source to use and the method of presentation, you must also take **time** into consideration. Some information will be required urgently and you may only have a few minutes in which to supply it; other information will take longer to find and you may need a day or more to find it. You should always be able to estimate the time you require to find the information and let the person know how long it will be before you return with the necessary facts. If there is going to be a delay and it will take longer than you thought, go back and tell the person, so that they do not think you have forgotten about it.

If you have several requests, put them in a priority order, so that the most urgent and important ones are first. Set your own deadlines if you do not have to meet a particular time or date; otherwise you may find that things get left and forgotten. You may have other duties to carry out, such as dealing with the post, answering the telephone, running errands or sorting out stock. You will need to include these duties in your priority list, especially when some have to be done at a particular time, eg the post or answering the telephone.

# ■ DIY 5.2.7

Make out a log like the example in Fig 5.17 on page 193 and complete the boxes when you have presented your researched information. This log can be attached to the log you have been completing for DIY 5.1.1 in Element 5.1. The 5.1 log will provide evidence of you researching, locating and selecting information to meet specified needs. The 5.2 log will provide evidence of how you have prepared and supplied information to meet specified needs. Both of these logs must be maintained over a period of time and copies of the finished work attached to them. Remember to enter details of any tasks you have completed for this unit or other units where you have presented narrative, statistical, graphical and tabular information.

| Date required | Information required | What methods were used to present information? |
|---|---|---|
| | | |
| | | |
| | | |
| | | |
| | | |
| | | |
| | | |
| | | |
| | | |
| | | |

**Fig 5.17 A blank log, for use with DIY 5.2.7**

## Knowledge and understanding question bank

1 How do you organise your information sources?
2 What types of material have you integrated and how?
3 What methods do you use to arrange material logically?
4 What presentational styles and formats do you use?
5 What is the Data Protection Act?
6 What is copyright law?
7 How do you identify confidential material?
8 How do you secure confidential material?
9 What methods do you use to reference your information sources?
10 How do you go about summarising information?
11 How do you acknowledge the source of information you have used?

## Claiming credit

For Element 5.2 evidence such as working papers, completed information presented in your chosen format and internal memoranda must be provided. Your format and presentation methods must include narrative, statistical, graphical and tabular form. The presentation of information must address the needs of both yourself and others and must comply with statutory and non-statutory requirements. Statutory requirements include regulations such as health and safety, equal opportunities, copyright and data protection. The following work products are potential sources of evidence:

- working papers
- completed information in the chosen format
- internal memoranda

Once you have completed your final assessment, you will need to write in your record book or folder how, when and what you have done to prove that you are competent.

The following statement is an example of how one trainee completed this claim:

*As an administrative assistant for 3 partners at Coopers & Co I am regularly involved in preparing and supplying information to meet the needs of the partners. Information can be presented as hard copy or as narrative. In some cases the information is requested by them; in others, such as the collection and checking of the accounts spreadsheet, I do this as part of my normal duties without being requested to do so. I ensure confidentiality and requirements under the Data Protection Act are always adhered to. I recently completed a report regarding the use of e-mail for one of the partners. The report contained statistical, graphical and tabular format and presentation. The partner asked me to talk through the report with him to clarify information, before he delivered a presentation to the other partners. The report was produced within deadlines although prices from one company had to be omitted as they were not delivered in time. The report was kept confidential and protected under a password.*

# Enter and integrate data, and present information, using a computer system

## ■ Element 6.1
### ENTER DATA INTO A COMPUTER

### Performance criteria

1 The need to store data is identified and available sources of data located

2 The application is suited to the type of data to be entered and the purpose for which the data is to be used

3 The organisation of files and the format of data within the computer system allow for its effective location, retrieval and transfer

4 Required data is entered accurately and is matched to the purpose for which the data is to be used

5 Source material is retained in accordance with organisational requirements

6 Work practices are in accordance with legal and regulatory requirements and organisational procedures

7 Security and confidentiality of data and source material are maintained

### Element introduction

This element is about how you use and operate hardware and software and why you select one particular type of software rather than another. It also includes how you organise your storage systems, the retaining and storing of original material and the back-up and security procedures you carry out. Finally it includes the safeguards you take to minimise risk to yourself regarding glare from, and exposure to, screens and posture and the protection of data. There are 2 main parts to any computer system, the hardware and the software.

## ▶ *Hardware*

The hardware includes the actual machinery: the screen (or VDU – visual display unit), keyboard, processor (or CPU – central processing unit), drives and a printer.

The CPU is the part of the machine which reads the information (data); the drives store the information. The CPU will contain a hard disk (also called a fixed disk) which cannot usually be removed from the machine, and it will also have 1 or 2 slots in the casing to insert floppy disks to store the information externally. The drives that contain the disks are usually called C for hard drive and A and B for the floppy disk drives. Other drives may be created but you do not need to know about these for this element. You only need to find out about making extra drives if you intend being a computer technician or programmer. You may also have a second hard drive fitted, which is likely to be labelled as the D drive.

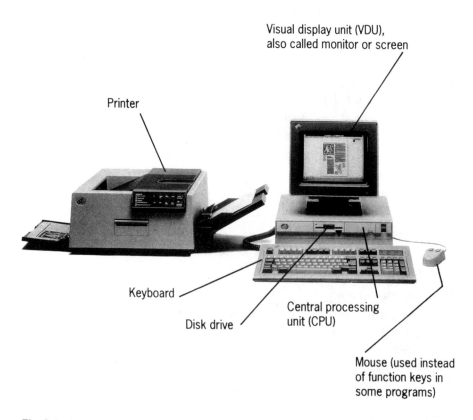

Printer

Visual display unit (VDU), also called monitor or screen

Keyboard

Disk drive

Central processing unit (CPU)

Mouse (used instead of function keys in some programs)

**Fig 6.1 Computer hardware**

## ▶ *Methods of inputting data into a computer system*

There are several methods that could be used to put data into the computer, some of which are specialist operations and are only likely to be used by those specially trained to carry out the work.

### Keyboard

The majority of the information you enter into the computer is likely to be done by using the keyboard. People who have learnt to use the keyboard via the touch typing method are likely to be the most accurate and fast in entering information this way. 'Touch typing' means that the operator does not need to look at the keyboard, their hands or the screen when entering text. Their eyes are constantly on the text being input and therefore less time is wasted looking from document to keys, and back again. Errors are likely to be fewer, as the operator does not jump sentences or paragraphs when returning their eyes to the work, as their eyes are constantly on the work.

### Scanners

Scanners are useful for importing graphic material on to a computer disk, but it will take specialist training for you to be able to master the techniques involved. Scanners can recognise more than just printed and typed alphanumeric text and so are different from Optical Character Recognition equipment. It would be unusual for you to carry out this type of work. If a company has a high demand for graphics, they are likely to appoint a specialist graphics worker to deal with all the documents and requests.

## ▶ *Software*

Software is the programs that make the hardware work. They are supplied on floppy disks which are usually 3.5" or 5.25" in diameter and are protected by a cover, either hard or soft plastic. The disk itself is visible and looks like a dark brown, smooth circular piece of plastic – it should not be touched or it will be damaged. Programs are written in languages that the CPUs can understand; the most common are BASIC (**B**eginner's **A**ll-purpose **S**ymbolic **I**nstruction **C**ode) and COBOL (**CO**mmon **B**usiness **O**rientated **L**anguage). You will not need to understand these languages unless you intend to become a computer programmer. Most of the people that use computers do not understand how they work; they only understand the programs they use.

197

# ■ DIY 6.1.1

---

Look at the equipment you use at work or in the training centre and identify all the hardware – the VDU, CPU, keyboard, drives and printer. If you are using a network and some of the equipment is not immediately visible, find out where it is located. Write down the name of the manufacturer and the name of the equipment and include the CPU specification, eg hard drive size, speed of operation.

---

Most of the programs used in a business or college are loaded from the floppy disks to the hard drive. This process is called **installing** a program. The program can then easily be used on a daily basis without having to be reloaded every time you want to use it. Each time a program is loaded on to the hard drive, it uses up space. A hard drive will have a limited amount of space; therefore it can only hold so many programs at one time. The number of programs held depends on the size of the program and the size of the hard disk.

## ▶ *Looking after the equipment*

You should check that the screen is placed at a comfortable distance from the keyboard, to make sure you do not suffer from eye strain. Also alter the brightness of the screen to suit you, using the brightness control and the contrast control. The screen should be facing away from windows, or direct artificial light, to reduce the glare. If this is not possible, an anti-glare screen may be attached. There should be sufficient space around your keyboard to place your work or to use a mouse (on a mouse mat) or joystick.

### Cleaning the equipment

Very few components can actually be cleaned. After switching off and unplugging from the mains, you can clean the screen with an anti-static spray (as recommended by suppliers or local stationers). The casing can also be wiped clear of dirty finger marks and dust. You will need to use a brush or small vacuum to remove dust from between the keys. **Never** remove the casing from computers. The screen is sensitive and should not be left on when not in use. Static from the screen will also attract dust. If the machine is not going to be used for a while, turn the screen brightness down or off, otherwise the characters may burn an image into the screen. Quite often you can see this 'burning' effect on the cash card machines used at building societies, banks and post offices.

Keep food and liquids away from all computer equipment. If an accident should occur, disconnect from the main supply immediately and call for assistance.

## ▶ Safety requirements

The Health and Safety at Work Act 1974 requirements state that you should take all necessary steps to operate in a safe manner, taking care of your own safety and the safety of other people who may be affected by your actions. Employers are also required to supply the correct equipment and systems to carry out the work and to ensure that employees operate in a safe working environment. The Electricity at Work Regulations 1989 have been incorporated into the HASAWA 1974 and were established to ensure precautions are taken against the risk of injury or death from electricity at work. There are maintenance guidelines for all electrical equipment. All electrical equipment must be regularly checked to confirm it is safe to use; even the office kettle, word processor and electric fan have to be inspected and maintained on a regular basis. Organisations are advised to label their electrical equipment with details of when they were last checked and the date of the next inspection. Green labels are used for equipment that has passed its test and red labels used for equipment that is not satisfactory. Further information can be found in leaflet IND(G)89(L) *Guidance for small businesses on electricity at work.*

Fig 6.2 Example of a completed green label

### Precautions that should be taken with computer equipment

Switch off all machinery at the end of the day. (The only exceptions may be the telephone answering machine, which will take telephone calls in your absence, and the fax machine which may send and receive messages during the night.) Make sure that any connecting wires are not trailing across the floor; they should be taped under the desk or placed along the outside of the room. Do not overload sockets. Multi-extension leads should be used when several items need to be plugged in at the same time, or extra sockets should be installed. Check the leads regularly for fraying or broken connections. Consult your tutor or health and safety representative if you are not sure about the state of any of the equipment you use.

## ▶ *Good posture*

To make certain you do not suffer from strain and injury, you should sit in the most comfortable position for typing. Strain can occur to the neck, back, arms and legs and on occasions can lead to serious complaints. To reduce the risk of injury, or RSI (Repetitive Strain Injury), you should use a chair which can be adjusted to suit you. It should allow you to sit with your feet flat on the floor (use a footrest if necessary), and it should have an adjustable backrest to support your lower back. Desks for typing are generally lower than normal desks to allow for the keyboard to sit at the correct height.

Your head should be upright, otherwise you will find your neck will ache from constantly looking down at the desk. This means that the document you are working from should be placed on a document holder, either to the right or left of your keyboard, whichever you find more comfortable.

## ▶ *Looking after disks*

Floppy disks are fragile. They can easily be damaged and damage may result in you losing all the information stored. The information is stored on the disks in tracks, which are similar to the grooves on a record. Each track has a circle which can hold a certain amount of information. Disks may be single- or double-sided – double-sided means that they can store information on both sides; therefore double-sided disks store more information than single-sided disks. They can also be single-, double- or high-density: the density of the disk refers to the amount of information that can be stored. If the disk is double-density, twice as much information can be stored on it as on a single-density disk. The high-density disk stores the most information. The speed at which the CPU runs will depend on which type of disk you use, in the same way that video recorders can run at different speeds. (If you halve the speed at which the tape runs through the machine, you can store twice as much.)

As mentioned earlier, disks are protected by a plastic cover. The covers of 5.25" disks are flexible, but should never be bent. The top of the disk is smooth and has no edges, whilst underneath you will find that three edges have been folded over and electronically 'stapled' in place. The exposed

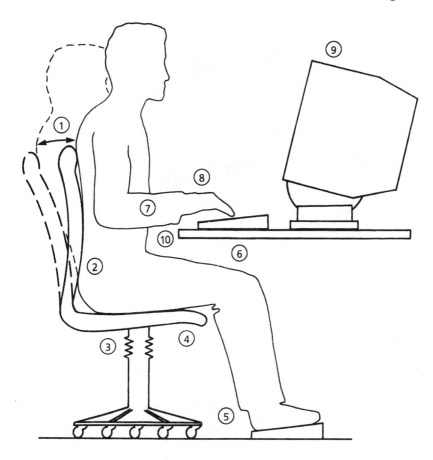

1 Seat back adjustability
2 Good lumbar support
3 Seat height adjustability
4 No excess pressure on underside of thighs and backs of knees
5 Foot support if needed
6 Space for postural change; no obstacles under desk
7 Forearms approximately horizontal
8 Minimal extension, flexion or deviation of wrists
9 Screen height and angle should allow comfortable head position
10 Space in front of keyboard to support hands/wrists during pauses in keying

**Fig 6.3 Good posture**
Crown copyright

201

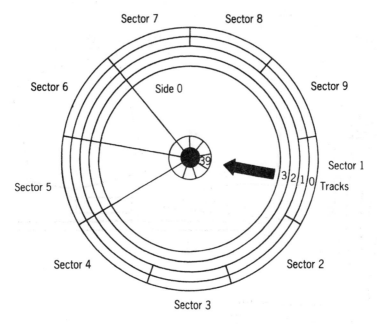

**Fig 6.4 Diagram of disk tracks**

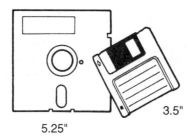

**Fig 6.5 Labelled disks**

parts of the disk should be in the middle and there is an oval slot on one side. This oval slot is the side pushed first into the disk drive in the casing of the CPU. A 3.5" disk is protected by a hard plastic cover which has an arrow printed on the front indicating which way it should be inserted into the CPU. It also has a metal protection cover over the exposed part of the disk. Slide one back carefully to see the disk. Both these disks may also be called diskettes.

Before any disk can be used for storing information it will need to be formatted (sometimes called initialising). Formatting a disk prepares it to accept information from the system you are running on your computer. It is usually done by using the 'format' command, but you will need to check with your IT supervisor or tutor before you carry out a format on equipment you are unfamiliar with. If you format an existing disk all the information stored on it will be lost, as formatting cleans the disk completely. Disks can be supplied ready formatted.

## ▶ Protecting the information on your disk

On the 5.25" disk you will see a small rectangular cut in the left-hand side. This is the write protection notch. If you do not want to put any further information on the disk or you want to make sure you do not delete any of the information, you can place a label over the notch and the CPU will then stop you from storing or deleting any further information. The screen prompt usually states: 'write protection error'.

On the 3.5" disk at the bottom right-hand corner at the back of the disk you will see a small plastic square that can slide up and down. In the up position the disk is write protected; if it is down you can delete and change files. Write protection is the same process as protecting a video at home: when you break off the plastic square from the front of the video, it stops anyone from recording over the top of your favourite film.

Another way of protecting information stored on disks is by saving the file with a password or keyword. Before the CPU will allow you to look at the information stored or to delete the file it will be necessary to type in the password. If you use passwords, make sure you remember them and if you write them down, make sure they are somewhere that is not easily found by everyone else in the office. Check that your company does not have regulations regarding the use of passwords before you start your own system.

## ▶ Labelling disks

To protect the exposed areas of the 5.25" disk you should place it in a paper cover and store all disks in a disk box. This may be a small box which can store 5–10 disks or a desktop box which can store many more. Each of the disks should be labelled, and it is useful to put the label in the corner which you hold when you place the disk into the CPU. When the disks are in their box the labels should be in the top left-hand corner.

Always write on the label **before** you stick it on to the disk. If you need to change what is written on the label of a 5.25" disk at a future date, you should use a fibre tipped pen. Do not use biro or pencil as the pressure of writing on the label may damage the disk.

## ▶ Using your disks in the CPU

To insert a 5.25" disk into the CPU, hold it over the label, insert it into the slot and push the lever down into position. To insert a 3.5" disk into the CPU, hold the disk in the right-hand corner and push it into the slot until it clicks down into place.

## ▶ Protecting your disks from damage

The disk box should be kept in a dry place which does not become too hot or cold and should not be exposed to excessive light. The disks should also be kept away from the top of the CPU, telephones, electrical equipment, steel or any magnetic surface as these may corrupt your disk (even a steel knife and fork could corrupt a disk!). If a disk is corrupted you may be unable to get your data back. If this should occur check with a computer technician as they will have access to special programs that may retrieve data or repair damaged disks. Data could also be lost through accidentally deleting a file, handling or overloading the disk. Again, check with a computer technician as deleted data can often be retrieved, as long as you have not reformatted the disk.

## ▶ Making back-ups

To reduce the chance of losing your data through a corrupted disk, it is usual to make 'back-up' copies. This means that you keep a copy of the data on a second disk. In some businesses they have a set procedure for making back-up copies. Check at work or discuss with your tutor how frequently you should make back-ups. Even hard disks may get corrupted so do not rely on keeping all your data on hard disk only. For this reason some companies change their hard disks and have back-up copies of them made, especially when they are dealing with millions of pieces of information every day.

## ▶ Saving your data

It is important to save your data regularly. If you are working all day on the same file, you may save it every half-hour or so, just to make sure you do not lose all the work through someone accidentally switching off your computer or through an electrical power cut. Some programs remind you to save your work by flashing a message at you while you work and slowing the system down, which generally annoys you so much you save quickly to enable you to get on! Some programs will create a back-up for you and save automatically every so often, eg 20 minutes or so. The time between automatic saves can usually be altered and set to your own preferred rate. Automatic back-ups are usually saved by the computer as a separate file, often called 'back-up' or with a file name extension of 'bk'.

To save a file it is necessary to give it a **file name**, the name which is used to recall the file when you wish to edit or change the information. The names you choose for files may depend on company policy or may be entirely up to you. However, if the choice is yours try to have a system that is logical. In some software packages you are able to enter a short description of the document you are saving; this helps you to recognise it again when you need to retrieve it. In some organisations you may be required to print the file name on the document, either as a reference number or in small print at the bottom of the page (footer). It is also likely that when you save your file, the date and time will also be saved at the same time. If you have several versions of a document you can easily see which is the latest version by the date. Another piece of useful information usually stored by the computer is the size of the file you have saved.

Computer memory is generally made up from bits and bytes. **Bits** are binary codes represented by 0 or 1; **bytes** are groups of 8 bits, often used to represent one character. There is normally an ascending number and a descending number, one representing the amount of space used on a disk or drive and the other representing the space left. You should check the amount of space left on a disk so that you do not try to save a file which is too big for the space left. If a disk is too full, its operation and use can become very slow.

The file name will usually indicate the content of the file and it should contain no more than 8 characters (preferably only letters as in some programs numbers and other characters have special meanings to the computer). Some software packages are also particular about whether small letters or capital letters are typed. Therefore, if you decide to call your file 'STOCKJAN', when you want to call the file back you must type this name exactly. If you enter the file name as 'stockjan' it may not be able to find it. This is called 'case specific', where the computer is looking for a particular 'case', ie lower case or upper case letters. (This is also called 'shift sensitive'.)

The second part of the file name is called an extension and your computer will automatically issue an extension to your file, if you do not key one in. Files in a word processing package may have the extension .DOC; database files may have the .DBF extension.

You should keep a record of the file names you allocate to your data.

# ■ DIY 6.1.2

Write a personal statement about the types of drives and disks that you use at work or college. Include in it a directory printout to use as an example of how the files are saved. Identify on your printout, where possible, the following:

1  File name
2  File extension
3  Date file stored
4  Time stored
5  Space left on the disk/drive
6  Space used on the disk/drive

Also include details of how you name your files and the procedure you follow.

**Note:** If you are unsure how to print your directory, once you have called up the directory on screen, press 'print screen' and this should print the information required.

## ▶ *Word processing*

The majority of businesses using computers will have some form of word processing package installed. This is used for all general correspondence, internal and external, as well as reports, minutes, notes, tables etc. The most popular packages currently used include: WordPerfect, Word, Amipro, Word for Windows and MicrosoftWorks.

Some of your work may involve researching information for inclusion in a report. Statistics and figures are generally easier to understand if they are presented in a tabular form.

Some documents may include items that need to be displayed, or documents may be required for display on a notice board, such as menus, advertisements, vacancies, programmes etc. There are several ways of producing such material: typing, word processing, desktop publishing, hand-drawn, transfers etc. Part of your job could be selecting the most effective method for displaying information, accessing or arranging for the work to be completed.

Many word processing packages allow you to change the size and style of the characters. The sizes are usually listed in point size (1 point = 0.0138"), the lower numbers referring to the smaller sizes of print. The size of print commonly used on typewriters and word processers is between 11 pt and 13 pt. For displayed items such as menus, programmes, tickets and posters you would need to select a size of print which would be effective for the purpose. On an A3 size poster 72 pt would be suitable for headings, and 36 pt for other information, wheareas A4 programmes may require 24 pt for headings and 14 pt for information. Typewriters often use cpi (characters per inch) as a measurement for print size, in pica or elite. Pica has about 10 characters to the inch, elite 12 characters to the inch. Therefore 10 is bigger than 12, ie the reverse of the point system.

Once you have selected an appropriate size of print for your documents, the style can be selected to suit. The fonts commonly used are Courier, Helvetica, Prestige, and Roman. Options may also be available for the styles to be in bold, normal, italic, or bold and italic. You will need to be able to experiment with the options obtainable on the machines available to you. If you are unfamiliar with the options, it is useful to keep a printout of all that are available as this saves time when you are selecting fonts and sizes for your documents. It may also be possible to shadow or outline your characters: this gives extra effect to displayed material.

Mathematical signs and foreign text may also be typed. Some word processors have a secondary keyboard, that is, the keys can be used to type special signs and characters after you key in a special code. You would need to consult your typewriter manual or software manual to ascertain the facilities available. Some signs or symbols may need to be added by hand, using a black pen.

## ▶ *Using material from copyright sources*

If you intend using figures or quotations from published books, trade magazines, microfiche, viewdata etc it is important that you acknowledge the source. Plagiarism is the act of taking and using the thoughts, writings, quotations, inventions etc of another and passing them off as your own. It is an offence under the Copyright Act to use material without permission or claim ownership of material written by others. The author's permission must be obtained before reproducing and you should also acknowledge their contribution by writing the source of your material on the document you are producing. There are universally accepted methods of layout for acknowledging sources, and one of the most frequently used by college and university students in their assignments is the Harvard method. The author's name and the date of the material is typed in brackets after the excerpt used. For example:

'It is unlikely that a residential module will be necessary for any modularised structure introduced in this institution.' (Bourne L, 1989)

If figures or statistics from public documents are used, such as Government papers or news items about these, the source is usually typed at the end of the figures, using a different typeface from that used for the document. However, if you are going to publish your material permission should still be sought.

The accuracy of the information used should also be investigated if there are any uncertainties or ambiguities. Quite often statistics are based on small samples and any conclusions based on these statistics may be biased. They may, however, be useful for ascertaining trends which can be used as the basis for further decisions and conclusions.

## ■ DIY 6.1.3

Make a personal statement about the type of word processing package you use and its facilities. State which facilities you use most and which you use on an infrequent basis. Collect 12 examples of documents you have created over a period of at least 2 months. On each example state:

1 Whether the document was saved and, if so, the file name and extension allocated. State whether you decided to save the file or whether you were requested by someone else to keep it.
2 Where you have been given a draft document or a handwritten copy to process, attach the original document to the final version you have prepared. Acknowledge any source documents you have used by stating the name of the author, the publication and the date of publication.
3 State the security and confidentiality procedures you have followed for confidential documents. Get your line manager to confirm that your statement is true. This can be done either by getting a statement and signature on your personal statement or by getting your manager to make a supportive testimonial for you.

## ▶ Database

A database package is similar to a filing system, in that it stores information and allows you to retrieve it at a later time, add a new file or delete an old one. You will probably have filed items in an alphabetical order manually, which can be time consuming. The computer does not need you to sort the information: it can do this by itself. This means that you can put the information into the computer in any order, and when you add a file it does not have to be in a particular place. Many different organisations use databases to store all sorts of information, such as customers' names and addresses, information on staff or patients, stock records, properties for sale, membership records, etc.

The type of information needed for each database will vary and you will need to look carefully at the information to be stored before you create a database. Each piece of information needs to have a line of its own; this line is called a FIELD. For example, if you were creating a database of your relations' birthdays you would probably want a field for name, one for the date, one for month and another for the year – 4 fields altogether. If you wanted to include the address you might wish to have further fields for street, town, county.

The computer is able to sort out for you the files stored with a common field. For instance, if you wished to have a list of all the relations who had birthdays in May, you would be able to LIST these by requesting the computer to SORT out all the files that have May in the field called month.

The fields will be listed individually on the screen in the shape of a FORM. The information for the relations' birthdays would therefore look like this:

| Name |
| Date |
| Month |
| Year |
| Street |
| Town |
| County |
| Postcode |

**Fig 6.6 Example of fields**

The space you need for each field will depend on the information you intend to put in it. For the name field you will have to make sure that it is long enough to type in the longest name; the date field would need a maximum of 2 spaces as the numbers would be between 1 and 31; the month field would require either a maximum of 9 if you wished to enter the name of the month (September is the longest month) or only 2 spaces if the month was typed numerically, ie September would be month 09 and October 10; and the year field would require only 4 spaces. Usually the database program will indicate by dots, dashes or a block how much space has been reserved in a field.

You also need to tell the computer the type of information you will be putting into the field, ie alphabetic letters, numbers or a combination of both. In our example the first field, name, would be alpha, the second field, day, would be numeric. The street field would be alphanumeric, as it would probably have the number of the house and the name of the street.

| |
|---|
| Name .......................................... |
| Date  .. |
| Month ........ |

**Fig 6.7 Different amounts of space are allocated to fields**

You may find that once you start using your database the space allocated to a field is not enough. Most programs allow you to change the space, even after you have started saving information.

## Accessing a database program

The database may be on your computer only or it may be connected (networked) to another or several hundred terminals (machines). Networked systems are used in large companies and allow many users to access the same information. The networked system shares the same CPU and all the information is saved centrally on the CPU, although it may be possible to save your particular information yourself on a floppy disk.

How you access your database depends on which program you are using and how the computer has been set up. Some computers will have been set up with a menu (a list of items from which you can choose a program) which appears when you switch on, while others will just have a prompt, such as C:\> which is waiting for you to enter a command. Find out from your supervisor or tutor how to access the database program installed on your machine and make sure you write it down, so you do not forget.

Your files in the database program will have different names. If you save your family information as 'FAMILY.DBF' you would not use this name for another file. A file with information on the 3rd Division football clubs might be called FOOTBALL.DBF (remember the file name cannot be more than 8 characters long and the DBF is an extension which indicates that the file is a **DataBase File**). The database software that you use may allocate an extension automatically when you save your file.

If you were looking at information in the FOOTBALL file and you wished to look at the FAMILY file, you may have to close one file in order to open the next. In most systems, if you open or close files you will need to select the correct option using the cursor keys and then press the return key or, if you are using a mouse, click on the option required.

When you enter information (text or numbers) into the database it is important to be accurate, otherwise you may have problems when selecting or looking for particular files. If you wanted to look at all the family records of people that lived in London and you had typed 'Londen' in some of the records, the computer would not be able to find them. Therefore you should always proof-read on screen after entering text before going to the next record or saving the file. If you have made an error it is easy to correct it by using the cursor keys: go back to the field containing the error, delete it and type in the correction.

## Searching, sorting and retrieving information

You may be asked to search through the records to find a particular form. If so, you can use the 'page down' key or 'next record' option on the database menus. This will allow you to look at each form. If you wanted to look at a particular set of records you could get the computer to 'sort' out the records for you. You will need to tell the database what you need; to do this you will choose a particular field, such as month, in the family file. The computer will need to know what you are looking for; you could say all the forms that have 'May' in the month field.

Once set up the computer will search for all the records that have May typed in the month field and it will show you on screen how many forms it has found. You can then look through these forms on screen or get a printout of them. If you wanted you could choose 2 fields at the same time for the computer to sort, eg all the records that have May in the month field and also have London in the address field. The computer will again show you how many records it has found for you to look through. Once you have found (retrieved) the forms you need you can write the details down from the screen or get a printout.

Being able to sort forms is one of the main advantages of a database record system over a paper-based system. An estate agent, for instance, could record all the details of the properties for sale. When a customer is looking for a house priced at £80,000 with 4 bedrooms in Erith, the office clerk could easily find the correct forms by stating the 4 special fields (type of property, price, bedrooms, location) and the details. A printout could then be made of all the houses available to give to the customer.

A club could use the computer database to find out which members need to renew their subscriptions each month. Businesses may use a database to select the customers located in the Lewisham area, to enable their representatives to call and inform them of a special offer.

Travel agents use databases which are linked nationally to each other and to the main providers of flights and holidays. They can find a holiday in a certain country or for a certain price or date in a few seconds, and inform the customer of the options.

The financial world uses databases to make sure it has the most up-to-date information about stocks and shares. The stock exchange computer system is called SEAQ, **S**tock **E**xchange **A**utomated **Q**uotations system. Each market maker (dealer in stocks and shares) has a terminal connected to the central computer and business is carried out via the computer. The main computer is updated every minute by agencies such as Reuters, Topic and Telerate who have the latest information on the market movements.

Colleges can keep details of their students on a database and are able to print out all those attending on Tuesday evening for Law, or any other options required. The uses of a database are many. No doubt you can think of several more.

## Adding new records to the database

To fill out a new form, or to add a record, you should open the file in the normal way for sorting or looking. You will find that your database menu will have an option called 'append', 'add record' or something similar. Select this option and a blank form will appear on the screen. You then complete the fields with the necessary information and save the file again. Your new record will then be added to the file. You will need to look at your own database to see the exact procedure to add forms, but generally databases are very similar.

## Deleting a record

To delete a record you can either go to the form you wish to delete and delete the page/record, or you may be able to specify a particular field, for example to delete all the records that have London in the town field. The computer will mark the records ready for deletion and when you save and exit the program these records will not be saved. The computer may give you an opportunity to change your mind when you are exiting, and a message may come on screen such as 'DELETE ALL RECORDS MARKED?' In reply to this you can answer Y/N. If you reply Y the file will be saved without the marked records; if you reply N you can continue to work in the file and the records will not be deleted.

## Backing up database files

All your records created on the computer should be backed up for the reasons discussed earlier. The database will have an option to allow you to do this. Make sure that you back up regularly or every time you finish entering new text, or deleting files. The back-up files should be stored safely and, if they are confidential, in a locked cabinet. Some companies delete all the records from the hard disk at the end of each year and keep a copy of all the records on floppy disk (such as a college, so that all the new students for the year can be entered on to the system). It is important to remove old files from the computer system and keep as much space free as possible for your new files.

## ▶ Planning and organising your work

You should make sure that you have all the necessary information before starting to update your database. The information may be supplied to you in different ways. The company may have a form which is completed by hand and the information is taken from it and typed into the correct file, form and field. Or you may take information from customers or clients verbally and enter this directly on to the database whilst on the telephone. If this is the case you must make doubly sure that the information you have entered is correct before your customer hangs up the telephone: always read back to them the information you have entered.

The database is only as good as the users make it: if the information is out of date and inaccurate then it will be of little use to anyone. It is very important to regularly update your database with information as it is received, such as new telephone numbers, changes of address, new requirements of customers etc.

The information stored may be confidential, in which case access should be restricted to those people that are authorised to use it. Access can be restricted by using passwords to gain access. Each department may be allocated a password or each separate user may have a password.

Some systems will also allow users to look at the information but not change any of it or delete it. This system is sometimes used for students' records, where the tutor enters all the information regarding assessments and the student is allocated a password which allows them to access their record and look at the results or get a printout of them. Only the tutor can amend the record. Access by other students is restricted as they will not know the password.

Floppy disks can be copied or stolen, so make sure they are kept in the disk box and then locked in a cupboard or drawer. Again, access to the disks should be restricted. A booking-out system should be introduced when confidential disks are taken away from the office by authorised users.

## ■ DIY 6.1.4

Write a full account of the type of database you have used, the files contained in it and its uses. Make a printout of some of the file listings, and one complete record. Include in your account how you add further files, delete files and back up. If possible give at least 2 examples of databases used, one that was already established and that you have accessed, another that you have established yourself. In the second example, state why you decided to set up this particular database, and how you ensure records are kept secure and confidential.

Collect examples of databases you have set up, altered, added to and deleted records from. While on work experience, make sure that you report on the type of database used and, as well as including printouts, state the uses of the database, and what security and confidentiality procedures you carried out. Ensure you get permission from your supervisor before taking copies. You will also need a statement from your supervisor to confirm the work has been carried out by you, to the standards required in the organisation.

### ▶ *Legal requirements for databases*

If you set up a database which contains personal information on individuals then it must be registered with the Data Protection Registrar. The records should not be kept longer than is necessary and proper security procedures should be introduced to make sure only authorised staff have access to the information stored. The information should also be kept up to date, be accurate, and never be passed to anyone who may use it for other purposes, eg a list of doctor's patients being passed to a mail order firm to allow them to send medical sales materials. Further information regarding registration can be obtained from your local or training centre library, the Post Office or direct from the Data Protection Registrar (Springfield House, Water Lane, Wilmslow, Cheshire, SK9 5AX).

# ■ DIY 6.1.5

Find out more details about the Data Protection Act. (The sources may include a library, your tutor, your computer technicians, the Post Office, DP Registrar.) Design a fact sheet for a new clerical assistant who will be starting in your office next week. Use simple language so you do not confuse your assistant. Your fact sheet should be typed or word processed.

## ▶ Spreadsheets

A spreadsheet is a table which has 'cells' made up from vertical and horizontal lines. These are called 'columns' and 'rows'.

|   | A | B | C | D | E |
|---|---|---|---|---|---|
| 1 |   |   |   |   | cell |
| 2 |   | * | cell |   | * |
| 3 | cell |   |   |   |   |
| 4 |   | cell | * |   |   |
| 5 |   |   |   | cell |   |

**Fig. 6.8 Example of a spreadsheet**

The spreadsheet in Fig 6.8 has 5 columns and 5 rows. Each box is one cell, therefore this example has 25 cells. To locate particular information in a spreadsheet you would state the column letter and the row number eg A3, B4, C2, D5 and E1 all have the word 'cell' printed in them (similar to the game of Battleships). Which cells have a * in them?

The number of columns and rows that you can have depends on the type of software you are using, but most can have up to at least 100. When you are working on a spreadsheet you will find that the cell you are currently using will highlight, in a similar way to the cursor in a word processing package. You can move round the cells by using the cursor arrow keys or a mouse. If you wish to go to a particular cell you will be able to instruct the cursor to go to it, rather than using the cursor to find it. This facility is particularly useful if the spreadsheet has several hundred cells. Cell size can be changed, if you need to enter a particularly long figure. You will need to consult your manual to see how to use these facilities.

## Uses for spreadsheets

Most spreadsheets are used for presenting, analysing and planning financial information. For instance a petty cash account could be kept on a spreadsheet, as could sales achieved by different sales representatives, expenditure of the department under budget headings etc. Once the information is entered it can be saved, recalled later, updated, deleted, moved or copied. It is also possible to make calculations using formulae. A formula is a set of instructions that you type in, which makes the computer perform a particular task. An example would be an instruction to add up a column of figures.

## Entering data

When you enter figures you will move to the cell required and key in the necessary information. If you are using dates or times you will need to check the Spreadsheet manual to see which format is acceptable. For instance, to type in 3 June 1995 you may need to key in one of the following:

- 030695, or 03-06-95, or 3-6-95, or 03/06/95 or 3/6/95

or the package may accept

- 3 June 95 or 3-Jun-95

If the format is 060395 this means the information is in the order of month, day, year. This is the acceptable layout for international use and if this is the order required by your program it may be due to the fact that the program you are using was designed abroad or is intended for use in more than one country. America for instance uses this format most of the time.

For time the options for 2.30 pm would include:

- 2.30 pm, or 02.30 pm, or 14.30, or 1430 or 14:30

Seconds are sometimes added

- 14:30:10

You may use some of the cells for labelling columns or rows, or a heading may also be typed at the top. If you are using calculations (formulae) these will also be contained in a cell.

|   | A | B | C | D | E | F | G |
|---|---|---|---|---|---|---|---|
| 1 |  | SALES | FOR | 1995 |  |  |  |
| 2 | £ | SE | SW | WALES | NE | NW | TOTAL |
| 3 | ITEM1 | 140,000 | 142,000 | 20,000 | 90,000 | 75,600 | 467,600 |
| 4 | ITEM2 | 20,900 | 12,000 | 49,000 | 35,000 | 26,900 | 143,800 |
| 5 | ITEM3 | 36,800 | 46,800 | 26,900 | 50,000 | 60,000 | 220,500 |
| 6 | TOTAL | 197,700 | 200,800 | 95,900 | 175,000 | 162,500 | 831,900 |

**Fig. 6.9 Example of a completed spreadsheet**

In Fig 6.9 a formula would have instructed the computer to add the columns down and put the total figure in row 6 and to add the rows across and put the total in column G.

### Entering formulae

A formula always begins with =. You will need to tell the computer exactly what you want to do. In the example in Fig 6.9 we wanted it to add cell B3, B4 and B5 and put the result in B6. The type of formula needed for this would be =+B3:B5, which would mean B3, B5 and all the cells in between should be added together. The formula would be in cell B6, which is where the total would be entered by the computer. What formula do you think is in C6, D6, E6, F6 and G6? To make the calculations across the rows, a formula would have been placed in G3, G4, G5 and G6. For G3 this would have been =+B3:F3.

## DIY 6.1.6

Consult your spreadsheet manual and find out:

1 What is the name of the package you will be using for spreadsheets?
2 What are the formulae for:
   - adding
   - subtracting
   - multiplying
   - dividing

**3** What would your formulae be for the spreadsheet in Fig 6.9?

**4** What would be your formula if you wanted to add B3 and B5 (missing out B4)?

**5** What would be your formula if you wanted to add C3 and E3 (missing out the other figures on that row)?

A spreadsheet program will also allow you to 'project' figures. This means that if you have a spreadsheet that has figures for sales in column B for 1995 and your company wants to know the expected increase in sales if there is a 5 per cent increase each year, then a formula can be entered which will increase all the figures in the column by 5 per cent for 1996, 1997, 1998, 1999 etc. This facility is called a **projection** and is used to estimate income and expenditure, sales and profits, growth and decline of products etc.

### Changing the size of your spreadsheet

If you wish to increase the size of your spreadsheet after you have already entered data, there will be an option (like that for adding a record in a database) for you to do this. In the same way you can reduce the number of columns and rows selected and delete data from the cells. Data in a cell can also be moved or copied to another cell. Information can also be sorted alphabetically and numerically. However you will need to consult your manual to see what instructions your computer needs to do this.

## ■ DIY 6.1.7

**1** To add a column to a spreadsheet I need to ...

**2** To add a row to a spreadsheet I need to ...

**3** To delete a column from a spreadsheet I need to ...

**4** To delete a row from a spreadsheet I need to ...

**5** To project a column I need to ...

**6** To move the data of a cell I need to ...

**7** To copy the data of a cell to another cell I need to ...

**8** To increase the size of a cell I need to ...

**9** To go to a particular cell I need to ...

### Correcting mistakes

The spreadsheet information will only be of use to you and your company if the data are 100 per cent correct. This means that the information you enter must be checked when you are entering it, before saving it and again in a printout. It is crucial that any errors are corrected immediately, preferably before you save the file. If, however, errors are identified afterwards you will need to call the file back and make the correction, remembering to save the file again before exiting from the program. Not only must the data be correct but the formulae must also be doubly checked, because if these are wrong it could lead to important decisions being made on incorrect figures. Many programs have 'fault' messages that appear if you have entered the incorrect formulae and will not allow you to proceed until the problem is sorted out.

Whichever type of document you are producing it is important to be accurate and consistent in layout and your spelling, punctuation and grammar should be correct. It is not always possible to rely on others to use the correct spelling and grammar in their drafts. Pay particular attention to words with which you are not familiar. Numerical information needs to be checked carefully against the original data. The terminology used by a specialised organisation may be unfamiliar to you and this makes checking your documents more demanding. Keep a list of common specialist terms you use or, if you have a computerised spell check, you can add them to the memory.

Interruptions can also create errors. In a busy office it is unlikely that you will be able to carry out any job for a sustained period without some kind of interruption. It could be the telephone, a visitor, a colleague's or manager's request, an emergency, a change of priority, or it could be the end of the day. When returning to the work make sure you reread the last few sentences of text, to familiarise yourself with the content again. You will then be able to restart and carry on where you left off.

If a fault occurs on the program or with the system it should be reported to your line manager or your technical support section. Always save your information before leaving the machine unattended.

## Measures for security and confidentiality with spreadsheets

Much of the information used in spreadsheets is likely to be highly sensitive, ie confidential. It should not be taken out of the office or shown to anyone who is not involved with the work. Passwords or keywords can protect files and back-up files should be made in case files become corrupted. Do not rely on your hard disk. Never leave your office with information displayed on the screen, as you do not know who may enter. Always save it, and either exit the program (if you are going to be quite a while) or move the cursor to another part of the spreadsheet which has empty cells (if it is only for a few minutes). You could also turn the screen down, so that the information cannot be seen.

▶ *Using display screen equipment*

The **Health and Safety (Display Screen Equipment) Regulations 1992** affect workers who habitually use VDUs for a significant part of their normal work. Employers still have general obligations under health and safety legislation to protect other workers who use VDUs to whom this description does not apply. The regulations do not contain detailed technical information, but instead set more general objectives.

Employers have to:

- analyse workstations of employees covered by the regulations and assess and reduce risks
- ensure workstations meet minimum requirements
- plan work so there are breaks or changes of activity
- on request arrange eye and eyesight tests, and provide spectacles if special ones are needed
- provide health and safety training
- provide information.

In order to reduce any possible negative effects on health through the use of VDU-based equipment for lengthy periods of time, the Health and Safety Executive has recommended a series of guidelines for ensuring that the office environment is compatible with the introduction of new technology. Leaflet IND(G) 36(L) 'Working with VDUs' is published by the Health and Safety Executive and provides useful information regarding the use of VDUs in an office environment.

The guidelines recommend that the VDU's adjustable brightness and contrast controls are used to improve the displayed image. These, together with screen filters, will reduce eye strain. VDU keyboards should be detached from the screen so that the distance between the screen and operator can be adjusted according to personal preference, and the keys themselves should have a matt surround to minimise glare and have concave tops with adjustable slope to maximise operator comfort.

VDUs generate heat and this will have to be taken into account when heating an office environment to an acceptable temperature. Adequate ventilation and humidity also need to be maintained. Lighting has to be adequate for the operator to read documents but not too bright or directed so that it glares on the screen and makes it difficult to read. Undue noise is also disruptive and therefore printers and other noisy office machinery should be sited away from operators, or provided with acoustic covers.

The time spent at a VDU will depend upon the nature of the work being performed. Lengthy periods of keying in text may require rapid keyboarding but will not involve extensive concentration on the screen itself. However, if the work involves composition of text, work with spreadsheets, databases or desktop publishing this may require shorter work periods as far greater concentration on the screen is necessary.

For the purposes of this element you must demonstrate that you are able to select the most suitable type of software application for the job required. You should include word processing, database and spreadsheet where possible and give examples of text, graphics and numeric information. Give examples of applications you have selected and those specified by others. Apart from specific word processing, database and spreadsheet applications you may include desktop publishing, accounts, stock control, MIS (management information systems) or organisational specific packages (eg hotels and public houses have special application packages for use in the industry).

## Knowledge and understanding question bank

1 What methods are there for inputting information into a computer?
2 What are the main security routines for computerised information?
3 What are the legal requirements related to computerised information?
4 What other legal requirements should you be aware of when operating computer equipment?
5 What is your organisation's procedure for retaining source material?
6 How do you reference your files?
7 How do you minimise the risk to yourself when operating computer equipment?
8 What types of software have you used and for what purpose?
9 How do you ensure that the data entered is accurate?
10 What non-statutory requirements does your organisation have which you must abide by?

## Claiming credit

For Element 6.1 you must prove that you have entered data into a computer using applications to process text, graphics and figures. You should have entered both textual and numerical information and selected the most suitable application yourself as well as using ones specified by others. You must prove that you have stored data in existing files and created new files.

The following work products are potential sources of evidence:

- copies of input data
- displays of data
- source information

Once you have completed your final assessment, you will need to write in your record book or folder how, when and what you have done to prove that you are competent.

The following statement is an example of how one trainee completed this claim:

*During my work at Octagon Training Centre and Turners Accountants I have used word processing and accounting packages. I have set up a database of customers for mailmerge purposes.*

*I access the correct application before entering the data. Once entered I check on screen before saving and printing. The file names are numerical and the next number is taken for the next file to be saved. A list of the files and numbers allocated is kept on the desk between me and my colleague (see Evidence 1). We keep the handwritten estimates attached to the final printout of quotations and estimates given – in case of error or query later. These are filed in the customer file. I ensure I follow the requirements of the Data Protection Act and HASAWA. The Electricity at Work Act Regulations are carried out by our maintenance team. All information and data relating to the computer files is confidential. Sensitive documents are filed with a keyword to restrict access only to those authorised. The evidence supplied for my portfolio has had the names and addresses of customers and suppliers erased to ensure confidentiality. The final figures in the spreadsheet examples have been altered, again to maintain confidentiality and security.*

# ■ Element 6.2
# INTEGRATE DIFFERENT TYPES OF DATA

## Performance criteria

1 The need to integrate data is identified and relevant data retrieved
2 Data is transferred effectively to facilitate integration and editing
3 Data is integrated and edited to meet specified needs, using the appropriate type of application
4 Work practices are in accordance with legal and regulatory requirements and organisational procedures
5 Security and confidentiality of information are maintained

## Element introduction

This element is about your skill and competence in identifying the need to integrate data. This means using stored information from different sources, transferring one to another, putting them together and editing to create a new document. This could mean transferring information from one package to another. Examples of this could be:

1 Using a standard letter together with a database to create a mailshot.

**2** Creating a report with graphics from a spreadsheet to illustrate financial points.

**3** Creating a report with word processing graphics to enhance display.

**4** Combining 2 separate word processing documents to make one.

An example of word processing with integrated graphics is shown in Fig. 6.10.

This is an example of using one application and integrating data across files within the same software package.

---

**We are looking for people that have time to help us to help others.**

**Distributors and Collectors are required in your area to sell products supplied by the third world countries.**

**We aim to provide these products at a realistic cost and to ensure that those making the products receive a good price for their goods.**

**HAVE YOU GOT THE TIME?**

**Collectors are required to collect bric-a-brac and other goods for resale and recycling to raise funds to support our cause. Please telephone 01412 149827 for further information or to register your help.**

---

**Fig 6.10 Example of word processing with integrated graphics**

*Identifying the need to integrate data*

When you are using the computer for your own or others' needs you will select the most suitable software to carry out the job you are intending to complete. It may be that during your preparation for the job, or while carrying out the job, you recognise the need to integrate data. In most cases this is likely to be due to the fact that graphics are being incorporated in the document you are creating.

# ■ DIY 6.2.1

Identify the software applications that you are using and their compatibility as regards transferring data across from one to the other. If you are unsure you may need to make further enquiries from your line manager, tutor or local computer shop.

## ▶ *Integrated packages*

There are several integrated packages on the market now, such as Works, which have word processing packages combined with database and/or spreadsheet. Working between them and integrating data is relatively simple, once you have been trained. Where standalone packages are used the integration between packages may be more difficult and you would need to check that the files are compatible before integrating. In some cases it is possible to save the file with a special name and extension to ensure that it is compatible for integration at a later stage. Quite often when integrating standalone packages the formatting instructions are lost and the work will need to be re-edited and reset using the new format codes. This will include hyphenation, justification, spacing, margins, page numbering, headers and footers, centring, styles and font sizes.

## ▶ *The Internet*

The Internet (also referred to as the 'information superhighway') is an international network of computer systems which is expanding rapidly. Computers of all types are connected to the Internet via telephone, satellite, optic fibre or cable. The system has an agreed set of procedures for establishing connections between computer systems.

Electronic mail messages can be sent over the Internet, and information from all over the world can be accessed and retrieved. Getting connected to the Internet can be expensive and complex unless the software you are using is correctly set up. Currently, the Microsoft PC Operating System and Windows 95 both include software to allow access to the Internet. One popular procedure for accessing the Internet is to use a feature called World Wide Web, which allows transfer of images as well as text. Users are able to click on a word or image to obtain further information.

## ▶ *Computer Conventions*

There are many terms and conventions used which are global, ie they are common to many applications. Most are based on the operating/drive system which may be DOS (**D**isk **O**perating **S**ystem) or another, such as Windows. To retrieve a file you will need to follow the computer convention necessary; this includes keying in the parameters. The parameters will include the drive, if other than the current drive, and directory that you want to access. Other commands you may use include: copy, del (delete), dir, diskcopy, rename, replace, restore, xcopy etc.

Unless you have experience of programing you are unlikely to use batch, configuration, internal, external or network commands or conventions. The syntax represents the order in which you should type the conventions being used. For retrieving a file this would normally be:

[drive:][path and/or directory][filename.extension]

For example L:BSA/link.doc means L drive, BSA directory, link is the file name and it is a document file.

## ▶ Types of files

The majority of files that you will deal with on the computer are text or data files. However, there are many more files used within the computer system, some of which you may find listed in your directory. It is important that you recognise these and do not delete or change them, unless you know exactly what you are doing.

### Program files

These files contain the programs run on the computer. Most of them have an extension such as .EXE or .COM.

### Data files

The applications that you use are likely to allocate an extension automatically to your file name if you do not allocate one yourself. The most common used is .DOC for document files.

### System files

These files contain information about your hardware and are device drivers. The extension is usually .SYS.

### Batch programs

These files usually contain DOS commands. They are used by programmers when they are setting up a computer system and starting a program or application. The extension used is normally .BAT.

If you go into DOS and type DIR at the drive prompt (usually C:>) you should get a list of all the files on your drive. You will also get information about the size of the files, and the date and time they were created or updated. You will notice that the full stop separating the file name and extension does not appear; only a space separates them. The file size is measured in **bytes**: one byte is the amount of space needed for one character. This information should help you keep track of your files. At the bottom of the list should be the total number of files saved, total number of bytes stored on the drive and the total number still free.

## ▶ *Information reference codes*

Many users of computers tend to give a reference to each document that they create so that it is easy to identify and retrieve when necessary. When you create a letter or memo the reference you use may also be the computer file name given to the document. If the document is a report, database or spreadsheet then the reference may be placed discreetly in one of the bottom corners, usually in a small point size (eg 7 pt or 20cpi). This is particularly useful for organistaions that issue mailshots or questionnaires on a regular basis, or when updating information which may have several versions, such as a staff handbook or health and safety instructions. It is not uncommon to have the version number or date of issue at the bottom of the page as a reference code.

Another form of reference may be used to identify cells or a group of cells within a spreadsheet. References tell the application which cell(s) to look for. They are used in formulae when you want to use data contained in different parts of the spreadsheet, or when you want to use one cell's data in several formulae. It is also possible to refer to other cells contained in other spreadsheets, hence transferring and integrating data across files. Such references are called 'external or remote references'. If the data required are contained in another application then a 'remote reference' may be used. For further information on using references within spreadsheets consult your application user manual.

## ■ DIY 6.2.2

Collect examples of reference codes that you have used when creating documents. State what the reference code is used for and its relevance.

## ▶ *Retrieving data*

When retrieving data it is necessary to type in the drive where the data are stored as well as the file name. It may not be necessary to use the extension code, unless files have the same name and different extensions. If you have data on screen already, the cursor should be placed exactly where you want the retrieved information to appear. The computer may question whether you wish to incorporate the recalled file into the current file, in which case you will need to respond accordingly. The recalled data should then appear on screen for you to format, print, resave and edit as required.

## *Transferring data across applications*

It is not difficult to use integrated packages to transfer data across applications, as long as you type in the correct code and file names. It is more difficult to transfer data across applications which are standalone. This may only be done if you have some computing knowledge of file compatibility or you are able to operate the drive system. Unfortunately not all applications use the same terminology. You will find references to transferring data, integrating data, importing data, pasting data, paste link, etc.

If you are familiar with Microsoft applications you may use the **D**ynamic **D**ata **E**xchange (DDE) to create links between applications. It is not a difficult operation to resave files to ensure compatibility but you may need some advice and guidance on which commands to use. Alternatively you will need to read the relevant chapter in your software application guide (although some of these can be hard going).

One of the most common formats used in saving standalone files that need to be incorporated into incompatible applications is called ASCII (**A**merican **S**tandard **C**ode for **I**nformation **I**nterchange). You are likely to be able to save a text file as an ASCII file (which usually has an extension of .TXT) and transfer it into the second application. Once transferred it will need to be recalled and transferred into the receiving application's format. However, at this stage you will need to consult someone who is totally familiar with the applications to and from which you are transferring data, and seek guidance from them. When converting a file to ASCII it is likely that you will lose all print and format codes and these will need replacing once the document has been imported to the new file.

## ▶ *Editing data*

Once the data have been integrated it will be necessary to edit to ensure that the correct format instructions and codes are in the right places. This is most easily done by revealing the codes on screen and editing from beginning to end. You should also check that the print codes and default settings are as you want them. All computer systems and applications have a set-up system, which are the default settings that the computer sets up once switched on, or the application is started. These may be pre-set by the organisation you work for, especially if there is a house style for print size and font style. It is not usually necessary to change the set-up unless it is your personal preference to have an alternative; most of the default settings can be changed within the data being created. Once changed in the data file they can be saved with the file. After editing has been completed it will be necessary to save the file, but ensure that you select a file name which is different from those of the files that have been used for integration purposes, otherwise your source data will be lost when it is overwritten with the new file.

## ▶ *Legal requirements*

In Element 6.1 you covered the need to observe the requirements of the Health and Safety at Work Act, the Data Protection Act, the Electricity at Work Act and the Copyright, Designs and Patents Act. All of these apply to integrated data and you should ensure that you abide by the relevant guidelines.

## ■ DIY 6.2.3

Collect examples of documents that you have integrated over a period of at least 2 months. Give at least 2 examples of text and graphical data, where the need for the data has been identified by you and by others. On each of the examples state whether the integration was across applications or across files within the same application.

## ▶ *Security and confidentiality*

If you do not have a password protection on your applications, you will need to decide whether the information you are creating and saving requires file password protection. This is usually done by selecting a keyword when saving the file, although you must remember the keywords you use to retrieve the data later. On networks, keywords may be made public, ie accessed by all users, or individual users may be allocated a keyword which may restrict the files that can be accessed by that user.

It is also possible to allow a user to access and view a file, but not to alter, delete or print from it. These global keywords are usually agreed and set up by a network manager who is responsible for and controls the applications used on the network.

## ▶ Housekeeping

As well as saving your file, ensure that you back up your files saved on the hard drive regularly on to disks. How frequently you need to do this will depend on how often you create, use and change the files, and how important the files are to you – what would happen if you lost everything saved on your hard drive? If some of the files are irreplaceable, they should have back-ups. Regularly delete old files or back-up files that are no longer needed to free up space.

## ■ DIY 6.2.4

Write a personal account of your competence related to the integration of data. State which applications have been used, how you ensure integration and editing, how you meet the legal requirements, and how you have maintained confidentiality. You will need to specify the amount of work that has been undertaken in your training centre and that undertaken within your work placement or within part-time employment. It is preferable that the majority of work samples and examples you give are based on real work activities rather than exercises and simulations carried out while training.

### Knowledge and understanding question bank

1 What back-up and safety procedures do you carry out?
2 What procedures do you take to limit exposure time to VDUs?
3 Are there any legal requirements regarding exposure to VDUs?
4 How have you integrated data across applications and which applications have you used for this?
5 How have you integrated files within an application and which application was used for this?
6 What procedure do you follow to retrieve data?
7 What is the correct posture you should use and what equipment is necessary for this?
8 What editing was necessary once you had integrated data from 2 applications?
9 What system of reference codes have you established and used?
10 What procedures do you carry out to protect and maintain your equipment?

### Claiming credit

For Element 6.2 you must prove that you are able to integrate different types of data, both textual and graphical, and that you can transfer, integrate and edit across applications and computer files as well as using functions across applications. The need for the data should have been specified by you as well as others.

The following work products are potential sources of evidence:

- display data
- printouts of integrated and edited data

Once you have completed your final assessment, you will need to write in your record book or folder how, when and what you have done to prove that you are competent.

The following statement is an example of how one trainee completed this claim:

*During my training and while on work placement I have used word processing, database and spreadsheet packages. The information stored in the database has been used to prepare a mailshot to all customers in the SW Region. I also used a macro to insert personalised information within letters. When using the spreadsheet figures I have integrated them and produced displayed bar charts, line graphs and bar charts. I have also designed posters for the social club at Turner's Accountants. At all times I ensure I abide by the relevant legal requirements and keep the information confidential and secure.*

# ■ Element 6.3
# PRESENT INFORMATION IN VARIOUS FORMATS

### Performance criteria

1 The intended use of the information is identified and specified
2 Formats are selected which are appropriate to the intended use of the information
3 The choice of presentation used conveys the information effectively and appropriately
4 The type of presentation is appropriate to its intended use
5 Work practices are in accordance with legal and regulatory requirements and organisational procedures
6 Security and confidentiality of information are maintained

## Element introduction

Element 6.3 is about how you present information in various formats. In this unit we have already seen that in word processing you are able to select different fonts and formats. For this element you will need to provide evidence that you have selected a suitable format for presenting text, graphics and numerical information, and that you are able to select a suitable typeface and size as well as paper size and layout.

If you have already completed Unit 5, 13, 14 or 15 you may already have covered some of the work required for this element. The work produced for those units may be cross referenced where applicable.

## ▶ *House style*

Written communication is one of the most important aspects of any business, as the appearance and quality of the documents represent the company image. Letters or other documents sent to customers with spelling, grammar or presentation errors will not project an efficient, businesslike image. The documents you produce should follow a 'house style'. This ensures that the documents received by the customer will reflect the same image regardless of the department that has sent them.

An organisation will decide upon the style in which letters, memos and other documents will be set out. Over the past few years more companies have moved from the indented, fully punctuated style to the blocked, open punctuation style, although combinations of both styles are sometimes used.

The blocked, open punctuated style is quicker to type and easier to learn, and fewer presentation mistakes tend to be made. Some companies are particularly strict with their house style, even stating what size and style of type should be used. Whichever style is chosen by your organisation, it is important to make sure that all members of staff follow the rules so that all styles are consistent.

## ■ DIY 6.3.1

Put together samples of the work you have completed which demonstrate the different types of house style you are aware of. When on work experience, ensure you collect at least 12 copies of work you have produced using the house style of the organisation you are working for. Alternatively you may obtain the samples from your part-time work.

# ▶ *Types of document*

Business correspondence, such as letters and memos, must be produced in the house style required by your organisation. You must be aware of the formats required for documents and enclosures and have the ability to use a variety of formats for the purpose of displays and graphics. The ability to use landscape and portrait display formats is also needed so that display material is produced as attractively and professionally as possible.

Most companies receive and despatch letters on a daily basis. The content of the letters includes requests for information, the supply of information or making arrangements; the aim is to get the information to the addressee, for it to be understood and acted upon. Most business letters are typed on letterheaded paper, which gives the basic facts about the company – the name, address, telephone number, fax and/or telex number, names of directors and company secretary, VAT registration number (if any) and possibly a logotype (commonly called a logo).

A professionally designed letterhead makes the company immediately recognisable; some companies invest in a skilled designer to establish the logo, which may also become a trade mark for the company. Letterheaded correspondence is usually produced on high quality paper: 80 gsm or above is usually used. The letters gsm stand for 'grammes per square metre' which means that the higher the number the heavier and better quality the paper.

Memoranda are used for internal communication only. Most companies have pre-printed forms in A4 and A5 size. They may have a company printed heading containing either MEMO or MEMORANDUM, To and From, Date and Reference. A subject heading can be included if required. The content of a memo may be formal or informal. Memos do not have a complimentary close, but may be initialled by the sender, to show approval or confirmation of the contents.

Special markings such as CONFIDENTIAL or PRIVATE are usually typed under the word Memorandum or centred at the top. If the memo is URGENT this would be typed in the top right-hand corner to ensure it was delivered quickly. Routed copies are indicated in the same way as letters, with 'Copy to' at the end of the memo, followed by the names/department of others that should receive a copy. A request for a blind carbon copy means putting the routing information on to the copies but not on to the original so that the person receiving the original is unaware of the other people to whom copies have been routed.

# 128 Long Acre, London WC2 9AN

Tel: +44(0)171 447 2000  Fax: +44(0)171 240 5771

**A Division of Pearson Professional**

Registered Office: Maple House, 149 Tottenham Court Road, London W1P 9LL

Registered Number 2970324. Registered in England and Wales

**Fig 6.11 An example of letterheaded paper with a logo**

Memo packs are available that have NCR paper ('No Carbon Required'). This paper enables the original to be produced on the NCR paper without the use of carbon paper. Copies may be coloured to indicate circulation, for example original to addressee, pink copy to catering, blue to security, green file copy.

## ■ DIY 6.3.2

Look back at the examples you collected for DIY 6.3.1 and ensure that you have a good range of documentation, including letters, memos, reports, minutes, displayed work, eg advertisements etc.

## ▶ *Form design*

Forms are usually typed in double line spacing to allow room to type or write on the lines. The lines are created by using the underscore or full stops and to ensure good presentation the right-hand margin is usually justified. When typing on forms the tails of descending letters such as p, q and j should be just above the line. When designing a form it is essential that adequate space is left for insertions to be made. How many forms have you used that do not allow enough space for you to insert your full details?

Forms that are designed using a word processor can be made to look very professional by using the various display functions such as shadowing, tables, boxes, style, font and so on. However, a word processor cannot be used to fill in forms, unless a template has been supplied, as there is not enough control over where the characters will be positioned on the paper when printed. Remember – they should be just above the line. A template allows the blank form to be set out on screen and inserts to be keyed-in by hand.

## ■ DIY 6.3.3

Collect together forms that you have produced during your training. If you have not completed one to date, discuss this with your tutor and arrange for some examples to be provided to you for word processing.

128 Long Acre, London WC2E 9AN

Tel: 0171 379 7383  Fax: 0171 240 5771

24 October 19--

Carly-Jo Born
Top Go Salon
224 Lyndsey Road
Branksome
POOLE
BH30 6DB

Dear Carly-Jo

I have been requested by the French authorities
to send you copies of a work placement agreement,
and I am enclosing three copies, one copy to be
retained by you, one copy for the students and
one to be returned to me in the envelope provided.

The document is required in France by all
students carrying out work placement.  Although
the document is not necessary under British law,
the French students are concerned that they will
not fulfil the requirements of their qualification
if this document is not part of their portfolio.

If you wish to delete any part of the document
please do so, or if there are any queries please
contact me.

Thank you for your co-operation.

Yours sincerely

*L Blakemore*

Leila Blakemore
Co-ordinator

Encs

**Fig 6.12 Letter in fully blocked style on letterheaded paper**

---

**MEMORANDUM**

**To**       Carol Baker

**From**     Lara Smith

**Date**     5 October 199–

**Ref**      LS/EF

MEDICAL CONFERENCE

Would you please arrange with the conference centre for a slide projector and screen to be available for Professor James's lecture on 15 October.

This will be required in addition to the OHP and flipchart.

*LS*

---

**Fig 6.13 Memo in fully blocked style**

▶ *Landscape and portrait presentation*

A4 portrait paper is 210 mm x 297 mm, and has 100 spaces across the top and 70 lines down (assuming you are using elite type which gives 12 characters to the inch).

A5 paper is exactly half this size, and A5 landscape has 100 spaces across the top and 35 lines down. The paper can be used either way: if the smaller side is put into the typewriter or printer first, this is portrait (as you would draw a person's face); if the longer side is put in first, this is landscape (as you would draw a view).

Portrait style is usual for business correspondence and is the style most commonly used in an office. Landscape style is used most often for display material that requires extra width. For example, an organisation chart is more likely to be produced on landscape paper as the chart grows in width each time a level is added.

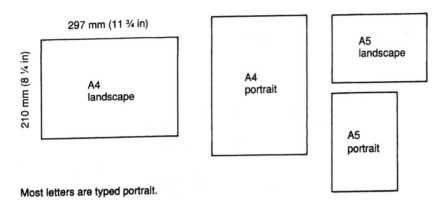

Most letters are typed portrait.

**Fig 6.14 Paper sizes**

You may find that although you have produced correspondence, such as a business letter, using portrait style, you may have to switch to landscape in order to display an accompanying enclosure.

## ▶ Tables and tabs

The terms table and tabulation are used to describe information that has been laid out in rows and columns rather than in written text. Tabs and tables are used because they are easier to understand than written information.

A tabular presentation is achieved by using the 'tab' key on your typewriter or computer keyboard. This key is used to align each column so that comparable information can read across or down. If you wish to prepare a lined tabulation using a typewriter, you will have to insert the horizontal lines as you go along. Some machines allow you to insert the vertical lines using a key on the keyboard, although in some cases you may have to insert vertical lines using a black pen and ruler.

Some word processing packages offer a tables option that will create a table on screen. Boxed-in tables are particularly useful if information needs to be broken down into separate parts. The boxes can be split or joined, shaded, enlarged and/or reduced to produce attractively displayed, and easy to understand material.

## ■ DIY 6.3.4

Put together the work you have produced at your training centre demonstrating that you are able to carry out effective display in the form of tables. You will need to add to this when you are on work experience with samples you have produced in work. Ensure your final portfolio identifies the difference between work produced at the training centre and that produced at work.

---

## ▶ *Effective display*

Some documents may include items that need to be displayed, such as a letter or memo that requires a table in order to display information effectively. Documents may be required for display on a notice board, such as menus, advertisements, vacancies, programmes etc. There are several ways of producing such material, but typing, word processing or using a desktop publishing package will produce display material of a high quality.

Some spreadsheet programs will allow you to type the information in the form of a table. The use of different commands enables the information to be printed in the form of line graph, bar or pie chart. Special flow-chart programs can also be purchased, although it would not be worth buying these unless the package was going to be used frequently. Part of your job could be selecting the most effective method for displaying information.

Word processing packages allow you to change the size and style of the characters. The sizes are usually listed in point size (1 point (pt) = 0.0138"), the most commonly used being between 11 pt and 13 pt (the lower numbers referring to the smaller sizes of print). When you use a typewriter you are likely to use 10, 12 or 15 pitch. These numbers relate to the number of characters per inch (cpi), 10 cpi being larger than 12 cpi, therefore the higher the number, the smaller the type.

To display material such as programmes, tickets and posters you would need to select a size of print which would be effective for the purpose:

- A3 size posters – 72 pt would be suitable for headings, and 36 pt for other information
- A4 size programmes – 24 pt for headings and 14 pt for information
- A6 (postcard size) – 15 pt for headings and 10 pt for information

Once you have selected an appropriate size of print for your documents, the **style** can be selected to suit your needs. The fonts most commonly used are Courier, Helvetica, Prestige and Roman. Options may also be available for the styles to be in bold, normal, italic, or bold and italic. You will need to experiment with the options available on the software or keyboard available to you.

If you are unfamiliar with the options, it is useful to keep a copy of all the available fonts and styles as this saves time when you need to select an attractive display for your documents. It is likely that your word processor or keyboard manual will give details of the fonts and styles available, although when you use a word processor the range available may be restricted by the printer you use. If you use a typewriter the style of type can only be changed if you have a variety of different daisy wheels or golf balls.

It may also be possible to shadow or outline your characters. This option gives extra effect to displayed material.

The following sizes are pica (10 cpi) converted to: small, large, very large and extra large.

NVQ LEVEL 3

NVQ LEVEL 3

NVQ LEVEL 3

# NVQ LEVEL 3

The following styles are bold, underline, double underline, italic, outline, shadow, small capital, redline and strikeout.

**BUSINESS OFFICE**

<u>BUSINESS OFFICE</u>

<u>BUSINESS OFFICE</u>

*BUSINESS OFFICE*

BUSINESS OFFICE

**BUSINESS OFFICE**

BUSINESS OFFICE

BUSINESS OFFICE

~~BUSINESS OFFICE~~

These examples have been created using a base font of pica, which is 10 characters per inch (cpi).

The following base fonts are: elite (12 cpi), elite double-wide, pica, pica double-wide.

UNIT 6.3

UNIT 6.3

UNIT 6.3

UNIT 6.3

## ■ DIY 6.3.5

Put together display work you have already produced in your training and add to the collection when you are on work experience. If you do not have any samples as yet complete the following activity:

Please design a suitable A4 letterheading and business card for a new catering business. The details are: Gourmet's Delight, 254 High Street, New Town, Wolverhampton WA24 5NN, Tel 01329 2934719; Fax 01329 2924788; VAT Registration Number 2–20495204. We would also like you to design a poster which can be displayed in the local newsagents etc. Would you please create one on A4 and enlarge it to A3 by photocopying. Ensure that you include all the relevant details on each of the pieces of work. Use effective display by changing font, size of print, shading etc.

---

## ▶ *Special signs*

Mathematical signs and foreign text may also be typed and some word processors have a secondary keyboard. This means that the normal keys can also be used to type special signs and characters by keying in a special code. You will need to consult your typewriter manual or software manual to find out the facilities available. You will find that some signs may still need to be inserted by hand using a black pen.

You may be able to find some of the following signs using your word processor or typewriter.

- ½ æ Σ © ¶ § ¥ Pt ® ● ☺ ♫

Word processors have the best facilities, which may include some graphics. The options will depend on the package you are using, the speed at which your computer operates and the printer you have available. Alternatively you may be able to use a desktop publishing package.

Many word processing packages also include graphics in the form of pictures which can be included in the text. These are among the easiest ones to use. If you become a specialist graphics operator then you will be able to create your own graphics to add to those already available.

The examples in Fig 6.15 can be found on WordPerfect.

# SCANNERS

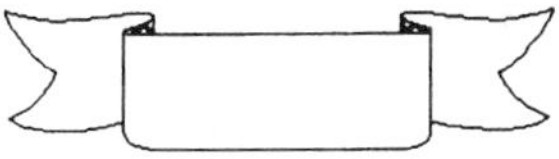

*WE ARE THE GREATEST!*

The scanner is similar to a photocopier but it copies the document to disk instead of to paper; this saves time as the document does not have to be keyed in and graphics are transferred automatically.

However, it would be unusual for you to carry out this type of work often; if a company has a high demand for graphics they are likely to appoint a specialist graphics designer to deal with all the documents and requests.

*WE'RE NOT LOST!*

**Fig 6.15 Example of graphics integrated with text**

## ▶ *Terminology*

There are of course specialist training courses available that prepare staff for different types of business; legal and medical secretaries who have followed such a course will have fewer problems with terminology than an inexperienced employment agency temporary called in to cover for holiday leave. It is important, however, to make sure that all work is error free and that costly mistakes are not made.

Accuracy is much more important than speed, and when you are dealing with unfamiliar vocabulary it is vital to ask for clarification if you are unsure and to slow down your typing speed so that you can concentrate on each letter of every word. A good, up-to-date glossary and a spell check that has had specialist words and terms added to it will help achieve accurately produced work.

## ▶ *Security and confidentiality*

Information passing through an office will fall into one of the following categories:

1 General or open – can be seen by anyone.
2 Restricted – limited access to a certain department or group.
3 Confidential – seen only by the authorised person.

You will be expected to carry out the day's duties with the minimum of fuss, in an organised fashion that rises above the pressures of the day. In reality you cannot always do this and there are bound to be some days when the office resembles organised chaos rather than a smoothly running operation. The telephone continually ringing, other members of the company coming in and out of the office asking questions and making demands, the boss having a 'bad day', together with a host of other distractions – all of these will ultimately affect the smooth running of the office and your own strength of character.

The ability to cope with pressure comes with practice, but more importantly, the ability to ensure that security and confidentiality are maintained at all times will take precedence. It is essential that you stay calm and keep control in order to ensure the tasks of the day are completed in accordance with deadlines and with no error. You must be able to rise to the occasion and 'step up a gear' if the workload of the day demands it. However, you should not allow aspects of security and confidentiality to lapse so that tasks can be completed quickly.

Whatever pressure you are under, confidential files, mail or information should still be kept under lock and key, even if the temptation is there to leave this material on the desk to come back to. Outgoing mail still has to be checked for enclosures and the correct letters put into their respective envelopes, without additional paperwork that has been attached to the paperclip by mistake! Customers and colleagues will be passing through the office at all times, therefore you will be required to keep all confidential matter from unauthorised eyes and you and any assistants will have to be especially careful to maintain security procedures during busy periods.

When you use a computer it is normal practice to use passwords to access confidential information. Passwords should be changed regularly and the words chosen should be ones that are easy to remember and that do not have to be written down. You must keep a separate file for all confidential material that should not be seen by any unauthorised person, including any assistants. There must also be separate files for restricted information that may be accessed by a limited number of personnel and by the assistant with discretion.

All back-up copies of confidential or restricted information should be kept under lock and key.

**Fig 6.16 Lock away confidential information**

# ■ DIY 6.3.6

Write a statement about how you currently deal with confidential information, how you protect your own work from the eyes of others. Secondly, state how your procedure would differ when dealing with confidentiality at work. Your statements should relate purely to work produced using a computer.

### Knowledge and understanding question bank

1 What typefaces are you familiar with and how do you change the font on your word processor?
2 What is the difference between 9 cpi and 9 pt character size?
3 Which paper size would you select for the following:

  **a** party invitation
  **b** business letter
  **c** noticeboard advertisement for summer fete?

4 Why is it important to ensure that the type of presentation is appropriate to its intended use?
5 What is meant by conveying information 'effectively and appropriately'?
6 What difference does the type of printer make to presentation?
7 How do you ensure that your data are presented accurately?
8 How do you instruct your printer via the device driver?
9 What types of format are you familiar with?
10 What requirements may be included in a 'house style' layout?

### Claiming credit

For Element 6.3 you must prove that you have presented information containing text, graphics and tables, and that you are able to select the most suitable presentation taking into account the typeface, character size, page size and layout. The information should have been presented on screen as well as on hard copy.

## NVQ Administration Level 3

The following work products are potential sources of evidence:

- display information
- printouts of integrated information

Once you have completed your final assessment, you will need to write in your record book or folder how, when and what you have done to prove that you are competent.

The following statement is an example of how one trainee completed this claim:

*During my training period and at work placement at Hooch & Co I have completed many different types of document. These have involved a wide range of typefaces, fonts and displays including text, graphics and tables. I have presented information on screen to others for approval (prior to printing) and on hard copy. Where information has been provided to me by others I have prepared and presented this by following house style where applicable, and at other times I have used my own sense of design and layout to ensure an attractive format for presentation. I have followed the organisation's and legal requirements for presenting information. I have acknowledged copyright, when it existed, by typing the name of the reference used within the document.*

# UNIT 7

# Draft and prepare documents

## ■ Element 7.1
## DRAFT DOCUMENTS TO MEET SPECIFIED REQUIREMENTS

### Performance criteria

1  The purpose of the documentation is accurately established

2  Completed documents meet specified requirements

3  Layout, spelling, grammar and punctuation are correct, consistent and in accordance with conventions and house style

4  The content of documents is comprehensive and accurate and is presented in a logical sequence

5  Recommendations, when required, are succinct and provide sufficient guidance to decision makers

6  Sources of information, on which documents are based, are verified as accurate and valid

7  Work practices are in accordance with legal and regulatory requirements and organisational procedures

8  Where work is not achievable within specified deadlines, reasons are promptly and accurately reported

9  Completed documents are provided within agreed deadlines

10  Security and confidentiality of information are maintained

### Element introduction

This element is about your ability to draft documents both for yourself and on behalf of others according to their instructions. Your spelling, grammar and punctuation must be correct and the layout used must conform with drafting conventions and house style. Your ability to present logically sequenced, accurate material based on sources of information that have been verified as correct will be assessed. Your work must be completed according to deadlines ensuring security and confidentiality are maintained. If you are unable to meet a specified deadline you must report reasons for this promptly and accurately. You must at all times obey legal and regulatory requirements relating to the provision of information.

## ▶ Establishing the purpose of documentation

Before drafting any document it is wise to consider if the document is necessary at all! A simple telephone call or visit to another person or office to communicate the information may be more efficient. However, if dealing with important, lengthy or requested documentation your next consideration should be the type of document most appropriate for the task.

There are many different methods that can be used to communicate. The communication process within an organisation flows in all directions, up, down and across the organisation. Some organisations employ a Communication Manager who is responsible for ensuring that communications, both internal and external to the company, are carried out effectively and efficiently. As a member of an organisation you too will inevitably have a part to play in the communication process. You will not only be on the receiving end of much of the communication but you will also be involved in creating communication which will go to other people.

Selecting the correct form of communication for the task is imperative if you are to communicate effectively and efficiently. The following list gives some ideas of the written communication methods available to you, although you may be able to think of more:

### 1 Communication with the public

- Business letters
- Press releases
- Advertising
- Leaflets
- Brochures
- Circular letters
- Annual reports
- Exhibitions
- Price lists
- Catalogues
- Mailshots
- Market research
- Quality questionnaires

## 2 Communicating with employees

- Reports
- Memoranda
- House journals
- News letters
- Notices/posters

- Bulletins
- Company handbook
- Annual report to employees
- Pay packet inserts
- Personal letters

It is more than likely that you will have already used a number of the different communication methods listed above. The business letter, memo and report are used extensively in the business world although not always to best use in terms of clarity of expression.

## ▶ *Clarity of expression*

When drafting a business document clarity of expression is all-important. Your ability to communicate purpose, requirements and conclusions clearly and concisely saves time, money and unnecessary work. It is essential to keep the document's intended function in mind constantly and to be aware of how the structure and style of language work to fulfil that function.

Before starting to draft the document establish and note down the objectives, main points to be made and any firm conclusions to be communicated. Refer to your notes frequently to keep you on target. Use a separate paragraph to deal with every major subject and make sure that each sentence connects to the next. Avoid forming sentences by joining clauses together with 'and' or 'but'. Form sentences of different lengths and varied structure using colons, semi-colons and commas in the correct places to make your documents more interesting to read and grammatically correct.

You should always look for the most direct way of expressing your meaning; use clear and specific vocabulary. Remember that you are writing a business document, not a piece of descriptive, illustrated fiction. Avoid using jargon and phrases that are ambiguous as these only confuse the reader. Omit words that are not necessary for the meaning; they obscure the topic and lengthen the text. Do not repeat vocabulary or subject-matter needlessly. Try using a thesaurus or dictionary for alternative words.

### Using a thesaurus

The best known thesaurus was written by Peter Mark Roget who developed a passion for words and for classifying them into categories as an aid for writers. *Roget's Thesaurus* is a useful aid to anyone involved in writing. Have you ever become stuck for an alternative for a particular word or expression that you would like to use again but cannot for fear of becoming repetitive or boring? The thesaurus can resolve the problem by offering a series of lists of words and phrases collected in groups, sharing a similar or identical root meaning. You may have a thesaurus facility on your word processing software; if you master the use of the thesaurus your command of English words and vocabulary will undoubtedly improve.

## Using a dictionary

If you wish to improve and extend your vocabulary you must take the trouble to use a dictionary to look up and digest the meaning of new words and the information about them. Every time you meet an unknown word, make the effort to look it up and then introduce it into your talking and writing as soon as possible. Try to use a pocket dictionary, supported by a larger dictionary in your workplace.

There are a number of dictionaries available that will help you not only with the spelling and meaning of words, but also with:

- pronunciation
- plurals
- derivatives
- linkage to other words or expressions
- the origin of the word
- abbreviations
- tables of weight, volume, distance, conversion
- words of foreign origin
- addenda (additional matter)

The alphabetical arrangement of the words in a dictionary follows a strict system. In the same way as A comes before D in the alphabet and an alphabetical filing system, so too will words beginning with A come before those beginning with D in the dictionary. If you are prepared to spend some time looking up words in a dictionary you will find it to be a most helpful and informative tool. Your extended vocabulary will increase self-confidence and your ability to prepare documents that hold the reader's attention.

If you are unsure of the spelling of a word write down what you think to be the correct spelling. Use this to help you locate the correct section in the dictionary. Aa will come before Ac and so on. Once in the correct vicinity work your way through the words until you find the correct spelling. Obviously, you are likely to have access to a spell check facility on your word processing software. This is a most useful facility but remember that it can make you lazy and not help you to understand the meaning of the word or remember the spelling in the future.

# ◢ DIY 7.1.1

Find out the meaning of the following words and their correct pronunciation:

vol-au-vent   lingerie   mnemonic   milieu

What do the following abbreviations stand for?

AAM   ABA   BAA   BBBC   CAMRA   TESL   WRAC

How many meanings can you find for:

frost   fan   chill   gobble   interim   lump

Find an alterative for each of the words below:

pleasure   improving   route   communicate   practice

resented   havoc   agitated   direct   association

There are guidelines for composing business documentation and certain rules regarding content, layout and presentation. The first place to start is the actual drafting of the document; for the purpose of this element business letters, memos and reports have been used.

## ▶ *Drafting business letters*

Most business letters are printed on letterheaded paper detailing:

- registered name of the company
- registered address of company
- logo (if any)
- names of directors, company officials or principals
- branch offices/subsidiary companies
- telephone number and code
- telex/fax number
- VAT number (if any)

When you use letterheaded paper part of the communication has already been done for you; it also saves time and presents a uniform image of the company to the people it deals with. Business letters are used to communicate information or to request information from other companies, customers or the general public. An organisation, if wishing to communicate privately with an employee, may also choose to use a

249

business letter presented on letterheaded paper rather than an internal memo.

The most widely used and economical layout for a business letter is the fully blocked style with open punctuation. That layout of the letter is easy to understand; all lines start at the left-hand margin with one clear line space left between information, such as the address, date, etc, and paragraphs. Punctuation is only used in the text (paragraphs) and abbreviations do not require full stops.

The usual salutation and complimentary close for a business letter is:

Dear Sir(s)/Madam      – Yours faithfully

Dear Miss, Mrs, Ms or Mr – Yours sincerely

If a FOR THE ATTENTION OF ... line is used it should be placed before the address followed by a clear line space. The letter, however, should be addressed to the company and the salutation Dear Sir(s)/Madam used.

Business letters should be typed in single-line spacing unless they are very short, when double-line spacing may be used to help fill the page. Continuation sheets should be produced on plain matching paper (not letterheaded) with details of the page number, date and addressee's name at the top, blocked to the left margin.

A good business letter should be concise, to the point but polite and written in the correct tone. All information must be correct with perfect spelling and grammar or a poor image of the company will be created. The content of the letter will depend on specified requirements but generally a business letter will have 3 parts:

1 **Introduction** – States the subject of the letter.
Acknowledges a correspondent's letter by quoting date received, references, etc.

2 **Content** – Deals with the subject referred to in the introduction, for example giving or requesting information or action.

3 **Conclusion** – Courteous close usually offering more information if required or requesting politely a quick response.

A subject heading can be used, especially if the letter deals with complicated material. This helps route the letter to the right person and gains the reader's interest. It can also save time.

It is important to be specific and give correct information such as dates, times, prices, description, specification, code numbers, and so on. Make

**Blue Bridge**
Picture Framers and Restorers

Reference:

26 April 199-

Mrs R L George
14 Wood Road
BRACKNELL
Berks
BR4 6TU

Dear Mrs George

PICTURE FRAMING

Thank you for your request for a brochure
describing our product range.  We have pleasure
in enclosing our latest brochure, together with
our price list.

We look forward to hearing from you and to
receiving your order.

Yours sincerely

Olivia Stone
Marketing Executive

Enc

Registered Office 11 Kilburn High Road London NE12
Registered Number 01255XX896

32 Knoll Road  London SW18 2DF
Telephone & Facsimile 0181 867 3625

**Fig 7.1  Letter in fully blocked style**

sure that when replying to a letter that you address and reply to all the requests that have been made. If you are unable to do this, explain that further information will be sent when you have it.

Take care to avoid opening the conclusion with hoping, wishing, thanking, trusting:

'We thank you for your prompt attention to our request.'

is preferable to:

'Thanking you for your prompt attention to our request.'

Keep your sentences short and to the point without being abrupt. Use a separate paragraph to deal with each subject or idea; within each paragraph make sure each sentence connects logically with the preceding one. Long paragraphs are more difficult to follow and understand than short paragraphs.

Using the correct tone does not mean the use of an occasional 'please' or 'thank you'. If you are asking for information or making a request you must do so politely by using a tone that will encourage a quick, polite response. When supplying information and replying to a request, again a polite response will create a good impression of the company and encourage customers to deal with you more often.

Would you write:

'I want to make clear several misunderstood points with you.'

or

'You seem to have misunderstood several points which need further clarification.'

'In your letter you forgot to enclose...'

or

'As you forgot to enclose.. would it be possible...?'

The tone of your letter reflects your own personality. If you are co-operative and efficient you are likely to draft a polite, constructive letter. Remember that business letters, if written competently, help to create a good impression of the company.

When you have drafted the letter read it through from the reader's point of view. Is the letter self-explanatory, to the point, polite and easy to read?

## ▶ *Drafting memoranda*

Memos (short for 'memoranda') are merely internal letters. They are often used unnecessarily to communicate information which could have been more quickly and cheaply dealt with through a short telephone call. Conversely, they may be used to confirm and document information that has been passed on verbally, so it is important to consider with whom you are dealing and the type of information being communicated.

Memos are useful for ensuring that important information or messages get passed between busy staff. They provide a useful record of an arrangement made during a quick telephone conversation and are often used as back-up protection as proof that a conversation took place and agreement or arrangements were made. It is therefore essential that the content of the memo in such circumstances is factually accurate, free from inferences, unambiguous and fair to other parties.

Many companies use typewritten or word processed memos when a short handwritten note would be adequate. Efficiency involves saving time; ask yourself if the memo really does need typing or whether a brief hand-written note will do the job just as well.

A short handwritten note, if adequate, can be written on to official memo paper and can save time. Pads of forms with NCR paper (no carbon required) are ideal, and often have space on the back or side for a reply so that the memo can go to and be returned by the relevant staff.

Electronic mail systems can allow memos to be displayed and stored electronically by means of desktop visual display units networked to the main company computer. The paper flow around the office is greatly reduced as the memo can be stored on computer file with no need for a printed hard copy.

Printed forms are used for memos. They can be written on, typed on, printed on or displayed on screen for insertions and information to be added and then printed off using word processing software. The form can also be used on screen but, when completed, be sent electronically using an electronic mail system. Whichever method of completion is used, the printed form requests the same information:

M E M O R A N D U M

TO:

FROM:

DATE:

REF:

SUBJECT HEADING:

The information is inserted opposite the relevant heading; reference and subject heading are only used if the information is available.

No formal salutation or complimentary close is used. However, if someone else is requested to type the memo, the originator may wish to read it through and add their initials at the bottom to verify they have confirmed the content.

If there are enclosures, these should be identified by typing ENC at the bottom of the memo next to the left-hand margin. If there are a number of enclosures this can be indicated with either ENCS or ENC(2) detailing the number of enclosures. A copy of the memo should always be kept on file.

When drafting a memo remember to keep it short and to the point. A5 paper is most often used for memos. Remember that they are normally used to convey a brief, single major point. However, A4 memos are used, sometimes with continuation sheets, when extensive, complex information is involved.

The tone used will depend upon the content of the memo, although politeness is a priority. Think about the following:

- the content of the message (congratulations, reprimand, crisis)

- the status of the recipient (superior, subordinate, or peer)

- nature of the message (facts, information, request)

- urgency of request (crisis, instruction, routine)

The *Concise Oxford Dictionary*'s definition of the memo is a 'note to help the memory'. With this in mind it is essential that the content of any message is condensed; that only its essentials and any arising action requirements are communicated to the recipient. The structure of the memo will vary according to its context but 3 principal components are necessary to form the basis of any memo:

**Part 1** – Puts the message in context (past, present, future)
Identifies the related components (who, what, why, when, where)

**Part 2** – Details the key points of the memo's message

**Part 3** – Details the actions requested or required from the recipient
– Gives a timescale or deadline for the action

---

**MEMORANDUM**

**To**      Michelle Goujon

**From**    Olivia Skone

**Date**    5 May 199–

**Ref**     OS/MR

SALES CONFERENCE

This will take place in the last week of June. We have booked the Royal Hotel, as last year.

Could you please ensure that we have 20 sets of promotional literature on our latest products for our sales representatives in advance of this date?

---

**Fig 7.2 Memo in fully blocked style**

# ■ DIY 7.1.2

You work as an Administration Supervisor in the Head Office of Lotus Natural Body Care Products. You have been asked by the Sales Director to draft the paperwork for the organisation's Annual Sales Awards Ceremony to be held on the 4th of next month at the Bath Hotel, Birmingham Road, Coventry, from 8 pm until midnight.

You will need to prepare drafts of the official tickets and notices, and write a memo to all sales staff inviting them to the event and asking them to indicate on the tear-off portion how many tickets they require. Staff will be allowed 2 tickets free of charge, but are asked to pay £10.00 each for additional tickets. Overnight accommodation can be booked for a special rate of £30.00 per room.

255

Your boss has asked you to write to the Bath Hotel to arrange the booking of their Connaught Suite for the ceremony. There will be approximately 200 diners and sample menus and wine lists, with prices, are required. You would like details regarding car parking facilities and what access and amenities are provided for disabled personnel.

You will also need to write a confidential letter of apology to Mrs J Jones, 103 Westland Road, Droitwich, in response to her letter of complaint regarding the venue used for last year's ceremony. Mrs Jones's husband uses a wheelchair and experienced great difficulty getting into and out of the venue used. She would like to know what arrangements will be made this year to ensure that this does not happen again.

Your draft may be handwritten, but must be proof-read and checked prior to being given to your assistant for typing.

---

## ▶ *Drafting reports, summaries and précis*

Reports are often required for meetings and conferences or to summarise the result of an investigation or research. They provide information, report on findings, put forward ideas and may make recommendations. Reports must be carefully laid out with the facts arranged in a logical sequence so that the reader can easily understand the content.

Reports can be used to deal with a wide range of topics:

| | |
|---|---|
| **1 Company** – | Required by statute to be made annually and presented to shareholders. The Directors' report, the audited statement of the accounts and the Chairman's annual review are often included with the report. |
| **2 Annual** – | Presented by the Honorary Secretary at the Annual General Meeting. It may also include the Treasurer's accounts and is used by voluntary organisations. |
| **3 Committee** – | A committee will investigate, hear evidence and issue joint findings on a given problem. A report will be produced with their findings. If it is an *ad hoc* (for the purpose of) committee, it will be dissolved once the report has been made. |
| **4 Expert** – | Commissioned from one or more experts who possess specialist knowledge. |
| **5 Routine** – | Companies need a constant flow of up-to-date information upon which their decisions can be based. Responsible persons (perhaps with certain expertise) |

may be asked to provide reports on problems within their area of work. The report may be presented formally or, if short, as a letter or memo. If the findings of the report are required urgently they may be given orally, perhaps over the telephone or during a meeting.

When drafting the report consider the following:

## PREPARATION

1 Subject –      Make sure of the exact terms of reference and clarify the scope and purpose of the report.

2 Reader –      How is the report to be used? What terminology can you use that will be understood by the reader? What information does the reader want from the report?

3 Material –      Collect all information, ideas and facts together in a logical sequence. Check each for accuracy before using them.

## STRUCTURE

1 Terms of reference –      Statement of instructions/purpose.

2 Findings –      Set out in logical order.

3 Conclusions –      Analyse findings and summarise facts.

4 Recommendations –      Offer advice based on findings and conclusions of the report and information contained therein.

## METHOD

1 Define the **purpose** of the report with the person requesting the report. Choose a suitable title.

2 Gather **information** and check validity.

3 **Research** information and select relevant facts.

4 Consider facts and decide upon **conclusions** and **recommendations**.

5 Arrange the material in a **logical order** under appropriate headings.

6 **Add** appendix and bibliography if required.

7 **Review** and revise the material before distribution.

## STYLE

**1** Tone –    No need for pleasantries. The tone should be impersonal and concise, giving factual information and/or ideas.

**2** Views –    Facts should speak for themselves: fair, free from bias and balanced.

**3** Language –    Should be brief, clear, definite and simple. Avoid jargon and terminology that will not be understood. Include a glossary if necessary.

## FORMAT

**1** Is the **layout** clear and easy to follow? Do you need to number each paragraph?

**2** Is the **numbering** of pages and paragraphs standardised?

**3** Does the report follow a **logical** sequence?

**4** Do all headings and sub-headings **stand out** clearly?

**5** Are the appendix, bibliography and glossary **clear** and helpful?

**6** Has the document been **proof-read**?

**7** Have all spellings and grammar been **checked**?

**8** Is text of suitable **quality** for multiple copying?

## ■ DIY 7.1.3

Prepare an informal report giving details on the health and safety requirements in your working area. Discuss a suitable title and content of the report with your tutor. When you have completed the report check it against the checklist in Fig 7.3.

| REPORT CONTENT CHECKLIST | Yes | No |
|---|---|---|
| **1** Does the report state clearly:<br>Subject and purpose?<br>Date?<br>Scope?<br>Who wrote it? | | |
| **2** Do the findings contain all the relevant facts? | | |
| **3** Do the findings follow a logical sequence? | | |
| **4** Do the findings contain only relevant material? | | |
| **5** Have information sources been acknowledged? | | |
| **6** Do conclusions follow on logically from the facts? | | |
| **7** Have abbreviations, symbols and terminology been explained? | | |
| **8** Are all facts, figures, data correct? | | |
| **9** Is all information up to date? | | |
| **10** Are all calculations correct? | | |
| **11** Do recommendations take into account all relevant information? | | |
| **12** Are conclusions and recommendations balanced, fair and free from bias? | | |
| **13** Are there sufficient facts to support conclusions and recommendations? | | |
| **14** Is the tone used impersonal and economical? | | |
| **15** Has the document been fully proof-read and checked for spelling or grammatical errors? | | |

**Fig 7.3 Report content checklist, for use with DIY 7.13**

## ▶ *Drafting a précis or summary*

The **précis** seeks to reduce a passage to approximately one-third of its original size, while retaining both its major features and approach throughout.

The **summary** selects points to meet a specific requirements or brief and is therefore more selective of the content of the material being summarised.

Skills required to draft a précis or summary include:

- Common sense
- An ability to listen
- Careful reading
- Frequent practice

Principles of writing a précis or summary are:

1 Check that you **understand** the specified requirement by questioning and clarifying requirements with the person making the request. Agree a title for the document.
2 **Read** documents carefully several times so that the theme or central argument becomes clear.
3 Study each section in turn, selecting the **principal** points. Underscore or highlight and number each point.
4 Remove any **repetition**, lists, examples and detailed description, but do retain technical terms or names.
5 Use your **own words** to note in short sentences the principal points.
6 **Check** each point against the original to verify accuracy.
7 Decide upon the most appropriate **format** to use.
8 Compose a **rough draft** leaving room for amendments. Use your own words where possible; do not copy word for word unless specialist terms have been used.
9 If you are working to a specified **number of words**, aim to exceed this in your first draft. It is easier to delete than insert at a later date.
10 Avoid disconnected statements and aim for a **logical flow** of sentences to provide continuity.
11 **Check** your draft against the original title. Have you met specified requirements?
12 **Polish** your draft into a final version by improving vocabulary, syntax, tone, etc.
13 Add details of **source information**.
14 Carry out final **proof-read** and amend accordingly.
15 Sign and date the **final copy**.

The final test of a précis or summary is that its recipient can understand it without ever seeing the original document.

# ■ DIY 7.1.4

Read through the draft report given in Fig 7.4 and write a précis for your boss who will be attending the next meeting but needs a general idea of what was discussed at the last meeting and the decisions made.

## ▶ *Preparing an oral report*

The format and methods of reporting are many and varied, as both spoken and written reports are produced in a number of different contexts. Often, if time is short and information is needed quickly, an oral report may be presented over the telephone, at a meeting or face to face. An oral report must still be prepared in a logical sequence and checked before the information is conveyed to others.

Oral reports are often used by managers who are unable to attend a particular meeting. Another person can be sent to attend the meeting and take notes, which are later used to deliver an oral report to the manager explaining the key issues discussed and decisions made at the meeting.

In order to deliver a competent oral report you must:

- listen alertly to what is being said
- make careful notes
- develop summarising techniques
- develop a clear memory
- practise delivering information orally
- use an organised and logical sequence.

# ■ DIY 7.1.5

Refer back to DIY 7.1.4. Prepare a commentary containing the main points of the report (your précis will help you to do this) and report these verbally to your assessor. You must provide your source information and working notes as evidence.

D R A F T

Sales Conference

Advertising, Sales and Marketing Managers with Managing Director.

Report on Sales/Marketing Program 429

1. The Sales Manager thought that in light of the success of Project 326, it wd be beneficial to run Project 429 in the same way. It was obviously a success that we would wish to repeat again this year.

2. He urged further advertising to keep the company's name at the forefront of the market. An additional budget allowance of £15,000 was endorsed by the Managing Director in light of the market research carried out.

3. The Advertising Manager confirmed that without the additional allowance of £15,000 the team could not meet targets. It was felt that the allowance would be well spent and would be earmarked for creating new and innovative ideas. The advertising team were on to the project already with some very exciting ideas.

4. The Managing Director has agreed the additional allowance in theory but added that there would have to be cuts elsewhere to raise the £15,000. She added that no further allowance would be made available, and asked the team for their projected sales figs. The following were put forward: Jan 8,096; Feb 9,264; Mar 7,578; Apr 5,889; May 7,886; June 8,889; July 8,557; Aug 9,997 Sept 10,335; Oct 9,447; Nov 8,999; Dec 10,778.

5. The team advised that these figures were purely speculative based on the previous year's performance. They do, however, take in the anticipated sales resulting from Project 429. The Managing Director said that she will consider the figs further and make a final decision next week. She then closed the meeting.

Copies to:     Sales Man

               Advertising Man

               Marketing Man

               File

**Fig 7.4 Draft report for use with DIY 7.1.4**

## ▶ *Using correction signs*

You may draft documents in writing, type or word process them. However, it may be the responsibility of someone else to prepare your documents and your responsibility to proof-read, correct, amend and ensure the document is produced professionally. If this is the case you will need to ensure that you follow the basic rules for the preparation of draft material and proof correction signs.

When preparing a draft copy for proof correction there are certain basic rules to follows, such as:

1 Agree on a style of presentation and adhere to it throughout.

2 The draft should be prepared in double-line spacing to allow insertions and amendments to be made easily.

3 A master copy must be kept in case the original is lost.

4 Each draft must be dated, or given a version number, to identity the most up-to-date copy.

5 Use headings and sub-headings throughout to break up text and simplify material.

6 Margins at top/bottom and left/right should be kept uniform throughout. Approximate word counts can then be made more easily. The margins can also be used for corrections.

7 Spelling, punctuation, use of abbreviations and acronyms must be consistent throughout.

8 Times, dates, measurements, mathematical and scientific symbols must be used consistently. The 24-hour clock and metric measurements are recommended.

9 Footnotes adding details to text should use a standard symbol such as *.

10 Illustrations should be kept separate from the draft but their inclusion and position marked on the draft for insertion in the final copy.

11 Pages must be numbered consecutively throughout the draft.

Proof correction signs are used to identify amendments, insertions and deletions in the draft. The British Standards Institution issues a classified list of standard marks for use in draft preparation and correction (BS 5261C:1976). Each correction is marked in the text with a corresponding mark in the left- or right-hand margin.

# ■ DIY 7.1.6

Type a copy of the list shown below. Next to each instruction insert the signs you would use to indicate the changes you wish to have made to a document.

| Instruction | Signs |
|---|---|
| **1** New paragraph | **1** |
| **2** Change to capital letter | **2** |
| **3** Change to small letter | **3** |
| **4** Insert a space | **4** |
| **5** Insert a comma | **5** |
| **6** Insert a full stop | **6** |
| **7** Run-on one paragraph into another | **7** |
| **8** Close up a space | **8** |
| **9** Delete | **9** |
| **10** Transpose letters, words, paragraphs | **10** |
| **11** Leave a correction as it was | **11** |

Copy the following paragraph (complete with mistakes) and then insert, with a red pen, the corrections that have to be made to it. Remember to use the correct sign for each correction.

---

asking questions to clarify the meaning of instructions is very important, In order to confirm under standing. youmust ensure that you are fully aware of what is expected From you. to do this you should ask quesitons and clarify the meaning if you do not not understnad what is expected. The person requesting you to carry out a task will be happie to answer questions, rather than receive a document that is totaly incorrect@ It may be the case that you are given written text to trans cribe into typewritten format. if this happens. it is a good idea to read thru the text first to make sure you understand it. If you do not, then you can ask questions before the person returns to their own work. It is also inportant that you clarify the persons instructions before they leave to make sure that you are clear as to whether you require copies of the document routing to other members ofstaff. and if they require a particular layout for the document. Remember that these insttuctions maybe verbal and should be writtend down so that you do not forget,

---

## House style

Written communication is one of the most important aspects of any business, as the appearance and quality of the documents represent the company image. Letters or other documents sent to customers with spelling, grammar or presentation errors will not project an efficient, businesslike image. The documents you produce should follow a 'house style': this ensures that the documents received by the customer will reflect the same image regardless of the department that has sent them.

An organisation will decide upon the style in which letters, memos and other documents will be set out. Over the past few years more companies have moved from the indented, fully punctuated style to the blocked style, with open punctuation, although combinations of both are sometimes used.

The blocked, open punctuated style is quicker to type, easier to learn, and less presentation mistakes tend to be made. Some companies are particularly strict with their house style, even stating what size and style of type should be used. Whichever style is chosen by your organisation, it is important to make sure that all members of staff follow the rules so that all styles are consistent.

## ▶ *Legal and regulatory requirements*

There are certain legal and regulatory requirements relating to the use and provision of information that you must take into account.

## Copyright law

Copyright is designed to protect the livelihood of the creators and producers of literary, dramatic, artistic and musical works. Following an EC Directive, copyright now in most cases lasts for 70 years from the death of an author and this covers photographs and other illustrations in a book.

Single copies of copyright material may be made for private study, provided no more than a 'reasonable proportion' is copied.

All copyright material is denoted by the symbol © followed by the date, and this can be found on videos, tapes, magazines, computer programs, etc, as well as on books. Multiple copies of this material may not be made without prior permission and payment may have to be made to the publishers for a licence to copy their material. It is normal practice for officers representing the British Copyright Council to visit organisations and ensure that the copyright law is not being broken.

When you use information sources that are covered by copyright law you must obey the regulations stated above. You must also ensure that you identify your source, using either the bibliography or appendix at the end of your work.

## Data Protection law

If you set up or use a database which has personal information on individuals then it must be registered with the Data Protection Registrar. The records should not be kept longer than is necessary and proper security procedures should be introduced to make sure only authorised staff have access to the information stored. The information should also be kept up to date, accurate and never be passed to anyone who may use it for other purposes. This also applies to your responsibilities when using information for documents drafted by you to meet specified requirements. If the information you are using is covered by the Data Protection Act make sure you adhere to the requirements. This information is confidential and should be kept secure at all times.

## Confidentiality

You must be sure that the information you are supplying is not confidential or, if it is, that you are supplying it to someone who is allowed to have it. You should check if you are unsure about a person's authority. Data held on computers about individuals is covered by the Data Protection Act and must be treated as confidential; would you like others to have access to your bank or medical records? Confidential information may also include the financial and accounts details of the organisation, staff location and detailed timetables, security arrangements, customers' records and requirements. In every situation you need to find out who is requesting the information and whether they are entitled to have it.

# ▶ *Appendices*

The appendix, placed near the end of a formal report is used as an additional source of information. It acts as a location point in the report for particular information which has relevance to all or part of the report's content. The appendix could comprise a list of useful names and addresses or extracts from another useful source, anything that will provide additional information to the reader of the report.

## ▶ *Bibliography*

This word means 'a list of books' and is used by the report writer to detail any books used in the compilation of the report. The list is arranged in alphabetical order of author's surname, and each entry contains also the title of the book and its reference or ISBN number. The bibliography provides useful information to the reader of the report by giving details of useful books that provide further information if they need it now or for further research.

## ▶ *Deadlines and prioritising*

When drafting documents to meet specified requirements, apart from deciding on the source to use and the method of presentation, you must also take time into consideration. Some information will be required urgently and you may only have a few minutes in which to supply it; other information will take longer to find and you may need a day or more to find it and then draft your findings. You should always be able to estimate the time you require to find and then draft the information and let the person know how long it will be before you return with the necessary facts. If there is going to be a delay and it will take longer than you thought, go back and tell the person, so that they do not think that you have forgotten about it.

If you have several requests, put them in a priority order, so that the most urgent and important ones are first. Set your own deadlines if you do not have to meet a particular time or date; otherwise you may find that things get left and forgotten. You may have other duties to carry out, such as dealing with the post, answering the telephone, supervising others or sorting out stock. You will need to include these duties in your priority list, especially when some have to be done at a particular time, eg the post or answering the telephone.

## ■ DIY 7.1.7

Copy the table in Fig 7.5 on to a sheet of A4 paper and enter details of documents you have drafted. Do not forget to include any tasks you have completed for this or other units. Identify, by ticking the appropriate box, whether you have had to take into account house style, copyright, data protection, confidentiality and/or meeting deadlines. You must also provide examples of the work you have completed which cover each of the requirements detailed in the table.

| Element 7.1 Draft documents to meet specified requirements | | | | | |
|---|---|---|---|---|---|
| Name of Document | House style | Copy-right | Data pro-tected | Confid-ential | Deadline |
| Drafted for yourself | | | | | |
| Drafted on behalf of others | | | | | |

**Fig. 7.5 Record of documents drafted, for use with DIY 7.1.7**

## Knowledge and understanding question bank

1 How do you establish the need for documentation?
2 What sources of information do you use?
3 How do you use different sources of information?
4 How do you go about verifying information?
5 How do you draft documents?
6 How do you ensure effective use of language?
7 How do you ensure effective use of grammar?
8 What is house style?
9 What is the Data Protection Act?
10 What is copyright law?

## Claiming credit

For Element 7.1 evidence must prove that you have drafted documents for both yourself and others which have been both self-generated and produced according to instructions from others. You must also prove that you have taken into account statutory and non-statutory legal and regulatory requirements such as health and safety, equal opportunities, copyright and data protection requirements. The following work products are potential sources of evidence:

- source information
- working papers
- reports
- commentaries
- précis

Once you have completed your final assessment, you will need to write in your record book or folder how, when and what you have done to prove that you are competent.

The following statement is an example of how one trainee completed this claim:

*In my work as an administrative assistant for Coopers & Co I am responsible for drafting my documents before either typing them myself or passing them to the office juniors. I always proof-read any documents prior to sending them to clients or passing to the partners for signature. We use our own house style to ensure that all documentation has the same layout. I have produced commentaries and precis according to instructions from the partners and also when preparing reports. The most recent report I prepared was on the use of e-mail in the office. When compiling a report I firstly discuss the requirements with the partner prior to obtaining relevant and valid information. When preparing the documentation or report I check validity of the information before selecting, editing, integrating and collating it. I always ensure that copyright law is not infringed and always detail the source of my information. When I produce a report I include conclusions and recommendations if these are required.*

# ■ Element 7.2
# INITIATE AND RESPOND TO CORRESPONDENCE

### Performance criteria

1 Correspondence for own action is correctly identified and prioritised
2 The language, style and tone of correspondence are suited to its purpose
3 Correspondence is accurate, clear and in accordance with house style
4 The speed, mode and cost of forwarding correspondence reflect its urgency and importance
5 Copies of all relevant documentation are stored in accordance with organisational procedures
6 Security and confidentiality of information are maintained

### Element introduction

Organisations rely on internal and external correspondence to allow personnel to communicate efficiently and effectively with other members of staff and with the outside business world. Correspondence may take the form of letters, memos, circulars, enquiries, quotations, invoices, statements, advertisements, notices and invitations, to name a varied selection. It is the compilation of and response to this form of written communication that make up a large proportion of the work carried out in an everyday office environment.

A valuable member of staff is one who recognises and processes the tasks they are able to carry out within their area of responsibility, and as this area expands with experience, training, career development and possible promotion, the variety and amount of correspondence needing their attention will increase accordingly. Delegation requires the responsibility for tasks, such as responding to correspondence, to be handed downwards so that slowly but surely staff are trained to take on more responsibility and expand their worth to the boss, department and ultimately the organisation.

## ▶ *Identifying correspondence for own action*

It is with experience that a member of staff will take on an increased proportion of their boss's workload. This may involve whole areas of work being placed in their control with the responsibility of initiating, responding and/or delegating tasks to others. It may simply require the identification of tasks that they can prioritise and then process as and when such tasks pass through the office. Whether you are in a supervisory position or working for one or more other people, you will find that as you get to know the workloads of the people around you, so you will recognise and take on more tasks yourself.

Initially, your job description will tell you what responsibilities are included in your position, but as your knowledge of the organisation and its personnel increases, you will find yourself better able to reply to correspondence or enquiries without having to consult your boss. This knowledge, together with getting to know how your boss works, will also help you to recognise correspondence that you are unable to process and should pass on to your boss for action. It should, however, always be remembered that the boss or the person delegating responsibility will retain ultimate accountability and, therefore, should always be informed of progress, decisions made or correspondence actioned on their behalf.

# ■ DIY 7.2.1

You work as the Personal Assistant to Mr John Ball, Personnel Director, and have received the post from the mail room. Sort through the mail and make 2 lists identifying those items that will be dealt with by you and those that will need to be actioned by Mr Ball.

1 Letter of enquiry regarding waiting lists for future vacancies in the canteen.
2 Letter requesting an application form for a vacancy that was advertised 2 weeks ago, with interviews taking place in 2 days' time.
3 Internal memo regarding a complaint from an employee about his pension plan.
4 Invitation requesting Mr Ball's presence at the Social Club's Annual Dinner Dance.
5 Letter marked CONFIDENTIAL for Mr Ball.
6 Urgent stationery requisition form from Personnel Office requiring authorisation.
7 Internal newsletter.
8 Agenda for the monthly Directors' Meeting next week.
9 Letter from the Union Representative regarding the dismissal of one of their members.
10 Letter addressed to 'Personnel' marked 'Private'.
11 Quotation from Business Supplies Ltd for the supply of continuous stationery for Mr Ball's home computer.
12 Letter from Environmental Health Officer requesting urgent appointment to carry out health and safety check.
13 Letter requesting a work reference for an existing employee.
14 Letter of resignation from Personnel Secretary who is unhappy in her job since your arrival.
15 Appointment for Mr Ball to attend local Magistrates' Court regarding employee's complaint of unfair dismissal.
16 Letter from a bank requesting a mortgage reference for an employee.

It is accepted that, without fully understanding the working practices of Mr Ball, this task is open to personal interpretation. Therefore, you will need to add a note of explanation next to each item of correspondence giving your reasons for either passing it on or taking action yourself. Once you have sorted this correspondence you will then have to prioritise it in order of importance. Number each item in your list to indicate in what order you would execute these tasks and what action you would take.

▶ *Producing accurate and clear correspondence according to house style*

In order to assist you in your daily response to correspondence received, organisations will make available a variety of pre-printed stationery, such as letterheaded paper, memorandum paper, order forms, and so on. It is important that correspondence, once identified as requiring your attention, is dealt with promptly and correctly. Always remember that any such communication presents an image of your organisation and its products, and it is your responsibility to ensure that poor presentation, grammar and spelling are corrected so that the impression given is a favourable one.

An organisation will usually have a 'house style' – a way in which it expects the correspondence of all personnel to be laid out and presented. A certain style of presentation or type of punctuation may be required; the date, reference, salutation and complimentary close may be typed in a specific way, and designation, enclosures and continuation sheets may be indicated according to company guidelines. Regardless of how you were taught at school or college, or how you were trained to present correspondence for your previous employer, the organisation's house style must be used if standardisation of presentation is to be achieved.

There are a few basic rules that may help you when preparing correspondence.

1 Presentation should always follow house style – if you do not already know this, find out. If there is not one, use your own style or that preferred by the person for whom you are preparing the correspondence.
2 Use the appropriately headed paper for the job in hand.
   For example, letterheads that look identical may contain different information for different members of staff.
3 Never allow your correspondence to be sent out with spelling, grammar or printing errors. Always check an assistant's work – remember you are responsible for it.
4 Ensure that all facts and figures such as dates (including the date the correspondence was typed), times and amounts of money are correct – this will save time at a later date explaining the error and avoid possible legal implications.
5 If errors are found, correction should be inconspicuous – a suitable method of correction needs to be selected according to the nature of the error.
6 Always indicate enclosures and continuation sheets to avoid confusion – and remember to insert all the contents into the envelope.

**Fig. 7.6 Examples of correspondence**

7 Ensure that your own correspondence is signed appropriately, and only use 'pp' and sign on behalf of your boss if this is acceptable. Check to make sure the boss has signed own correspondence before it is sealed in an envelope.

8 Prepare addresses for envelopes and packages according to Post Office regulations. Indicate in pencil on the envelope or package the class of postage and if a special service is required.

9 Confidential, private or personal instructions should be indicated on both correspondence and envelopes. Memos that carry these instructions should be placed in an envelope, marked accordingly.

10 Always select your method of communication according to the speed, mode and cost of response required for each individual piece of correspondence – a telephone call, fax or telex may be more suitable for the job in hand.

## ■ DIY 7.2.2

Collect examples of various business correspondence that you have prepared according to house style or as required for training centre or examination purposes. Write an information sheet to go with each example explaining how to achieve this style.

## ▶ *Composing correspondence*

This area of responsibility has been covered in depth in element 7.1 but it is wise to look back briefly at the main points made.

Correspondence will either convey information or ask for it and should do so in a manner which leaves no doubt on the part of the reader. The reader should clearly understand the meaning of the correspondence and be confident that any action taken is correct – ambiguity leads to confusion and the wrong action may be taken as a result. The correspondence should be concise and to the point without being abrupt, impolite or too vague and tact must always be used, particularly if dealing with a complaint or problem. The material should cover all points.

In general terms, correspondence should be:

- concise and to the point
- written in straightforward language
- written in an easy to understand style
- accurate
- tactful
- courteous in tone
- pleasing to the eye
- presented in a logical sequence

The opening paragraph(s) should indicate what the correspondence is about; the middle paragraph(s) should contain the information being given or sought; and the concluding paragraph(s) should reflect the general tone of the rest of the correspondence bringing it to a polite close. Words should never be used unless the writer is absolutely sure of both their meaning and their spelling, while care should be taken never to use words that might confuse the reader or be open to misinterpretation.

When you first start to compose your own correspondence it is useful to make a list of all the points you need to cover in a logical order – refer to previous correspondence that is relevant and which will indicate the information being sought or given. If you are using a word processor then, with time, you may find that you are able to compose at the keyboard and can use a spell check facility to eliminate spelling errors and a thesaurus to broaden your vocabulary.

# ■ DIY 7.2.3

Copy the table in Fig. 7.7 on to a piece of A4 paper. Complete the following tasks and enter details of these, together with any other relevant tasks you have completed in this or other units, on to the table.

| ELEMENT 7.2 Initiate and respond to correspondence | | | | |
|---|---|---|---|---|
| Name of Document | Informing | Requesting | Advising | Explaining |
| **1** Initiated by self | | | | |
| **2** Initiated by self on behalf of others | | | | |
| **3** In response to correspondence received by self | | | | |
| **4** In response to correspondence received by others | | | | |

**Fig. 7.7 Record of correspondence dealt with, for use with DIY 7.2.3**

You work as an Administration Assistant in the Personnel Department of Lotus Natural Body Care Products and have received the following correspondence (Figs. 7.7a to 7.7d). Read through it and type your responses according to the basic rules for preparing correspondence already listed in this unit.

---

```
Anne Schneider

Kopernikusstrasse 10

Berlin

1034


1 April 199-


Personnel Department
Lotus Natural Body Care Products
The Bargates
Christchurch
Dorset
England


Werter Herr/Frau

Hiermit bitte ich um die Zusendung von
Bewerbungsunterlagen, da ich gerne in England
arbeiten wuerde, wenn ich mein Studium an der
Sekretaers Fachhochschule in Deutschland beendet
habe.

Hochachtungsvoll


Anne Schneider
```

---

**Fig. 7.7a**

```
M E M O R A N D U M

TO      Personnel Department

FROM    Mary White, Canteen Supervisor

DATE    7 May 199-

REF     Salaries and Conditions of Service


I have recently discovered that one of the other
canteen supervisors earns more than me, even though
our duties and conditions of work are exactly the
same.

I think that this situation is totally unacceptable
and demand that my pay is increased in line with
other members of staff immediately.
```

**Fig. 7.7b**

```
M E M O R A N D U M

FROM        John Ball, Personnel Director

TO          All Administrative Assistants

DATE        7 May 199-

REF         Safe Working Practices


Arrangements have been made for the Local Authority
Health and Safety Inspector to visit these premises
next week. In order to ensure that all office staff
are aware of the potential hazards in the office and
how these can be avoided, I have taken this
opportunity to write to all Administrative
Assistants to ask that they prepare a brief report
on their immediate office surroundings. In this
report would you please identify any potential
hazards and how these may be remedied.
```

**Fig. 7.7c**

```
M E M O R A N D U M


FROM          Joe Walsh, Union Representative

TO            Personnel Administration

DATE          8 May 199-

REF           Confidentiality of Personnel Records


I have recently been contacted by Mrs Vera Brown,
Canteen Supervisor, regarding the leakage of personal
information regarding her salary. She has been
approached by another member of staff who appears to
know her exact annual salary and other personal
details about her. I have informed the Personnel
Director of this situation and he has asked me to
contact you in order to obtain information explaining
the security and confidentiality procedures
implemented in your office.
```

**Fig. 7.7d**

You have received the following telephone messages (Figs 7.7e to 7.7g). Reply to them in writing.

```
TELEPHONE MESSAGE


TO

FROM Rob Brown, Sen Manager

DATE 8.5.9-   TIME 9.12 am   DEPT/CO Admin Dept

EXT/TEL NO 5674

MESSAGE

Could you please let him know asap what
information/books, etc, are required, by law, under
health and safety legislation, so that he can check
these are available ready for H&S inspection.
```

**Fig. 7.7e**

```
TELEPHONE MESSAGE

TO                                    FROM    Mrs Barber

DATE   8.5.9-  TIME 9.15 am

DEPT/CO        Allington Hotel

EXT/TEL NO -

MESSAGE

Called to ask why we were not using her hotel for the
Annual Sales Awards Ceremony - we used it last year.
Wants to know what the problem was with disabled
gentleman. Address: Ruxley Road, Coventry.
```

**Fig. 7.7f**

```
TELEPHONE MESSAGE

TO                    FROM James Borrows, Manager

DATE 8.5.9-   TIME 9.20 am

DEPT/CO Coarse Cosmetics

EXT/TEL NO

MESSAGE

Could you let him have sales figures for last year,
including details of best sellers and profit and loss
figures for the year. He would also like names of
sales personnel who achieved best results. Reply to:
Sloane Street, London SW1.
```

**Fig. 7.7g**

## ▶ *Proof-reading*

Proof-reading is usually thought of as a tiresome, tedious affair, but the quality of your work and the image you, your boss and the organisation wish to present both internally and externally should mean that errors in correspondence are simply not acceptable. Proof-reading is time consuming and some may feel unproductive, but if a customer or client were to receive correspondence with errors, particularly in figure work, this could lead to a loss in confidence and possibly a loss of business.

Given time and experience your proof-reading techniques become more finely tuned, although a useful ploy is to ask another person to proof-read for you and vice versa. When you have spent time preparing a document and know the content very well, it is easy to read what you 'think' it should say rather than what it 'does' say. Provided the correspondence is not confidential, another member of staff can read through it with a more critical eye as they are not so familiar with the text and will, therefore, use more concentration.

When composing correspondence always use a dictionary if you are unsure of the meaning or spelling of a word – keep a list of commonly misspelt words at hand for easy referral. If using a word processor use the spell check as a matter of routine – it will save time and help you towards error free correspondence. However, it is wise to remember that a spell check may not identify:

- grammatical errors
- words that have been typed twice
- incorrect information
- incorrect or transposed figure work
- omissions – word, line, paragraph
- word substitutions
- incorrect punctuation
- inconsistent presentation

Therefore, correspondence will still require final proof–reading and inconspicuous corrections to be made if necessary.

## ▶ *Making corrections*

You will find various methods and materials in use for error correction, the choice of which will depend upon the nature of the error and the type of equipment in use. The method chosen should be the one that best suits the type of correction to be made; above all, the correction should be inconspicuous to the eye and not detract from the content of the correspondence.

Large blobs of correction fluid smudged over the paper or holes made with rubbers are not acceptable. Typed correspondence with incorrect words crossed out and rewritten in pen should never be allowed out of the office.

The type of correction method chosen will depend upon the error and the equipment used to produce the correspondence in the first place. Word processors have the advantage of allowing you to key in, proof-read and correct as you go along – a very simple process that allows the final copy to be printed out error free. Draft copy is often printed out first, for example a long report that needs to be proof-read and edited. Eventually the document is simply called up on screen, corrections are made and a final copy is printed.

If you do use a word processor a balance needs to be maintained for the purposes of economy and time. Multiple sheets of paper are often used in the quest for error-free work. Poor screen proof-reading may suggest that the document is error free, but once it is printed, errors may be found that need to be corrected and another copy printed. To prevent wasting time and paper make sure that correspondence is proof-read correctly on screen before printing it out. If a draft is required use the back of obsolete forms, etc, to save paper. It is useful to remember that when using a word processor the advantages that allow totally inconspicuous correction and easy editing can sometimes lead to the disadvantage of an increase in workload, purely because it is such an easy process to edit, correct and print out yet another copy.

Modern typewriters normally offer a correction facility and/or a display to aid proof-reading and error correction as you go along. There are correction tapes made from a sticky film that lifts the error from the paper. Provided the correct carbon cassette ribbons are used, the typist simply presses a correction key and the error is lifted from the paper. Chalk-based correction tapes are also available that deposit a white chalk substance over the error. These tapes are used with ink ribbons and simply cover over the error. Some typewriters with correction facilities also have a memory that allows automatic correction of errors in previous lines or paragraphs. However, once the paper has been removed from the typewriter it is a very difficult process to realign it again to type in corrections.

## DIY 7.2.4

Your assistant has prepared the following memos for you (Figs. 7.8a and 7.8b). Proof-read them and amend them where necessary. Comment on whether you feel the memos have been written using the correct language, style and tone for their purpose.

```
M E M O R A N D U M

FROM

TO    John Ball, Personnel Director

DATE

REF   Applications for junior Clerk typist post


      To date i have received 5 aplications for the
cletk typist post    advertised in last weeks evening
Echo. I have suggested a dealine date of tues. next,
with interview to be arranged for the following weds.
(date please).


      Can I suggest that you drawer up a list list of
your requirements to aid us in to select a shortlist
and so that we can base our interview questions
around what you want.


      We need to discus salary as details will need
      to be given to the    applicants at inteview -
      it is it possible to meet with you tomorrow\
      and weather accom. can be arranged for the
      interview panel.
```

**Fig. 7.8a**

```
M E M O R A N D U M

FROM

TO      Carol Barker, Head Receptionist

DATE

REF     Annual Sales Award Ceremony


        Regarding the above ceremony , would it be
possible for you to ask your stff to prepare sep.
name badges on the Kroy lettering machine req'd for
all staff attending the eveing ?


        The ceremony will be held on the 14th of next
month and Mr Ball would like all staff to were name
badges so that they can recognise colleagues who
operate in different regions.  I will       sent you a
list of names once we receive all the tear-off
portions detailing the how many tickets are required
and the    names of members of staff attending.
Their should be about 200.


        You may find yourself receiving telephone
enquiries regarding the ceremoney, and to help you
answer these,  |I have attached a draft copy of the
memo and notice soon to be sent out to all staff.

Yours faithfully
```

**Fig. 7.8b**

## ▶ *Form letters*

A form letter is the framework of a prepared letter: one with the essential material but lacking a date, inside name, address and salutation (which may be presented as 'Dear' – and a space left for the name to be inserted). Form letters are business letters sent from one organisation to another, or to members of the public, for example someone who has applied for a vacancy but has been unsuccessful.

Form letters are pre-printed either by a duplicating process or by a word processor on letterheaded paper. They are used when a large number of similar letters need to be prepared with only a small amount of variable information such as the name and address. The variable information is added using a typewriter, where care must be taken to align the type correctly, or by using a word processor which will display the form letter on screen and allow the relevant information to be inserted before printing out. The use of form letters saves time; they also give the impression that the letter has been specifically typed for the recipient.

Nowadays it is usual for an organisation to have a bank of form letters stored on disk that simply require the insertion of variable information to personalise them. Another common practice is the setting up of standard paragraphs which can then be recalled and assembled to form a combination appropriate to the situation. For example, standard paragraphs that may be used by an accounts department may be:

- 'Thank you for your payment in settlement of your account dated ...'

- 'We write to inform you that your account is now ... weeks overdue, and that we will take legal action in 28 days.'

It is normal practice for each paragraph to have an identity number. The person writing the letter simply selects the most appropriate paragraphs from those available on the computer and writes in their reference number and the paragraph appears instantly on screen to form part of the letter. These paragraphs can be saved under separate file names (if they are quite lengthy) or by using a facility called a Macro.

## ▶ *Responding to contacts*

Correspondents and recipients to whom you may have to write are:

- internal to the organisation
- external to the organisation
- own principal and more senior staff
- regular clients or customers

- first-time enquirers
- occasional contacts
- overseas contacts

The type of response you will make to these contacts will depend upon the nature and size of the organisation that you work for and will be based on your job role and responsibilities within that organisation. Generally speaking, you will find that you will be responsible for compiling standardised replies, such as the form letters already mentioned, or individual replies that may require you to carry out investigation, refuse a demand or perhaps make an apology or explain items.

Your correspondence may take the form of oral or written responses, depending on the content of the correspondence received, the nature of the correspondent and/or recipient and the equipment available to you.

For example, an emergency order may be taken verbally over the telephone or face to face, but it will need to be followed by a written confirmation on official stationery sent by post or fax. A written invitation from a boss or someone making a complaint may require initial verbal contact for confirmation or placatory purposes, followed by a written

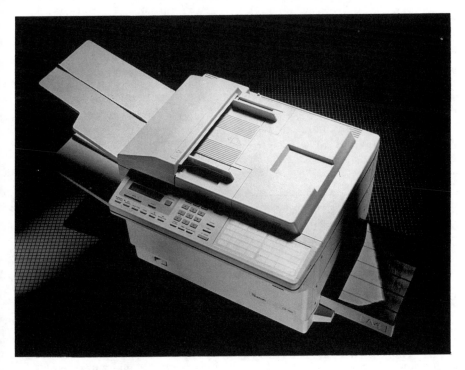

**Fig. 7.9 A fax machine**

**Fig. 7.10 A telex machine**

response. Correspondence requesting information may require a brief verbal or written acknowledgement to allow time for investigation.

The use of a telex machine will allow typed correspondence to be transmitted at the touch of a button, and a fax machine enables instant transfer of hard copy, including written text and diagrams, in less time than it would take to relay the information verbally over the telephone.

## ■ DIY 7.2.5

Explain the advantages and disadvantages involved in using fax, telex and post (including special services) to deliver correspondence. Give examples of the type of correspondence and situation that help you to decide the most appropriate method to use.

### ▶ *Storing copies of documentation*

Most business transactions involve the keeping of records and these records are usually kept in written or printed form – letters, minutes, memoranda, reports, buying and selling documents are all examples of

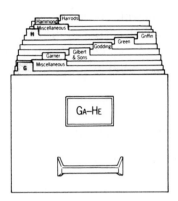

**Fig. 7.11 An alphabetical filing system**

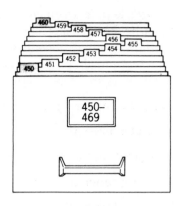

**Fig. 7.12 A numerical filing system**

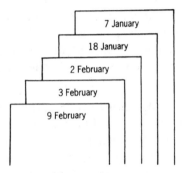

**Fig. 7.13 A chronological filing classification**

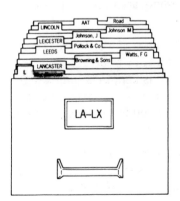

**Fig. 7.14 A geographical filing classification**

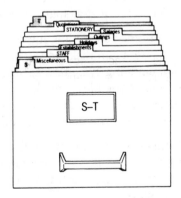

**Fig. 7.15 A subject filing classification**

records kept in an office. If an office is to run efficiently, documentation must be stored using a quick and reliable method of classification. The method used will depend on the type of documentation being stored. It is vital that members of staff understand the classification in use so that all documents are stored in their correct sequence.

Filing is used for a number of reasons:

- to **preserve** information so it is readily at hand when needed

- to **protect** information so it is safe from damage or loss

- to **sequence** information in a logical order so it is easy to locate.

In general terms there are 5 commonly used classifications (*see* Figs 7.11–7.15).

No one classification is better than another. The art is in finding the best method to suit the type of document to be stored. All classifications do however have one thing in common; they all allow documents to be stored in a **logical** sequence. Remember that it will not always be the same person putting files in or taking files out of a filing system. Therefore, a logical sequence is necessary if files are to be retrieved quickly and efficiently when needed and not lost in the system.

Computer-based filing uses a **database** program that is designed to store and sort information. Files are produced by keying in the information and can be sorted easily using simple instructions. The database is set up using fields such as name, date of birth, account number and so on. The computer can be instructed to sort records alphabetically, by name, or numerically by account number or date or birth. Computerised filing saves space and time and is particularly useful for personnel records, wages records and stock records. Files cannot go missing, are easy to update and you can request as many copies of the file as you wish.

Computer-based filing involves the keeping of copies of word processed documents on disk file rather than printing out a copy to be kept in a manual filing system. A record of each document is kept in an index with details of the file name. If a copy of the correspondence is required at a future date, the name of the recipient can be located in the index and the file name of the document found.

When using electronic mail a memo or message can be sent, using a networked computer, to another terminal. The message can be read from screen and then saved. A hard copy printout is only requested if necessary.

It is important that copies are kept of all correspondence sent out by a company. Future requests, information and action will usually be based upon previous communication and if a record is kept the process of getting it right is simplified. It is vital that you ensure copies of all relevant documentation are stored in accordance with organisational procedures. Great care must be taken with confidential matter and material covered by the Data Protection Act.

# ■ DIY 7.2.6

You are responsible for a new junior member of staff in your office. Your boss has asked you to prepare a guide explaining how the alphabetical filing system works, the importance of keeping copies of correspondence sent to customers and the need for security. The system in use requires copies of correspondence to be printed on to blank, yellow paper. The yellow copy is then sent to customer records. The original is sent to the customer and a copy saved under the customer's reference number on your computer. Explain why and how this system must be kept secure.

## Knowledge and understanding question bank

1 Explain the scope of your own authority when dealing with correspondence.
2 What conventions do you follow when drafting correspondence?
3 What sources of information are available to you?
4 How do you ensure effective use of language?
5 How do you ensure effective use of grammar?
6 What methods of transmitting correspondence do you use?
7 What do you understand by the term 'house style'?
8 What is the Data Protection Act?
9 What is the Copyright Act?
10 How do you make sure you prepare correspondence in the right context?

## Claiming credit

For Element 7.2 evidence must prove that you have dealt with correspondence related to others internal and external to the organisation. The correspondence generated must be that initiated by yourself, or initiated by yourself on behalf of others, in response to correspondence received by yourself and correspondence received by others. The correspondence that you deal with must have the purpose of informing, requesting, advising and explaining. The following work products are potential sources of evidence:

● correspondence received and copies of responses made
● copies of self-generated correspondence

Once you have completed your final assessment, you will need to write in your record book or folder how, when and what you have done to prove that you are competent.

The following statement is an example of how one trainee completed this claim:

*As an administration assistant at Coopers & Co it is my responsibility to sort and open the mail each morning. Correspondence for my own action is put to one side while I deal with the correspondence for the partners. When replying to correspondence myself I can draft this and pass it to one of the office juniors. I always proof-read the correspondence before sending it to clients. The correspondence I initiate and respond to includes giving and requesting information and advice together with that used for explaining matters. The language, style and tone of correspondence used in the office tends to be very formal as we are dealing with accounting matters. However, my own correspondence which deals with items such as office supplies, placing advertisements, etc is a little less formal. The mode of forwarding correspondence is chosen according to its urgency or importance. Correspondence is most often sent by mail, sometimes registered or recorded, and agencies such as TNT are used if a special service is required. I also use the fax to send non-confidential matter, for example an order, but this is usually followed up with a postal copy for legal reasons. Copies of all documents are stored in our paper-based filing system under the clients' company name or surname. Accounts details are kept secure on the database. Internal communication is written or typed on to NCR memo paper and a copy kept in the internal correspondence file.*

# UNIT 8
# Develop, implement and maintain procedures

■ **Element 8.1**
**DEVELOP PROCEDURES TO MEET SPECIFIED NEEDS**

### Performance criteria

1 Procedures meet identified needs and conform to legal and regulatory requirements

2 Designs and specifications for procedures are developed in conjunction with users

3 Benefits and costs are formulated and agreed with decision makers

4 Specialist advice is obtained, when required, and acted upon, where appropriate

### Element introduction

It is important that most of this unit is assessed in the workplace. Assignments and projects can be used as supplementary evidence to support workplace activity, but the ability to develop, implement and maintain procedures can only be judged and assessed in practice. If you look through the units for the Level 3 award you will see that there are no units that specifically concentrate on areas of work such as filing, dealing with the mail and using telecommunications equipment. The Level 3 award assumes that you are already competent in such areas and that at this level your ability to design, implement, operate and monitor procedures to improve efficiency are the skills to be assessed.

This unit has to be assessed over a long enough period of time to allow for meaningful evaluation of the procedures put into place. The unit can be assessed in a working environment such as a training office, an assessment centre or a real working office. The procedures being monitored can be ongoing or one-off situations, for example the ongoing monitoring of outgoing mail procedures or the one-off monitoring of a sales campaign.

The time-scale used for such assessment must be taken into consideration; monitoring of the ongoing procedure can be undertaken over a period of time, whereas monitoring of the one-off procedure will take much longer as the procedure will need to be assessed, evaluated and changed as necessary before the next campaign – which may be some time away.

You should now be aware that this unit can be easily cross-referenced with a number of other units in the NVQ Level 3 Administration award. As you work through the other units look for opportunities to develop, implement and maintain procedures that will improve efficiency in areas such as filing; photocopying; mail handling; health and safety and security; managing appointments; researching and presenting information; data entry, integration and presentation; drafting documents and responding to correspondence.

It is important that your cross-referencing is clear and follows a logical sequence in order to avoid confusion for both you and the assessor. You should discuss and agree an action plan that identifies the units and elements currently in hand and then agree an appropriate assessment plan with your assessor. If you have identified areas of cross-reference beforehand you may be able to use the same assessment plan for more than one element.

## ▶ Managing change

Organisations have to change to survive. **Basic change** relates to changes in basic operating procedures, which, although implemented and monitored quite easily, can still cause irritation and resentment from the people who have been asked to change their way of working. People vary in their ability to cope with changes in their working environment: some see it as a threat, others as a burden they could do without.

Basic change could be something as simple as changing the way in which a task is carried out. A task-centred change could involve changing the design of a form or the way in which it is completed, reorganising a database or manual filing system, or implementing the use of postage books or photocopier logs, to name but a few. Such changes should be implemented in order to enable people to cope more easily and the office to become more accountable. If change is managed correctly, with appropriate measures being taken to inform staff and explain the need for the change, it is likely to be implemented smoothly; if managed badly it is likely to be mishandled or even ignored!

Basic change involves change in task-centred activity. However, **fundamental change** is a much larger challenge and involves implementing changes in areas such as contracts, hours of work, structure of the organisation and job responsibilities. Fundamental change creates stress, anxiety, worry and distress for those people who are most affected. Therefore, for the purpose of this unit, we will concentrate on basic change as it is more than likely that any fundamental changes made in an organisation will have been discussed and agreed at management level.

## Dealing with basic change

When dealing with basic change you will need to look at the way in which tasks, procedures and systems are used in your working environment. When developing procedures that involve change you must always remember that the biggest demotivator for staff is the feeling that they have no control over their work. It is important that you have a thorough knowledge of the task, procedure or system; that you listen to what others have to say and that you show them you have taken their ideas into account. Always consult the people who are doing or will be doing the job first and never automatically think that you know best.

## ▶ *Identifying tasks and procedures*

A **task** is a single administrative activity such as: making a photocopy; opening an envelope; or answering a telephone call.

A **procedure** identifies a number of administrative tasks required to complete a routine such as photocopying, collating, binding and completing the photocopier log book; dealing with outgoing mail; or using the telephone equipment to make and answer calls.

This element is about developing procedures to meet specified needs. Depending upon the size of the organisation that you work for, your responsibilities and the type of change in which you will be involved vary greatly. In a small company you may be involved in developing a complete system to deal with one area of work, such as use of the telecommunications equipment. The fact that the company is small means that any change and the number of people affected by the change will also be small; it may be that the change involves only you!

A large organisation is unlikely to allow a **system** to be changed without specialist advice and discussion at management level. Therefore, it is more likely that while you may be called upon to make changes in tasks, and possibly in procedures, such as dealing with incoming and outgoing calls, the likelihood that you would be asked to make changes to actual systems is very small.

However, if your work is involved in the system change, it is good management practice for you to be asked about your views and ideas either verbally or by requesting you to produce a report.

# ■ DIY 8.1.1

Think about the actions you would take when dealing with the incoming mail for a particular department. Write a list of the tasks you would complete.

## ▶ *Why use procedures?*

Organisations use lists of tasks that form a procedure for a number of different reasons. Perhaps one of the most important reasons for this is consistency. In order to maintain standards at a required level it is important for staff to know how to go about the completion of related tasks. If the tasks and relevant procedures are listed then it is an easy process for staff to follow the written rules. When staff are on holiday, off sick or are new to the organisation the completion of work is not so daunting or hard to learn if the procedures are written down in black and white.

Procedures can also include **quality measures** that allow supervisors and line managers to check that the procedures are being followed to the desired standard. A quality measure could be that all incoming mail must be delivered to staff by 9.15 am. Quality should also improve as errors are reduced by the use of set procedures.

Job descriptions can also be linked with procedures so that it is easy to see who is responsible for a certain area of work. There is a clear definition of level of responsibility and a list of daily tasks can be identified in the job description.

The most important reason for procedures at present, when there is so much emphasis on quality, is that of **improved efficiency**. Work activities that can be analysed and then organised into a logical sequence of procedures can be made more efficient with little effort. A set of clear procedures reduces the amount of time taken by staff to learn a particular activity or task. Also, if the task is standardised throughout the organisation the transfer of staff from one department to another requires less training. Staff will spend less time disturbing others to ask how to complete a particular task. If the procedures are interlinked with other areas of work or departments then teamwork and organisational efficiency are improved.

## ▶ Developing procedures

When developing procedures it is vital that they are clearly written down in a logical sequence to make efficient use of time. They must state how the tasks are to be carried out, who is responsible for completing the tasks and when and where they should be completed. If the tasks are to be checked by a supervisor or line manager then this must also be stated. The defined tasks should be clearly listed in order to form the full procedure in an easy to understand manner. It is vital that they are not written in a manner that will confuse; if so, they are of no use to anyone!

When writing a list of tasks to form a procedure it is important that the tasks are those that would need to be carried out in a number of situations so that they can be followed at all times. (Think back to filing, photocopying and mail handling, which will all follow similar steps regardless of the person or organisation using them.) If you go into too much depth or include too many exceptions to the rules the procedures become less user-friendly and will without doubt cause confusion. Keep them clear and concise so that they can be followed logically and consistently by a variety of people involved in a range of working environments.

There are 2 main types of procedures:

- functional
- general

**Functional** procedures are used to bring together related activities or tasks undertaken in a department. Look at an organisation chart that illustrates **function departmentation**. This means that all tasks have been classified and grouped as the responsibility of one department, for example personnel, accounts, administration. However, this does not mean that each department works in isolation. The personnel department will have to liaise with accounts regarding salaries and pay rises, and perhaps more importantly, the administration department would have to be aware of the needs of every department if it is to provide an efficient support role for the organisation. Functional procedures bring together tasks that are specific to each individual department.

**General** procedures are those that encompass the general activities and tasks undertaken in all departments. Communications, information handling and reprographics are just a few examples of areas of work in

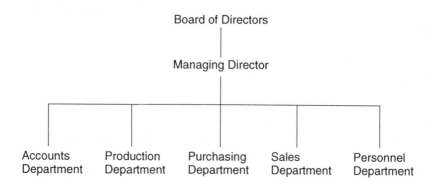

**Fig 8.1 An organisation chart**

which all departments are involved on an individual basis. Therefore, when producing general procedures it is important not to link them with any one department but to keep them 'general' so that they may be used throughout the organisation.

# ■ DIY 8.1.2

In DIY 8.1.1 you listed the tasks you would complete when dealing with the incoming mail. Rewrite these tasks into a set of general procedures that could be used by any departmental office.

## ▶ *Centralised and decentralised procedures*

It is wise at this point to look at how some organisations deal with general procedures by adopting a **centralised** or **decentralised** system. System design takes into account whether activities such as mail handling, reprographics and filing can be more efficiently carried out in a central department or individually by each separate department. There are certain advantages and disadvantages offered by both systems:

1 Advantages of centralisation

- Saves space as all equipment is kept to one department
- Saves money as less equipment needs to be purchased
- Specialist staff can be employed
- Saves time by eliminating repetition of work
- Special equipment can be purchased to improve efficiency

2 Disadvantages of centralisation

- Staff have to wait for others to do specialist tasks
- Increased paperwork writing out instruction/request forms
- Individual requirements may not be catered for
- Time wasted telling others how to do a task you could do yourself in less time

# ■ DIY 8.1.3

Refer to the organisation chart in Fig. 8.1. Copy the chart and under each department heading write a list of the different functions carried out by each department. Add to the bottom of the chart a list of general procedures that would be carried out by all departments.

## ▶ Designing procedures

### Identify the need

So what is the starting point when designing a procedure? It may sound obvious but the first place to start is by finding out if the procedure is needed in the first place. People can be quite reluctant to accept change if they can see no reason for the change in the first place. Conversely, procedures that may have been set in place some time ago may no longer be necessary.

Take, for example, the completion of the mail in and out book. Procedures for logging all incoming and outgoing mail were set up in some companies so that a daily record could be kept of all mail received and sent out. However, it was not long before some of the companies discovered that this information was rarely needed and the time it took to complete the book each day meant that other work was not completed. This does not mean that the mail book is no longer in use, but it does illustrate that if there is no real need for the procedure then it should not be used purely because it exists.

### List the tasks and activities

Once a need for a procedure is identified the next step is to list the tasks and activities required to fulfil the need. (It is a good idea to use a flow chart to do this.) Look for variations but always remember to keep the information logical and concise. Above all, you must discuss your ideas and thoughts with other people who may have specialist knowledge or who will be affected by the procedure when implemented. Involving

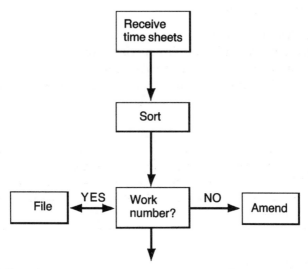

**Fig 8.2 A flow chart**

others will help you to see the whole picture and will make implementation much easier.

## Approval from others

When you have identified the need, listed the relevant tasks and actions to form the procedure and discussed and agreed these with those involved and your line manager, what is the next step? You could 'pilot' the procedure before full implementation so that any faults, omissions or mistakes can be corrected.

For example, let us say that you have just designed a new expenses claim form to be used by all staff. Would you produce the form and have 2,000 copies printed immediately, or would you circulate the form to staff and invite their comments? You would be naive to think that you can get it right first time!

You could organise a formal or informal discussion where the procedures can be discussed as a team. Notes or minutes should be taken, to record comments made and ideas put forward. In some cases a working party may be asked to carry out research and make a presentation to those concerned prior to a formal discussion taking place.

Alternatively, you could use a questionnaire to involve staff who will be affected by any changes. Ask other members of staff to comment on ideas and preferences. The questionnaire can be sent to staff with a memo explaining the need for the procedure and asking them for their comments. If they choose not to reply then they are not in such a strong position at a later date to criticise any action you have taken.

Obviously you would not have to take such measures if the procedure you were designing would affect no one other than yourself, but care must still be taken to ensure that you are not operating your own system in conflict with others. If there is already a set procedure which you think you can improve, talk to your line manager about it and ask if you can put forward some recommendations that would improve the procedure for all staff concerned and not only for yourself.

For example, imagine if you were to completely change the directory of your database, against company procedure, and then went off sick for the next 2 weeks. Do you think you would be very popular upon your return to the office?

### Evaluate the procedure

You must build into your procedure some kind of check that will help you to evaluate its success. For example, if staff are not receiving incoming mail by a certain time, this in itself provides an indicator that the procedure is not being followed or requires modification. Procedures are not set in stone. Internal and external factors affect the organisation and require changes to be made; new legislation, technology, actions by competitors, social changes, etc often signal the implementation of new procedures or rewriting existing procedures to bring about the desired change.

## ■ DIY 8.1.4

Look back at the procedures you wrote for DIY 8.1.2. Explain how you have or would have included the following:

1 Identifying the need
2 Listing the tasks and activities
3 Incorporating checks
4 Obtaining approval from others

## ▶ *Sources of information*

Designing a set of procedures can be a simple task of identifying what is already done and then putting this into written form. It may also be an extremely complex activity requiring much reading and research. Once you have identified the need, listing the tasks and activities and incorporating checks may be a little more difficult, especially if you are dealing with a procedure that is being set up from new.

It is at times like this that you should look for sources of information that will assist you. You might simply talk to other members of staff who have their own ideas or carry out a 'brain-storming session' to give you material to work with. You may be able to find a person or department that has already set up similar procedures, or approach an external source such as another company for information and advice.

Internal sources of information can be found easily. Talk to colleagues, people in other departments and specialist staff, and refer to computerised and manual records that provide a wealth of information.

External sources of information include services such as libraries, Chambers of Commerce, Government departments such as the DTI, information services such as Prestel and the Internet. You may also wish to approach business associates, suppliers, other companies and agencies who provide specialist information such as legal, security, computing and health and safety advice. Reading specialist books, magazines and periodicals will also be of help. You will not be expected to know all the answers yourself, but should be able to show that you know how to find out the information and whom to contact.

## ■ DIY 8.1.5

Refer to DIY 8.1.2 where you wrote a set of procedures for dealing with incoming mail. If you referred to internal and/or external sources of information explain how you did this. If you did not, you should now do so and change your procedures accordingly. Make a list of the internal sources, for example your tutor and other trainees; and external sources, for example the Post Office, from which you could obtain information.

### ▶ *Legal and regulatory requirements*

There are a number of legal and regulatory requirements that you must adhere to when developing procedures. The most important laws are:

- Health and Safety at Work Act
- VDU legislation
- Data Protection Act
- Copyright law

## ▶ *Health and safety in the workplace*

There are legal minimum health and safety requirements that have to be followed in both the office and other working areas. Health and safety legislation covers lighting, heating, space, cleanliness, ventilation, and so on to ensure people are offered a safe and comfortable place in which to work. It is in the company's interests that standards and procedures are followed in order to reduce absenteeism through poor working conditions, illness or accident.

Legal action that may be taken against an employer who fails to provide a healthy and safe place of work includes fines, closure of premises and even imprisonment for persistent offenders. However, health and safety at work is such an important aspect of the welfare of employees that most employers do not need the threat of legal punishment to provide good working conditions.

There are about 30 Acts of Parliament governing the working environment. Some of the more important ones are:

## ▶ *Health and Safety at Work Act 1974*

The **Health and Safety at Work Act 1974** (HASAWA) is an enabling Act, which means that it is designed to bring together all the previous legislation and make sense of it. However, at the moment many of these earlier Acts exist side by side with the HASAWA. The basic idea of the Act is that there should be a joint effort by employers and employees to provide a safe and healthy working environment.

The employer has to provide safe:

- equipment and systems of work
- working conditions and adequate arrangements and facilities for welfare
- use, storage, transport and handling of substances and articles
- means of access to and from work.

If an accident should occur the employer must investigate this fully and all staff should be fully informed, supervised and trained in accordance with their work role.

Employees are responsible for:

- taking care of their own safety
- safety of other people affected by their actions

**Fig 8.3 Employees are responsible for taking care of their own safety**

- cooperating with employers and any other persons involved in carrying out duties under this law.

The HASAWA includes the **Electricity at Work Regulations 1989** and the **Reporting of Injuries, Diseases and Dangerous Occurrences Regulations 1985** (RIDDOR).

### ▶ *VDU legislation*

The Health and Safety (Display Screen Equipment) Regulations 1992 affect workers who habitually use VDUs for a significant part of their normal work. Employers still have general obligations under health and safety legislation to protect other workers who use VDUs to whom this description does not apply. The regulations do not contain detailed technical information, but instead set more general objectives.

Employers have to:

- analyse workstations of employees covered by the Regulations and assess and reduce risks
- ensure workstations meet minimum requirements
- plan work so there are breaks or changes of activity
- on request arrange eye and eyesight tests, and provide spectacles if special ones are needed
- provide health and safety training
- provide information

In order to reduce any possible negative effects on health through the use of VDU-based equipment for lengthy periods of time, the Health and Safety Executive has recommended a series of guidelines for ensuring that the office environment is compatible with the introduction of new technology. Leaflet IND(G) 36(L) *Working with VDUs* is published by the Health and Safety Executive and provides useful information regarding the use of VDUs in an office environment.

The guidelines recommend that the VDU's adjustable brightness and contrast controls are used to improve the displayed image. These, together with screen filters, will reduce eye strain. VDU keyboards should be detached from the screen so that the distance between the screen and operator can be adjusted according to personal preference, and the keys themselves should have a matt surround to minimise glare and have concave tops with adjustable slope to maximise operator comfort.

**Fig 8.4 A word processor**

VDUs generate heat and this will have to be taken into account when heating an office environment to an acceptable temperature. Adequate ventilation and humidity also need to be maintained. Lighting has to be adequate for the operator to read documents but not too bright or directed so that it glares on the screen and makes it difficult to read. Undue noise is also disruptive and therefore printers and other noisy office machinery should be sited away from operators, or provided with acoustic covers.

The time spent at a VDU will depend upon the nature of the work being performed. Lengthy periods of keying in text may require rapid keyboarding but will not involve extensive concentration on the screen itself. However, if the work involves composition of text, work with spreadsheets, databases or desktop publishing this may require shorter work periods as far greater concentration on the screen is necessary.

If an organisation has no procedures in place to regularly check that health and safety laws are being met, this could be an area which requires procedures to be set up.

## ▶ Data Protection Act

If you set up or use a database which contains personal information on individuals then it must be registered with the Data Protection Registrar. The records should not be kept longer than is necessary and proper security procedures should be introduced to make sure only authorised staff have access to the information stored. The information should also be kept up to date and accurate and never be passed to anyone who may use it for other purposes, eg a list of hospital patients being passed to a medical supplies distributor to allow them to send sales material on treatments for their condition.

## ▶ Copyright law

Copyright is designed to protect the livelihood of the creators and producers of literary, dramatic, artistic and musical works. Following an EC Directive, copyright now in most cases lasts for 70 years from the death of an author and this also covers photographs and other illustrations in a book.

Single copies of copyright material may be made for private study, provided no more than a 'reasonable proportion' is copied.

304

All copyright material is denoted by the symbol © followed by the date, and can be found on videos, tapes, magazines, computer programs, etc, as well as books. Multiple copies of this material may not be made without prior permission and payment may have to be made to the publishers for a licence to copy their material. It is normal practice for officers representing the British Copyright Council to visit organisations and ensure that the copyright law is not being broken.

▶ *Other laws*

Depending on the type of business carried out by the organisation, there are other laws that may have to be taken into account when writing procedures.

- Offices, Shops and Railway Premises Act
- Employment legislation
- European legislation and rulings
- Companies Acts
- Sale of Goods Act
- Unfair Contract Terms Act
- Fair Trading Act
- Trade Descriptions Act
- Consumer Credit Act
- Employment Protection Act
- Race Relations Act
- Equal opportunities legislation
- Official Secrets Act

Privatised industries have to follow regulations defined by Government watchdogs such as OFWAT (which covers the water industry) and OFTEL (telecommunications). The British Standards Institution regulations allow organisations that agree to follow specifically agreed regulations for their particular area of work to display the BSI 'kitemark' and a BS number. There are also regulations set by specialised bodies who require companies to abide by specific requirements in order to be able to register as members. For example, travel agents are governed by ABTA (Association of British Travel Agents) regulations.

# ◄ DIY 8.1.6

You have been asked to set up procedures for the following areas of work. Explain what laws you would have to take into account when dealing with each and why.

1 Rearranging staff details on the personnel database
2 Staff interview and selection
3 Reprographic centralised service
4 Promotion and appraisal system
5 Operating new cutting and collating equipment
6 Accidents and first aid
7 Use of solvents in the office
8 Customer service facility
9 Computing workstation layout

## ▶ *Formulating benefits and costs*

When designing or changing procedures you must take into account the benefits and costs incurred by the implementation of the procedures. The introduction of expensive equipment may increase efficiency but if the cost outweighs the benefits the procedure is unlikely to be of benefit in terms of economy. This is another reason why it is important to discuss your ideas with others who will be affected by the change. Your line manager may be aware of constraints that may make your ideas unfeasible or may be able to provide advice that will help you to make your procedures more consistent and usable by other departments.

You must look at costs that involve staff, maintenance, equipment, space and storage and consumables. Also look at short- and long-term costs:

- Is it cheaper to buy the equipment outright or lease it over a period of time?
- Is it cheaper to hire a temp or employ a member of staff?
- Should you take out the maintenance contract with the supplier of the equipment or is it cheaper to go elsewhere? Is maintenance free if the machine is bought outright?
- Should you recommend the use of a transport service or the purchase and garaging of company delivery vans?
- Should consumables be ordered in bulk to save money, or will storage costs outweigh any economies made?

What may look cheapest in the short term may be the most expensive option in the long term.

Costs must be weighed against benefits to the company. Think about recommending the purchase of a highly specialist photocopier: could this mean having to employ a specialist technician to operate the machine or would it mean that one less person is now required in the reprographics department and a redundancy has to be recommended? Perhaps the answer would be to lease the photocopier and pay for the specialist training of one member of staff who could then help other staff to use the machine. There are many options available. Would you know which would be the best?

When looking at the benefits and cost of a small area of your work such as improving the filing system, for instance, it may be within your own area of responsibility to order items such as files, dividers, labels and so on. If, however, you wished to purchase a new filing cabinet, or transfer your files on to database or microfilm it is more than likely that you would need authorisation from your line manger do so this.

If you are in a position where you can prepare and monitor your own budget, perhaps for a one-off activity such as a sales promotion, then this will need to be prepared alongside your intended procedures.

First, you must estimate your costs by making a list of fixed costs such as purchase of items of equipment and variable costs such as purchase of stationery and consumable items. You would need to clarify with your line manager or sales department their specific requirements and the numbers involved. Your estimate should be as near as possible to the actual figure required.

Once your budget has been fixed, if it is up to you to monitor expenditure and keep a record of what your budget is being spent on, this can be done on a daily, weekly or monthly basis. If you think that you have under-estimated, talk to your line manager immediately rather than delay the sales promotion – upon which other departments may have already followed procedures and made ready their contribution.

# ■ DIY 8.1.7

You have been asked by your sales executive to organise a mailshot to existing customers telling them of your new discounts. There are 1,200 customer names and addresses on your database and you have designed an A5 sheet giving full details. This sheet can be folded into DL size envelopes. You will be able to produce labels using your own printer but you are unsure whether to use self-adhesive envelopes or those that have to be moistened. You need to find out which is the cheaper, bearing in mind that you will need a moistening pad and time to stick the latter. To save ordering A5 paper, you have decided to print 2 sets of details on to 1 piece of A4 paper and then cut this in half. However, you do not have access to a guillotine. You have spoken to your line manager who agrees that you could do with a guillotine in the office and that you should add the purchase to your budget.

1 Write a memo to your line manager giving an estimated budget that details fixed costs and variable costs.

2 List the tasks and activities you will follow to form a procedure to be followed for this sales promotion. Why do you think it is a good idea to do this?

## Knowledge and understanding question bank

1 What is a functional procedure?
2 What is a general procedure?
3 To whom would you refer to check on the limit of your own authority when developing procedures?
4 What methods could you use to consult others about procedures? Give 4 examples.
5 Give 4 examples of internal sources of information.
6 Give 4 examples of external sources of information.
7 How do you go about designing, specifying and developing procedures?
8 How do you go about getting approval from others?
9 Name 3 cost considerations you would take into account.
10 How do you measure the benefits of procedures?

## Claiming credit

For Element 8.1 you must prove that you have identified needs and that your designs and specifications have been developed in conjunction with users. You must show that you have agreed benefits and costs with decision makers and obtained and used specialist advice when appropriate. Procedures must conform to legal and regulatory requirements.

The following work products are potential sources of evidence:

- records of discussions
- correspondence relating to seeking advice
- internal memos
- correspondence with external sources of information
- designs of procedure
- specifications of procedures
- schedules of costs and benefits

Once you have completed your final assessment, you will need to write in your record book or folder how, when and what you have done to prove that you are competent.

The following statement is an example of how one trainee completed this claim:

*On my work placement at Coopers and Co, chartered accountants, I was asked to look into the possibility of setting up procedures for the mail department. I spoke to the mail room assistant and also to my tutor at college. My work placement was for one day per week over a period of 6 months so this in itself set my deadline for developing and monitoring the procedures once in place. I interviewed members of different departments and went to the post office to find out if they had any useful ideas or literature. I put together a file of information and designed a flow chart around this. I also had to investigate the costs of buying in additional mail room equipment and balance these costs against the benefits that the procedures would offer the company. I submitted the flow chart, schedule of costs and written procedures to my Manager who presented them at the next managers' meeting. It was agreed that the mail procedures would be put in place immediately. I was then asked to produce a set of specifications of procedure for staff to follow and to make myself available for staff to ask questions.*

# Element 8.2
# IMPLEMENT AND MAINTAIN PROCEDURES

### Performance criteria

1 Accurate, clear and comprehensive guidance is supplied to users
2 Users are provided with support to enable them to implement agreed procedures
3 Installed procedures conform to relevant legal and regulatory requirements
4 The effectiveness of procedures in meeting their purpose is assessed and evaluated
5 Opportunities for improvements are identified and appropriate action taken

### Element introduction

In Element 8.1 you should have been able to identify and decide on what procedures you are going to develop. In addition you should have carried out sufficient research, costing and negotiations with relevant personnel. This element requires you to implement the procedures, give advice and guidance to users and monitor legal and regulatory requirements. Once the procedures have been operating you will need to assess and evaluate their effectiveness and identify opportunities and action improvements to the procedures.

### Implementing procedures

The way in which you start your procedures will depend on the type of procedure you have decided to introduce; how many people it affects and the size of your organisation; how much it will cost; and the time of year.

## Type of procedure

If you have decided to change the whole procedure relating to incoming and outgoing mail this will affect nearly everyone in your organisation. You will have to ensure that you have fully thought through all the steps necessary, acquired the equipment, trained the staff, informed all the staff of the changes and expected differences and requirements, etc – all prior to the start date. On the other hand, if your chosen procedure is related solely to your own work area – for example setting up a computerised address system, reorganising the filing system, monitoring health and safety in respect of equipment, resources and your work area – you will still need to have thought everything through carefully and designed your new procedures, but errors and omissions may not have such a critical effect on the organisation.

The differences between and the effects of functional and general change will affect the method you choose for implementation.

## The number of people affected and the size of your organisation

As mentioned above, new **general** procedures that are intended to affect many people within the organisation need careful planning and may be introduced in the form of a pilot initially. A pilot is usually carried out with a minimum number of personnel, usually in a restricted part of the organisation and for a limited period of time. It allows problems, difficulties and omissions to be identified and rectified before introducing the procedure throughout the whole organisation. A pilot will also allow for **feedback** from the individuals involved. Constructive feedback from those not involved with the design or initial negotiations regarding the new procedures can be very useful and will allow you to update or modify the procedures before your major launch.

The larger the number of people involved, the more thought needs to be given to the method by which you will communicate the change in procedures, requirements and recommendations. You will certainly need written notes of guidance or information for large groups of people (and those likely to be out of the building for one reason or another). This may be in the form of a notice, memo, staff circular or note in a staff magazine, or a combination of several of the options. Verbal information may also be given to support the written instructions. This may be presented during a meeting or training session.

If your procedure will affect a smaller number of people you may decide to introduce it to everyone at the same time. In this way everyone involved will carry out the new procedures from the same time. In some areas this type of introduction is referred to as a 'total take-up'. The ways in which you inform the people affected will probably still include written and verbal communication. However the verbal information may be given informally rather than in a formal meeting or training session.

## Cost of the new procedure

If your new procedure involves the purchase or replacement of equipment then careful research should have been carried out before implementation. If possible, you should have visited other organisations (small and large) to see the procedure in practice and obtained feedback and comments from the users. If several pieces of the same equipment are necessary – for example new computers for administration staff, or new software packages on existing equipment – you may decide on a phased introduction of the procedures. This would involve one section at a time being given the new procedures (and related equipment), eg one department every 3 months. It would not be as expensive as a total take-up introduction and would also allow for diagnosis and remedy of problems, difficulties and omissions before the next phased introduction.

## Time of year

Ensure you select the timing of your introduction correctly. Your organisation will have busy and quiet times of year – peaks and troughs – and it will be preferable to introduce your new procedure during a quiet period. However, ensure you do not select a period of time during which many people are absent through holidays, annual conferences etc. Busy periods, such as the end of the financial year, or those prior to any annual meetings (eg an AGM), should be avoided if possible. Depending on your organisation you may have other busy times of year, such as Christmas, beginning of term, beginning/end of the month etc.

Ensure you find out the busy periods of the staff that will be affected by the introduction of your new procedures and take these into account before making your recommendations.

# ◾ DIY 8.2.1

Using the procedure outlined in Task 2 of DIY 8.1.7, assume you have to introduce this new procedure to all personal assistants in the following departments: purchasing, servicing, personnel, marketing and accounting. Identify the most suitable implementation procedure in relation to each department and the people affected, cost and timing. What type of implementation would you recommend and why?

## ▶ *Supplying guidance*

The guidance you supply to expected users of the new procedures must be accurate, clear and comprehensive. Accuracy is essential in written and verbal information and both forms are recommended.

### Written information and instructions

All written information and instructions should be attractive and well designed, informative but also interesting and usually written in the third person. Avoid jargon, slang and difficult language; take into account your audience and their needs. Whenever possible itemise information using numbers or letters.

If the materials are going to be used in a training session, leave space for the users to make notes of their own. Ensure you use differing sizes of print and different fonts to make the document attractive; enhance important points by emboldening, underlining or using capitals. Above all make sure that the document is error free: proof-read it several times. It should also be factually accurate; try out the procedure yourself by following your written information. Also get someone else to follow it through – preferably someone who has no knowledge of your procedures.

When you are developing your written guidance ensure that you include a reference point for queries. This may be a named member of the organisation (yourself) or a telephone extension as a 'help line'.

Include a reference or version number on the written information, then when it is updated people will know which version to throw away. Dating the information should be avoided if possible, because if updating is not necessary people may query whether 'May 1995' is the latest.

Lastly, make sure that sufficient copies are available. All relevant staff should be informed, not just those using the procedures. Relevant staff may include security, reception, line managers, personnel, union representatives, head office etc.

### Verbal information

Always write down the information you are going to give to users verbally, especially when you may be giving several verbal sessions at different times. This will ensure that you follow a logical sequence and do not forget anything. Once you have written down everything you intend to cover you may be able to reduce it to a few points or headings – just to prompt you.

Do not divert too much from your written outline and keep within the time specified. Ensure your audience know your name and how to contact you in the event of queries.

If necessary use aids such as a flip chart, overhead transparencies and demonstrations. Give examples of expected outcomes or sample products when possible. Ensure that you use simple language and invite questions at regular intervals.

Do not try to give too much information at one session; people are only able to listen and concentrate for a limited period of time (no more than 20 minutes), especially if the area of work or procedure is totally new to them.

If you intend to demonstrate the procedure, allow time for those listening to practise once you have finished and observe them. Give immediate feedback (positive before any negative, but always constructive) on their performance and resist the temptation to interfere while they are practising.

It may be necessary to set up special training sessions. If you have already covered Unit 1 of Level 3 you will have completed the necessary activities as a trainer. If you are going to carry out formal training sessions it would be advisable to complete this unit or get advice and guidance from a qualified trainer.

# ◄ DIY 8.2.2

Develop written notes and verbal guidance for organising the mailshot discussed in DIY 8.1.7. These notes should be thorough and complete, accurate and clear.

Your procedures may include the use of certain equipment, processes, consumables, stationery etc and it is important to ensure that the users have an adequate supply or access to the necessary resources. If you expect all fax messages to be sent on the new header sheet, for example, sufficient supplies must be available. If all correspondence must be typed in Sans Serif 12 cpi, this should be available on all machines.

In addition to supplying all the necessary resources and equipment, you should also be available to carry out any trouble-shooting and to deal with queries and problems that may arise through the implementation of the new procedures. Therefore do not introduce them just before going on holiday, maternity/paternity leave or off sick! You will also need to decide how long you are going to run the new procedures before carrying out an assessment and evaluation of their effectiveness. Try and make sure that the evaluation period does not occur at one of the troughs or peaks. Detailed information on the procedures for assessment and evaluation is discussed later.

# ■ DIY 8.2.3

Identify all the resources that the users will require when implementing your new procedures. How will you ensure sufficient supplies and distribution? Has this been costed in your original development?

## ▶ *Further training and support*

Once the procedures have been operating for a period of time the staff may require further assistance or support. Check on a regular basis that they are following the procedure correctly and organise training sessions if required. The number of people attending any training session should be limited to 5 if possible. This will allow all to practise the procedure and allow time for questions. Ensure you structure a training session to meet the needs of the audience. This includes catering for any special needs or those that may find change difficult.

Before starting a training session check that your resources are working, including any equipment which is part of the procedure, aids you may be using, and lights. If some of the staff attending are not familiar with your environment ensure that you cover the fire and evacuation procedures in the event of an emergency and inform them of the location of rest rooms and refreshments.

Legislation has been dealt with fully in Element 8.1 and you should have already researched the legal and regulatory requirements for your procedure. Special attention should be given to this aspect during training or within your written and verbal guidance. If demonstrating, use the proper equipment, eg an adjustable chair with a computer. Make references to the legal and regulatory requirements and ensure that the users understand the implications of not following the correct procedures.

# ■ DIY 8.2.4

Look back at Element 8.1, and in particular at DIY 8.1.6. What are the legal requirements for the procedure you have developed? State the name of the Acts, where relevant, and the action the users should take. State also the legal implications of not following the correct procedure. Check your written and verbal guidance developed in DIY 8.2.2 and ensure the legal and regulatory requirements have been included. If not, redraft your guidance. If you have to redraft keep both copies of your guidance for your portfolio.

## ▶ *Assessment and evaluation – what, how, who and when*

Your method of evaluation should have been included in your initial design and research carried out in Element 8.1. Any procedure that is going to be implemented should have aims and objectives eg reduced cost, increased productivity, reduced complaints, enhanced image etc. It is important to consider how you are going to monitor the effectiveness of your procedure before you implement it.

Once the procedure has been running and operating for a period of time, say 2 weeks, or has been carried out on, say, 4 separate occasions, you should assess the effectiveness to ensure that your aims and objectives are being met. Do not leave the assessment and evaluation too long after implementation. The assessment and evaluation is when any problems that have arisen may be ironed out or deficiencies in the process can be identified and rectified. Quite often people may believe they are carrying out the correct procedure and following the guidance received but they are missing some vital element or point. For example, some users may not recognise a particular font size or style of print easily; therefore they may believe they are using the recommended Sans Serif 12 cpi but in fact they are using something entirely different!

### Evaluation

You will need to look at the aims and objectives of your procedure before you can evaluate its effectiveness. Were your aims to reduce cost or time, enhance quality, reduce errors etc? How are you going to measure the effectiveness? If your aim was to reduce the number of photocopies being taken, thereby reducing costs, then a regular meter reading before and after your implementation will be able to evaluate its effectiveness. If your procedure was to ensure mail is delivered more quickly to staff, then a questionnaire may be suitable. Whatever procedure you have designed and implemented, you must ensure that the legal and regulatory requirements are being adhered to as part of the assessment and evaluation.

There are several methods of gathering information regarding the effectiveness of your procedures – the 'How'.

### Assessment

Among the methods of assessment are the following:

**1 Observation** – you can watch, listen and record the actions of staff. You should use a checklist of exactly what you are looking for, thereby standardising your observations of different staff. This method would be suitable for assessing telephone answering technique, reception of visitors, and other procedures which involve personal effectiveness.

**2 Sample products** – obtaining from users samples of letters, memos, photocopies, computer printouts produced, telephone message forms completed, fax headers completed, looking at filing systems. With any procedure which has an end product, the product itself can be examined for effectiveness. There may be additional questions you wish to ask the users, such as the time taken to produce the item, difficulties encountered etc. Therefore examination of a product could be used in conjunction with a questionnaire.

**3 Verbal and written feedback** – this can be obtained by using a verbal or written questionnaire. It is important to standardise the questions to ensure the users address the issues on which you are trying to get information. A questionnaire may be suitable for internal use, ie with the users of the new procedure, or external use, ie with the receivers of the new procedure (customers, visitors, clients etc).

## People involved in evaluation and assessment

If your procedure is general you may need assistance in assessment and evaluation. Identify key staff that will be able to assist in this process and inform them of the procedure you wish them to carry out. Once again written or verbal guidance may be necessary for this, or a short meeting to ensure those participating fully understand the aims and objectives of the evaluation.

You may wish to discuss the effect of your procedures with those carrying them out, eg line managers, customers and clients, or independent observers. If you are working in a large organisation then you may only be able to sample. Sampling is when you decide to obtain assessment and evaluation from only some of those involved. You may select one from each section, 4 from each department, every tenth person etc. Whichever way you decide to sample, you should ensure that your sample is a reasonable percentage of the whole.

If you are sampling products you may only look at them in the first week of the month, the first 50 produced, every tenth product etc. Staff who have had difficulties or are newly appointed may have their work sampled more frequently than others. Whoever you decide to include in your assessment and evaluation should be fully aware of your requirements, and the method selected should be deemed fair and reliable by all involved.

No matter how many people are involved, you should be responsible for the co-ordination and collection of the results and feedback. This information should be assimilated and passed on to the appropriate people, once you have identified and recommended any necessary actions.

## The timing of evaluation and assessment

In the same way that you have to decide on the best time for implementation you should also carefully consider the time for assessment and evaluation. The procedures should have run for a long enough period of time for staff to become familiar with them, but not too long. Ideally this period should have covered both busy and quiet periods of time.

You will also need to decide on the frequency of your assessment and evaluation: will you monitor effectiveness daily initially, or weekly, or monthly? The frequency should be related to the type of procedure. When procedures are carried out frequently – such as answering the telephone, greeting clients, photocopying, dealing with the post – the assessment should be frequent, perhaps even more than once a day. When the procedure is infrequent – such as a mailshot to 2,000 customers, monthly billing, maintenance of equipment – the assessments will be fewer and will take place over a longer period of time.

## ◗ DIY 8.2.5

Decide on the 'what, how, who and when' of your assessment and evaluation. Design any questionnaires or checklists that are to be used. Decide on who will be involved and the timing of the assessment and evaluation. For each decision you make state why and how you came to that particular decision – ie justify your actions.

## ▶ *Identifying improvements and action*

Once you have gathered all the assessment and evaluation information you will be in a position to identify any deficiencies that may have occurred and improvements that could enhance the procedure. Collate the information carefully and present your findings in a memo or report to those involved in the initial agreement and authorisation of the procedure. In addition you should supply some feedback to those involved in the assessment and evaluation; they will want to know the results.

Your report should provide a factual account of the effect of the procedure measured against the initial aims and objectives; it should have a conclusion and should recommend appropriate action. If your aims and objectives are not being met, why not? Your evaluation may have identified appropriate action such as that further staff training/updating is required, that the procedures need redrafting from scratch or just part of the procedure needs redrafting, that a rewrite of your written guidance materials is necessary, that the procedures are extremely effective and should be introduced on a wider basis, etc.

If you have insufficient information to make any observations, recommendations or improvements it could be that your assessment and evaluation needs to be reconsidered. You may need to ask more people – increase your sample; observe more frequently.

Whatever the appropriate action required, ensure that you consider the implications and costs before discussing with your line manager and updating and passing on information to the users.

# ■ DIY 8.2.6

You have implemented procedures in the typing pool with the aim of changing from a system of typing from handwritten material to one of typing from audio-taped material. The original problem was that the typists could not read the handwriting of several of the managers. You have carried out an evaluation with the typists (8) and the managers (4) involved. The problems identified after your trial period of one month are as follows.

1 The typists are much happier, but some find that the managers change their minds in the middle of dictation, and cannot really dictate properly (one in particular has been named).
2 Some managers are still sending long letters and reports that are handwritten.
3 Some find Mr McLaughton's accent difficult to understand.
4 One manager has not yet received the audio equipment necessary.
5 One manager does not like using it very much.
6 All managers have found the spelling and grammar errors made by the typists have increased.

Identify the problems arising and list proposals of steps that could be taken to rectify these.

### Knowledge and understanding question bank

1 How does the type of procedure affect the implementation?
2 What methods are there of implementing procedures?
3 What methods are there of supplying guidance to users?
4 What methods of support can be given to users?
5 What methods of assessment and evaluation are there?
6 Which legal and regulatory requirements may relate to the implementation of procedures?

**7** How do you ensure that guidance supplied is accurate, clear and comprehensive?

**8** How can effectiveness be measured?

**9** How do you identify opportunities for improvements in procedures?

**10** What appropriate action may be taken to improve procedures?

## Claiming credit

For Element 8.2 you must show that you have provided accurate, clear and comprehensive guidance to users, together with support to enable them to implement agreed procedures. Evidence must show that you have assessed, evaluated and made recommendations for improvements in procedures and as a consequence taken appropriate action. Procedures must conform to legal and regulatory requirements.

The following work products are potential sources of evidence:

- internal memos
- copies of guidance material
- implementation plans
- monitoring documentation
- records of discussions

Once you have completed your final assessment, you will need to write in your record book or folder how, when and what you have done to prove that you are competent.

The following statement is an example of how one trainee completed this claim:

*When implementing my mail procedures at Cooper and Co, chartered accountants, I was asked by my Manager to produce a set of guidelines that staff could follow in order to implement the new procedures correctly. I did this by designing an attractive 'help manual' that contained flow charts and written details on the procedures to be followed. I also included my extension number so that staff could contact me if they needed to. I made sure that all the procedures were being carried out in light of legal and regulatory requirements such as health and safety – where machinery was being used. Dealing with confidentiality and data protection were also written in to the procedures. I monitored the success of the procedures by sending a questionnaire to all staff involved with the new procedures. I evaluated the results of the questionnaire and made some adjustments to the procedures, ie the times for receiving and delivering mail in the afternoon. I ensured that personal contact was maintained with the staff so that I could monitor how successful the procedures were in practice and report this back to my Manager.*

# UNIT 9

# Obtain, organise and monitor the use of materials and equipment

## ■ Element 9.1
## OBTAIN AND ORGANISE MATERIALS AND EQUIPMENT

### Performance criteria

1 The need for materials and equipment, to meet current and anticipated work loads, is identified

2 Obtained materials and equipment meet current and anticipated work loads

3 Materials and equipment are obtained at appropriate times and in quantities relevant to available space, work requirements and financial constraints

4 Materials and equipment are obtained in accordance with organisational procedures and within limits of own authority

5 Materials and equipment are safely located to facilitate access and maintain workflows

6 Arrangements for the maintenance of equipment are in accordance with organisational procedures

### Element introduction

The main object of keeping an efficient office supplies system is to ensure that there is always a constant supply of the necessary materials and equipment for the office or business to run effectively. Any system should also be cost effective: it should not take too much time to operate; it should be easily understood and secure; it should not allow too much money to be tied up; and it should make good use of available space. Organisations use the term 'stock' when referring to the materials and equipment they require in order to operate the business. The type of stock kept will depend on the type of business.

# ▶ *Types of stock*

The terms 'stock take', 'out of stock', 'summer stock' etc are probably all familiar to you. The term 'stock' has the same general meaning whether in a large organisation or a small office.

In your college and/or workplace you will find different kinds of stock which is usually kept in the 'stock room', 'store room' or 'stores'. The stock is kept in one place to protect it and to make sure it is ready to be taken out when required. Stock is worth money to the organisation and in the company accounts would be shown in the 'credits' section. For this reason, it is imperative that the system of storage and control in use is secure.

Stock that is held by any organisation will fall into one of 5 categories:

## Raw materials

Raw materials are held ready for use in the manufacture of goods. Sufficient stock of raw materials and components must be held for a regular supply to the Production Department. If the supply fails, production would be halted and the order deadlines missed. An example of a raw material would be cotton cloth used by a clothes manufacturer.

## Consumables

Consumables are supplies that are necessary for the smooth running of the organisation, which are used in the day-to-day running of the business. They are not usually profit-making in themselves, but are used rapidly so there must always be a reserve in stock. Examples of consumables would be typewriter ribbons, stationery in an office and paper serviettes in a restaurant.

## Finished goods

Finished goods are the goods that have been manufactured by the business and are awaiting orders from customers. The business will want to sell this stock as quickly as possible to make a profit, in order to buy more raw materials and make more finished goods. The business should always keep in stock regular lines which sell quickly, so that delivery can be made immediately upon receipt of an order – this is called ex-stock. Examples of finished goods are cars, bikes and furniture.

## Goods for resale

Retail shops and wholesale warehouses purchase a variety of stock which they display and sell at a higher price – to make their profit. These outlets usually offer a wide range of stock from which customers choose as and when they require it. Examples of resale stock would be clothing, food and drink, and electrical equipment.

### Spare parts

Spare parts are required so that they are readily available in the event of breakdown in machinery, vehicles, plant, etc. Examples of spare parts would be printer collector units, control panels, switches and motors.

# ■ DIY 9.1.1

What type of materials and equipment are most likely to be used in an average size office? Copy the table in Fig 9.1 on to a piece of A4 paper. Complete the list by detailing the equipment and materials in general use in your workplace or training centre.

| Types of equipment and materials in the workplace or training centre ||
|---|---|
| Equipment | Materials |
| | |
| | |

**Fig 9.1 Form for use with DIY 9.1.1**

▶ *Ordering stock*

The stock used in your organisation will be purchased from suppliers. There may be agreed suppliers for different types of stock but if the item required is costly the organisation may send out an initial **enquiry**, to perhaps 3 or 4 suppliers to find out which can offer the best deal. In return the suppliers will send a **quotation** detailing the goods required, price and discounts offered, delivery date and any guarantees. They may also send price lists and catalogues of other goods or arrange for a sales representative to call.

Once a supplier has been selected an **order** will be sent. The supplier may send an **acknowledgement** to confirm the order has been received. Once the order is ready to send an **advice note** will be sent by the supplier which will give the delivery details – the date, and how it will be transported, post, rail, carrier, own van, etc. When the goods arrive a **delivery note** will accompany them. The goods should be checked against the delivery note and, if correct, it should be signed. One copy of the delivery note will be retained and the other given back to the person delivering the goods. Any discrepancies must be noted at this stage; otherwise, once the goods have been signed for, the business will be charged for the goods detailed on the delivery note.

When the signed delivery note is returned to the suppliers, they will produce an **invoice** which will give full details of the goods supplied with a breakdown of costs, including **VAT** and discounts. If your organisation uses the supplier only occasionally then you will pay on receipt of the invoice; if it is a supplier used several times a month, then you will wait until the **statement of account** is received, usually at the end of the month.

The statement gives details of all the invoices, credit notes and debit notes sent during the month, and has a total figure due. The statement of account is checked back against the invoices received for the month, which will in turn have been checked against the delivery notes received with each delivery. If the statement of account is authorised for payment, your accounts department will write one cheque for all the goods received from the supplier during the month.

Credit notes are used when goods have been received damaged or have been returned. Debit notes are used when more items have been received than were ordered, and you have decided to keep them, or goods of a higher quality than you ordered have been sent in their place.

This whole process is used when an organisation is first looking for a supplier of a particular range of goods. Once contact has been established and a suitable supplier found you are likely to place regular orders with the supplier by using an authorised order form or account number. Regular suppliers will also accept telephone and fax orders for items required in an emergency. However, if a supplier fails to supply items required or is continually late in delivering, alternative sources should be sought. Likewise, you should remember that in a competitive world a good business system will always be on the lookout for alternative sources that are able to supply the same quality for a lower price.

# ■ DIY 9.1.2

Complete the flow chart in Fig 9.2. Explain why each document is used and the information it contains.

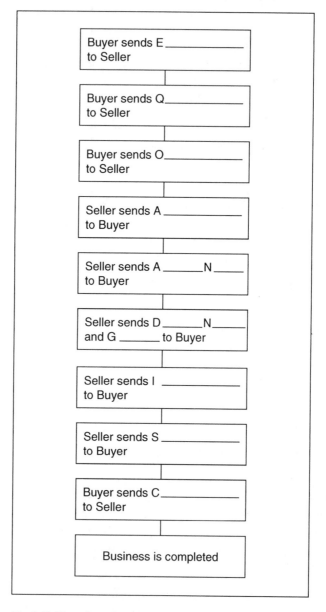

Buyer sends E_____ to Seller

Buyer sends Q_____ to Seller

Buyer sends O_____ to Seller

Seller sends A _____ to Buyer

Seller sends A _____N_____ to Buyer

Seller sends D_____N_____ and G _____ to Buyer

Seller sends I _____ to Buyer

Seller sends S_____ to Buyer

Buyer sends C_____ to Seller

Business is completed

**Fig 9.2 Flowchart for ordering stock (DIY 9.1.2)**

# ▶ *Checking deliveries*

It is usual practice to check deliveries against the initial order, to ensure that the correct goods and quantities are being delivered. The delivery note (complete with corrections if there are any) will then be checked against the invoice sent to your company to make sure the correct amount has been charged.

If at any stage a mistake is identified, this must be reported to a line manager immediately. It may be that incorrect goods have been delivered, which will need to be returned, or that your organisation has been charged for goods that it has not received. In both cases it may be your responsibility to find these errors and mark them on the delivery note before signing it. Remember that the delivery company uses the delivery note as a receipt of goods delivered and will, therefore, work out your company's final invoice on these details.

It is not sufficient to just check the delivery note; the goods themselves must be unpacked, counted and checked carefully. There are a number of reasons for the delivery note to be different from the actual order.

**1 Missing goods** – Goods may have been out of stock when ordered or may simply have been forgotten. If goods are out of stock, they are usually marked 'to follow' on the delivery note. Sometimes a company will substitute an alternative, but this does not have to be accepted and can be sent back.

**2 Additional goods** – If goods are received that have not been ordered, they should be sent back to the supplier. If the goods are detailed on the delivery note they should be crossed off, otherwise your company will be asked to pay for something they did not want.

**3 Incorrect goods** – Sometimes the wrong items will be received; these too should be returned immediately and crossed off the delivery note. A quick follow-up order will be needed because of the delay caused.

**4 Items ordered incorrectly** – The supplier has no obligation to take goods you have ordered incorrectly back! However, depending upon the relationship your organisation has with the supplier it may be acceptable to return incorrectly ordered items.

**5 Damaged or faulty goods** – Items should be checked immediately and if damaged or faulty returned to the supplier. Such items should be crossed off the delivery note. The supplier will exchange the item(s) with little difficulty if notified immediately. If they are not notified until some time later this can cause problems. Records of faulty goods should be kept so that receipt of the exchange item can be monitored.

# ■ DIY 9.1.3

Check the following order forms (Figs 9.3 and 9.4) against their respective delivery notes (Figs 9.5 and 9.6). Make a list of any errors you find. Write a memo to your line manager giving itemised details of your check. What would you do if you received faulty goods in one of the deliveries?

---

### PEMBROOKE MARKETING SERVICES LTD

115-119 Cavendish Square, Bridport, BR4 9PQ

ORDER NUMBER: 123890                    Date: 12.9.— —

Please supply the items listed below:

| QTY | DESCRIPTION | CAT NO | UNIT PRICE | TOTAL PRICE |
|-----|-------------|--------|------------|-------------|
| 12 | HB12 Pencils | 16354 | | 10.69 |
| 4 | Markers (red) | 11987 | 0.60 | 2.40 |
| 4 | Markers (green) | 11988 | 0.60 | 2.40 |
| 4 | Markers (yellow) | 11989 | 0.60 | 2.40 |
| 10 | Reams A4 Bond (white) | 20675 | 4.15 | 41.50 |
| 2 | Reams A4 Bank (yellow) | 20667 | 4.10 | 8.20 |
| | | | TOTAL | 67.59 |
| | Authorised by | | | |
| | . . . . . . . . . . . . . . . . . . . | | | |

**Fig 9.3  Order form 1 for use with DIY 9.1.3**

---

### PEMBROOKE MARKETING SERVICES LTD

115-119 Cavendish Square, Bridport, BR4 9PQ

ORDER NUMBER: 123892                    Date: 15.10.— —

Please supply the items listed below:

| QTY | DESCRIPTION | CAT NO | UNIT PRICE | TOTAL PRICE |
|-----|-------------|--------|------------|-------------|
| 12 | HB14 Pencils | 19875 | | 10.69 |
| 2 | Staplers | 35627 | 5.95 | 11.90 |
| 5 | Sticky tape | 36728 | 98 | 4.90 |
| 24 | Correction Fluid | 09758 | 1.54 | 39.96 |
| 7 | Staple removers | 67301 | 1.37 | 9.59 |
| | | | TOTAL | 77.04 |
| | AUTHORISED BY | | | |
| | . . . . . . . . . . . . . . . . . . . | | | |

**Fig 9.4  Order form 2 for use with DIY 9.1.3**

## THE STATIONERY COMPANY LTD

97 Fontmell Street
Bridport Dorset

DATE: 20 September 199--
ORDER NO: 123890          DELIVERY NOTE NO: 1675

DELIVERY ADDRESS: Pembrooke Marketing Services
                  115-119 Cavendish Street Bridport

| QTY | DESCRIPTION OF GOODS | CATALOGUE NUMBER | TOTAL |
|-----|----------------------|------------------|-------|
| 12  | PENCILS HB12         | 16354            | 10.69 |
| 4   | RED MARKERS          | 11987            | 2.40  |
| 4   | YELLOW MARKERS       | 11989            | 2.40  |
| 5   | BLUE MARKERS         | 11986            | 3.00  |
| 10  | A4 BANK WHITE        | 10675            | 31.50 |
| 20  | A4 BANK YELLOW       | 20667            | 82.00 |

Please mark errors or damaged goods before signing

. . . . . . . . . . . . . . . . . . . . . .

Do not pay until you have received our official invoice.

**Fig 9.5 Delivery note 1 for use with DIY 9.1.3**

## THE STATIONERY COMPANY LTD

97 Fontmell Street
Bridport Dorset

DATE: 27 September 199--
ORDER NO: 123892          DELIVERY NOTE NO: 1897

DELIVERY ADDRESS: Pembrooke Marketing Services
                  115-119 Cavendish Street Bridport

| QTY | DESCRIPTION OF GOODS | CATALOGUE NUMBER | TOTAL |
|-----|----------------------|------------------|-------|
| 12  | HB12 PENCILS         | 16354            | 10.69 |
| 5   | STAPLERS             | 35627            | 29.75 |
| 5   | STICKY TAPE          | 36728            | 5.90  |
| 24  | STAPLE REMOVERS      | 67301            | 32.88 |
| 7   | CORRECTION FLUID     | 09758            | 10.78 |

Please mark errors or damaged goods before signing

. . . . . . . . . . . . . . . . . . . . . .

Do not pay until you have received our official invoice.

**Fig 9.6 Delivery note 2 for use with DIY 9.1.3**

## ▶ *Stationery packs*

Companies often use stationery packs which contain all the relevant documents for one order. Each document either is made from NCR (no carbon required) paper, or will have carbon paper placed between the sheets. When the delivery order details are typed or written on to the top sheet they are automatically copied on to the other sheets – delivery note, stores requisition, accounts advice, invoice, and so on. This saves time, as the documents do not have to be prepared separately. Sections of information that are not needed on certain forms can be blanked out. For example, it is usual practice not to have price details on the delivery note.

## ▶ *Supplying stock*

It is essential to have a reservoir of all the items required for the business to operate efficiently. Delays in the supply of items required in manufacturing will cause hold-ups in production and possible loss of profits. If office consumables and stationery run out the administrative support of the business would fail. Imagine the problems that would occur if the photocopier paper ran out or the last typewriter ribbon was used. It is also cheaper to buy goods in bulk as advantage can be taken of the higher discounts given. However, care must be taken not to over order and use capital (money) that may be required in other areas.

The need for stock to meet current and anticipated work loads must be identified and stock obtained to meet these needs. The stock must be obtained before its need becomes an emergency, in quantities relevant to work requirements, but taking financial and available space constraints into account.

## ▶ *Quantities of stock*

When ordering stock you must decide upon the quantity required to address the need. Remember you need to get this just right so that money is not tied up in stock, but ensuring that there is sufficient stock to run the organisation efficiently. The quantities you order will vary according to the type and size of business.

You should consider:

**1 Money** – as mentioned above, stock is worth money and it is unwise for a business to have too much money tied up in stock. Some stock may be perishable and have a limited 'shelf life'. Examples are fashionable clothing, fruit and vegetables, and even paper which becomes yellow in time.

**2 Time** – it may be difficult to obtain stock quickly and valuable orders may be lost to other businesses which are able to deliver goods on the date required. You will find that to prevent this situation arising most businesses will carry sufficient quantities of stock to ensure that when orders are received they can be fulfilled immediately. It is important that delivery time is taken into consideration and that suppliers are reliable.

**3 Space** – storage space is expensive; it uses valuable space in areas which must be maintained with heating and lighting, protected and secured. Staff are employed to take charge of stock and insurance must be paid to provide cover in the event of damage or theft. The business will anticipate the maximum amount of each item of stock that should be kept at any one time to reduce the costs of storage.

**4 Sales** – it will also be necessary to anticipate the quantity of stores, spares and raw materials required to keep the business operational. While it is important not to carry too much stock, it is more important to ensure that there is enough stock available to prevent the business coming to a halt. Seasonal variations must also be taken into account; it would be unwise for a shop to stock up with Christmas cake at Easter as the stock would be unlikely to move until nearer Christmas.

**5 Usage** – in an office you would find yourself needing typewriter ribbons, correction tapes, paper, envelopes, etc on a regular basis. It is a good idea to keep a check on how much stock is used in an average week. You will then be able to calculate when the regular orders need to be made.

## ▶ *Pareto analysis*

The level of stock that needs to be held depends very much on the work carried out by the organisation or department. There will always be standard items such as paper, envelopes, filing materials, office sundries (such as paper clips, staples and correction fluid) that are needed on a regular basis.

You can categorise these items into those needed for everyday use, where a high turnover is expected, and those required infrequently. You can assess the need for items according to a technique called Pareto analysis, or the 80/20 rule.

The 80/20 rule works on the basis that 20 per cent of the items are used 80 per cent of the time. If you can identify the 20 per cent and give them special attention you will automatically be providing stock for 80 per cent of the time. The remaining 80 per cent of stock can be virtually ignored, and ordered on a 'needs-must' basis as they are unlikely to affect the efficiency and effectiveness of the organisation or the office.

To help you understand this analysis look at your own lifestyle:

- It is likely that you wear 20 per cent of the clothes, shoes and underwear in your wardrobe 80 per cent of the time.

Now look at your working time:

- It is likely that 20 per cent of the tasks detailed in your job description take up 80 per cent of your working day.
- It has also been said that 80 per cent of the world's wealth is held by 20 per cent of the population!

It is worth considering the type of materials and equipment used most in your working environment. If you can do this and make a list of the 20 per cent most widely used items of stock, it is likely that you will achieve efficiency and effectiveness without keeping a storeroom of 'just in case' items.

The Pareto analysis is a very useful technique used to identify items used frequently; but how do you go about ordering the exact quantity to ensure efficiency? The following formulae are often used to estimate the minimum, maximum and reorder levels for stock.

- **Minimum** = the lowest amount possible, without risking running out completely.
- **Maximum** = the greatest amount possible, taking into account storage space and cash available.
- **Reorder level** = the amount when an order should be placed. This should be the minimum level plus the amount used on a daily basis before delivery of the item is received.
- The amount required to keep the business operational until delivery of the order is called the **buffer stock**.

An example would be:

- Minimum level is 10 packets, and you use 1 packet each day. Delivery from the supplier will take 2 weeks. Therefore, your reorder level will be 20 (10 minimum + 1 per working day for 2 weeks awaiting delivery = 20). This will ensure you do not run out before the delivery is received.

When you order it would normally be an order large enough to take you back up to the maximum level. However, if you find you are ordering a particular item more frequently it may be necessary to change your maximum level. Changes occur in usage for many reasons and one of your responsibilities will be to recognise when such changes are occurring and respond to them accordingly.

It is unwise, however, to order items in large quantities because they are on 'special offer'; they still cost money and expensive storage could nullify any economy intended. The only occasions when this action may be warranted is if a known price increase is on its way and the business wishes to buy in stock at the cheaper price.

## ■ DIY 9.1.4

In your office you use 1 ream of A4 paper per day. You only have a small stationery stock cupboard and can keep 2 months' supply at maximum, and a safe minimum level is 2 weeks. It takes 1 week for your supplier to deliver. From this work out the minimum, maximum and reorder levels. Assume a 5-day week and 30-day month. How will you be able to use these figures to identify the need for stock to meet current and anticipated work loads?

## ▶ *Storage of stock*

We have already stated how valuable stock is and that as an asset to the business it is important that it is kept in perfect condition. The type of storage will depend upon the kind of stock and the size of organisation. Large organisations will have a stock room with staff employed purely to take charge of the stock. A small organisation may only have a stock cupboard with one person in charge of the key.

Every item of stock must be stored neatly and be easily accessible when required. Shelves should be labelled so that it is easy to find what is needed, and the stock room or cupboard should always be locked. It is important that the storage area is kept dry at all times to prevent paper-based items from becoming damp and going mouldy. Large or heavy items should be kept low and when new stock arrives it should be placed at the back or at the bottom so that the older stock is used first.

It is important that you treat hazardous stock with care. Any liquids that are dangerous or inflammable, for example thinners, glue or duplicating fluid, must be kept in a separate area and you must never smoke in this area or in the stock room itself. If you anticipate any problems, or problems arise with storing certain stock items, this should be reported to your line manager or the Health and Safety representative immediately. Likewise if damage occurs to any stock while it is being stored this should be reported; it may still be under guarantee and the supplier could arrange for exchange or repair, or alternatively the business may be able to make an insurance claim.

# ■ DIY 9.1.5

You are in charge of the general office stock and have decided that it could be better organised to improve safety and accessibility. Using the list you compiled in DIY 9.1.1, explain why you would keep each item of material and equipment in a particular location.

## ▶ *Arranging maintenance of equipment*

Office equipment will need to be serviced and maintained regularly if it is to operate efficiently. Service contracts may be set up with a company which, for a fee, will provide a maintenance service for a period of time (usually 1 year). If the service given is of the required standard, the contract will be renewed.

The agreement made will depend upon the needs of the company. Some equipment may require regular servicing; some will only need attention when something has gone wrong. The agreement made will depend upon the type of equipment and whether the organisation prefers preventative action or remedial action. Maintenance records must be kept to ensure that the company gets its agreed number of visits or is not charged for more visits than have actually taken place.

When new equipment is bought it is likely that a guarantee or warranty will be issued with it. If the equipment breaks down, free repair and parts should be available under the warranty, which may also provide a number of free maintenance or service visits during a set period of time. This information must be recorded and checked to ensure the organisation is not paying for a service or repair which is covered under the warranty or guarantee agreement.

It is also useful to keep maintenance and repair records in order to identify equipment that is constantly in need of repair. If more repairs are necessary than expected it may need replacing, or if it is relatively new it may need to be returned to the supplier.

# ■ DIY 9.1.6

Find out how the equipment used in your workplace or training centre is maintained. Find out if it is maintained under contract and explain how this system works.

# ▶ *Disposal of stock*

Once a year, or more often in some organisations, an audit is carried out to count all stock. This means that the stock can be given a value which is shown on the organisation's accounts. The audit calculates how much stock has been used during the year and details any adjustments that have to be made if stock has been disposed of. The audit will also identify if there has been any pilfering.

Stock may be unusable if it has been damaged (eg through water leakage) or has become obsolete. Before any stock is disposed of, it should be examined to see if it is still fit for use. Obsolete stock may be given an alternative use, eg forms made into scrap or message pads. In some cases stock may be resaleable to the staff or perhaps other organisations, eg typewriters sold on because they are being replaced by computers.

Records of the disposal of stock must be kept in order to make adjustments on the audit. By this means the organisation can calculate how much it has spent on stock in relation to the budget allowance it has allocated. Any income from selling obsolete stock is set against this expenditure to calculate the final cost.

## Knowledge and understanding question bank

**1** What is the scope and limitation of your own authority for obtaining items?
**2** What organisational procedure do you follow when obtaining items?
**3** How do you estimate requirements for items?
**4** How do you site items for safe access?
**5** How do you site items to maintain work flows?
**6** What organisational procedures do you follow for the maintenance of equipment?
**7** What organisational procedures do you follow for recording the obtaining of items?
**8** What documents do you use when obtaining items?
**9** What documents do you use when arranging maintenance of items?
**10** How do you ensure that you operate within financial limits?

## Claiming credit

For Element 9.1 you must prove that you have identified the need for and obtained materials and equipment to meet current and anticipated work loads for yourself and others. The material and equipment must be obtained at appropriate times and in quantities relevant to space, work requirements and financial constraints. You must follow organisational procedures within the limits of your own authority, locate materials safely to facilitate access and maintain workflow, and arrange for maintenance of equipment. The following work products are potential sources of evidence:

- documentation relating to obtaining materials and equipment
- financial statements
- records of faulty goods
- records of disposal of items
- maintenance records
- internal memoranda

Once you have completed your final assessment, you will need to write in your record book or folder how, when and what you have done to prove that you are competent.

The following statement is an example of how one trainee completed this claim:

*As the administration assistant for Coopers & Co Accountants it is my responsibility to ensure that materials and equipment needed to meet current and anticipated work loads are obtained and organised efficiently and effectively. I carry out a monthly check on the stationery store room, or ask one of the office juniors to do this for me, and then prepare an official order form ready for signature by the chief accountant. If items of equipment are required, I complete a purchase requisition form and request 3 separate quotes from suppliers before passing this to the chief accountant. At the end of each week the office juniors check the stationery requirements of the staff and partners and complete stationery requisition forms on their behalf. The stationery store is kept safe and secure and only accessed by authorised personnel. I arrange maintenance of equipment either through the lease agreement or by contacting the supplier to request a visit from their engineer. I keep a fault/repair/service log so that I can monitor how often a piece of equipment has been serviced or repaired. I attend a weekly team meeting with the partners where current and anticipated workflow is discussed so that I can plan ahead the ordering of materials and equipment.*

# ■ Element 9.2
# MONITOR THE USE OF MATERIALS
# AND EQUIPMENT

### Performance criteria

1 The receipt, use and cost of materials and equipment are monitored in accordance with organisational procedures

2 Where the need for materials and equipment exceeds financial allocations, appropriate persons are informed promptly and accurately

3 Records of the use of materials and equipment are complete, accurate and legible, and in required format and within timescales

**4** The disposal of faulty and excess materials and equipment is in accordance with organisational procedures

## Element introduction

Obtaining, organising and monitoring the use of equipment and materials require different levels of responsibility in different organisations. You are likely to find that the number of tasks for which you are responsible are greater in a small organisation than in a large one. A large organisation is likely to set up a centralised division to store, maintain and control the majority of the stock, whereas a small organisation will identify one person to be responsible for ordering, monitoring and maintaining supplies.

It is important that a system is set up and followed that covers not only the ordering and storage procedures for stock but also keeps comparative notes on suppliers, monitors usage and checks costings and valuation of stock for auditing purposes. Small offices do not often operate any system; consumable items are ordered on a 'needs-must' basis, and are stored randomly where there is space; staff help themselves and operate on a first-come, first-served basis. Do you think this is effective and efficient? How do you think the accountant completes an audit? Do you think the office could run out of materials and equipment?

Stock is very important and has a close relationship with the office accounts. Stock represents an expense and must be shown as such on the company's accounts. The only way this can be achieved competently is to keep records that document the use of materials and equipment.

**Fig 9.7 A badly-organised stockroom**

## ▶ *Cost control*

All organisations need to make profit in order to survive. In order to do this the organisation must monitor its costs very carefully, from raw materials to manufactured goods, taking into account the cost of equipment, materials and consumables that make no profit in themselves but are essential for the organisation to function.

The organisation looks at the selling price of an item, deducts the cost price of the same item and then multiplies this figure by the amount that have been sold. The total gives the **gross profit** the organisation has left. It is now time to work out the expenses incurred in running the organisation, such as:

- wage bill
- electricity bill
- rent
- telephone/fax bill
- business rates
- travelling expenses
- maintenance
- depreciation
- expenditure on equipment
- expenditure on materials

The higher the expenses the lower the **net profit**. It is only by keeping tight control on the expenses that the net profit can be increased. An efficient stock system is one way of helping the organisation's profitability. Therefore, even in an area such as stock control, an efficient system is one way of making a direct contribution to the organisation's profitability by your actions.

There are 3 ways of costing stock (consumables):

**1** AVCO – Average cost system. AVCO means that the cost of stock is averaged out over a given period of time, eg one year. When a company is involved in buying stock over a period of time it is obvious that the price for the stock will fluctuate. When it is necessary to know the value of the stock this system works out an average across the period of time.

**2** FIFO – First in first out. FIFO means the value of the stock is costed and used in relation to when it was received.

**3** LIFO – Last in first out. LIFO is another method used for costing, but not for consumables.

The following example may help you to understand these terms more clearly:

1 An organisation receives a delivery of 100 reams of paper twice a year. The first delivery cost £600; the second cost £700.

2 The organisation also purchases two identical photocopiers. The first one cost £2,500 and the second (bought later in the year) £3,000.

At the end-of-year audit there are 50 reams of paper left and the 2 photocopiers.

**FIFO** will assume that the first delivery of paper (the cheaper) was used first, so the 50 remaining reams will therefore be valued at the higher price (£700). The photocopiers are not consumables in the same way as paper and would therefore retain their value (less depreciation) unless written off. If one of the photocopiers was damaged and written off it would be valued at £2500 as it would be assumed that the first photocopier in would be the first one out.

**AVCO** – The paper stock for the whole year would be combined and valued at £1,300 (divided by 200 gives a value of £6.50 per ream). The 50 remaining reams would therefore be valued at (50 x £6.50) £300. The damaged photocopier would be written off with a value of £2,750 as the purchase prices of both photocopiers would have been added together and then divided by 2 to give the average.

**LIFO** – Last in first out is another costing method, but as already mentioned, it is not used for consumables. However, it could be used as a method by which the value of the photocopiers can be calculated. If this method was used, the value would be £3,000 as it would be assumed that the last photocopier in was the first out.

It is wise at this stage to look at the type of mistakes, that cost money, which can be made if an efficient stock system is not in place:

- stock may be pilfered and misused by staff
- stock may be stolen by thieves or visitors
- too much stock may be held, reducing the capital available to run the organisation
- more stock is ordered than necessary because staff cannot find what they want in a poorly-organised storage system
- incorrect invoices are paid
- payment of invoices does not take advantage of discounts (cash discounts)
- no advantages is taken of trade discounts
- obsolete stock is not written off correctly

**Fig 9.8 What has happened in the stockroom?**

- stock deteriorates through poor storage or storage for long periods
- stock is ordered in error through lack of control across offices/departments
- no advantage is being taken of bulk buying
- deliveries are not checked correctly, so that damaged and/or faulty items are accepted and paid for

All of the above will add to the expenses of the organisation and reduce profit margins.

# ■ DIY 9.2.1

Imagine that you are working in a small office that has no system for monitoring the receipt and cost of materials and equipment. List the types of problems you are likely to encounter. What are the financial implications? Write a memo to the office manager giving details of your findings and explain the difference in the terms FIFO, LIFO and AVCO.

## ▶ *Organising a stock control system*

Organisation of the system may be carried out at management level in a large company, perhaps after requesting a report from the office manager detailing requirements and making recommendations. In a smaller organisation it may be your responsibility to identify what is wrong and

338

set up a procedure to put it right, with the authority of your line manager. However, it is important that, whatever system is in use, it should be used by all concerned and operate as a whole.

When setting up a system the following points need to be considered:

- What items are to be classified as stock?
- What items are to be held in stock?
- What items are to be bought in on a 'needs-must' basis?
- What are the maximum and minimum quantities for each item?
- What is the budgeted allowance for stock?
- What storage space is available?
- What is the projected usage for each item?
- What are the lead times for supplying orders?
- Is a manual or computerised system to be used?
- How often will an audit be necessary?
- What procedure will be employed?
- What contingency plans are needed for emergencies?
- How often should the system be reviewed and updated?

The first thing to do is to categorise items into those relating to everyday needs, where a high level of turnover and demand is expected, and those needed on a less frequent basis. Divide your list into highly active, less active and non-active items. You will need to take into account seasonal fluctuations and forthcoming sales promotions.

Non-active items do not have to be kept in stock, but you must be aware of the lead time (the time it takes from placing your order to the delivery of the item) so that they can be ordered in time for when they are needed. This is often referred to as a 'JIT' system (just in time). This system reduces the capital tied up in stock and the amount of storage required.

A buffer stock must be calculated for all other items. The buffer stock level will depend upon the time it takes for the delivery of the item, eg letterheaded paper will need to be printed prior to despatch to your organisation whereas plain paper will be taken straight from the shelf; therefore a larger buffer stock would be needed for headed paper due to the time it takes to receive a delivery.

Each item on your list will need a maximum and minimum level. The minimum indicates the lowest possible amount you will always need to keep in stock. The maximum indicates what you consider should be held in stock given the constraints of space and budget allocation. It is unlikely that you will wait for the stock to reach its minimum level before you place an order. This is because you have to allow for delays in the delivery of the order and the fact that while the order is being processed staff will continue to use supplies. The information you have compiled can be used to set up a stock control card system which can be used either manually or on a computer system and which monitors the use of stock across offices, departments and the organisation itself.

## Stock card system

Small businesses may use a 'visual' system of stock control, in other words, stock is ordered when a need is seen. Larger businesses use a 'bin' system where all stock is given a bin number which identifies the position it can be located in the stock room. Many organisations will use stock cards as a system of keeping a record of the stock in hand and the issues and receipts made.

A stock card should be made up for each item held. It will show details of the supplier used, the minimum, maximum and reorder levels used. The date of receipts and issues made, who received the item and the current stock level will also be detailed. You are then able to see at a glance when items need reordering.

**STATIONERY STOCK CARD**

| | | |
|---|---|---|
| Item A4 Bond Paper ① | Maximum level 50 ⑤ | Bin No 100 |
| | Minimum level 10 ⑥ | |
| Unit Ream | Reorder level 20 ⑦ | |

| Date | Receipts ② | | | Issues ③ | | | Balance in stock ④ |
|---|---|---|---|---|---|---|---|
| | Qty | Inv no | Supplier | Qty | Req no | Dept | |
| 199- | | | | | | | 26 |
| Jan 1 | | | | | | | 26 |
| 3 | | | | 6 | 141 | Accounts | 20 |
| 4 | 30 | A133 | J Smith & Co | | | | 50 |
| 10 | | | | 3 | 159 | Personnel | 47 |

**Fig 9.9 A stock card**

A stock card (see Fig 9.9) will show details of each item used by the organisation (1). Each time stock is delivered by a supplier this will be **added on** to the record (2), and each time stock is issued to a department in response to a **stock requisition form**, this is **deducted** from the record (3), thus showing exactly how much is in stock at any one time (4).

We have already discussed how important it is for an organisation not to have too much stock, or too little stock. To prevent either of these situations arising a stock record card is used to indicate the **maximum** (5) and **minimum** (6) level for each item of stock required by the organisation.

The stock record card also indicates the **reorder level** (7) which shows at what quantity of stock an order needs to be requested so that delivery is made before the remaining stock runs out.

# ◼ DIY 9.2.2

---

Make out a stock card for A4 packets of paper, calculating the minimum, maximum and reorder levels and complete the following details. Select an appropriate stock number. You have in stock 15 reams at the start; during the month you have issued 2 to the typing room (on the 6th), 2 to your manager (on the 10th), 1 for your assistant (on the 19th), and you will be taking 2 for your own use. Your order for 20 reams arrived on the 20th.

Using this stock card as an example, write a memo to your line manager explaining how the stock card system works and why it should be used. What recommendations can you make regarding improvements in the use of materials and equipment?

---

It is important that your calculations are correct. If they are not you may find yourself in trouble for ordering stock unnecessarily or, even worse, not ordering stock that is required.

## ▶ Stocktaking and reconciliation

A regular check should be made on your stock; this is called stock taking or reconciliation. This is where every item of stock in the business is counted to calculate how much of the business's money is tied up in stock. An index will be made of all the items held: this index is called an inventory. It is necessary to physically count the number of items in stock and compare the total against the total written on the stock card. Any discrepancies should be reported and the reason for the discrepancies should be sought. It is possible that items have been taken without authority, or the figures on the card are incorrect.

It is possible to keep an up-to-date record of the stock levels by using a computer. The procedure is similar to that used with the bar code reading tills in the supermarkets. The computer will automatically deduct from the total stock level every time something is taken out, and add to the stock level every time stock is received. This is a very good method of keeping check of the stock, but one disadvantage is that the figures given are those that it has calculated – it cannot take into account theft, damage and loss unless the details are fed into the program.

Therefore, a manual stock check will still take place at least once a year so that the actual stock can be entered into the business's annual accounts sheets. It is during the stock check that damaged stock and obsolete stock can be 'written off'. Some businesses will have a special sale to reduce the 'written off' stock or an insurance claim may be made.

## ▶ Stock requisition

In large businesses it is likely that specialist staff would be employed to carry out these functions. As a member of a large business you will need to be aware of the procedures required in order to request supplies for your own section. Your stock is likely to be the consumables used in your working area, and will not be large items. Most stock in large businesses is ordered centrally by the Purchasing Department, as the business can then benefit from bulk purchase discounts. A stock or stationery requisition will need to be completed by you, authorised and sent to the central stores.

If you request an item that is not held in stock, then it will have to be ordered specially and the stock controller may have to obtain quotations prior to ordering. You should bear this in mind and not wait until you urgently require the item. It will also be necessary to complete a purchase requisition which will probably need countersigning by an authorised person from your section. The stock controller will send any purchase requisitions to the Purchasing Department.

Even the best system will not always meet the demands made upon it. Always keep an open mind and be prepared to review and change a system according to the demands currently being made. You should also be able to anticipate demands for special functions, such as a large annual meeting, where certain items are going to be used above the normal level. Special requisitions or orders may need to be made for these events.

## STATIONERY REQUISITION

No................................................

Date .........................................

| Quantity | Description |
|----------|-------------|
|          |             |
|          |             |
|          |             |
|          |             |

Signed .........................................  Storekeeper's initials

Department ...............................

Authorised ...............................  ...................................................

**Fig 9.10 A stationery requisition form**

# ■ DIY 9.2.3

Design a suitable stock requisition form and stock purchase requisition. Make a list of instructions for completion of each form together with a list of materials and equipment that are mostly to be ordered using each of the 2 forms.

## ▶ Monitoring expenditure

It is important that expenditure is monitored to ensure that the end-of-year budget is not overspent. If you are working to a budget it is not good practice to have spent your budget allowance within the first 6 months! It is vital that you work alongside the Accounts Department who are responsible for 'posting' payments made to your departmental account and will be able to provide an up-to-date printout or details of total expenditure with any one supplier as and when you ask.

The Accounts Department keeps itemised records of expenditure for each supplier. However, the records that they keep give details of the total expenditure your organisation has made with each supplier and not the expenditure made by each department or office. Therefore, it may be useful to keep your own departmental records if you wish to keep track of your own department's expenditure compared against the budget allowance. This would be common practice in a small organisation where records of expenditure on consumables is tracked, not necessarily by an accounts department but as a task within an employee's job description.

Expenditure can be tracked by either item or supplier. A good computer software program can provide this information easily. If you are using a manual system, there should be a section on the stock card which details the cost price of each item and the supplier. It is vital that the cost price is always up to date if exact expenditure is to be tracked.

When an update on expenditure is required, it is a fairly simple process of working through all the stock cards and adding up the supplies that have been received, multiplying each figure by the cost price and then adding all totals together to give a final figure of stock expenditure. If you do keep up-to-date records of expenditure then you will find that much of the work that needs to be prepared for the annual audit will have already been completed.

# ■ DIY 9.2.4

You are setting up a new office and have been asked to calculate a budget allowance for consumable stock over the next year.

Make a list of the items you feel will be required.

Look back at your list and arrange it in order of importance of active and non-active stock.

Now decide upon minimum and maximum quantities of stock to be held.

Obtain an office supplies catalogue and find the cost price for each item on the list. Calculate the cost of obtaining maximum stock levels for all the items you have listed.

Write a memo to the office supervisor giving details of your research and the recommendation you would like to make with regard to the budget allowance for the new office. Explain the procedure to follow in the event of a critical overspend being identified during the coming year's budget allocation.

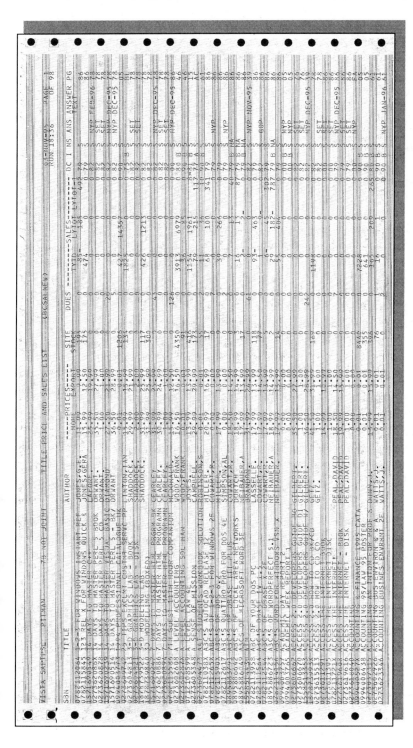

**Fig 9.11 A stock computer printout**

## ▶ *Disposal of unwanted or damaged stock*

You should already be aware that disposal of unwanted or damaged stock does not mean merely giving it away or throwing it away. Stock value is included in the company accounts and if it is disposed of, for whatever reason, details must be made available to the accountant so that the stock can be 'written off' and deducted from the total stock figure.

Obsolete stock can often be used for other purposes. For example, old headed paper can be used in offices to print out draft copies of reports, etc. Companies which are moving from using typewriters to using more up-to-date computers will want to see some income from the sale of the typewriters. The unwanted typewriter ribbons and correction tapes may be sold with the typewriters or arrangements could be made to return them to the supplier, probably at a reduced cost.

Some organisations will look to sell on the materials or equipment in order to retrieve some of the cost. This often happens with out-of-date equipment that is sold to staff or other companies that still use the equipment. Sometimes this equipment can be sold to smaller organisations or office supplies companies which have a market for second-hand office furniture and equipment. The income gained from such sales can be set against the loss to the company.

It is important that a set procedure is followed when materials or equipment are to be sold. It is unlikely that a member of staff from a large organisation would be allowed to leave the office with a computer under his arm without being challenged! In such cases the correct documentation and arrangements must be made for equipment to be removed from the premises by staff.

**Fig 9.12 Is the removal of this computer authorised?**

It is normal practice to complete the relevant documents for removal of equipment prior to writing across the equipment that it has been 'written off' with a date and initials for authorisation. The serial number of all pieces of equipment should be recorded and these details included on the documentation if the equipment is 'written off'. This system gives an identity to each piece of equipment which can then be tracked throughout the company and during its disposal.

## ■ DIY 9.2.5

You have just walked into the office to find that the office junior has had a spring-clean. He has put 10 reams of old headed paper by the bin for disposal and asked the caretakers to remove the electric typewriter from the office because it is never used. He has taken home the typewriter ribbons because he can use them on his typewriter at home.

Write a memo to him explaining why he should not have taken this action and what consequences it has on the budget allowance for the department. Explain the procedures that should have been followed and why.

### Knowledge and understanding question bank

1 How do you monitor the receipt of items?
2 How do you monitor the cost of items?
3 How do you monitor the usage of items?
4 What is your own scope and limit of authority relating to financial expenditure?
5 How do you ensure that best use is made of items?
6 What are your organisation's procedures for recording usage of items?
7 How do you go about making recommendations for improvements in the use of items?
8 How do you organise the disposal of excessive items?
9 What action would you take if you identified a critical overspend?
10 How do you organise the return of faulty goods?

### Claiming credit

For Element 9.2 you must prove that you have monitored the receipt, cost and use of materials and equipment, and where need exceeds financial allocations show that you have informed the appropriate person promptly and accurately. You must provide records of use of materials and equipment which are complete, accurate, legible, in the required format and within time-scales. You must follow organisational procedures for the disposal of faulty and excess materials and equipment.

The following work products are potential sources of evidence:

● financial statements
● documentation relating to the receipt of goods

- records of use of materials and equipment
- internal memoranda

Once you have completed your final assessment, you will need to write in your record book or folder how, when and what you have done to prove that you are competent.

The following statement is an example of how one trainee completed this claim:

*As the administration assistant at Coopers & Co it is my responsibility to monitor the use of materials and equipment. When ordering equipment I request at least 3 quotes from our suppliers so that the chief accountant can select the best deal. The unit cost of each item of stationery is kept on the stationery stock card. There is a separate card for each item. I use stationery stock cards to detail the item, issues, receipts and final balance. Each time stock is removed from the store room it is deducted from the balance and details of the person or department receiving the stock entered. When a delivery is received I check this against the delivery note and only sign it if it is correct. The delivery note is then checked against the original order; if something is missing or additional items are sent this will be checked with the supplier and a debit/credit note requested. When materials are placed into the store room the quantity is added to the balance on the stock card. All stationery requisition forms are checked by me; I keep a record of stock issued to each person or department so that I can identify excessive requests. A check is also kept on the budget allowance for each department and I will memo the head of that department if requests for materials and equipment are excessive to their financial allocation. The disposal of faulty or excess materials and equipment must be authorised by the chief accountant as these must be written off correctly against the budget and documented correctly ready for the next audit. Where equipment has been sold off to staff I have completed an authorisation slip to enable the staff to remove the equipment from the premises. Details of serial numbers are kept on file so that movement of equipment can always be tracked.*

# UNIT 10
# Organise and record meetings

## Element 10.1
## ARRANGE AND PREPARE FOR MEETINGS

### Performance criteria

**1** The purpose of meetings is clarified with the appropriate persons

**2** All requirements for meetings are met and are in accordance with organisational procedures

**3** The range and sources of documentation and other material for meetings are identified

**4** All required material is obtained and, where necessary, approved within specified deadlines

**5** Relevant documentation and other material is prepared, produced and forwarded to the appropriate persons, within specified deadlines

**6** Security and confidentiality of information are maintained

### Element introduction

In most businesses meetings are held on a regular basis. The type of meeting will depend on the matters to be discussed.

There are 2 types of meeting, informal and formal.

### ▶ *Informal meetings*

Informal meetings are generally held in order to make decisions, reach agreements and decide future action. They are usually relaxed as the participants are normally known to each other and the meeting may be called at short notice.

The procedure will depend on the nature of the meeting. For example, staff meetings will probably have an agenda (a list of items to be discussed) and a Chair (the person leading the meeting). Notes will probably be taken and later distributed. On the other hand a meeting of parents and teachers might be far less documented; they could meet just to discuss some ideas for the coming year.

### The types of group likely to hold informal meetings

The following are two of the types of group that may hold informal meetings.

**1 Working parties** – these are formed to address a certain matter. Once the solution or alternatives have been resolved, the committee is dissolved. The findings of a working party are reported to the parent committee. Recommendations can be made but only limited action can be taken without the approval of the parent committee.

**2 Managers** – groups of staff, such as sales representatives, will meet on a regular basis. Managers of a business will also meet regularly as it is essential for good communication that they should do so. The degree of formality varies, but the decisions made usually have considerable influence.

## ▶ *Procedure for formal meetings*

Formal meetings are controlled by regulations. A business which has limited liability (Ltd or plc) will be required to set out its meeting procedures in the Articles of Association – the document that sets up the company. Clubs will have a constitution and local authorities have standing orders. If the meeting is not run in line with the regulations the decisions made may be invalid.

All the people invited to attend must receive a written notice of the date of the meeting. The notice must state the date, time and place of the meeting and the type of meeting to be held. The length of notice required will depend on the type of meeting and the regulations. It is essential that the person arranging the meeting ensures that sufficient planning and booking are done before the notice is sent out to the members.

### Presenting a notice of meeting

A notice may be typed as part of the agenda, or as a separate letter or memorandum. As the notice only contains the details of the time, date, place and type of meeting it is sometimes combined with the agenda.

Notice is hereby given that a meeting of the Development Committee will be held on 8 December 199–, at 1400 hrs in the Conference Room.

Please let me know if you will be unable to attend.

Name of Chairperson

Date

**Fig 10.1 Example of a notice of meeting**

The wording of such a notice is not formally set. An example is shown in Fig 10.1.

## Preparing an agenda

The agenda is a list of items to be discussed at the meeting and there is a traditional order for an agenda. It should state the purpose of the meeting and give the members an opportunity to bring with them any documents they may need and enable them to prepare themselves for effective discussion on the points arising. (See Fig 10.2)

A special agenda may be typed for the Chair, in which the information would be typed on the left hand side of the page only, to allow the Chair to write notes during the meeting on the right-hand side. This agenda may also have prompts and reminders for the Chair included under the listed items. (See Fig 10.3.)

# ◄ DIY 10.1.1

You are the Secretary of the Parent Teacher Association who will be meeting on the first Monday of next month. Draw up a combined notice of meeting and agenda. The meeting will be at the Memorial Hall, Town Lane, New Milton at 7.30 pm. The Chair particularly wants to discuss the fund raising required to replace the new trampoline, and wants the Treasurer to report on the existing state of the funds held.

---

### AGENDA

**1 Apologies for absence**
(The Chair will read out the names of those people that were invited but are unable to attend.)

**2 Approval of the minutes of the previous meeting**
(Copies of the last minutes would have been circulated to all members; approval is necessary to ensure that all agree with the record. If approval is given the Chair will sign the master copy on each page; this will then be filed in the minute book. If changes are required this will be noted and approved.)

**3 Matters arising from the minutes**
(Quite often, members will be required to take action, for example to find out costs of new equipment. These items will be discussed before any new business.)

**4 Correspondence**
(Any letters, circulars, memos etc received will be brought to the attention of the members.)

**5 Reports**
(From officers such as the Treasurer or from sub-committees.)

**6 New business**
(Items that members have requested be placed on the agenda for discussion or decision.)

**7 Any other business (sometimes abbreviated to AOB)**
(Urgent items that need to be discussed. Generally these have arisen after the agenda was circulated and cannot wait until the next meeting.)

**8 Date of next meeting**
(A date is agreed by those present; often this will be the same time next month, quarter or year.)

---

**Fig 10.2 Example of an agenda**

## ▶ Types of formal meeting

The most common type of meeting is the **Annual General Meeting** (AGM), sometimes called an **ordinary general meeting**. These are held once a year for all members, whether they are club members or shareholders.

A **statutory meeting** is one that a group is by law required to hold. The regulations drawn up when the group began would include the requirement for such a meeting.

352

```
┌─────────────────────────────────────────────────────────────┐
│                                                             │
│   CHAIR'S AGENDA                              Notes         │
│                                                             │
│   1  Apologies for absence                                  │
│      Apologies have been received                           │
│      from Ms Williams, Mr Stevens                           │
│      and Miss Beeney.                                        │
│                                                             │
│   2  Approval of last minutes                               │
│      No suggested                                           │
│      alterations have                                       │
│      been received.                                         │
│                                                             │
│   3  Matters arising                                        │
│      Minute numbers 24, 26, 31                              │
│      and 45 need following up.                              │
│                                                             │
│                                                             │
│   (Etc)                                                     │
│                                                             │
└─────────────────────────────────────────────────────────────┘
```

**Fig 10.3 Example of a Chair's agenda**

**Board meetings** are held on a regular basis. The members of the Board are those elected by the general members (eg staff, club members, shareholders) or members whose presence is required by the company's regulations – usually because they hold a particular position in the company, such as the Company Secretary.

An **extraordinary meeting** would be called to discuss an urgent matter that has arisen, which the group considered could not wait until the next ordinary meeting. Extraordinary meetings may also be held to discuss one particular problem that would take up the whole of the time devoted to an ordinary meeting, to ensure that there is time for full debate of the topic.

## ▶ Committees and their purpose

A **sub-committee** belongs to a main group and may be set up as a standing committee or an advisory committee.

A **standing committee** is one which is permanently set up to deal with a specific issue, such as accommodation, repair and redecoration. *Ad hoc* (Latin for 'for this') committees would be set up to deal with a specific problem (a committee 'for this' purpose) and once the problem is resolved the committee would be dissolved.

353

An **advisory committee** may be set up by the main/parent committee to look at a specialist area and advise on matters of policy. This type of committee can make recommendations but does not have authority in its own right.

## ▶ *Positions held by members of a committee*

As mentioned earlier the **Chair** is the person responsible for running the meeting. The Chair is appointed by the members of the committee and must ensure that the meeting follows the agenda, that the correct procedure and order is followed. Anyone wishing to speak at the meeting must address their comments to the Chair and not to the meeting in general. The Chair will summarise the points made at the end of discussion and take decisions on points of order. If a vote is necessary the Chair will receive the votes and declare them. The meeting is always closed by the Chair and can be adjourned if it is considered necessary. A good Chair will make sure that the meeting does not digress and that the speakers are kept to relevant matters.

The **secretary** is the 'legal' representative of a committee. They should not be confused with a personal secretary who may deal with office administration in general. The committee secretary should be totally familiar with the regulations and be on hand to assist the Chair in matters of procedure. They are usually responsible for the documentation of the meeting, drafting the notice and agenda, preparing the room, taking the minutes (although a minute secretary may also attend the meeting), listing who attends, and ensuring that the necessary action is taken on the agreed points. Quite often many of these tasks will be delegated to a personal assistant or personal secretary.

There may be other officials, such as people appointed as officers, treasurer, social secretary, publicity manager, etc, although the appointment of other officials will depend on the type of committee and its purpose.

## ■ DIY 10.1.2

Prepare a folded A4 leaflet for your office junior which explains types of meeting and the officials who may be present. Use suitable language and explanation.

# ▶ *Preparing for a meeting*

If the meeting you are arranging is a small internal meeting, you are likely to contact all those invited to agree a suitable time and date. Once this is agreed you will be able to locate a suitable venue. Quite often this may be the manager's office or a special meeting room within the organisation. These rooms are usually easy to book by either writing in a diary or contacting a central point to reserve the room.

If the meeting is larger you may first of all locate a suitable place to hold the meeting; this may be on the premises or you may have to find an external venue. Many hotels and other centres now offer meeting and conference facilities. Before you are able to book a venue you will need to know how many people are likely to attend and from where they are travelling. It is essential that the venue be central to those attending, and that rail and road connections are good. If you were arranging a meeting for members coming from other countries you would also have to take into consideration the location of airports and seaports.

It is quite possible that some members may have disabilities and will need easy access to the meeting room; others may have special dietary requirements. It is important that these issues are checked with the venue, before you book it.

Once the date, time and venue are agreed the agenda is drawn up. A notice of meeting and copies of the agenda are sent to all those invited to attend along with any documents to be discussed at the meeting. When members receive the agenda, those with prior commitments are likely to write or telephone to give their apologies. Make a note of these and pass them on to the committee secretary.

Check the agenda and make a list of the equipment required. This could include an overhead projector (OHP), which may require transparencies (OHTs), slide projector, flip chart, video, microphones – it is a good idea to check with the meeting secretary what equipment is likely to be needed.

Usually the personal secretary or administrator will be responsible for organising the room. If the venue is external then the organisation will be done by the conference department at the centre used, but you will still need to check prior to the meeting that everything is in order. Apart from the room layout, check that the equipment supplied is working; projector bulbs have a habit of breaking when constantly being moved from room to room. Also make sure that the cables reach the plugs and are placed so that no one will trip over them; rubber mats are usually available to cover trailing wires on such occasions.

The tables used should be large enough to enable all members to sit around. If small tables are used then they may be placed in a 'U' shape. The Chair would normally sit at the head of the table, although some Chairs now prefer to sit at the side of a large table to make their presence less formal. The secretary and minute secretary would be close to the Chair. Each member should be supplied with pen/pencil and paper, and place names should be made ready for all those attending.

Special pens will be required if an OHT or flip chart is going to be used; at least one of each colour available should be to hand. Sufficient stationery should be ordered well in advance of the date and fresh water and glasses should be placed in easy reach of all members. If you are using an external centre, these should all be provided and it is likely they will supply mineral water in addition to orange squash. However it is not necessary to have such a selection for meetings held internally. A check will need to be made with the committee secretary to see what refreshments are required. Although traditionally coffee is supplied in the morning and tea in the afternoon, tastes are now changing and most members would expect both to be available. If the refreshments are to be supplied by an outside agency or your refectory they will need to be ordered. If you are intending to provide them yourself, you will need to check supplies.

If the meeting is going to last all day, lunch will have to be provided. You should agree with the committee secretary what type of lunch, formal or buffet, and whether there are any members with special dietary requirements. Some meetings may last several days, in which case accommodation will also need to be booked. Ashtrays will also be required, unless the Chair has a policy of 'no smoking' at meetings. If members are unfamiliar with your premises ensure that prominent notices indicate where the toilets and cloakrooms are located.

Finally, a list of members attending should be sent to your receptionist and/or security officer so that they are fully aware of who is expected. Some of the members may have requested parking spaces, if you have them available, or cars/taxis to collect them from the station. All these details should be agreed and notified to the relevant people.

It is quite likely that on the day of the meeting, one or more of the members will forget their meeting documents. An efficient organiser will always have at least one spare set available and be able to access a photocopier if more are required.

# ■ DIY 10.1.3

Draw up a checklist for your own use. It should include all the points made above for a formal meeting. Inherited checklists are almost useless, unless they are written for your specific requirements. Include particular arrangements you would have to make for members attending who have special needs because they are wheelchair bound, blind or deaf.

Prepare documentation for a meeting. The details of the meeting are:

A meeting will be held in 2 months time, on the first Wednesday, and will last all day. The members regularly visit the company and can all travel there without problems. You are expecting 20 members. The internal meeting room has sufficient space and is free on the date required. Please write a memo to the Receptionist, booking the room and an OHP. Also book 4 car spaces. The Chair has asked you to supply coffee for 15 and tea for 5 in the morning, and in the afternoon tea for 10 and coffee for 10. he has agreed that a cold buffet lunch will be suitable, with a selection of vegetarian and non-vegetarian food available. Write a memo to the refectory manageress to order these refreshments. Check your list and tick off those items dealt with. Write a memo to the committee secretary requesting any further information you require to set up this meeting.

## ▶ *Special terminology used in meetings*

There are special terms which may be used at meetings. The more formal the meeting, the more likely it is that some of the following terms may be used.

| | | |
|---|---|---|
| *ad hoc* | *intra vires* | resolution |
| adjournment | lie on the table | show of hands |
| committee | majority | standing committee |
| ballot | motion | sub-committee |
| casting vote | *nem con* | teller |
| closure | point of order | *ultra vires* |
| co-option | poll | unanimous |
| *ex officio* | proposal | |
| in attendance | proxy | |
| in camera | quorum | |

# ■ DIY 10.1.4

Type or word process a suitable hand-out for your junior staff, listing the above terms and providing a simple explanation. The hand-out should be suitable for the junior staff to use as part of their training for promotion to secretarial positions, when part of their duties will be assisting the secretary of meetings.

---

▶ *Security and confidentiality for meetings and documentation*

Meeting documents should be kept securely in a locked cabinet and should not be accessed by anyone who does not have the authority to look at the contents. Circulation of the documents is usually restricted to the members of the committee only, and at no time should the documents be left unattended on desk top, photocopier, typewriter or on the screen of the word processor. Many companies insist that meeting documents are numbered and each committee member has an allocated number, therefore only the exact number of copies required are made and these are circulated according to a strict circulation list. For instance:

| | |
|---|---|
| Chairman | 1 |
| Secretary | 2 |
| Sales Manager | 3 |
| Purchasing Manager | 4 etc |

Extra copies of minutes may be made to take to the next meeting, in case someone forgets their own, but once the meeting has finished these should be shredded. Any outdated documents should also be destroyed by either shredding or incinerating. The only copy kept permanently would be the master set, usually kept by the Chair or Secretary, and stored in a fireproof cabinet. Each page of the minutes is numbered, so that any missing pages can be easily identified.

If the documents are stored on computer disks or microfiche, then these should be stored safely under lock and key and the documents on computer disk saved using passwords or keywords.

In large companies industrial espionage is quite common as secret information can be traded for large sums of money. For instance, the news of a take-over or financial problems in a company may be useful information for a competitor.

## ■ DIY 10.1.5

---

Write a memo to your temporary replacement who will be carrying out the arrangements for the next month's meeting. Include in your memo the actions that should be followed from setting up a meeting to those for security and confidentiality.

---

## Knowledge and understanding question bank

1 What is your role and responsibility for arranging and preparing for meetings?
2 How do you determine the purpose and objectives of the meeting?
3 How do you select an appropriate venue?
4 What facilities do you require for your meetings?
5 What documentation do you prepare prior to a meeting?
6 How do you arrange for participants to attend a meeting?
7 What refreshments do you need to organise and how is this done?
8 How do you prepare an agenda?
9 What legal and regulatory requirements are related to meetings within your organisation?
10 What are the consequences of inadequate preparation for meetings?

## Claiming credit

For Element 10.1 you must prove that you have arranged the venue, facilities and refreshments for meetings held to make decisions and those held for communication purposes.

The following work products are potential sources of evidence:

● agenda, reports and minutes
● agenda items and supporting documentation
● internal memoranda
● correspondence relating to the meetings

Once you have completed your final assessment, you will need to write in your record book or folder how, when and what you have done to prove that you are competent.

The following statement is an example of how one trainee completed this claim:

*I have carried out preparation for meetings at the training centre and while working at Jones & Co. I agreed with the managers and others when the meetings would take place, then drafted an agenda from information supplied. The main meeting room was booked by telephoning reception to make sure that it was free and then confirming by memo. Prior to the meetings I set out the room and made sure any equipment required was available and working. I copied and circulated documents to the members of the meeting a week before to enable them to consider the documents. These were posted in sealed envelopes and marked 'confidential'. I booked refreshments and buffet lunch using the form required.*

# ■ Element 10.2
# ATTEND, SUPPORT AND RECORD MEETINGS

## Performance criteria

**1** Requirements for meetings are available in accordance with agreed arrangements

**2** Necessary documentation and other materials for the conduct of meetings are available at the outset

**3** Attendance of people at meetings is confirmed and, where appropriate, recorded

**4** Information and advice are supplied to participants accurately and clearly, and within limits of own authority

**5** Unforeseen occurrences are dealt with effectively

**6** Key issues and decisions are accurately recorded, in accordance with organisational procedures

**7** Security and confidentiality of information are maintained

## Element introduction

Once all the arrangements have been made and the items on your checklist have all been dealt with, the day of the meeting will arrive.

## ▶ Action required before the meeting

It will be necessary to carry out some last minute checking, just to ensure that the meeting goes smoothly. Some of the members attending may already have cancelled, and a note will have to be passed to the Chair to read out the apologies of those not able to attend. Some last minute changes may affect everyone attending and it will be your duty to ensure that everyone is notified.

You should confirm the arrangements made – the room booking, equipment, refreshments and stationery required. Check that the Company Secretary and Chair have all the documents they require, including copies of the minutes of the last meeting. Make sure that colleagues are aware of who is attending the meeting and where they can be contacted, in case of emergencies. Ensure that any necessary signs are in place. (You should also have a 'Meeting in Progress' sign ready for the door.)

The room itself will also need checking. It may be that you have to arrange the furniture yourself, or if someone has already done this for you, check that it has been done as you requested. Make sure the water is fresh and the glasses clean. Pads, pens and place names should be placed on the table. Equipment should be tested, and ensure you know who to contact urgently if it is found to be faulty. Finally check that the room is at the right temperature and ventilated.

Before leaving for the start of the meeting you should remember to take with you the extra copies of the agenda and papers, in case someone has forgotten theirs. It would also be useful to take your boss's diary (and your own) as it may be necessary to arrange a date for the next meeting.

# ■ DIY 10.2.1

Write out some notes on how you would deal with the following emergencies.

1 The caterers did not receive your instructions and are unable to provide the refreshments ordered, tea/coffee in the morning and buffet lunch.
2 An urgent message arrives for one of the committee members, who will need to return to his office immediately.
3 The fire alarm goes off in the middle of the meeting.
4 Someone you expected to attend, cannot, but has sent a representative, who only speaks French.
5 In the middle of the meeting a participant has decided he wants to use a flip chart, which has not been ordered.
6 A security threat has been received by your receptionist who has telephoned to inform you.

## ▶ Recording attendance

If you are responsible for recording the attendance of those in the meeting (and apologies received) it is important that you know all personnel attending by sight. If you are unsure you should circulate a piece of paper with a suitable heading. You will need to have prepared this prior to the meeting. (See Fig 10.4.)

---

**Meeting of Planning Sub-Committee**
**held on 12 December 1995 at**
**Lovell Chambers, Southampton**

List of participants (please PRINT your name).

1

2

3

4

etc

---

**Fig 10.4 Example of list of participants at a meeting**

Alternatively your organisation may have a formal **Record of Attendance** which all participants sign prior to the meeting.

# ■ DIY 10.2.2

Find out the type of meetings held in your training centre and how recording of attendance is carried out. The meetings may include managers' meetings, team meetings, course meetings, union meetings.

## ▶ *Recording apologies for absence*

Normally you as the organiser will have been notified of those not attending the meeting and the apologies will have been passed to the Chair, prior to the start of the meeting. If the meeting is a large meeting, then some of the members attending may write the apologies of colleagues on a circulated record of attendance or in the record book.

The apologies for absence will usually be read out by the Chair and a note may be made of them at this time. Alternatively the names may be obtained from the Chair after the meeting.

## ▶ *Taking and preparing the minutes*

The minutes should be a true record of all that occurred at a meeting. They should be written in the third person and in the past tense and should contain the details of the type, date, time and place of meeting; names of those present (the Chair's name goes first followed by a Deputy, if there is one, and the Secretary; after that the names are in alphabetical order); and a summary of the business discussed in agenda order.

## Taking the minutes

If a minute secretary has been appointed, they will take the minutes. Quite often though, and especially at informal meetings, it will be the job of the personal secretary or assistant. Before you take the minutes of a formal meeting, it is a good idea to practise on some informal meetings, where the subject-matter can be understood easily and you know those attending. Some committees may allow you to take minutes alongside a minute secretary, to allow you to practise before being on your own. In this way you can go through the whole procedure without the worry of getting something drastically wrong.

When you have the job of taking the minutes you will need to sit fairly close to the Chair, who will be controlling the meeting. You will need to record who is attending and who has sent apologies. At some meetings a list is circulated for those attending to write their names. If this is done, make a quick head-count to make sure you have the right number of names.

You will need to be alert and not get involved in any of the discussion (unless required). Concentrate on what is being said and pick out the important points. It will help if you are familiar with the matters being discussed. You should have read the minutes of the last meeting and the papers for discussion. The minutes may be a **verbatim account** (word-for-word) of what was said. To take such minutes you will need an exceptional shorthand speed or be able to use a stenograph (the machine sometimes used in court proceedings). It is not often that such minutes are required, unless the matters being discussed have legal implications.

The most common minutes are an **account of what was said**, and usually the Chair will summarise the main points, which will be your cue to write down what the Chair says. Conclusions and decisions will also be recorded. These may have been proposed and seconded and the names of those concerned must be recorded as part of the minutes. The minutes should also include any action that has to be taken and by whom. An example of this type of minute would be:

> It was agreed that Mr Green would acquire quotations for
> the new building from at least 3 local builders. These
> would be presented to the committee at the next meeting.

Some committees use an 'Action' column in their minutes, and the names of those having to take 'action' on a matter are then easier to notice.

---

**ACTION**

It was agreed that 3 quotations for the new building would be acquired from at least 3 local builders. These would be presented to the committee at the next meeting.                                          Mr Green

---

If you get behind with the minutes, indicate immediately to the Chair that you need to catch up. Do not rely on your memory. Even if you type up your notes immediately after the meeting, there will be distractions and your memory will not be able to hold the details required to provide an accurate record.

### Style of minutes

The style will always be the 'house' style, that is, how the previous minutes have been typed. There are so many different ways of typing minutes that you should ensure that you are familiar with the style early on in your involvement with any committee. Generally the order of the minutes will follow the order of the agenda but whatever the format, when you have typed the minutes they should be given to the Chair for approval. The Chair may amend them or ask for them to be passed to the Company Secretary for clarification on any points of order.

Once the minutes have been agreed, they should be typed formally, numbered as required and circulated to the members of the committee so that they can be read before the next meeting. Ensure you follow the organisation's requirements for security and confidentiality of information.

## ■ DIY 10.2.3

Type up the notes shown in Fig 10.5 in the form of draft minutes for the approval of the Chair. Ensure that the notes are expanded into correct sentences.

8.22 Roundhouse Supporters Club
Meeting 25/4 at 7.15 The Grey Room,
Royale Hotel, TRIDEND

Present: Miss J Pruit (Chair); Mrs B Goldney
(Hon Sec); Mr Y Jay (Hon Treas); Mr D Dale;
Miss L Burdett; Miss M Stevens; Mr N Tidswell;
Mrs S Gibbon.
Apologies from: Mrs W Widscombe and
Ms N North.

1. Minutes of last meeting read and
   approved.

2. Matters arising. 1 – Still no reply from
   building contractor re Extension? 2 – Mr
   Jay had written to 6 electricians to get
   quotes. 3 – Mrs Gibbon received payment
   all subscriptions. 4 – Mr Jay has
   received approval of a/cs from auditor.

3. Treasurer's report. £1211 in bank; £6005
   in building society a/c. Interest received
   on 1st 6 months was £70.50. Subs
   received were put into BS a/c.

4. Functions for fete agreed 1st week July.
   Suggestions include: bouncy castle,

**Fig 10.5 Handwritten minutes, for use with DIY 10.2.3**

swing boats, 'shot at goal', raffle, fancy dress. Stalls – bottle, cake, plants, tins, pies, children's books, toys & games. Food & drink – candy floss, hotdogs, ice cream, tea/coffee, cold drinks. Contact – local police①/fire②/St Johns③/mayor④; local shops for raffle prizes; local school for band & gym team; local sports club for display – perhaps judo/karate/aerobics; printers for programme.

5. Miss Burdett offered to write letters to 1–4 above & ask if they'll support again this yr. Mr Dale & Mr Tidswell will contact local shops etc + Mrs Goldrey printers.

6. Car boot sale date agreed – 3rd Sun in June. Details to be discussed at next meeting

7. AOB – Mrs North now out of hospital & progressing well. Thanks received for card & flowers.
Bring to next meeting items required for stall – to be stored in basement.

8. Next meeting 24/5 same time/venue.

**Fig 10.5 continued**

▶ *Participating in the meeting*

If you are required to participate in the meeting and take the minutes, you will need to have your input well prepared. You may be asked to provide information relating to one of the agenda items or confirm arrangements that have been made for future events. The Chair should have discussed this with you before the meeting, but if not you should try to anticipate the requirements from the agenda items. As stated previously, it is a good idea to take your diary (and any other relevant diaries) into the meeting. This will provide you with dates and the timing and location of meetings already arranged for the future.

If you have been requested to supply information to a participant after the meeting make a note of it on a separate piece of paper, so that this can be actioned immediately. If you have a planned break you may be able to get someone else working on the action required while you are in the meeting, thus saving time when the meeting is finished.

▶ *Evaluating your arrangements and attendance*

It is a good idea to evaluate your arrangements after the event. How well did your arrangements run? Did any problems occur that you had not envisaged? Were the presentation methods used effective? Were the refreshments on time, suitable, attractively displayed? If you carry out an evaluation after each meeting it should help you to ensure that all future events will run smoothly and meet the demands of the participants.

### Knowledge and understanding question bank

1 What are your role and responsibilities in attending, supporting and recording meetings?
2 What type of meetings have you attended and what was the role of the participants?
3 How were the meetings conducted?
4 What contributions have you made yourself to meetings?
5 What contingencies or emergencies have you dealt with and what action did you take?
6 What is the purpose of the minutes of a meeting?
7 How do you record notes during the meeting – how do you decide what to record?
8 What legal and regulatory requirements relate to meetings held in your organisation?
9 How do you maintain security and confidentiality of information regarding meetings?

**10** How does your organisation record the attendance of people at
**a** informal meetings and **b** formal meetings?

## Claiming credit

For Element 10.2 you must prove that you have attended meetings, provided the necessary documentation, recorded the issues and decisions as well as a list of those attending.

The following work products are potential sources of evidence:

- minutes
- records of meetings
- correspondence relating to arrangements

Once you have completed your final assessment, you will need to write in your record book or folder how, when and what you have done to prove that you are competent.

The following statement is an example of how one trainee completed this claim:

*While working as an assistant in the Administration and Assessment Centre I organised and attended meetings. Before the meetings I made sure that all the planned arrangements were in hand and checked the room. I took extra copies of the documentation to the meeting in case anyone had forgotten theirs. I recorded the names of those attending in my notes (as I was familiar with them all I did not need to circulate an attendance list, nor do we have a record book).*

*I gave details of the next month's bookings when requested and supplied information regarding the best available time for meetings in the future. During the meeting I took notes of the main points, items of decision and action. After the meeting I did not discuss the contents with anyone else inside or outside the organisation. My notes were kept secure by locking them in the desk until I could draft them into minutes.*

# ■ Element 10.3
# PRODUCE AND PROGRESS RECORDS
# OF MEETINGS

## Performance criteria

**1** Accurate and clear records of meetings are produced within specified deadlines

**2** Approval of records, when required, is obtained from appropriate persons

**3** Records are produced in a form which conforms to organisational requirements

**4** Records are issued to appropriate persons, within planned timescales

**5** Actions arising from meetings are accurately identified, progressed and monitored

**6** Progress on actions is reported to the appropriate persons

**7** Security and confidentiality of information are maintained

### Element introduction

In Elements 10.1 and 10.2 we have covered how to organise and set up a meeting and what action you should take in attending, supporting and recording meetings. In the last element of this unit you need to provide evidence that you can produce and progress records of meetings. This will include producing the records (notes or minutes), getting them approved, providing them to the appropriate persons, following up any action required, reporting on the action and maintaining security and confidentiality of information.

## ▶ *Producing the records of meetings*

You should try to type or word process the records of the meeting from your notes as quickly as possible – while all the events are in your mind. When attending the meeting you should have recorded the decisions made and summarised the main points. These may have been summarised by the Chair who may have indicated that items should be noted or minuted.

The draft records should be made available to the Chair as soon as possible. Try to present the records in a format which is as close as possible to the final format required. If you are unfamiliar with the style, look at previous records, if they are available. If previous records are not available you should discuss with the Chair the format required for the records – or present a format for approval.

Once the records have been amended and approved by the Chair, sufficient copies should be made for circulation to those attending. In the case of an AGM the minutes may be kept on file for reference purposes and may not be circulated to all attending, other than on request.

## DIY 10.3.1

Submit the minutes you drafted in DIY 10.2.3 to your tutor for approval. Once returned make any corrections and amendments and produce the final version. You should make sufficient copies for circulation to those attending. State how you have made the copies and how you will circulate the minutes (eg internally and/or externally, post – first/second, marked personal or confidential etc).

### ▶ *Circulating and retaining the records*

Your organisation may number the copies, as discussed in Element 10.1. This assists in identifying the recipient and supports security and confidentiality. The original copy of the records should be kept for the next meeting, and when approved at the meeting, should be initialled by the Chair.

Distribution to the members of the meeting should be made as soon as possible. If the documentation is confidential then it should be posted under cover (sealed envelopes) and marked accordingly. The documentation **must** be received by the participants before the next meeting, but preferably in time for them to review the contents and take action on any matters identified for their action.

### ▶ *Matters arising*

In most records, whether formal or informal, there will be actions arising from the meeting. On the next agenda these will be identified as 'matters arising'. At this time the Chair will go through the records and ask for a report from the person(s) concerned as to the present situation, what action had been taken and the result.

It may be part of your responsibility to follow up the 'actions arising' to ensure that they have been completed and that any necessary reports or documentation are supplied to you ready to copy and circulate with the next agenda. Some individuals will require constant gentle reminders while you may need to pursue others daily in order to get the action completed. Only experience in the job and familiarity with the people concerned will guide you in this aspect. However you should be courteous, co-operative and supportive at all times.

You will need to keep track of the progress being made by the individuals who are taking follow-up action. Any concerns should be discussed first with the individuals and secondly with the Chair or other appropriate person. You may need another person to take action, if the individual who attended the meeting is away from the office for a period of time – on holiday, business or ill, especially if they have forgotten to delegate the task to a colleague.

### ■ DIY 10.3.2

Arrange for a group meeting to be held and draw up an appropriate agenda in discussion with your tutor. Take notes, provide records for approval to your tutor, amend and correct the approved records as necessary and circulate the final version to the rest of the participants. Identify the action required and complete a chart as suggested below. Collect all the documentation together, including a summary of all the action you have taken to complete this task, and submit as evidence for this element.

| Action by (name of person) | Action required | Progress and date of check–notes |
|---|---|---|
|  |  |  |
|  |  |  |
|  |  |  |

**Fig 10.6 Action chart for meeting**

## ▶ *Legal and regulatory requirements*

Many committees and organisations are not required to publish or take formal records of meetings held. However there are certain organisations that, according to their Articles of Association, are required to hold meetings on a regular basis, make the records available and keep them for a set period of time. All formal records are required to be approved and signed by the committee at its next meeting and the signed version must be kept secure – usually by the Secretary of the Committee on behalf of the Chair.

## DIY 10.3.3

Investigate the legal and regulatory requirements of a public limited company and a private limited company in respect of the production and issue of records of meetings. Submit your investigation in the form of a memo to your tutor.

### Knowledge and understanding question bank

1 What are the role and responsibilities of a minute secretary?
2 How do you prepare records of meetings? What style do you use?
3 How do you obtain approval of the draft records?
4 What procedure do you follow for issuing the records of meetings?

**5** How do you identify action arising from the records of meetings?

**6** How do you ensure action arising is monitored and progressed?

**7** To whom do you report progress, or non-progress, on action arising from the records of meetings?

**8** How do you maintain security and confidentiality of draft and final versions of records of meetings?

**9** How do you ensure security and confidentiality of progress of actions arising from records of meetings?

**10** What legal and regulatory requirements are there in respect of producing and issuing records in your organisation?

## Claiming credit

For Element 10.3 it is necessary to prove that you have produced the records of meetings (decision-making and communication meetings) and that you have reported progress on action arising from the meeting. This should include action by you and by others.

The following work products are potential sources of evidence:

- notes of meetings
- records of meetings
- approved records
- list of recipients
- notes relating to the monitoring of progress on actions

Once you have completed your final assessment, you will need to write in your record book or folder how, when and what you have done to prove that you are competent.

The following statement is an example of how one trainee completed this claim:

*During my work as an assistant I had to prepare minutes from my notes of meetings. It was essential that the information I recorded and prepared was accurate and clear. The information was required within 48 hours of the meeting held (quality assurance standard).*

*Draft minutes were provided to the Chair in double line spacing to allow for addition, deletion and alteration. Once approved I made the necessary changes and photocopied a full set (enough for all attending, one for the file and one for the next meeting). At the right-hand side of the minutes there is an action column, in which I type the initials of anyone needing to take action on a particular point. These points are followed up to ensure that relevant action is taken before the next meeting. This is done by me by either telephoning or sending a memo. If there were any problems (eg staff absence through illness) I either got one of the other staff to follow up the action or spoke to the Chair who decided on the course of action to take. At all times the information I handled and had access to was kept secure and confidential. All master copies were kept in the locked cabinet and my disk has a keyword protection on it.*

# UNIT 11

# Arrange and monitor travel and accommodation

## Element 11.1
## ORGANISE TRAVEL AND ACCOMMODATION ARRANGEMENTS

### Performance criteria

**1** Requirements for travel and accommodation are accurately obtained from the relevant persons

**2** Selected methods of travel and accommodation provide optimum use of time, within financial and travel policy constraints

**3** An accurate and comprehensive itinerary is prepared and made available to the relevant persons within agreed deadlines

**4** All supporting documentation is arranged and provided within agreed deadlines

**5** Security and confidentiality procedures are in accordance with organisational requirements

**6** Medical arrangements, where required, are appropriate to the routes being travelled

**7** Monetary arrangements, for costs incurred, are in accordance with organisational procedures

### Element introduction

This element is about your ability to arrange travel and accommodation within the UK and overseas. You should be able to demonstrate competence in arranging the travel and documentation including monetary arrangements. The arrangements you make should include those organised by yourself and the work you do in organising others. You may need to co-ordinate with travel agencies, a financial department or bank, contacts at the destination or staff within your own organisation.

▶ *Requirements for travel*

As businesses become more and more successful, their contacts and customers are likely to come from a wider geographical spread. One of the consequences of this is that the company's staff will have to travel further and more frequently to discuss business. It may be a part of your job to organise all the necessary arrangements for business travel, whether it be a day visit locally, a three-day visit in Europe or an international visit lasting several weeks. A company representative should always arrive at their destination feeling their best; able to negotiate and participate in meetings to the benefit of the company, even if they have had a long, tiring and perhaps difficult journey.

Large companies, whose personnel travel frequently, may have a travel department that would make all the necessary arrangements for the staff, in consultation with a travel agent. In this case you would still need to be able to give them full details of what is required to ensure the most suitable arrangements are made for the individual travelling. If you are making the arrangements direct with a travel agent, make sure that the one selected has a good reputation and that it is registered with ABTA (Association of British Travel Agents).

Most companies will have an agreed policy regarding travel which will state the class of accommodation and travel members of staff are entitled to, the mileage rate paid to those using their own cars, and the method of travel permitted. Companies would request that employees select a mode of travel which has the optimum cost and travel method – that is, the most efficient (taking cost into consideration) for the circumstances. When you are responsible for organising travel and accommodation you need to take into account not only the most suitable mode of travel and accommodation but also the number of people travelling, the status of those concerned, the aims of the visit and the destination.

Whatever arrangements are made, it is useful to gather all the relevant information and documents together in a travel file and all the information for your boss in a travel pack. The travel file will provide an up-to-date record that will enable you to compile travel plans and monitor the progress of the bookings. It will also allow you to fully brief staff with information regarding their travel plan.

▶ *Selecting the mode of travel*

**Car**   For most local journeys it is practical for employees to drive, either their own car, or a company car if it is available. If employees are using their own cars, they should check that their insurance cover is valid for such journeys. A company will pay employees a fixed rate per mile for journeys made on business. This rate should take into account petrol used (distance and cubic capacity (cc) of the car) and wear and tear on the vehicle. The rate agreed by companies seems to vary enormously and currently varies between 20p and 50p per mile. Some companies also have a limit on how much can be claimed per month, or have a decreasing scale, for example 30p per mile for 1 to 300 miles, 25p per mile for 301 to 500 miles, 20p per mile for 500 miles plus.

Companies with a number of cars available for employees' use will probably have an account at a local garage which will service the cars regularly, sort out mechanical problems and allow employees to obtain petrol. Some of the cars may be allocated to specific personnel; for example, directors usually have cars as a 'perk' of the job and sales representatives will have cars to enable them to visit customers. Companies that offer a maintenance and repair service are likely to have a fleet of vehicles, usually vans, for use by the engineers and technicians.

If an employee does not have their own car or access to a company car, it may be necessary to hire a car. Car hire rates vary considerably and it is worth checking several companies before deciding on which one to use. You should take into account the distance to be travelled and the frequency of visits as it may be that the hire company would be prepared to negotiate special rates if you are to use their cars on a regular basis. If the cost of hiring cars is regularly increasing, it may be worth investigating the options available, ie purchasing or leasing. Leasing vehicles is becoming extremely popular with companies. The leasing company allocates vehicles to the business in exchange for a regular payment over a fixed period (for example 1 – 3 years). At the end of the period the business has the option of purchasing the vehicle or leasing a new vehicle for another fixed period.

When planning a journey by car, you will need to look at the routes available. The AA and RAC *Handbooks*, published annually, provide maps as well as information on the cities and main towns, hotel accommodation and garage services available. Computerised route planners are also available and these will produce a printed map, plus the mileage incurred, so that the quickest and shortest routes can be selected. The cost of the journey can also be included in the print-out if the mileage rate is entered.

Whichever planner is used, it will not advise you of any major roadworks or diversions in operation, so it would still be worth checking with AA, RAC, or local travel help lines. During the holiday periods traffic builds up at particular spots and the motorways and major roads can become congested, so time should be allowed for such delays.

**Train** British Rail operates accounts for companies whose staff use the rail system frequently. A warrant card can be issued to the person travelling, and on presentation of this to the booking office, the cost of the ticket will be charged to the company account. Tickets can also be pre-booked by telephone and the charge made to the account. If a company does not hold an account and staff only travel occasionally by train, individuals may purchase their own tickets and be reimbursed by the company at a later stage, when they submit their travel claim form.

When booking rail tickets you may also book a particular seat: many people prefer to sit facing the direction of travel and this should be stipulated. The terms 'face to engine' and 'back to engine' are used by the rail booking clerks. First and second class, smoking and non-smoking carriages are also bookable on most of the Intercity trains. You should make yourself familiar with the requirements of the person for whom you are making the booking before contacting the booking office. You will need to inform those travelling of the departure and arrival times. They may also wish to know whether a buffet bar will be available on the train or not. Additional services such as sleeper trains and motorail (transporting of cars) are also available on some trains. It will be necessary for you to check the timetables, in the *ABC Rail Guide* (published monthly), which lists the services available. In addition to the times of arrival and departure, double-check with the booking clerk when reserving your tickets that the information printed in your timetable is still current.

The advantage of rail travel is that it is quicker than road on direct routes, the person travelling is able to rest and review documents if they wish and on longer journeys the cost will be cheaper than a car mileage claim.

The disadvantages are that often it is necessary to change one or more times during the journey to reach the destination and connecting trains may not be available immediately which will result in a 'waiting period' at stations. If connections are good this may not be such a problem, but bear in mind the transfer time required, especially if it is necessary to change stations. This would most likely occur in London, as there are several main line stations serving different parts of the country.

It is unlikely that you will need to book trains outside the country but if the occasion arose, liaison with a travel agent would be recommended although *Cook's International Timetable*, published monthly, will give details of the principal rail services of Europe, Africa, America, Asia and Australasia.

**Sea**  There are many companies that operate routes from the UK by sea, and the services offered are increasing as the demand for access to Europe, in particular, increases. Sea travel is limited to the routes available, and it is unlikely that your manager would travel by sea, unless air travel was feared, or they wished to take a car abroad. To avoid inconvenience it is wise to make an advance booking on a car ferry, especially during the peak holiday periods. Cabin accommodation may also be booked on some ferries, and this would be essential for executives travelling overnight, who wish to arrive fresh to carry out their business. Service timetables and brochures are available from operators at seaports, travel agents or in the *ABC Shipping Guide* which is available on a monthly basis.

**Air**  For long distances and international travel, time can be saved by flying. Frequent internal flights (known as shuttle services) are available and it is reasonable to expect an executive based in London to fly to Glasgow to attend a meeting and fly back the same day. There are nearly 60 airports in the UK, although not all have shuttle services. There is no need to book these flights and 'booking in' time at the airport is reduced to the minimum required for security reasons. Special company accounts can be opened for those using these services frequently. However, the availability of internal flights is still limited and this restricts the alternatives open when planning a journey. Transfer time from the airport to the meeting venue must also be taken into consideration.

Internationally, however, there are many airline operators – some who specialise in travel to specific parts of the world. Increased competition between the operators has resulted in special conditions and prices being offered to attract business customers. Most airlines offer economy, executive and first class travel on long-distance flights, although all Concorde's seats are first class. Companies generally make use of the executive and first class options to ensure that their staff arrive as relaxed and alert as possible to carry out business. In these two classes there is more room round the seats for increased leg comfort and to enable travellers to carry out work undisturbed – some flights offer fully reclining chairs or bunk beds for sleeping. To assist the travellers on the ground there are separate booking-in arrangements and usually a separate waiting lounge – all designed to speed up the travelling process and make the journey as comfortable as possible. When it is necessary to change flights to reach a destination, time should be allowed. Quite often, as with rail stations, it will be necessary to change airports although it is customary for the travel operators to offer a transfer service, either by minibus, car, helicopter or plane – such a service operates regularly between Gatwick and Heathrow.

Although there are many advantages to air travel, there are some considerations that should be taken into account which may affect the travel plan of a business person. There is a restriction on how much luggage may be carried without incurring a charge, although most business travellers do not carry much luggage. The weather often creates problems and once plane departure times are delayed there is a knock-on effect which can result in planes being delayed for some time. Bookings need to be made well in advance, especially to popular destinations. Although waiting lists operate for some flights, it would not be appropriate for someone who had to attend a meeting at a specific time to be placed on a waiting list.

Do not forget that when the manager reaches the destination it will be necessary for them to reach the meeting venue. They will need advice as to whether a taxi, company car, hire car or a representative will be available for transfer.

The *ABC World Airways Guide* and *ABC Guide to International Travel* contain information and timetables for airlines. However, unless you are working within a specialised travel department, most air travel would be booked through a travel agent or direct with the airline operators who would supply you with all the information required. Before booking you should familiarise yourself with the requirements of your manager – whether they wish to sit near the window, prefer smoking or non-smoking, and which class of travel is required.

# DIY 11.1.1

Draw up a checklist of information required from someone travelling. Your list should include all modes of business travel, be comprehensive but easy to understand, for example **car** – own/company/pool/hire, engine power required, manual/automatic, left/right hand drive, 2/4 door, etc; **train** – 1st/2nd class, facing/back to engine, etc.

## ▶ *Selecting suitable accommodation*

The type of accommodation required will depend on the status of your traveller, how long they need the accommodation, the facilities required and the cost. As with mode of travel, companies will usually have laid down procedure for accommodation. Directors and senior staff would normally expect a good class of hotel; sales representatives on the other hand may only require bed and breakfast in a small lodging. When booking accommodation you will need to know the duration of stay, time and date of arrival, method of payment, special dietary requirements, facilities required and names of those staying.

Accommodation available in most cities and towns includes:

**1 Hotels** – some companies have special accounts and agreed costs with a group of hotels. If this is the case, the only concern will be which hotel is closest for your purposes. If a hotel has to be selected the AA and RAC *Handbooks* and *Hotels and Restaurants in Great Britain*, published by the British Tourist Authority, are all good references. A star grading system is used and details of the facilities available are provided, as are information regarding market days, and the hotel's location in relation to the centre of town. A telephone number and fax number (if available) will be given and further details can be ascertained by contacting the hotel direct before arranging a booking. Bookings are normally first made verbally and later confirmed in writing, either by letter or fax. A confirmation of booking should be sent by the hotel to you and this should be placed in the travel pack.

**2 Motels** – motel accommodation is increasing in the UK. Motels have facilities for overnight accommodation or longer term if preferred. They are located on the main routes around the country as well as in the centres of towns and cities. They do not usually have the luxury or style of a top-class hotel but are comfortable and have shower/toilet facilities in most of the rooms. The dining facilities depend on the size of the motel, but the majority will offer a variety of menus for breakfast, lunch and dinner.

**3 Residential centres** – there are centres that are built specifically to meet the demands of conferences and meetings. Such centres may be converted from country houses or similar properties, are usually located in the country, and cater solely for the executive levels. They offer properly equipped meeting rooms in addition to excellent accommodation and food. There are normally facilities for entertainment and relaxation which may include a sports centre or even a cinema. Booking such a centre would have to be completed at the initial stages of any plans as most have bookings at least a year in advance. It is not usual for these centres to accept bookings not associated with the functions being held. Information regarding such venues can be obtained from professional conference agencies or conference placement agencies.

**4 Bed and breakfast lodgings** – these can be found in most towns, but especially in the coastal areas. This type of accommodation is very popular with tourists, but is also used by sale representatives. The accommodation may be specialist built but many are family homes. The rooms are standard and may have washing facilities or a small *en suite* bathroom. The food served is normally home cooked. Lists of bed and breakfast accommodation can be obtained from the tourist information office of the area.

## ■ DIY 11.1.2

Using suitable reference books and contacts recommend accommodation for a senior manager visiting the following places:

London, West End; Bristol; Edinburgh; Rome, Italy; Orlando, USA; Muscat, Oman.

Once the details of the trip are agreed you may make the arrangements directly yourself or co-ordinate through a travel agent or department within your organisation. Whichever method is used, arranging the travel and accommodation is only part of what is required when organising a business trip. Depending on the destination you may need to arrange vaccinations and on most journeys insurance will be required.

### ▶ *Checking and arranging for travel and health insurance*

Many of the travel agents, sea and air line operators offer insurance automatically; in fact some will not accept your booking without having confirmation of insurance. Cover will be required against personal accident, medical and hospital expenses, loss of luggage and personal belongings.

A life policy may be required, which would be payable to the dependants: usually these policies are for a minimum of £100,000. If a member of staff is using their own car, their insurance must be checked to ensure it covers them for business use. When arranging company car insurance ensure that it covers any driver. If special notification is required when driving abroad, confirm this well in advance of any planned visit. Anyone driving abroad should always take their insurance certificate and driving licence with them. (An international driving licence is required in some countries.) They should also ensure the car meets that country's requirements – for example, display a GB plate, have tinted headlights, and carry a red warning triangle. In some countries a first aid kit must be carried. The AA and RAC will be able to advise on the regulations of the countries to be visited.

Some organisations may provide a health insurance card to employees travelling on business. These cards usually have a policy number and an international emergency contact telephone number. The extent of cover will depend on the type of policy taken out by your organisation, but may include card holder's medical costs and treatment, transportation home and transportation of next of kin to card holder. If a group of people are travelling, they may be issued with a card each or one for all, usually held by the group leader.

# ◾ DIY 11.1.3

Research the area of travel insurance for business people, including the cost, type of cover, availability. As a minimum you should contact at least 2 insurance companies to compare the cost, conditions, exceptions etc.

## ▶ *Medical requirements*

Many places abroad need confirmation of vaccinations or inoculations before allowing people into the country, especially against malaria, typhoid, polio, cholera and yellow fever. An embassy, a practice nurse, doctor or travel agent will inform you of the requirements of the countries to be visited. Health certificates may be required and should be obtained from a doctor, along with any special health requirements such as insulin for diabetics, tablets for heart patients. Spare spectacles should be taken, in case of accident or loss. In some hot countries it would be as well to take some insect repellent cream, antiseptic cream, 'gyppy tummy' medicine, in addition to the normal medicinal aids such as indigestion and headache tablets. A suitable pack should be put together and stored where it is easily accessible. A leaflet is available at main Post Offices for those travelling abroad which lists usual information including general health recommendations. It is important to find out this information well in advance, to enable the necessary vaccinations or inoculations to be given.

# ■ DIY 11.1.4

Obtain a copy of the information leaflet *Travelling Abroad* from your main Post Office. Find out the medical requirements for someone visiting the Gambia and write a memo to Louis Stevens detailing the action he must take before travelling.

## ▶ *Other travel documentation*

**1 Passports** – you should check with the person travelling that their passport is still valid. British passports are valid for 10 years and can be renewed by completing a form, available at main Post Offices, and sending it to one of the passport offices. It can take 4 – 12 weeks for a new passport to be issued, and the Passport Office recommends that applications are made as quickly as possible. Two 2½" x 2" photographs are required, along with a birth certificate and marriage certificate. Passports valid for one year are available direct from main Post Offices but are not valid worldwide; a list of countries accepting these passports is printed on the form. It would be useful to keep the number of the passport in your file in case it is stolen or lost during the visit.

**2 Visa** – you may have to organise entry/exit permits or visas. Some countries require additional documentation to allow people access to their country. The list of countries requiring permits and visas is constantly changing, so you must check with the appropriate embassy or with a travel agent whether one is required or not. Alternatively your contacts in the country being visited may be able to inform you of the requirements. If one is required apply as quickly as possible as some embassies take a long time to process them, and some embassies will also wish the person travelling to attend in person to support the application. It is usual for 1 or 2 passport photographs to be provided with the visa request.
When arranging a visa, you may need to supply the name and address of the organisation or people being visited – especially on a business trip. These organisations or individuals are referred to as 'sponsors' and without named sponsors a visa is unlikely to be approved. Quite often the sponsor will arrange the visa on behalf of the person visiting, and it will be held at the destination airport by the immigration personnel. However, the person travelling should have some evidence of a visa being approved prior to leaving this country. Many airlines will not allow the passengers to board without this evidence, and this could result in your colleague or manager missing their flight!

**3 Exit permits** may also be required and it is important to check before travelling.

# DIY 11.1.5

Find out the requirements for someone travelling to Dubai in the Middle East. Write a memo to Dorothy Cleghorn informing her of the information required, whether photographs are required and what action she must take prior to travelling.

## ▶ *Arranging the monetary requirements*

The person travelling will require some money. If your company has a large finance department arranging travel money may be part of their responsibilities. In a smaller organisation you may have to arrange this for your boss. Eurocheques or travellers cheques can be ordered from a bank or travel agent. It should only take a few days to arrange, but it would be worthwhile advising the bank or travel agent when you know how much is required. Expenditure during the journey may include taxis, hotel, meals, newspapers and airport taxes. Ensure that there is some small change in the currency being supplied as this may be needed as soon as the person arrives at the destination airport. Some organisations arrange for the hotel bill to be paid directly or via the travel agency. In other cases the traveller will be expected to pay before leaving. It is important to find out before travelling what the procedure will be, as the amount of money required will differ enormously depending on whether the hotel bill has to be paid before leaving. Many hotels can cost at least £100 per night for the room alone.

It is also recommended that a charge card (such as American Express) or credit card (such as Access or Visa) is carried, as these are acceptable in almost all countries and will assist in case of problems. Always check that the cards are valid and will not expire during the visit and ensure that they are acceptable in the countries being visited.

Your manager may be travelling to carry out business and there may be some financial transactions requiring credit transfers, bills of exchange, letters of credit or exchange of currency. These may be arranged by your organisation's finance department. Currency can be purchased on a futures market, which will ensure a specific exchange rate for large sums of money. Information on currency restrictions can be obtained from the national bank of the country concerned or from your travel agent, who will advise you of the best method of transfer.

On return to your organisation those travelling will have to account for their expenditure. Where possible receipts should be obtained for everything – or at least the major expenditure items. There may be some instances where receipts are not available, eg newspaper, tip for the bell boy at the hotel, but where possible these items of expenditure should be noted down so that the money allocated can be fully accounted for.

# ■ DIY 11.1.6

Find out the currency required for a visit to Madras in India. Assume the person travelling will have to pay for all costs, including the hotel (£80 per night including breakfast). Make recommendations on how much currency should be taken and how much in travellers cheques. Which currency should the travellers cheques be in?

## ▶ *International time zones*

When making any travel arrangements you should bear in mind the implications of the international time zones. Jet lag can be particularly bad for those travelling east across time zones and time should be given for rest before starting on a busy work schedule. The time in the UK is Greenwich Mean Time (GMT), but arrival times and meeting times may be in local time. You should check when confirming the booking with your agent. Your telephone directory has a page showing the difference in times across the world, but remember that these times are approximate as they may be altered during the summer. The international telephone operator (telephone 155) can confirm exact times for you.

## ▶ *Maintaining security and confidentiality*

As with any other part of your job the details and contents of any business travel are confidential. Files should not be left lying around the office and access to the information should be restricted to those authorised. This is particularly important for visits of a sensitive nature. Documents should be kept under lock and key and word processed documents protected with a password or keyword. The insurance documents and currency are valuable and should be kept secure at all times. Once you have all the relevant information you will be able to draft an itinerary for approval by the person travelling. It is important to supply a draft, as the person may have arrangements or plans that you are not initially aware of and this will give them an opportunity to include them or comment on the arrangements you are planning. The itinerary should be accurate and comprehensive, and preferably be on one sheet of paper. If the trip is several weeks long then more than one itinerary may be used, one for each stage of the visit(s).

▶ *Itineraries*

The itinerary you provide should be a travel plan, which includes dates, times, addresses, telephone numbers and contacts, mode of travel and any other useful information. Most people prefer the itinerary to be typed on postcards, as they fit neatly into pockets or bags and are readily available. If the trip is a particularly long one then several cards may be required and these can be divided into separate weeks or separate locations. An overall itinerary (see Fig 11.1) should also be available which can be kept in the travel pack. Copies of the itinerary should also be prepared for yourself, the travel file, the main office, any line manager and deputy, the traveller's home, and your contact(s) (if there is one) in the country to be visited. The contact(s) may only get an abridged version of the itinerary as there may be information that you do not wish them to receive.

You will need to confirm all the business meetings, to ascertain where they will be held and then decide how your manager is going to travel to and from the venues. A hire car may be required for the whole visit and certainly street maps and travel guides will be needed. Do not have a tight schedule, allow sufficient time between each meeting for travel and in case meetings overrun. If meetings do not include lunch or dinner, separate arrangements may be required – your travel agent will be able to make reservations at recommended restaurants. Do not forget that countries have national holidays when most companies and facilities will be closed; the weather may be unfavourable or siestas common. A good reference book to verify some of this information would be Croner's *Handbook for Exporters.*

It may be necessary for you to find out some background information on the companies and contacts to be visited, or on the country in general – its economic condition, its exports/imports, etc. From this information you will be able to compile a detailed meeting brief. Your manager needs to be familiar with any local customs to ensure that he follows protocol, and if he is unfamiliar with the language an interpreter will be required.

If the trip is a sales promotion visit, samples and literature (in the correct language) will be required – it is far better to send these separately. They will also need a supply of business cards, the customers' records and reports. If electrical equipment is to be used it should be checked to ensure that it will operate correctly on the voltage and that the correct plugs are available. Customs authorities may require time to authorise entry of any equipment as it may be necessary to prove the specifications meet the required standard.

# ITINERARY

### Mr Kris Bourne's visit to India

**Tuesday 15 March**

0800   Taxi from home to Heathrow

1000   Check in Gulf Air – GA342 to Bombay

1220   Depart Heathrow (there will be a one hour stop at Kuwait)

**Wednesday 16 March**

0130   Arrive Bombay (4 hours ahead GMT)

Taxi to Hotel Interasia, Nehru Road, Bombay

Tel: 298 9823, Fax 298 9843

1300   Lunch with Mr Bezra at Hotel Interasia

(Mr Bezra tel: 293 0984)

1600   Meeting at Omray International (Mr Bezra will accompany and drive)

1930   Dinner with associates of Omray (they are booking restaurant)

**Thursday 17 March**

0800   Meeting at Halad Associates, Madinat Bangalore, Bombay

Tel: 294 2098

Papers in meeting file

Working lunch will be provided at Halad Associates

1430   Return to hotel

1700   Contract agreement and negotiation with Omray/Halad, conference room booked at Hotel Interasia

Dinner to be arranged as required at the hotel

**Friday 18 March**

0900   Check out and pay hotel bill

0930   Taxi to airport

1000   Check in domestic flight to Calcutta – IA523

1100   Depart Bombay to Calcutta

**Fig 11.1 An itinerary**

Your colleague/manager may wish to send back to you documents, orders, samples and literature. You should provide them with sufficient addressed envelopes or packing materials to enable them to do this. It is also useful to have a dictating machine for recording the outcome of each meeting, rather than rely on memory at the end of each day. Tapes can be posted back for transcription and if necessary transcripts faxed for checking.

## Knowledge and understanding question bank

1 How do you book travel and accommodation requirements?
2 How do you prepare an itinerary?
3 How do you determine what method of travel to select?
4 What documentation may be required for an international trip?
5 Name three types of monetary arrangement suitable for international travel and the purposes of each.
6 How do you find out the current rate of exchange for currency?
7 Where would you find the international time zones? What do you understand by 'local time'?
8 What medical requirements and arrangements are necessary for travel outside the UK?
9 What security and confidentiality precautions do you take when arranging travel?
10 What legal and regulatory requirements relate to travel and accommodation?

## Claiming credit

For Element 11.1 you must prove that you have arranged travel and accommodation within the UK and overseas, and arranged foreign currency and direct payments by the organisation. The arrangements should be made by yourself and through organising others (eg travel agency staff).

The following work products are potential sources of evidence:

- schedules
- itineraries
- letters of confirmation
- orders
- correspondence
- instructions
- notes of individual needs

Once you have completed your final assessment, you will need to write in your record book or folder how, when and what you have done to prove that you are competent.

The following statement is an example of how one trainee completed this claim:

*I work part-time in an estate agent's office and part of my duties is arranging the travel and accommodation for the agents. I also arrange accommodation for people visiting the area to view properties. Prior to a trip I make sure that I have all the essential information from the person travelling (see my checklist). Once I have this information I can decide on the best method of travel for the trip. When I have draft details I start to put the itinerary together; at this time confirmations may be coming in or the person travelling may have altered their arrangements. I gather all the information in a file (which is kept locked in my cabinet), maps or route planner, information regarding the meetings or properties etc. The file is provided to the person travelling about 2 – 3 days before departure. If the visit is abroad (we have properties in France) then we have a medical kit which is kept in the office and taken in the cars (when they are used). The contents are regularly checked by me and topped up as necessary. We have arrangements with a local bank to issue travellers cheques and I order currency about a week prior to travel. If the country to be visited is outside the EU then I would order currency a couple of weeks prior to departure – to ensure that it arrived on time.*

# ■ Element 11.2
# MONITOR AND VERIFY TRAVEL AND ACCOMMODATION ARRANGEMENTS

## Performance criteria

1 Confirmation of travel and accommodation arrangements being met is obtained from appropriate persons

2 Where arrangements are not met, reasons are ascertained and appropriate action taken

3 Actual costs of arrangements are monitored against those estimated and any changes investigated

4 Claims for expenditure are checked and verified before forwarding for payment

5 Problems arising from the arrangements are investigated and appropriate action taken

## Element introduction

In Element 11.1 we covered the steps necessary to organise travel and accommodation arrangements. However, once these are settled it is necessary to monitor that the requirements are in fact confirmed, the necessary documentation is received and is correct, and that all parties are informed of any changes.

Once the travel and accommodation arrangements have been finalised and the parties have returned from the trip, it is necessary to check the invoices received from the travel agents or the costs incurred from your section's or department's budget. The individuals travelling may also put forward personal expenses related to the trip which need to be checked and verified. On occasions this may involve dealing with discrepancies and investigating problems.

# ■ DIY 11.2.1

State what action you would take in the following instances:

1 Flight time has changed by 2 hours, now leaving Heathrow at 1200 hrs instead of 1000 hrs.
2 The car hire firm do not have a driver available to take your manager to the airport in the morning.
3 The hotel required in Paris is fully booked.
4 The visa cannot be approved until copies of the traveller's passport have been received in the country being visited.
5 The currency you have requested has to be specially ordered and may not be ready for next week.

## ▶ *Confirming travel and accommodation arrangements*

You will need to confirm the arrangements being made with all involved, right up to the point of receiving the travel documentation. Quite often there will be last minute changes which will have a knock-on effect on the itinerary and possibly on the meetings and arrangements schedule.

During the time that you have been organising the travel and accommodation arrangements you will have been collecting together a travel file for those travelling. This should include all the documentation and information required for their trip, including: tickets, maps, visas, currency, travellers cheques, insurance documentation, medical papers and medical kit, itinerary and meeting papers. Any one or more of these may change up to and including the day of travel! Quite often last minute changes will be confirmed by telephone or fax. If the changes are confirmed to you by telephone make sure you double-check any times and flight details – especially any reference numbers and airline. When changes occur in flight details it may be necessary to collect the tickets from the relevant airline desk at the airport prior to departure. This will take more time than just checking in for a flight and the itinerary should show the necessary change and an amendment to the initial departure time made.

# ■ DIY 11.2.2

Your manager is required to travel to Athens on Monday to be available for a meeting at 1400. It will be necessary to stay overnight and return after lunch on Tuesday. Your manager already has appointments that will need rearranging on Monday and Tuesday. It is now Thursday 1600. List the action you would take and then prioritise it in order and state the approximate time required to carry out the tasks.

## ▶ *Ascertaining the reasons for the change*

When alterations are made by those making the travel arrangements on your behalf you should ascertain the reasons for the change. Reasons for changes are many and varied and could include one or more of the following: fully booked flights, cancelled flights, bad weather, road works, industrial action, non-clearance of visas, illness of persons being visited, etc. When passing on changes or alterations to those travelling, especially when you have already provided an itinerary and documentation, it is always best to give a justified reason for the change. Quite often you may be asked to confirm that an alternative is acceptable. If you are unsure you should check this with the group leader or individual travelling.

Only when you have all the documentation organised, confirmed and in hand should you verify arrangements with those travelling and anyone receiving the personnel at the destination. A new itinerary should be provided.

## ▶ *Checking the actual costs against estimated or budgeted costs*

Your organisation will probably have arrangements for invoicing the costs of travel and accommodation. There are generally three main methods of payment:

**1** There may be an agreement with a travel agency to **invoice** your organisation. Invoicing may occur after each trip or at the end of the month. The invoices may be received by each person organising the travel and accommodation or by a central person in the finance department. Whichever system is approved you should ensure that you have sight of the invoice relating to the travel and accommodation you have arranged to ensure it is correct (including any agreed discounts or reductions).

**2** The parties being visited at the destination may **pay directly** for the cost of the trip or will reimburse your organisation when invoiced. In the first case the arrangements may be for the travel and accommodation to be paid for directly by the host organisation. In this case you may not have sight of any of the costs or invoices involved, but you should ensure that your travellers are aware of the arrangements and do not pay the costs themselves. In the second case, you will need to receive the invoices (purchase invoice) from the travel agencies or airline involved and raise an invoice (sales invoice) for the host organisation to pay the costs involved. Your organisation may have agreed to add any expenses incurred to the invoice, in which case you will not be able to raise the invoice until the travellers have returned and submitted their expenditure.

**3** Your organisation may have a **central finance department** that receives and pays all travel and accommodation costs. The arrangement may then be for your section or department to raise an **internal transfer** across to the finance department to reimburse them. The original invoice, or a copy of it, may be sent to you to approve for payment. This should be checked against any quoted costs made by the agency. In addition it will still be necessary to account for any expenditure incurred by those travelling and a record of this should be completed and submitted on the organisation's approved documentation.

Whichever method of payment is used, if alterations have been made to the agreed costs these should be investigated immediately. Quite often agencies and airlines will give discounts for travelling at night; on Saturday; booking a combined flight and hotel; travelling one way; having a stopover at another airport, etc. These discounts can be quite substantial and should be investigated if not already being offered.

Any currencies being collected on behalf of the travellers should be counted and verified at the time of collection. As with any other financial transactions, errors cannot usually be rectified later. Get the cashier to count the currency out to you and count it yourself. Check the exchange rate being used by the cashier at the time and make a note of it for the expenditure claims. It is likely that the traveller's cheques will need to be signed by the person travelling and may have to be collected personally from the cashier. Alternatively an arrangement may be made for a courier to bring them to your office to be signed by those travelling. You should keep a note of the numbers of the traveller's cheques before they are handed to those travelling – in case of loss, damage or theft.

# ■ DIY 11.2.3

Research the agreed arrangements for payment of travel and accommodation in any organisation that you have worked for (either full time, part time or on work experience) or at your training centre. Write a memo to a new member of staff explaining the arrangements for travel in the UK and abroad and attach any organisational guidance notes as appendices to your memo.

## ▶ *Approving expenditure*

Your organisation may have quite formal guidelines for those travelling on business. Some organisations have a rate per day for expenditure which is increased by a percentage for international travel. It is essential that the individuals travelling are aware of any restriction on their budget prior to travelling. In addition many organisations will not approve expenditure on entertainment, alcohol, hotel tips, personal telephone calls, newspapers, personal toiletries, etc. Once again guidelines must be given to any individuals travelling for the first time to ensure that they are not out of pocket when they return. It will also be necessary for expenditure to be supported by receipts whenever possible. It is a good idea for those travelling to keep a running record of their expenditure, either on a form provided or in note form, especially when the trip covers several days and the itinerary is hectic. It is likely that when the person returns there will be several courses of action that will need to be taken, such as orders to process, promises to follow up, etc; expenditure will soon slip from the mind and may be difficult to remember later on, without the benefit of notes made at the time.

## ■ DIY 11.2.4

Design a form that would be suitable for someone travelling on business to note down their expenditure. Do not forget to include space at the top for the traveller's name, type and amount of currency and/or traveller's cheques issued, dates of travel and place(s) visited.

When people return from a business visit try and get them to pass their claims for expenses to you as quickly as possible. This will enable you to process them and arrange payment, if necessary, or in the case of query, you will be able to sort out the problems while the details are fresh in their minds.

## ■ DIY 11.2.5

Investigate the regulations related to expenditure by personnel while on organisation business (one that you have worked for full time, part time or on work experience). If you do not have access to an independent organisation, investigate the regulations related to personnel employed within your training organisation. Where possible obtain examples of the documentation used.

If you find discrepancies in an individual's claims for expenditure you should initially take them up with the person completing the claim. There may have been a straightforward mistake (in addition or in a currency exchange calculation) or misunderstanding (as to what is considered to be approved expenditure). Use diplomacy when investigating problems or discrepancies and attempt to resolve them quickly and quietly. If you are unable to resolve the problem with the claimant then you should refer the matter to your line manager or the financial controller to whom the approved claim would have been passed.

If the traveller has needed to pay for expenses from their own personal funds, their claim should be expedited to ensure that they are recompensed as quickly as possible – especially if a large credit card payment is involved. Credit card companies are now processing payments much more quickly than in the past and it is likely that a payment will appear on a statement within a few weeks of returning from the visit. (In some cases it has been known to be on the statement waiting for the person to come home!)

## ▶ Legal and regulatory requirements

Apart from the Health and Safety at Work Act regulations, under which you should be operating, you will also need to ensure that you are aware of any other legal and regulatory requirements. These may include requirements relating to the amounts of money (currency) being transferred to and from different countries, the medical requirements of any countries being visited, local customs and requirements for visitors to particular countries, inland revenue requirements for personnel receiving benefits, etc.

## ◀ DIY 11.2.6

Arrange to interview a travel agent or individual responsible for arranging travel and accommodation. Discuss with them the legal and regulatory requirements when arranging travel and accommodation in the UK and abroad. Write a report to your tutor on your findings, listing any references you may have used.

### Knowledge and understanding question bank

1 What methods of monitoring travel and accommodation arrangements do you use?
2 How do you deal with changes to arrangements?
3 What methods of monitoring financial allocations do you use?
4 What methods of checking and verifying expenditure do you follow?
5 What types of problems in relation to travel and accommodation arrangements have you encountered and how have you dealt with them?
6 How do you confirm travel and accommodation arrangements?

**7** How do you monitor actual costs against estimated costs?

**8** What are your organisation's procedures for checking expenditure?

**9** What type of expenses may not be approved for payment?

**10** What types of problems in relation to expenses have you dealt with and how were these resolved?

## Claiming credit

For Element 11.2 you must prove that you have monitored and verified travel and accommodation arrangements, including invoices relating to the cost of travel and accommodation and expense claims from individuals for whom arrangements were made.

The following work products are potential sources of evidence:

- schedules
- itineraries
- reports relating to travel and accommodation
- records of corrective action
- comparisons of actual against planned expenditure
- copies of checked and verified claims
- reports of investigations and complaints

Once you have completed your final assessment, you will need to write in your record book or folder how, when and what you have done to prove that you are competent.

The following statement is an example of how one trainee completed this claim:

*As part of my duties when arranging travel I liaise with the travel office or sometimes direct with the ferry company or airlines. I tend to use the fax to confirm my requirements. When the requested times of departure are not available I ensure that the next best is available. Alternatively I would try other airlines or ferry companies before settling for the second choice. The estimated costs are kept on file until the final invoice is received. This is then checked with the estimate and with the person who travelled to ensure that all the services and requirements were met. The personnel travelling are required to complete an expenses form when they return. This should contain all the details of their expenditure and supporting receipts are required – these are checked against the claims. If I have any problems I always try to sort them out with the person concerned rather than involving my Manager – most of the time it is an easy mistake such as a wrong date or amount. I have to keep careful, accurate and up-to-date records as most of the costs and expenditure are invoiced to our clients.*

# UNIT 12

# Contribute to the acquisition and control of financial provision

## Element 12.1
## CONTRIBUTE TO THE ACQUISITION OF FINANCIAL PROVISION

### Performance criteria

**1** Estimates of expenditure for own area of responsibility are based on detailed assessments of resources to achieve planned work

**2** Estimates of expenditure are supplied to decision makers, within agreed deadlines

**3** The format of the estimates provides clear and accurate information to decision makers

### Element introduction

Financial provision and control are amongst the most important aspects of good businesses. In your role within the organisation you may find that you are responsible for acquiring finance for special projects. Alternatively you may be responsible for an area of financial provision, such as stock control, or petty cash. Any financial transactions should be recorded accurately and must meet any legal or regulatory requirements.
The procedures you set up or follow should take these needs into account.

## ▶ *Estimating expenditure*

If you are responsible for a **special project** you may be asked to set out the proposed procedures and costs for approval to your line manager or a committee. This may involve obtaining estimates of expenditure, time and resources. Estimates are approximations, but should be as close to the actual expenditure as possible. You may need to contact suppliers, contractors or other members of staff to obtain your estimates and this may be done verbally or in writing, or you may obtain the costs from catalogues or information provided by the supplier. If you are obtaining information from literature supplied, you may need to check that the prices quoted are the most recent and that there are no further costs to be added – such as delivery.

Alternatively you may be responsible for buying **stock**, such as stationery required by the department. Your manager may require you to estimate the cost of the stock and allocate you a budget to order and purchase requirements over a set period – perhaps 6 months or a year. You will need to obtain estimates of use as well as estimates of cost. Estimates of use may come from stock records – if they are kept – or from the individuals that use the stock. The estimates for the purchase of the stock will come from the suppliers or their literature.

Another common area of financial control is in **petty cash**. Petty cash is run on the **imprest** system. The imprest is the amount of cash required for the accounting period. The accounting period may be one week, one month or any other agreed period. You will need to estimate the amount of finance required for the imprest, account for the cash spent and keep accurate records.

You will need to decide which one of these areas is relevant to your area of work and will provide you with sufficient evidence for your portfolio and qualification. It is not necessary to set up a system from the beginning but you must be able to demonstrate that you have met all the performance criteria. If you do set up a system from the beginning you may be able to link your performance and evidence with the requirements of Unit 8 – Develop, Implement and Maintain Procedures.

## ▶ *Special projects*

Special projects may relate to replacing equipment, refurbishing a room, setting up a new reception or other area within your organisation. Your manager may delegate to you the responsibility for researching the requirements, obtaining the estimates, setting the timescales, submitting the project for approval and overseeing its completion.

Ensure you look at all the alternatives available and seek the views of any other individuals involved. Once you have a scheme in mind, set it down on paper and support your ideas with sketches, diagrams and explanations. Write to the necessary suppliers of services, materials and equipment to obtain their estimates and complete a budget for your project. Remember that the estimates quoted may only be held for a certain period of time. If this time expires you will need to check whether the cost has altered. Make sure that your report is concise, easy to read and does not omit any important facet.

# ■ DIY 12.1.1

You have been asked to replace the desktop copier in the mail room. You know that the copier is used every day, but only 20 or so copies are taken each day. The copies are usually only A4 and single-sided. Research the type of machines available that would complete the tasks necessary in the mail room. Obtain estimates of the cost of renting and purchasing a suitable machine and take into account the costs of consumables. Write a report on your proposal and provide supporting documentation regarding the pricing and period of time it would take to complete your project.

## ▶ *Stock control*

Many organisations do not have a formal procedure for controlling stock, especially stationery and office consumables. This may be an ideal opportunity for you to usefully organise an area of work which is not currently formalised and aim to save the organisation money through careful control of stock and finance. However, your proposed procedures should include how you intend to acquire the services of suppliers, identify and obtain materials and equipment necessary for the work area, and take into account any particular services supplied by people such as special delivery.

It is essential to have a reservoir of all the items required for your business to operate efficiently. If office consumables and stationery run out the administrative support for the business would fail. Imagine the problems that would occur if the photocopier paper ran out or the last typewriter ribbon was used. It is also cheaper to buy goods in bulk as advantage can be taken of the higher discounts given. However, care must be taken not to over-order and not to use capital (money) that may be required in other areas.

### Estimating sufficient stock

You should consider:

**1 Money** – Stock is worth money and it is unwise for a business to have too much money tied up in stock. Some stock may be perishable and have a limited 'shelf life'. Examples are fashionable clothing, fruit and vegetables, and even paper which becomes yellow in time.

**2 Time** – It may be difficult to obtain stock quickly and valuable orders may be lost to other businesses who are able to deliver goods on the date required. You will find that to prevent this situation arising most businesses will carry sufficient stock to ensure that when orders are received they can be fulfilled immediately. It is important that delivery time is taken into consideration and that suppliers are reliable.

**3 Space** – Storage space is expensive and it uses valuable space in areas which must be maintained with heating and lighting, protected and secured. Staff are employed to take charge of stock and insurance must be paid to provide cover in the event of damage or theft. The business will anticipate the maximum amount of each item of stock that should be kept at any one time to reduce the costs of storage.

**4 Usage** – In an office you would find yourself needing typewriter ribbons, correction tapes, paper, envelopes, etc on a regular basis. It is a good idea to keep a check on how much stock is used in an average week. You will then be able to calculate when the regular orders need to be made.

The following formula is often used to estimate the minimum, maximum and reorder levels for stock.

- **Minimum** – the lowest amount possible, without risking running out completely
- **Maximum** – the greatest amount possible, taking into account storage space and cash available.
- **Reorder level** – the amount when an order should be placed. This should be the minimum level plus the amount used on a daily basis before delivery of the item is received. The amount required to keep the business operational until delivery of the order is called the **buffer stock**. An example would be: minimum level is 10, you use 1 a day, and delivery from the supplier will take 2 weeks; so your reorder level will be 20. This is 10 minimum (10 buffer stock) + 1 per working day for 2 weeks (ie 10 days) awaiting delivery = 10 + 10 = 20. This will ensure you do not run out before the delivery is received.

When you order it would normally be an order large enough to take you back up to the maximum level. However if you find you are ordering a particular item more frequently it may be necessary to change your maximum level. Changes occur in usage for many reasons and one of your responsibilities will be to recognise when such changes are occurring and respond to them accordingly.

It is unwise, however, to order items in large quantities just because they are on 'special offer': they still cost money and expensive storage could well eliminate any economy intended.

Small businesses may use a **'visual'** system of stock control: in other words, stock is ordered when a need is seen. Larger businesses use a **'bin'** system where all stock is given a bin number which identifies the position in which it is kept in the stock room.

However most organisations will use **stock cards** as a system of keeping a record of the stock in hand and the issues and receipts made.

A stock card should be made up for each item held, showing details of the supplier used, the minimum, maximum and reorder levels used. The date of receipts and issues made, who received the item and the current stock level will also be detailed. You will then be able to see from a glance at the card when something needs reordering.

It is important that the calculations are correct. If they are not, you may find yourself in trouble for ordering or approving stock unnecessarily or, even worse, not ordering stock that is required.

A regular check should be made on your stock; this is called **stock taking** or reconciliation. This is where every item of stock in the business is counted to calculate how much of the business's money is tied up in stock. An index will be made of all the items held. This index is called an **inventory**. It is necessary to physically count the number of items in stock and compare the total against the total written on the stock card. Any discrepancies should be reported and the reason for the discrepancies should be sought. It is possible that items have been taken without authority, or the figures on the card are incorrect.

# ■ DIY 12.1.2

In carrying out this activity, assume that you are working for a small office with 3 administrative assistants. Within the office you have a typewriter, 2 computers and an ink jet printer. The photocopier is in another room and is maintained and supplied by central reception. Using supplier catalogues make a list of the stationery and consumables you believe will be required. Obtain or calculate the estimated cost of purchase and present your proposals and findings in a formal report to your tutor.

## ▶ *Petty cash*

Many organisations do not have a formal petty cash system as it is not required – staff are not expected to pay out sums of money for business purposes. Such organisations may issue 'floats' to those with regular expenditure requirements or a company credit card may be issued. In other cases the member of staff may be reimbursed by completing an expenses or expenditure claim form. If your organisation has an informal method of paying for small claims from staff it may be worth investigating the possibility of setting up a more formal system for controlling the acquisition and approval of the cash spent.

As stated earlier petty cash is usually run on the imprest system and you will need to estimate how much cash is required over the accounting period. The accounting period may be one week, several weeks or a month. It will depend on how much petty cash is held and spent. If the amount is small, £10 or so in a month, it would not be worth setting an accounting period of less than one month. However, if £100 is accounted for over one month, this could be broken down into 4 accounting periods or weekly periods.

A petty cash book should be kept which details all the incoming and outgoing cash. At the end of the accounting period the total spent is accounted for and a corresponding amount is requested from the cashier or the accounts department to replenish the petty cash, ready for the start of the next accounting period. For instance, if the imprest for your office was agreed at £30 and you accounted each week for the amount spent, if you spent £10 during the week, a request would be made for £10 to be refunded for the beginning of the next week, bringing the total held back to the imprest of £30. You may find that as prices increase you will need to increase your imprest accordingly. Authority should be sought before any increase is carried out.

Before paying any amounts out from your petty cash, you should request a petty cash voucher (see Fig 12.1). The voucher should be completed and signed by the person requesting the payment and receipts should be attached where possible. A voucher will give details of the item purchased or details of what the money was spent on, for example bus fares. It may be that small amounts can be paid without authorisation, but large amounts will probably need a countersignature of a supervisor. It will be up to the person in charge to decide on the amounts for countersignature, or the business may have internal regulations which need to be followed. It is usual for each of the vouchers to be numbered, to make the book-keeping easier to operate.

If there are any discrepancies, eg money has been paid out without a voucher being completed or money is missing, these should be reported to your supervisor immediately.

At the end of the accounting period it will be necessary for you to take your accounts to the cashier for verification. You will need to keep a petty cash book or a weekly analysis sheet to record expenditure. A typical petty cash book would have columns ruled and headings as shown in Fig 12.2.

400

**Petty Cash Voucher**

Folio ________

Date ________ 19

| For what required | AMOUNT £ | p |
|---|---|---|
| | | |
| | | |

Signature ______________________

Passed by ______________________

**Fig 12.1 Petty cash voucher**

Dr. PETTY CASH BOOK Cr.

| Received | Date | Fo | Details | Vo no | Total paid out | | | | | |
|---|---|---|---|---|---|---|---|---|---|---|
| | | | | | | | | | | |
| | | | | | | | | | | |
| | | | | | | | | | | |
| | | | | | | | | | | |
| | | | | | | | | | | |
| | | | | | | | | | | |
| | | | | | | | | | | |
| | | | | | | | | | | |
| | | | | | | | | | | |
| | | | | | | | | | | |
| | | | | | | | | | | |
| | | | | | | | | | | |
| | | | | | | | | | | |
| | | | | | | | | | | |
| | | | | | | | | | | |
| | | | | | | | | | | |
| | | | | | | | | | | |
| | | | | | | | | | | |
| | | | | | | | | | | |
| | | | | | | | | | | |
| | | | | | | | | | | |
| | | | | | | | | | | |
| | | | | | | | | | | |
| | | | | | | | | | | |
| | | | | | | | | | | |
| | | | | | | | | | | |
| | | | | | | | | | | |

**Fig 12.2 Petty cash book**

The **VAT** (Value Added Tax) column is particularly important if your business is registered for VAT, as the accounts office will wish to claim back all VAT paid out by the business. By law, businesses need to keep records of VAT received and paid. It is therefore essential that you have a separate column for VAT and correctly calculate the amounts involved. Remember that the rate of VAT may change. (It is currently set at 17.5 per cent.) It is therefore helpful to put the rate used on the petty cash account pages. Not all goods are VAT rated if you contact your local HM Customs and Excise they will advise you as to the current regulations.

An example of VAT calculations would be:

- **VAT charged to a customer**
  Goods bought = £10
  + VAT 17.5% = £1.75
  Total payable = £11.75.

- **VAT paid to a supplier**
  Total payable = £15.00 (this figure includes the VAT, therefore you will need to divide by 117.5 and times by 17.5 to find out how much has been charged)
  $$£15.00 \div 117.5 = 0.1276 \times 17.5 = £2.23 \text{ VAT}$$
  $$£15.00 - 2.23 = £12.77 \text{ cost excluding VAT}$$
  Therefore the cost of the goods was £12.77 to which the supplier added 17.5% VAT of £2.23, making a total payment of £15.

You will also select headings depending on the type of expenditure made. For instance, if you pay out for stamps, recorded and registered post, you may have a heading for **post**; for bus and taxi fares, **travel**; for window cleaning, fresh air sprays, etc, **cleaning**; string, pens, pencils, etc, **stationery**. This assists the accounts department when completing the end-of-year accounts.

At the end of the imprest period you should total the columns and ensure that they are correct; count the cash left and add the two together. They should total the imprest. If not, then your figures may be wrong or you have cash missing. The cashier will want to check your figures and the vouchers before transferring the information into the company cash book. Any discrepancies will be noted at this point.

Cash will then be issued to you to make up your imprest and this amount should be entered on to the debit side (left-hand side) of your petty cash account.

## Security for petty cash

In the petty cash procedures, we have already stated that no cash should be issued without a voucher being completed. It is also important that access to the cash is restricted to those that have authority to pay out amounts, in accordance with the regulations of the business. A special lockable petty cash box should be bought. These usually have sections for the cash in a lift-off tray, and notes can be placed underneath – a similar layout to a cash till, but much smaller.

The box should also be kept in a locked drawer and keys kept with a responsible person, although no one person should be responsible for cash or financial records within a business. It is usual practice to have at least one other person checking the accounts and methods on a regular basis; this would normally be the person who issues you with cash at the end of each accounting period. This will help to ensure that the methods employed are secure and pilfering is prevented. Discourage 'loans' to staff who are short of cash for lunch, as this will only confuse the accounting system you have and a check should be made if some of the cash is missing.

Provision should be made for when the person responsible for petty cash is away, whether sick, on holiday or on a course. All the employees of the business should know what the agreed procedure is and should not be permitted to help themselves.

## Dealing with emergencies

Quite often emergencies will occur which will require you to react and think quickly. Apart from the routine requests for petty cash you may be asked for emergency funds at a time outside the normal issuing time. Claims may be made that you do not agree with, such as an employee whose car broke down at home, so she used a taxi and reclaimed the amount. It may be that the business will agree to pay such an amount, but it should be checked. Even claims that have been countersigned should be closely verified by you, as many supervisors are extremely busy and may not actually look closely at the voucher they are signing. A claim may be made for more than you have in your cash tin at the present time. If this occurs regularly it could mean that the imprest needs to be changed and a new amount agreed with the cashier.

# ◾ DIY 12.1.3

Up to now the petty cash has been dealt with on a very informal basis in your office, but you propose that you should implement the formal procedures. Design a petty cash voucher that will be suitable for use by all the staff, and write a memo to staff informing them of your new system. Fix the maximum amount payable from your float. (Amounts above this should be claimed from the accounts office and a cheque will be issued.) Also determine the amount at and above which countersignatures are required from immediate supervisors. Indicate the type of expenditure that will be acceptable from staff and estimate the requirements for one month. Request receipts to support claims whenever possible. Decide when payments will be made, whether at a fixed time per week, or on demand, and try to anticipate any other questions the staff may have and include them in your memo to reduce the number of queries that may be raised. You will also be expected to pay the office cleaner £10 per week, and to collect a floral display for the reception at a cost of £15 per week.

Put together a report for your manager regarding your proposal and include your estimated figures plus your draft memo to staff and other documentation as appendices to your report.

## Knowledge and understanding question bank

1 What is the role and responsibility you have undertaken in respect of obtaining and supplying estimates of expenditure?
2 What method of estimating have you used?
3 What are your organisation's procedures for authorising financial expenditure?
4 What are your organisation's requirements for presenting estimates for approval?
5 What sources of information have you accessed to obtain your estimates?
6 How have you presented the information to your decision makers?
7 What financial timescales does your organisation operate within?
8 What estimates have you obtained and presented in relation to costs involved with services, materials, equipment and people?
9 What do you understand to be clear and accurate information?
10 What deadlines have you worked to when providing estimates of expenditure and have you encountered any difficulties in meeting them?

## Claiming credit

For Element 12.1 you must prove that you have provided estimates for your own area of responsibility in relation to services, material, equipment and people.

The following work products are potential sources of evidence:
- work programmes
- resource assessments
- cost estimates
- estimates of financial resources required

Once you have completed your final assessment, you will need to write in your record book or folder how, when and what you have done to prove that you are competent.

The following statement is an example of how one trainee completed this claim:

*While working at Cold Service Co I organised the purchase and installation of new mail room equipment. I gathered estimates from local suppliers for the equipment required and presented my findings in a report to the Director. I presented all of the costs in a table and compared the different service and maintenance packages available for the franking machine. We discussed the implications of the new procedures and which staff were to be involved.*

# Element 12.2
# CONTRIBUTE TO THE CONTROL OF FINANCIAL PROVISION

## Performance criteria

**1** The allocated financial provision, for own area of responsibility, is monitored and variations from planned expenditure identified

**2** Expenditure is accurately recorded in accordance with organisational requirements

**3** Expenditure is within limits of own authority

**4** Variations from planned expenditure are promptly and accurately reported to the appropriate persons

**5** When expenditure is required outside limits of own authority, accurate details are promptly provided to the appropriate person

## Element introduction

In the Element 12.1 we covered the ways in which this unit may be achieved and suitable evidence gathered for your portfolio. This element is a continuation of your chosen project. In Element 12.1 you identified the project to be completed, obtained the estimates and provided all the necessary information to the decision makers. You will probably have carried out further discussion regarding the project with your line manager and tutor and made any adjustments required.

The requirements for this element include monitoring the approved expenditure, accurate recording, reporting variations from agreed expenditure and ensuring work is carried out within the areas of your own authority.

# ▶ *Special projects*

If you have agreed to complete a special project then for this element you will need to implement your plans and monitor the expenditure. If your organisation does not have an approved system for recording this type of expenditure, a simple income and expenditure account (see Fig 12.3) will suffice for recording these transactions.

Any amounts received for your project will be shown in the income column, along with the date and the details of the transaction. Any payments made for the project will be shown in the expenditure columns, along with the date, the details of the expenditure, ie who payment was made to and what for, and the amount.

| Debit | INCOME AND EXPENDITURE | | | Credit | |
|---|---|---|---|---|---|
| Income | | | Expenditure | | |
| Date | Details | Amount £ | Date | Details | Amount £ |
| 3/3 | Budget received from finance | 1500.00 | 6/3 | Office Supplies – desk purchased | 275.50 |
| | | | | | |
| | | | | | |
| | | | | | |

**Fig 12.3 Simple income and expenditure account**

At the end of each week (or month if it is a long-term project) the columns should be totalled and the account balanced (see Fig 12.4).

The entry 'balance c/f' stands for balance carried forward, and 'balance b/f' for balance brought forward. The double lines under the totals show that it is the end of the balancing period and indicate the balances on both sides. It is important that the total is written on both sides. The balance figure shows that the amount of expenditure left for your project is £564.00.

| Debit | | INCOME AND EXPENDITURE | | | Credit | |
|-------|-----|------|-------|---------|------|-----|
| Income | | | Expenditure | | | |
| Date | Details | Amount £ | Date | Details | | Amount £ |
| 3/3 | Budget received from finance | 1500.00 | 6/3 | Office Supplies – desk purchased | | 275.50 |
| | | | 10/3 | Building Services – decoration carried out | | 575.00 |
| | | | 12/3 | W Granger – desk supplies (see list) | | 85.50 |
| | | | 12/3 | Total to date | | 936.00 |
| | | | 12/3 | Balance c/f | | 564.00 |
| 12/3 | Balance | 1500.00 | 12/3 | Balance | | 1500.00 |
| 13/3 | Balance b/f | 564.00 | | | | |

**Fig 12.4 Income and expenditure account at end of balancing period**

# ■ DIY 12.2.1

Set up the records necessary to monitor expenditure for the activity carried out in DIY 12.1.1. Generate the necessary invoices and correspondence to track the project fully from start to finish.

In many circumstances the project will not run as planned – items will be delayed, or out of stock, prices will change etc. You will need to keep track of the proceedings and be aware that changes may incur variations to the planned expenditure. When the variation is a saving in expenditure the managers or decision makers are unlikely to be concerned – they may even be pleased – as long as the quality and objective are still on target. However, if the variation is an increase in cost then it must be you who monitors it, confirm when definite and work out and the variation (ie the difference between the estimated or budgeted cost and the actual cost). Any differences should be communicated to the appropriate persons as soon as they are positive – especially when approval will be required for you to exceed your budget. As well as informing the appropriate person of the variation you should state why it has arisen and your recommended action.

While monitoring your project you should ensure that all the expenditure you approve is within your authority. Special items that cost more than expected as well as unexpected additions should be approved by the decision maker. You may report the variations verbally or in writing. As the change is an important part of the project, and you do not wish to be compromised at a later date, confirmation in writing from your decision maker should be obtained if possible.

Another aspect which you need to take into account is when expenditure from another person's budget is required. This can be quite common in large organisations where perhaps a number of small orders may be grouped and one order will be placed to gain the benefits of bulk discounts etc. Once again you should gain approval from the appropriate person before giving the go-ahead for the work to be completed, the order to be placed or payment confirmed. You will then need to make the necessary arrangements for payment by the other person or for your budget to be credited by them with the funds required.

## ■ DIY 12.2.2

The cost of paper has risen by 20 per cent and your approved expenditure will not cover the cost of your project. Write a memo to the Finance Manager justifying the increase. State what the amounts involved are and recommend that you buy 12 months' supply as prices are likely to increase again next month.

### ▶ *Stock control*

In Element 12.1 you will have identified the procedures you wish to implement, the items you wish to purchase and control. For this element you will need to order the required goods, check the financial documentation relating to the purchases and keep track of your budget.

Various documentation will be used by different companies involved in buying and selling transactions. It is normal practice for these organisations to allocate document reference numbers in order to assist identification and clarify payments. Sales and geographical references can be used to identify each customer and each individual order placed. Corresponding documents carry the same number so that all parties know what order or delivery is being dealt with. If a company were to receive 2 invoices for the same delivery, it would be easy to identify this because each invoice would carry details of the same order number.

Larger organisations will allocate official order numbers to an order which may have to be signed by an authorised member of staff. Printed order forms may carry a warning stating that if the order does not carry an official order number and is not authorised then the delivery of goods will not be accepted.

Documents that you are likely to come across are:

1 Order
2 Acknowledgement
3 Advice Note
4 Delivery Note
5 Consignment Note
6 Pro-forma Invoice
7 Invoice
8 Statement of Account
9 Credit Note
10 Debit Note

In the Element 12.1 you may already have sent out an initial **enquiry**, perhaps to 3 or 4 suppliers, in order to find out which supplier can offer the best deal. In return the suppliers will send a **quotation, estimate, catalogue** or **price list** detailing the price and terms they are prepared to offer. The supplier may also take this opportunity to send free samples or arrange for a sales representative to call.

You need to decide upon the supplier(s) to use and send out an **order**. When the supplier receives this order they will send an **acknowledgement** back to confirm that they have received the order. Once the order is ready to be sent the supplier will send an **advice note** by post, containing the delivery details.

A **delivery note**, containing the same details as the advice note, will be sent with the goods. It will be your responsibility to ensure that the goods delivered correspond with the goods detailed in the delivery note. Any discrepancies must be detailed on the note and confirmed to the suppliers or to the person delivering the goods.

The supplier will produce an **invoice** for each delivery of goods sent to the business, which will give full details of the goods supplied together with a breakdown of costs, including any discounts, transport charges and VAT. At the end of each month the supplier will send the organisation a **statement** which details the amount payable for all the invoices for that month, less any refunds for goods returned or damaged (detailed on the **credit note**), plus any charges for additional goods or under-payments (detailed on the **debit note**).

You may pay separately for each invoice received (this will depend on how often the business uses the supplier and how many deliveries are made in one month). When the invoice or statement of account has been checked arrangements are made for payment to be sent to the supplier in settlement of the account. This may involve you writing a cheque yourself or writing a memo to the finance section to approve payment.

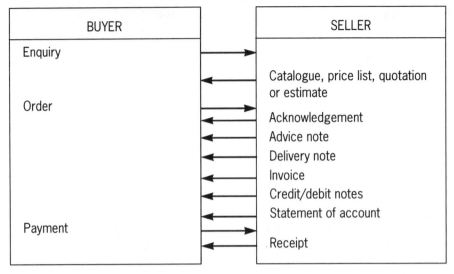

**Fig 12.5 Document flow between buyer and seller**

In general terms, the usual flow of some of these documents is as shown in Fig 12.5.

You may also be responsible for calculating transport charges which will be added to the invoice. The following pricing terms are used to indicate transport charges:

- **Carriage paid** – This means the price includes all transport costs.

- **Loco** – This is the factory price and does not include transport costs (often used for motor cars).

- **Free on Rail (FOR)** – This means the seller pays all costs up to named railway station.

- **Carriage forward** – This means the cost of delivery is not included in the price.

- **Cash With Order (CWO)** – This means payment must accompany the order.

- **Cash On Delivery (COD)** – This means payment must be paid to whoever delivers the goods.

### Checking the documentation

**Manual systems** involve the use of **files** to keep all business transaction documents. Box files and lever arch files are often used to keep documents such as invoices and delivery notes in order. It is likely that a separate file will be kept for each supplier, with invoices kept either in date order or numerically by their invoice number.

When an invoice or statement of account is received it is checked against the original order form and delivery note to make sure the correct goods have been delivered before payment is made. Some organisations will also check the invoice against the delivery note, although the invoice is often used instead of a delivery note.

**Computerised accounts systems**, such as Pegasus and Sage, can be used to store all information detailed on buying and selling documentation. Information regarding sales can be keyed into the computer and stored indefinitely. Invoices and other documents can be printed out and invoices received by the company can be checked against the original order information held on the computer. A computerised accounts system can automatically calculate VAT, discounts and transport charges.

### Credit and debit notes

The use of **credit notes** and **debit notes** allows adjustments to be made without having to create another invoice. If you discovered you were overcharged or were invoiced for an item you had not received, you would request a credit note to make up the difference. If you found that you were undercharged or accepted items not listed on your invoice, then a debit note would be forwarded. The amount under- or over-paid will be rectified on the next statement of account.

### Calculating the VAT

When you receive of an invoice note that VAT is often entered in a separate column. When invoices are being processed you will have to identify purchases that include VAT, calculate how much VAT is included in the price, then check that this is correct before the invoice is paid.

If you are presented with an amount which includes VAT, divide the total by 117.5 and then multiply by 17.5 – this will tell you how much of the total price is VAT (you can also multiply by 7 and divide by 47 to arrive at the same answer!). If you are given a figure that requires VAT to be added to it, divide the figure by 100 and then multiply by 17.5 – this will tell you how much should be added on.

The VAT column is particularly important if the company is registered for VAT as this registration enables the company to claim back all VAT paid on goods and services. Therefore it is essential that accurate records are kept not only for the benefit of the company, but also because they are required by law.

411

The rate of VAT is currently set at 17.5 per cent, but remember that some goods, such as food, children's clothes and shoes, newspapers and books are exempt. In effect, the government uses registered businesses to collect VAT from the consumer on its behalf. These businesses have to pay on the VAT collected every quarter-year, but are allowed to deduct all the VAT paid out by the business from this amount.

Some businesses do not have to add VAT on to the price of their goods or services. Such businesses will not get a refund of the VAT they have themselves paid on goods and services they have bought.

- Small businesses do not have to become VAT registered provided their annual turnover is less than £46,000. Once it exceeds this amount they have no option but must become registered and keep relevant, up–to-date VAT records that can be checked by HM Customs and Excise Department at will.
- Some businesses, such as banks, do not charge VAT on their services, but are exempted from reclaiming VAT paid out.

Zero-rated businesses do not have to add VAT on to the selling price of goods, but can obtain a refund of all VAT paid on the purchase of goods or services. A zero-rated business, such as a publisher or a business selling food, is in a better position than an exempted business.

The only business that is allowed, by law, to charge you VAT is one that is registered to do so. You will be able to check whether a business is registered by asking for its VAT registration number, although this should be printed on the invoice and any other business documents used by the business.

## Discounts

Businesses often use various methods to attract custom. Two methods are:

1 **Trade discount** – this is usually given by the seller to buyers who order in large quantities. A discount percentage is given on orders over a certain amount and therefore encourages bulk orders.

2 **Cash discount** – this is given by the seller to the buyer to encourage quick payment. The discount is usually shown as '**terms** 2% one month', meaning that if payment is made within one month the buyer can deduct 2 per cent from the total price.

If an invoice for £50.00 was received showing a trade discount of 10 per cent and a cash discount of 5 per cent one month, provided the payment was made within one month, the buyer would deduct £7.25 from the invoice and only pay £42.75. The formula used for this calculation is:

£50.00 ÷ 100 x 10 (trade discount) = £5.00

£50.00 − £5.00 = £45.00

£45.00 ÷ 100 x 5 (cash discount) = £2.25

£45.00 − £2.25 = £42.75

## Tax point

In most cases the date of the invoice will be the same as the **tax point**. This is the date on which the goods transfer hands and VAT is payable. The seller and the buyer of the goods will have to enter details of VAT charged and paid on to their records for that particular date. This date is very important as VAT is paid to HM Customs and Excise department every 3 months (quarterly), so it is important for a business to know in which quarter to place the VAT paid or collected. If, for example, a company were to receive their goods in separate deliveries the tax point date would be different from the invoice date, as the VAT would only be charged once the total amount of goods had been delivered.

# DIY 12.2.4

Check the orders shown in Figs 12.6 to 12.8, placed by the Purchasing Department of Bales Paint Supplies, against their respective invoices (Figs 12.9 to 12.11). List any errors you find and report these in a memo to the Accounts Supervisor, Mrs Cathy Sewell. When checking the invoices make sure you deduct both trade and cash discount from the price before calculating the VAT.

---

### BALES PAINT SUPPLIES
144 Knight Lane
Kinstone KJ32 7BB

Pickford Chemicals
Salisbury Way
Bury

ORDER NUMBER
C/6785/245

DATE
27 January 199-

Please supply the following:

| ITEM | CODE | QUANTITY |
|------|------|----------|
| White Spirit | WD99/B | 8 x 4 litres |
| Methylated Spirit | MS56/A | 9 x 4 litres |
| Caustic Soda | CS/02/C | 5 boxes |

DELIVER TO: above address    AUTHORISED BY: *A N Other*
NOTE: Goods deliveries will only be accepted if accompanied
by an official order number.

**Fig 12.6  Order 1, for use with DIY 12.2.4**

---

### BALES PAINT SUPPLIES
144 Knight Lane
Kinstone KJ32 7BB

Pattersons Stationery
The Long Yard
Ilkeston

ORDER NUMBER
F/2693/23

DATE
29 January 199-

Please supply the following:

| ITEM | CODE | QUANTITY |
|------|------|----------|
| A4 Copier Paper (white) | 45/A/9 | 10 reams |
| A4 Bank Paper (yellow) | 23/67/8 | 4 reams |
| Staplers | 15/87/A | 6 |
| Staple removers | 25/784/1 | 10 |
| Comb Binding machine | 123/87 | 1 |
| Lever Arch Files | 12/5/89 | 2 x 10 |
| Box Files | 72/6/90 | 2 x 10 |

DELIVER TO: above address    AUTHORISED BY: *A N Other*
NOTE: Goods deliveries will only be accepted if accompanied
by an official order number.

**Fig 12.7  Order 2, for use with DIY 12.2.4**

414

# BALES PAINT SUPPLIES
144 Knight Lane
Kinstone KJ32 7BB

Ace Computer Supplies
Catchpole Gardens
London SE9

ORDER NUMBER

C/7648/54

DATE

31 January 199-

Please supply the following:

| ITEM | CODE | QUANTITY |
|------|------|----------|
| Concept 35 computer chair | 24-m-2309 | 3 |
| Laser Toner Cartridges | 34-n-3425 | 6 |
| Double Density Diskettes | 38-p-4879 | 3 x 10 |
| Diskette Library Case | 56-o-3099 | 2 |
| Economy PC Stand | 11-r-5888 | 3 |

DELIVER TO: above address    AUTHORISED BY: *A N Other*
NOTE: Goods deliveries will only be accepted if accompanied
by an official order number.

**Fig 12.8 Order 3, for use with DIY 12.2.4**

# PATTERSON'S STATIONERY SUPPLIES
The Long Yard
Ilkeston IK3 9DD

VAT REG NO: 333/555/22

### INVOICE

Our Ref: pg/aw/897
Your Ref: F/2639/23

DATE/TAX POINT: 9.2.9–

To: Bales Paint Supplies
144 Knight Lane
Kinstone

| QTY | DESCRIPTION | UNIT PRICE | TOTAL PRICE | VAT | AMOUNT TO PAY |
|-----|-------------|------------|-------------|-----|---------------|
| 10 | A4 Copier Paper White | £2.99 ream | 29.90 | 5.12 | 34.42 |
| 5 | A4 Bank Paper (Yellow) | £2.55 ream | 10.20 | 1.75 | 11.75 |
| 6 | Staplers | £4.75 | 28.00 | 4.88 | 32.81 |
| 10 | Staple Removers | £1.15 | 11.50 | 2.01 | 13.24 |
| 2 x 10 | Box Files | £10.70 | 21.40 | 3.66 | 24.63 |
| 2 x 10 | Lever Arch Files | £8.50 | 18.00 | 2.91 | 19.57 |
| | | | | | 136.42 |

Terms: 2% One Month
E&OE

Total Payable    £136.42

**Fig 12.9 Invoice 1, for use with DIY 12.2.4**

415

### PICKFORD CHEMICALS
#### Salisbury Way
#### Bury BY14 8BB

VAT Reg. No: 675/75876/32
Invoice No: 27/56/90/A
Goods delivered to:

Date/Tax Point
20.2.9-

Bales Paint Supplies
144 Knight Lane
Kinstone KJ32 7BB
Order No: C/6785/245

| QTY | DETAILS | UNIT PRICE | TOTAL PRICE | VAT | TOTAL |
|-----|---------|------------|-------------|------|-------|
| 5 | CAUSTIC SODA | 0.98 | 4.90 | 0.85 | 5.75 |
| 8 | METHYLATED SPIRIT | 4.00 | 32.00 | 5.60 | 37.60 |
| 9 | WHITE SPIRIT | 4.20 | 37.80 | 6.61 | 44.41 |
| TERMS: 30 days net monthly NOTE: 1 x Methylated Spirit to follow | | | 74.70 | 13.06 | £87.76 |

**Fig 12.10 Invoice 2, for use with DIY 12.2.4**

### ACE COMPUTER SUPPLIES
#### Catchpole Gardens
#### London SE9

VAT Reg. No: 423/75894/11
Date and Tax Point:

Invoice No: 55.2.78.93
Order No: C/7658/54

30.2.9-

| Qty | Description | Code | Price | Total |
|-----|-------------|------|-------|-------|
| 3 | Comp. chairs | 24-m-2309 | 57.69 | 173.07 |
| 6 | Cartridges | 34-n-3425 | 45.90 | 27.54 |
| 3 x 10 | Diskettes | 38-p-4879 | 8.90 | 26.70 |
| 3 | PC stand | 11-r-5888 | 27.50 | 82.50 |
| 2 | Diskette Cases | 56-o-3099 | 5.99 | 11.98 |
| 1 | Continuous Paper | 45-p-8759 | 9.99 | Free |
| TOTAL PRICE EXCLUDING VAT | | | | 569.65 |
| VAT @ 17.5% | | | £89.72 | £659.37 |

Goods delivered to:
Bales Paint Supplies
144 Knight Lane
Kinstone

Terms:
5% - 28 days.
10% - 14 days
E&OE

**Fig 12.11 Invoice 3, for use with DIY 12.2.4**

416

### Reporting variations in expenditure

If you find that the cost of an item has risen between your order and the supplier's invoice then you should first check this. Your supplier should have notified you of any changes in price. You may need to report unexpected changes and variations in cost to your manager or decision maker. As well as reporting the variation ensure you explain why it has occurred and state the action you would like to take. Your action may be to approve the expenditure, alter the supplier, change the item for a replacement etc. It is preferable to refer variations to the appropriate person in writing. They are likely to reply in writing, and you will have a record of the referral and approval.

## DIY 12.2.5

Complete an income and expenditure account for the invoices you have approved in DIY 12.2.4. Investigate the requirements, within your training centre, for staff wishing to spend in excess of their budget and how they deal with expenditure outside the limits of their authority. Present your findings in the form of a report.

## ▶ *Petty cash*

If you have selected to set up and run a **petty cash system** you will need to put in place the necessary procedures and obtain the documentation required. Relevant staff will need to be notified of the new procedures and know where they can obtain petty cash vouchers from.

### Completing an analysis sheet

An **analysis sheet** is a summary of all the payments made, both in and out. It enables you to check whether the amount of cash in the tin is correct and it is also the document that the chief accountant and auditors (those that examine the company's accounting procedures and documents) will want to check. It is vital that you write clearly and are 100 per cent correct as the analysis sheet is an important document and needs to be read by several people. Look at the example in Fig 12.12.

You can see that the imprest agreed is £20 and this has been entered on 2 January. The folio reference is CB1 which means that the Cash Book entry has been made on page 1. The amount of £20 has been entered on the left-hand side on the analysis sheet (the debit side).

The first voucher to be agreed is Voucher number 1 of month 1 (1/1), and it totals £5.50 for magazines bought for the reception area. The amount has been written in the Amount column on the right hand-side and also in

## PETTY CASH ANALYSIS SHEET

| Debit | | | | | | | Credit | | | | | |
|---|---|---|---|---|---|---|---|---|---|---|---|---|
| Date | Folio | Amount £ p | Details | V No | Amount £ p | Travel | Stationery | Post | Refreshments | Reception | VAT £ p | |
| Jan 9 | CB1 | 20.00 | Received cash imprest | | | | | | | | | |
| " 3 | | | Magazines for reception | 1/1 | 5.50 | | | | | 5.50 | | |
| " 3 | | | Milk | 1/2 | 2.50 | | | | 2.50 | | | |
| " 4 | | | Cleaning | 1/3 | 11.75 | | | | | 10.00 | 1.75 | |
| " 5 | | | Total for week | | 19.75 | | | | 2.50 | 15.50 | 1.75 | |
| " 5 | | | Balance carried down (c/d) | | 0.25 | | | | | | | |
| | | 20.00 | | | 20.00 | | | | | | | |
| | | 0.25 | Balance brought down (b/d) | | | | | | | | | |
| " 8 | CB2 | 19.75 | Cash received | | | | | | | | | |

Fig 12.12 An example of a petty cash analysis sheet

the Reception column. The second voucher is for milk purchased for the office. This totals £2.50 and the amount has been written in the Amount column and the Refreshments column. The third voucher is a little different as it has VAT (Value Added Tax) included. VAT is currently set at 17.5 per cent but this amount is reviewed regularly by the Government and may go up or down. The VAT must be shown separately – this is because businesses may be able to get their VAT repaid (if they are registered) and the accountant will wish to know exactly how much VAT you have paid out over the last year. Any amount that includes VAT should be divided by 117.5 and times 17.5 to find out what the VAT is, eg:

£25 ÷ 117.5 = 0.2127659 x 17.5 = £3.72.

If the figure does not divide equally, always round down to the nearest penny. This means that the original price of the goods was £21.28 and 17.5% VAT on this is £3.72; add price and VAT together (£21.28 + £3.72 = £25) and the total amount paid for the goods is £25.

Putting the amounts under the separate headings also allows you to double-check that your arithmetic is correct. The balance paid out for the week (calculated by adding down the Amount column) should equal the totals of the itemised columns. Each column should be added and the total written on the same line as the total for the week. If you now add the totals across the page, it should equal the balance in the amount column (do not include the amount column total when adding across). In the example, this would mean adding the Refreshments, Reception and VAT totals together.

Headings on the analysis sheet will be chosen depending on the type of expenditure made. For instance, if you pay out for stamps, recorded and guaranteed delivery mail, you may have a heading for **post**; for bus and taxi fares, **travel**; for window cleaning, fresh air sprays etc, **cleaning**; for string, pens, pencils etc, **stationery**. These headings assist the accounts department when completing the end-of-year accounts, as each amount may need to be placed in a special budget account.

At the end of the imprest period you should total the columns and ensure that they are correct; count the cash left and add the two together; it should total the imprest. If not, then your figures may be wrong or you have cash missing. The cashier will want to check your figures and the vouchers before transferring the information into the company cash book. Any differences should be noted and reported at this point.

Cash will then be issued to you to make up your imprest and this amount should be entered on to the debit side (left-hand side) of your petty cash account. The cashier will tell you the Folio Number (the Cash Book page number on which the payment to you has been entered) which should be entered on your analysis sheet and on the petty cash vouchers as you accept them (see Fig 12.13).

You are now ready to deal with the vouchers for the following month and have restored the £50 float. Make sure that every time you end an accounting period you complete the balance and restore the imprest.

## ■ DIY 12.2.6

Complete petty cash vouchers with the following information:

| Person claiming | Amount (£) | Item | Date |
|---|---|---|---|
| Vicky North | 4.50 | Envelopes | 3/9 |
| Carl Gough | 11.00 | Train fare | 4/9 |
| Kerry Vivian | 2.40 | Registered post | 2/9 |
| John Tutton | 1.20 | Stamps | 5/9 |
| David Scott | 5.12 | Refreshments for meeting | 12/9 |
| Gemma Ashford | 3.40 | Light bulbs | 6/9 |
| Jim Sutton | 8.20 | Window cleaning | 12/9 |
| James Hampton | 25.00 | (Not known) | |
| Jenny Spade | 10.00 | Office cleaning | |
| Bouquets to go | 15.00 | Flowers for reception | |

Follow the guidelines you outlined in DIY 12.1.3 and use the same amount of imprest you recommended there. Complete the analysis form provided in Fig 12.14 and write memos to anyone where the expenditure is outside your authority. Identify any variations or difficulties arising.

## PETTY CASH ANALYSIS SHEET

| Debit | | | | | Credit | | | | | | | |
|---|---|---|---|---|---|---|---|---|---|---|---|---|
| Date | Folio | Amount £ p | Details | V No | Amount £ p | Travel | Stationery and Post | Cleaning | Refresh-ments | Miscel-laneous | VAT £ p |
| 28/2 | | | Balance for month of February | | 36.85 | 1.20 | 12.80 | 10.00 | 7.20 | 3.20 | 2.4 |
| 28/2 | | | Balance carried down (c/d) | | 13.15 | | | | | | |
| | | 50.00 | | | 50.00 | | | | | | |
| 1/3 | | 13.15 | Balance brought down (b/d) | | | | | | | | |
| 1/3 | | 36.85 | Cash received | | | | | | | | |

**Fig 12.13 A completed petty cash analysis sheet**

## PETTY CASH ANALYSIS SHEET

| Debit | | | | | V No | Amount £ p | | | | | | | | | | | | | | | | Credit |
|---|---|---|---|---|---|---|---|---|---|---|---|---|---|---|---|---|---|---|---|---|---|---|
| Date | Folio | Amount £ p | Details | | | | | | | | | | | | | | | | | | | |
| | | | | | | | | | | | | | | | | | | | | | | |
| | | | | | | | | | | | | | | | | | | | | | | |
| | | | | | | | | | | | | | | | | | | | | | | |
| | | | | | | | | | | | | | | | | | | | | | | |
| | | | | | | | | | | | | | | | | | | | | | | |
| | | | | | | | | | | | | | | | | | | | | | | |
| | | | | | | | | | | | | | | | | | | | | | | |

**Fig 12.14 Blank petty cash analysis sheet, for use with DIY 12.2.6 and DIY 12.2.7**

# ■ DIY 12.2.7

1 Complete the records for your system for the next 2 months using the analysis sheets provided by your organisation or make copies from the blank sample (Fig 12.14). Identify any variations from planned expenditure (expenditure you identified in your first submission in Element 12.1) and report these to your line manager or decision maker. If you are requested to pay out sums which are outside your authority provide details of how you dealt with it. If this situation has not yet occurred, state the action you would take if it did.

2 Investigate the system used in your training centre for petty cash. What are the limits and restrictions, how are variations reported and what type of expenditure request has occurred which is outside the responsibility of the petty cashier?

## Knowledge and understanding question bank

1 What do you understand by 'variation from planned expenditure'?
2 How do you deal with such variations?
3 How do you record expenditure within your organisation?
4 What limits are there on your authority?
5 What variations and deviations from planned expenditure have you dealt with and what action did you take?
6 What are your organisation's reporting procedures for identified variations and deviations?
7 Give examples of expenditure you have approved and monitored in relation to services, materials, equipment and people.
8 How do you acquire the allocated financial provision?
9 Who are the appropriate persons that you need to report variations to?
10 How do you ensure that the details regarding variations are accurate and correct before you pass them on to the appropriate person?

## Claiming credit

For Element 12.2 you must prove that you have contributed to the control of the expenditure on services, materials, equipment and people, that you have recorded expenditure correctly and reported variations or expenditure outside your limits of authority to the appropriate people.

The following work products are potential sources of evidence:

- financial statements
- analysis of statements
- records of variations and actions taken

Once you have completed your final assessment, you will need to write in your record book or folder how, when and what you have done to prove that you are competent.

The following statement is an example of how one trainee completed this claim:

*Once the Director had agreed the estimates and my plan for the new mail room I checked with the suppliers that the quoted figures had not changed. Once agreed I placed orders with the chosen suppliers. I checked the delivery notes and invoices against my original order before passing to finance for payment. I recorded all the invoices passed in my income and expenditure record to ensure that I did not exceed my budget. All the expenditure I approved was within the limits of my authority. The only difficulty I had was in getting the correct logo installed on to the franking machine. This was due to the company changing its logo on its 50th anniversary. The additional cost was estimated and approved by the Director which enabled me to complete the order request and my project. I installed the new mail room and trained staff on how to use the equipment.*

# UNIT 13

# Prepare, produce and present documents using a variety of sources of information

## Element 13.1
## RESEARCH AND PREPARE INFORMATION

### Performance criteria

1 The need for the document is identified and specified
2 Information is located from a variety of sources and relevant information is selected
3 Any discrepancies in source material are identified and rectified
4 Source material is integrated and edited to meet specified needs
5 Work practices are in accordance with legal and regulatory requirements and organisational procedures
6 Security and confidentiality of information are maintained

### Element introduction

In order to carry out your work correctly and efficiently you will need to access information sources both internal and external to the organisation. These may be price lists, catalogues, a database, a spreadsheet, customer records, telephone and fax directories, reference books, maps and diagrams – any information kept and stored in your section is a potential resource and information point for your work.

It is therefore important that these resources are kept up to date, and have enough relevant information in them. If you are responsible for ordering stationery from external suppliers, you will probably keep more than one catalogue for information. You will also make sure that you obtain the new catalogue when issued, otherwise the codes and prices you have on record could be incorrect.

The information kept internally must be reviewed on a regular basis. If it has not been used for some time, is it still required?

## ▶ Types of information

There are 3 main types of information:

**1 Technical** This is anything that is relevant to your work or your department. Reference books needed for your work may include telephone directories (local, national and international), price lists, filing systems (database), timetables (train, bus and air), etc.

**2 Organisational** This will include company procedures, policies and objectives. Organisational information may be in the form of health and safety guidelines, quality standards and guidelines, an internal organisation chart, staff locations and telephone extensions. Staff circulars and magazines will all be treated as organisational information sources and should be kept up to date in the filing system.

**3 Personal** This information will be relevant to you and confidential. Therefore it should be contained in a cabinet or database that can be kept secure. This information would include personal training action plans, personal agreements and appraisals, pay scales and payslips, holiday entitlement and details of disciplinary action.

The technical and organisational information that you obtain and organise may also be accessed by other members of staff. Therefore, as well as being up to date it must have an index system that is easy to understand. You should select the method which is best suited to the type of information being stored. If you intend changing a system, make sure that you discuss this with your line manager and others using the system. It may be necessary to issue guidelines to the users once you have reorganised the system.

No day will go by without you being asked for some kind of information. You may immediately know the answer to the question being asked, or you may have to refer to reference material as a source of information.

## ▶ Sources of information – internal/external to organisation

There will be times both at home and at work when you will need to find out information such as the arrival time of a train, what number bus to catch, the address and telephone number of the local college and so on.

Nobody would expect you to know the answers to these questions immediately, but when at work you will be expected to know how to go about getting the answers.

There are obvious sources of information like the telephone directory, dictionaries and timetables. You should also be familiar with standard reference books, publicity material and when to contact official organisations to gain more information.

To ensure your success and save you from wasting valuable time and effort you must know exactly what is expected of you before you begin your search. You must also be aware of the timescale you are working within and keep others informed of your progress, or lack of it as the case may be.

## ▶ Useful sources of information

You must have a dictionary if you want to amend incorrect use of language or spelling. If you are ever unsure of a word – look it up. Do not rely upon others to spot and correct errors: it is your job to proof-read, correct and check information. Always check work that you have delegated to others to ensure your standards are maintained and that researched information is correct.

Apart from a dictionary, other useful reference books are:

- Thesaurus – this gives alternative words with the same meaning, and can help widen your written and verbal vocabulary.
- Glossary – a specialised list of words and their meanings for your particular business, for example, legal, medical and computing glossaries.
- General office reference books such as *Chambers Office Oracle* or *The Secretary's Handbook*.

On a day-to-day basis you may need to refer to:

- BT's Directory enquiries
- Railway timetables
- *Yellow Pages*
- *Thomson's Directory*
- *Financial Times*
- Ceefax or Teletext
- Road maps/A–Z street guides
- Travel agents
- Internal telephone directory
- Company organisation chart

A great number of both general and specialist reference books exist, but those which would be of use in your own office would depend on the nature of the company's business. All reference books can be found in your local library, but those which may be of use on a regular basis are:

- *Whitaker's Almanack*
- *Who's Who*
- *Kelly's Business Directory*
- *Good Food Guide* or *Hotels and Restaurants in Great Britain*
- *Roget's Thesaurus*
- *The Stock Exchange Official Year Book*

Most organisations will provide you with information so long as it is not confidential or sensitive. Organisations that you may wish to contact in order to gain information are:

- AA or RAC
- Local Authority
- Chamber of Commerce
- Citizens Advice Bureau
- British Telecommunications plc
- Post Office
- English Tourist Board
- Inland Revenue
- The Department of Trade and Industry
- The Consumers' Association

Your first problem may be finding the correct reference material for the information required. The following list gives details of common reference books and the type of information they provide.

| Book | Information |
| --- | --- |
| Telephone directory | Local telephone numbers and addresses |
| *Yellow Pages* | Local business telephone numbers and addresses |
| *Business Pages* | Local business telephone numbers and addresses (excluding retail outlets) |
| *Thomson's Directory* | Local business telephone numbers, addresses and post codes |
| *Mail Guide* | Information on all Post Office Services |
| Railway timetables | Train times and destinations |
| *ABC Guide* | Information on air travel, shipping and coaches |
| *AA* and *RAC Guides* | Details of roads, towns, routes, hotels, garages, etc |

428

| *Whitaker's Almanack* | Information on world affairs, calendar year, statistics, prizewinning authors, plays, films, music, details about United Kingdom and a wide range of other topics |
| *Who's Who* | Biographical details of famous people |
| *Debrett's Peerage* | Gives correct forms of address |
| *Good Food Guide* | Information on places to eat |

**Fig 13.1 Looking up information in a library**

## ▶ *Locating information*

Locating information may be a simple process of knowing whom to ask; manager, colleague, assistant or library staff may know the answer to your question, or they may be able to tell you from where you can get the information.

During the course of a day you may be called upon to access information either:

- orally over the telephone or face to face
- using a computer, eg Prestel or database
- using a paper-based source, eg files or reference books.

If you do need to ask for information make sure you are polite and know exactly what information you require – remember, you are asking someone to spend their time helping you! If you use the telephone to contact a person or organisation, be prepared with notes of the information you require and use the correct telephone manner.

It is important that when you are asked to find information you are aware of **when** the information is required. If the request is urgent you must prioritise it accordingly and fit it in with your daily tasks as quickly as possible. If the request is not urgent, wait until you have time to spare. All staff have to work to deadlines. Remember that if you are late in obtaining information for a colleague you affect their deadline as well as your own.

# ■ DIY 13.1.1

Prepare a table like the one in Fig 13.2. Each time a colleague, manager, customer or client asks you for information make a note of the date, details of information required and the source you used to obtain the information. You will have to design the table so that there is enough room for your entries. It should fill at least one sheet of A4 paper. Also, keep notes, instructions, lists, copies of information and documents relevant to copyright (this could include copyright licences).

| DIY 13.1.1 – Research and prepare information | | |
|---|---|---|
| Date | Information | Source |
|  |  |  |
|  |  |  |
|  |  |  |
|  |  |  |
|  |  |  |
|  |  |  |

**Fig 13.2 Record of information found, for use with DIY 13.1.1**

## ▶ *Locating computerised information*

In an office environment you will find information from paper-based files, microfiche or files held on a computer database. Some organisations provide computer and/or television access to information called viewdata. You may have already used Prestel, Teletext and Ceefax.

Prestel links television screens or personal computers to large computers via BT lines. The information held on these is updated every 24 hours and includes:

- company information
- directories
- market research
- business news/services
- share prices
- government statistics
- travel information
- weather information
- sport and entertainment
- banking and investment
- mailbox
- customer guide

This service allows the user to make bookings using their keyboard, for example purchasing theatre tickets and air tickets. The user is charged according to how long they have used the line, in the same way as with a telephone.

Teletext and Ceefax give similar information to Prestel. This information is often available at no additional cost on television screens, but does not allow users to make bookings.

Information services such as the speaking clock are also provided by BT (sponsored by Acurist), and 0891/0898 numbers, advertised in newspapers, can be used for information such as weather reports and traffic news.

## ▶ Using microfilm and microfiche

Microfilm is used to store reduced photographic copies of documents. Each document is photographed on to strips of 16 mm film, to nearly a twentieth of the original size. A special reader is used which enlarges the document on screen back to its original size. Some readers will allow a copy of the document to be printed out.

Microfiche works on the same principle but documents are photographed on to single sheets of microfilm measuring 150 mm x 100 mm. Each sheet can be labelled with details of its contents and is placed on a reader when information is required. This system is most commonly used in libraries. If you look up an author's name or a book title on the microfiche you are able to see if the library has the book and, if so, where it is located.

**Fig 13.3 Using a microfiche reader**

Microfiche and film are also used to store information from old newspapers, records, correspondence and any document where the original is not required.

# ■ DIY 13.1.2

Sources of information we have spoken about include:

- Database    ● Viewdata    ● Microfiche

Make a list under each of these headings detailing what information you would find in each of these sources. Carry out research to identify if any of these facilities are available to you and how you would go about accessing them.

## ▶ *Extracting information*

When you are first asked to find information, write down details of what is required, using questions to make sure you are clear in your own mind exactly what you are looking for. When you have found the information it is likely that your source will give more than is required. It is your

432

responsibility to go through all the information and pick out only the **relevant** points.

If, for example, your manager asked you to find the train times for London to Dover, your first question should be 'what day and between what times?' It is unlikely that your manager will need the time of every train for that day, only a train to get to/from an appointment or meeting. You may be able to photocopy information directly from the source you have found, but take care that the information is not protected by copyright.

It is useful to underline or highlight information to pick out the important points. Make notes as you read through information and always remember to say where the information was taken from. Your manager may want to get further details from the same source or you may be asked to find the same or similar information again. If you have kept a note of your source this will be an easy process.

## ▶ *Making notes*

You should make notes of the information you find as you go along. Always use a note pad, never scraps of paper that can be easily lost. Leave plenty of room between notes so that additional information can be slotted in if necessary. A wide margin will also allow space for insertions or markers for important facts. Try to number the information so that it can be read back in a logical sequence; leave out unnecessary words and use abbreviations to cut down on time. If you are unsure of standard abbreviations you can find these listed in your dictionary.

Write up notes as you find each piece of information and when your research is complete, transfer the notes to your chosen form of presentation as soon as possible. It is better to present your information while it is still fresh in your mind. When taking notes from speech, edit any irrelevant information and listen for key words. Factual information such as times, dates, etc, should be noted in full.

## DIY 13.1.3

You work in the Travel Department and have been given statistics (see Fig 13.4) regarding newly appointed couriers.

| First Name | Surname | Passport? | Languages spoken | Age |
|---|---|---|---|---|
| Amanda | Blacker | Y | German | 19 |
| Sally | Sager | Y | French | 20 |
| David | Presley | Y | French | 24 |
| Mark | Harrison | N | Italian | 18 |
| Rachel | Miller | N | Spanish | 19 |
| Jade | Chandris | Y | German | 28 |
| Perri | Scott | N | French | 29 |
| Amanda | Blacker | Y | German | 19 |
| Leila | Scott | Y | Hindustani | 19 |
| Crystal | Harper | Y | French | 18 |
| John | Emrie | Y | Hindustani | 23 |
| Lynne | Patience | N | Greek | 19 |
| Shervin | Patel | N | Spanish | 28 |

**Fig 13.4 Statistics for DIY 13.1.3.**

The Travel Manager has asked you to prepare notes for a meeting tomorrow, but has asked you to check the list first as it was typed very quickly by your assistant.

She requires the following information:

- What percentage of the couriers can speak French?
- What is the ratio between men and women couriers?
- What is the average age?
- List the names of couriers aged 19 and under.

The Travel Manager wishes you to send a memo to each of the 14 couriers confirming the information about themselves in the table and inviting them to lunch next Thursday. Find the name and address of a suitable restaurant in the area, one serving Italian food if possible. You have also been instructed to prepare an information sheet to give to all the couriers who do not have a passport. This sheet must give information on the nearest post office, the type of application form required, the cost and what they will need to complete the form – an example of the form will also help.

▶ *Unavailable information*

First make sure you have looked everywhere you can think of. Your manager will not be pleased if you are constantly asking for help instead of looking for yourself. Your manager may be able to point you in the right direction, or they may not know either! Once you have tried everyone and everything you can think of report back to the person who requested the information and explain your actions to date. This is particularly important if the person needs the information for a specific time or date.

In your search for the information you should identify other options and alternatives that may be of help. For example, if your manager has requested the name and number of a local stationery supplier, it is sensible for you to supply 2 or 3 alternatives in case the first one cannot be contacted. Likewise, alternative hotels, venues, restaurants, travel times and so on will provide a wider selection to choose from.

# ■ DIY 13.1.4

You work for Tredre & Simms, Chartered Surveyors, 15 Westmead Road, Basingstoke, BA12 8BB. The Sales Executive, Jenny Fraser, has been invited to visit the London branch of the company based at 113 Leicester Square, London. She will be travelling from the local office and wishes to stay overnight in a 4-star hotel.

**1** Look through this extract from her diary for the week and decide what day she should attend the meeting.

| D I A R Y – brief details | |
|---|---|
| **Monday 9 Feb** | Meeting with Managing Director<br>12.00 to 3.00 pm<br>Dentist 4.00 pm |
| **Tuesday 10 Feb** | Sales Meeting – Room 66<br>9.30 am – 3.30 pm (working lunch)<br>Need sales figures for 94/95 |
| **Thursday 12 Feb** | Presentation at the London Chamber of Commerce,<br>Cannon Street, London<br>10.30 am – 2.30 pm<br>Dinner with Peter – La Lupa, The Quay<br>(pick up at home 9pm) |
| **Friday 13 Feb** | Lunch with Purchasing Manager<br>12.00 – about 2.00 pm<br>Take dog to the vet – 4.00 pm |
| **Saturday 14 Feb** | Write up Sales Meeting report |

**Fig 13.5 Diary extract**

**2** Check BR timetables and find the best times for her to travel by train to/from London.

**3** What underground tube(s) will get her from the BR station to Leicester Square?

**4** Select a 4-star hotel within walking distance of Piccadilly Circus.

**5** Write to Mrs D Vincent, Sales Director at the London branch, to inform her when and how Jenny will be travelling; give details of what time she should arrive at her office (it's about a 5-minute walk from the underground station). Also give the name and address of the hotel you have selected and ask her if she would like to join Jenny for dinner.

**6** Prepare an itinerary for Jenny's trip to London.

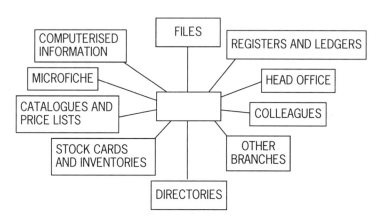

**Fig 13.6 Sources of information**

## ▶ *Carrying out and giving instructions*

Usually you will deal with written documents, corrected typed documents, and your own notes or notes from others. Occasionally someone may add a verbal instruction when they are handing you the work. Make sure that you write down the instructions, either on your note pad or on the document itself. You may need to find out additional information such as train times or technical data that has to be integrated into the work. Verbal instructions are just as important as written instructions, but are easier to forget or overlook if they are not written down.

On some occasions you will take notes that have to be expanded into a required document. All you need are the relevant facts and information, the remaining text you will enter yourself. Many documents have a standard content, eg letters of apology, invitation to an interview, requests for information. Your instructions may be a simple reply to this and accept the invitation – all you need is the invitation which contains all the information you need to produce the reply.

On some occasions it may be your responsibility to identify the need for a specific document, eg confirmation letters must be sent but it may be up to you to go ahead and send them without instructions from someone else. You may also need to research and find out information to be included in a report or a letter, or it may be that your manager needs to have information at hand in a meeting and will require only short notes from you.

When researching information you may come across difficulties such as incomplete information, inaccurate information, ambiguities in text and/or incorrect use of language. These discrepancies in information may be rectified by you or you may call upon someone else, perhaps your manager, colleague or assistant to carry out further research in order to identify the correct information.

If you have been asked to locate and abstract information you will find a variety of sources that may be of help to you. When you discover the information needed you will be required to present your findings using one of a variety of methods, but if at any time you are tempted to merely copy the relevant information you must be sure that you are within the copyright laws or you will be committing an unlawful act.

## ▶ Planning and organising your work

It is important for you to get into the habit of sorting through your work first thing in the morning to put all your tasks into order of priority. As the day goes by other work will be given to you and you will be expected to fit this in if it takes higher priority than the work you already have. Keep an eye on your in-tray and rearrange tasks into order each time you are given more work to do.

**Fig 13.7 Mr Disorganised**

**Fig 13.8 Mr Organised**

You must schedule your work so that important tasks are not left to the last minute or forgotten completely. You will not be given one piece of work at a time. It is likely that you will receive a number of tasks at the same time, followed by more tasks as the day progresses. These tasks must be continually prioritised so that urgent work is completed quickly, less urgent work goes to the bottom of the pile and easier tasks are delegated.

Always sort your work into priority order, taking into account the time needed to complete each task. After you have prioritised your work you can set about delegating tasks, with a completion deadline, to others. When delegating make sure the person understands your instructions or time will be wasted. Monitor the progress of others to check whether deadlines will be met or if more help is needed.

Never under any circumstances allow yourself to forget security and confidentiality even if you are under pressure to get a task finished.

## ▶ *Preparing documents*

You will always be preparing correspondence such as letters and memos, but other documents you prepare will depend on the type of organisation and the type of department you work in. Each department has documents that are specialist documents, for instance a Purchasing Department will prepare orders, a Wages Department will prepare pay slips. The work of the department will determine the type of document produced in addition to the usual memos and letters.

In addition to the departmental documents there will also be general documents that need to be prepared. These may include reports, statements, end-of-period figures, meeting documents, articles, advertisements, notices, invitations etc. Some of these documents will be typewritten, some may be handwritten – it will depend on the instructions you have received.

At first you will probably have to prepare figures or reports for your own area of work or section. This could be a report on how many orders have been placed in the last month, what is the total value, how many are new customers etc. To find out this information you will need to access the files and other information sources within your department. The directors or managers of your organisation will hold regular meetings and will need to discuss the progress of each of the departments.

It is quite likely that your organisation will have an aim or plan of work for the year, and the managers will want to monitor progress in line with this plan. If progress is slow then explanations and corrections will need to be made. The report that you make will be submitted to your manager who will also be receiving reports from other individuals. It will then be your manager's turn to write a departmental report for submission further up the line. Your manager will not have time to check that the content and figures of your report are 100 per cent accurate, this is your responsibility. If, however, you have asked others to supply information you must check this before passing it on.

Make sure that you fully understand any instructions given to you before starting the task. If you come up against a problem, inform the correct person and agree what action you will take. Make sure you are clear as to whether the information you are researching should be presented as a full report or merely a set of handwritten notes. If only notes are required these will of course be much quicker to produce and time will have been wasted if you have set about preparing the information in a manner which was not requested.

## DIY 13.1.5

Research and present the following information in the most suitable form. Remember to quote the source.

1 Currency exchange rates for all the European Union countries.
2 The names and addresses of 3 local senior schools.
3 The organisation of your section within the company, listing the names and the titles of the people concerned.
4 The time difference between Britain and America.
5 The price of one packet of A4 copier paper.
6 The address of the Data Protection Registrar.
7 The person in charge of health and safety in your department.

**8** Name, address, telephone and fax number of 3 local stationery suppliers.

**9** The procedure to follow when taking double–sided copies on the departmental photocopier.

**10** Summary of the equal opportunities policy in place at your company or at the training centre/college.

## ▶ *Integrating information*

You may find that when you create a report or a long document it will be necessary to include a chart or diagram. This may be done by 'cutting and pasting'. This means that you leave a space or cut the paper where the diagram needs to be inserted and tape the parts together. The sheet can then be photocopied to give a good master copy, ready for recopying or circulation.

Certain software will however allow you to import images from other files into reports. For example, you may prepare charts using a spreadsheet or software program and these may be integrated into a word processed document to clarify information. Using such a method will result in excellent presentation of your researched information.

Source material that you have researched is likely to need editing prior to its integration into a document. The editing of source material will enable you to cut down the information so that specified needs are met. If you have been asked to insert train times into correspondence, you will only insert those times relevant to the material and not all the train times available to you. Likewise, when preparing reports and other documents you will only include relevant information and not all that you find on the subject.

## ▶ *Security and confidentiality*

If you are responsible for processing confidential documents make sure you keep them in a folder marked CONFIDENTIAL, and lock them away when not required. Text on a VDU can easily be read if the screen is left on and poor printouts thrown into the bin can be retrieved and read at a later date. If you take carbon copies, remember the carbon paper can be read after use, giving full details of the document. Remember that carbon typewriter ribbons can also be read. Do not allow anyone to look over your shoulder when typing and put all documents out of the way if you have to leave the office for any reason. Remember to use passwords to protect documents held on disks.

**Fig 13.9 Don't allow unauthorised people to read confidential documents**

## ▶ *Health and safety in the workplace*

Switch off all machinery at the end of the day. (The only exception may be the answer machine, which will take telephone calls in your absence, and the fax machine which may send and receive messages during the night.) Make sure that any connecting wires are not trailing across the floor; they

**Fig 13.10 Some safety hazards in the office**

441

should be taped under the desk or placed along the outside of the room. Do not overload sockets: multi-extension leads should be used when several items need to be plugged in at the same time. Alternatively extra sockets should be installed.

Check the leads regularly for fraying or broken connections. New regulations under the Health and Safety at Work Act (HASAWA) and the Electricity at Work Act state that all electrical equipment must be regularly checked to confirm it is safe to use. Consult your manager or health and safety representative if you are not sure about the state of any of the equipment you use.

# ■ DIY 13.1.5

Produce a summary of the following:

- Health and Safety at Work Act 1974
- Office, Shops and Railway Premises Act 1963
- Electricity at Work Act

How do these Acts affect your working conditions?

## ▶ *VDU legislation*

The Health and Safety (Display Screen Equipment) Regulations 1992 affect workers who habitually use VDUs for a significant part of their normal work. Employers have general obligations under health and safety legislation to protect other workers who use VDUs, but who are not covered by this description. The regulations do not contain detailed technical information, but instead set more general objectives.

Employers have to:

- Analyse workstations of employees covered by the Regulations and assess and reduce risks.
- Ensure workstations meet minimum requirements.
- Plan work so there are breaks or changes of activity.
- On request arrange eye and eyesight tests, and provide spectacles if special ones are needed.
- Provide health and safety training.
- Provide information.

In order to reduce any possible negative effects on health through the use of VDU-based equipment for lengthy periods of time, the Health and Safety Executive has recommended a series of guidelines for ensuring that the office environment is compatible with the introduction of new technology.

**Fig 13.11 A word processor**

The Health and Safety Executive publishes leaflet IND(G) 36(L) *Working with VDUs* which provides useful information regarding the use of VDUs in an office environment.

The guidelines recommend that in the operation of VDUs, adjustable brightness and contrast controls are used to improve the displayed image. These, together with screen filters, will reduce eye strain. VDU keyboards should be detached from the screen so that the distance between the screen and operator can be adjusted according to personal preference, and the keys themselves should have a matt surround to minimise glare and have concave tops with adjustable slope to maximise operator comfort.

VDUs generate heat and this will have to be taken into account when heating an office environment to an acceptable temperature. Adequate ventilation and humidity also need to be maintained. Lighting has to be adequate to enable the operator to read documents but not too bright or directed in such a way that it glares on the screen and makes it difficult to read. Undue noise is also disruptive and therefore printers and other noisy office machinery should be sited away from operators or provided with acoustic covers.

Time spent at a VDU will depend upon the nature of the work being performed. Lengthy periods of keying in text may require rapid keyboarding but will not involve extensive concentration on the screen itself. However, if the work involves composition of text, work with spreadsheets, databases or desktop publishing this may require shorter work periods as far greater concentration on the screen is necessary.

If you do not already have a copy of the leaflet *Working with VDUs* contact: HSE Information Centre, Broad Lane, Sheffield, S3 7HQ, or contact their free leaflet line on (Tel) 0114 289 2345 (Fax) 0114 289 2333 and ask for a copy.

## ▶ *Posture*

To make certain you do not suffer from strain and injury, you should sit in the most comfortable position for typing. Strain can occur to the neck, back, arms and legs and on occasions can lead to serious complaints. To reduce the risk of injury, or RSI (Repetitive Strain Injury), you should use a chair which can be adjusted to suit you. It should allow you to sit with your feet flat on the floor (use a footrest if necessary), and have an adjustable back rest to support your lower back. Desks for typing are generally lower than normal desks to allow for the keyboard to sit at the correct height.

Your head should be upright, otherwise you will find your neck will ache from constantly looking down at the desk. The document you are copying should be placed on a document holder, either to the right or left of your keyboard, whichever you find most comfortable.

## ■ DIY 13.1.6

**1** The office manager has just employed 2 new junior members of staff and has asked you to show them round the office. He is particularly concerned about safety in the office and the correct maintenance of computing equipment. He has asked you to put together a list of do's and don'ts with regard to looking after the computers in your office. Prepare this list on a piece of A4 paper ready to hand to the new juniors.

**2** You are unhappy about the quality of your assistant's work. He says that he keeps getting a bad back when he types for too long, and that this affects his accuracy. You decide that he needs information regarding posture, seating and the ergonomics of his office environment – type an information sheet (with illustrations) that will help him.

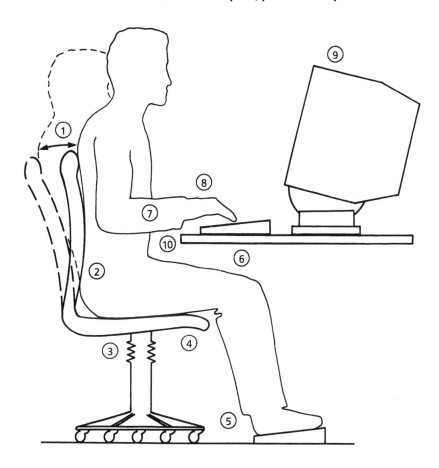

1  Seat back adjustability
2  Good lumbar support
3  Seat height adjustability
4  No excess pressure on underside of thighs and backs of knees
5  Foot support if needed
6  Space for postural change; no obstacles under desk
7  Forearms approximately horizontal
8  Minimal extension, flexion or deviation of wrists
9  Screen height and angle should allow comfortable head position
10  Space in front of keyboard to support hands/wrists during pauses in keying

**Fig 13.12 Seating and posture for typical office tasks**
Crown copyright

## ▶ *Data Protection Act*

If you set up or use a database which contains personal information on individuals then it must be registered with the Data Protection Registrar. The records should not be kept longer than is necessary and proper security procedures should be introduced to make sure only authorised staff have access to the information stored. The information should also be kept up to date and accurate and never be passed to anyone who may use it for other purposes, eg a list of hospital patients being passed to a medical supplies distributor to allow them to send sales material on treatments for their condition. Further information regarding registration can be obtained from the Post Office or direct from the Data Protection Registry who can supply you with an information pack (Telephone 0162 553 5777).

## ▶ *Copyright law*

Copyright is designed to protect the livelihood of the creators and producers of literary, dramatic, artistic and musical works. Following an EC Directive, copyright now in most cases lasts for 70 years from the death of an author and this covers illustrations in a book.

Single copies of copyright material may be made for private study, provided no more than a 'reasonable proportion' is copied.

All copyright material is denoted by the symbol © followed by the date, and can be found on videos, tapes, magazines, computer programs, etc, as well as on books. Multiple copies of this material may not be made without prior permission and payment may have to be made to the publishers for a licence to copy their material. It is normal practice for officers representing the British Copyright Council to visit organisations and ensure that the copyright law is not being broken.

## ■ DIY 13.1.7

Your boss, Ms D Camus, is unhappy with the quality of work produced by your assistant and has asked you to proof-read and retype each memo reproduced in Figs 13.13 and 13.14. A copy of each memo is to go on file with another copy to Mr Brady, Managing Director. Please indicate this on the memos and route them correctly. Ms Camus has also asked you to note the following:

- She has now received 9 applications.
- Deadline date has moved to a week next Tuesday.
- Carol Barker is off sick: send the memo to her Deputy.

- We now expect 275 to attend the ceremony.
- The Kroy machine is broken; tell the Deputy to make enquiries as to how much it will cost to have the badges made by an outside firm.

---

```
CONFIDENTIAL
M E M O R A N D U M

FROM
TO      John Ball, Personnel Director
DATE
REF     Applications for junior Clerk typist post

    To date i have received 5 applications for the cletk typist
post        advertised in last weeks evening Echo. I have
suggested a      dealine date of tues. next, with interview to
be arranged for the      following weds. (date please).
    Can I suggest that you drawer up a list list of your
requirements     to aid us in to select a shortlist and so
that we can base our     interview questions around what you
want.
    We need to discus salary as details will need to be given to
the        applicants at inteview - it is it possible to meet
with you this evening, at (find out the name and address of a
local indian restaurant)        Please let me if you can as
soon as you can if possible.
```

**Fig 13.13 Memo 1 for use with DIY 13.1.7**

---

```
CONFIDENTIAL
M E M O R A N D U M

FROM
TO      Carol Barker, Head Receptionist
DATE
REF     Annual Sales Award Ceremony

    Regarding the above ceremony , would it be possible for you
to        ask your stff to prepare sep. name badges on the Kroy
lettering        machine req'd for all staff attending the
eveing ?
    The ceremony will be held on the 14th of next month and Mr
Ball       would like all staff to were name badges so that they
can        recognise colleagues who operate in different
regions. I will  sent you a list of names once we receive all
the tear-off     portions detailing the how many tickets are
required and the        names of members of staff attending.
Their should be about 200.
    You may find yourself receiving telephone enquiries regarding
the        ceremoney, and to help you answer these, |I have
attached a draft        copy of the memo and notice soon to be
sent out to all staff.

    Yours faithfully
```

**Fig 13.14 Memo 2 for use with DIY 13.1.7**

## Knowledge and understanding question bank

1 Explain how you would determine information needs.
2 List sources of information external to your organisation.
3 List sources of information internal to your organisation.
4 How would you go about researching information?
5 What is the Data Protection Registrar?
6 What is the copyright law?
7 How would you go about planning and organising your information search?
8 How would you go about locating information?
9 How would you go about selecting relevant information?
10 How would you go about recording the information you have found?

## Claiming credit

For Element 13.1 you must prove that needs are specified for yourself and others using source material collected by yourself and others. The sources of information used must include paper-based and computerised and that held by other people. Your ability to deal with discrepancies identified by yourself and others, such as incomplete information, inaccurate information, ambiguities in text and incorrect use of language must also be proven. Statutory and non-statutory legal and regulatory requirements such as Health and Safety, Equal Opportunities, Copyright and Data Protection requirements must also be taken into account. The following work products are potential sources of evidence:

- records of discussions
- records of searches
- lists of sources of information
- notes of information
- copies of information
- documents relevant to copyright

Once you have completed your final assessment, you will need to write in your record book or folder how, when and what you have done to prove that you are competent.

The following statement is an example of how one trainee completed this claim:

*As the administrative assistant at Coopers & Co accountants I have my own work-station with a 486 personal computer. I have access to a number of different software packages on the network. The need for the document would either be specified by myself, for example upon opening the mail and identifying the need for a reply, or by one of the 3 partners that I work for. I have to use a variety of computerised information sources such as the clients' database, accounts spreadsheet and word processor directories. I also use the manual correspondence files which are kept in alphabetical order and the client index which gives quick*

448

*access to details about every client the company has ever dealt with. When I carry out an information search I keep notes in a pad for easy referral and always record the source of the information for future reference. After discussing with the partner the purpose and extent of information needed I list the potential sources that are available to me, this includes paper-based, computerised and that held by other people. When I have identified information I always make sure it is valid and up to date and check discrepancies such as incomplete or inaccurate information, ambiguities in text or incorrect use of language. If copying the information I make sure that I do not infringe copyright law or the Data Protection Act.*

# Element 13.2
# PRODUCE AND PRESENT DOCUMENTS USING A KEYBOARD

## Performance criteria

1 Error-free documents of approximately 1,500 words are produced, under workplace conditions, from selected material, in 2.5 hours

2 Selected presentation conveys the information effectively, appropriately and in accordance with house style

3 Spelling, grammar and punctuation are consistent and correct

4 The language, style and tone of the finished document are suited to its purpose

5 Work practices are in accordance with legal and regulatory requirements and organisation's procedures

6 Security and confidentiality of information are maintained

7 Work is achieved within agreed deadlines

8 Documents are finished for presentation and appropriate routes determined

**The performance criteria for Elements 13.2, 14.2 and 15.2 are exactly the same. Complete this Element to complete Unit 13, 14 or 15.**

## Element introduction

The equipment available for typing will vary from company to company but you may encounter manual typewriters, which have a distinctly sloping keyboard and a carriage return lever. People who have been trained on manual typewriters find it quite easy to transfer to electric or electronic keyboards, but it is more difficult the other way round.

Electric typewriters are similar to manual typewriters in that the keyboard slope is more or less the same; the difference is that less pressure is required to depress the keys. The carriage still moves from side to side but is controlled by a carriage return key instead of a lever. Automatic correction facilities may also be available in the form of correction tape. If a normal nylon ribbon is used a correction tape can be used to cover up the error; if a carbon ribbon is used a lift-off tape is required.

Electronic typewriters usually have a flatter keyboard than manual or electric machines; they also have a fixed carriage. A typing head moves along the carriage and a daisy wheel, golf ball or ink jet will type the characters. Daisy wheels and golf balls can be changed, which enables different type faces and sizes to be used to enhance display.

Electronic machines also have several features available which may include centring, justifying, memory, wider carriages, automatic correction, underscore, emboldening, carriage return and liquid crystal display. A typewriter with numerous, sometimes complicated, facilities may require operators to have specialist training – therefore it may be worth the company investing in word processors rather than complicated typewriters.

Word processors have a wide range of facilities and guidance should be sought before purchasing. The software available on the market today has many advanced features which can be time saving, offer increase productivity and provide excellent quality display material.
The majority offer mailmerge, spell check (specialised dictionaries may be available), various type faces and sizes, automatic lines for tables and pictures, moving and copying facilities.

## ▶ *House style*

Written communication is one of the most important aspects of any business, as the appearance and quality of the documents represent the company image. Letters or other documents sent to customers with spelling, grammar or presentation errors will not project an efficient, businesslike image. The documents you produce should follow a 'house style'. This ensures that the documents received by the customer will reflect the same image regardless of the department that has sent them.

An organisation will decide upon the style in which letters, memos and other documents will be set out. Over the past few years more companies have moved from the indented, fully punctuated style to the blocked, open punctuated style, although combinations of both are sometimes used.

**Fig 13.15 Electronic typewriter**

**Fig 13.16 Word processor**

451

The blocked, open punctuated style is quicker to type and easier to learn, and fewer presentation mistakes tend to be made. Some companies are particularly strict with their house style, even stating what size and style of type should be used. Whichever style is chosen by your organisation, it is important to make sure that all members of staff follow the rules so that all styles are consistent.

A major part of your job could be producing correspondence and other types of business documentation. Your typing skills should be quick but also 100 per cent accurate. This does not mean that you will never make an error, but that you should recognise and correct the error when proof-reading the copy or onscreen.

When using a word processor it is likely that you will use a spellcheck to proof-read your work for spelling mistakes. However, spellcheckers will only highlight a word that is not recognised by the computer's dictionary; any grammar or punctuation errors still need to be identified by you.

## ▶ *Types of document*

Business correspondence, such as letters and memos, must be produced in the house style required by your organisation. You must be aware of the formats required for documents and enclosures and have the ability to use a variety of formats for the purpose of displays and graphics. The ability to use landscape and portrait display formats is also needed so that display material is produced as attractively and professionally as possible.

Letters are received and despatched on a daily basis from most companies. The content of the letters may be requesting information, supplying information or making arrangements; the aim is to get the information to the addressee, for it to be understood and acted upon. Most business letters are typed on letterheaded paper. This gives the basic facts about the company – the name, address, telephone number, fax and/or telex number, names of directors and company secretary, VAT registration number (if any) and possibly a logotype (commonly called a logo).

A professionally designed letterhead makes the company immediately recognisable; some companies invest in a skilled designer to establish the logo which may also become a trademark for the company. Letterheaded correspondence is usually produced on high quality paper; 80 gsm or above is usually used. The letters gsm stand for grammes per square metre, which means that the higher the number the heavier and better quality the paper.

## 128 Long Acre, London WC2 9AN

Tel: +44(0)171 447 2000  Fax: +44(0)171 240 5771

**A Division of Pearson Professional**

Registered Office: Maple House, 149 Tottenham Court Road, London W1P 9LL

Registered Number 2970324. Registered in England and Wales

**Fig 13.17 Letterheaded paper with a logo**

453

Memoranda are used for internal communication only. Most companies have pre-printed forms in A4 and A5 size. They may have a company printed heading with either MEMO or MEMORANDUM, followed by To, From, Date and Reference. A subject heading can be included if required. The content of a memo may be formal or informal. Memos do not have a complimentary close, but may be initialled by the sender, to show approval or confirmation of the contents.

Special markings such as CONFIDENTIAL or PRIVATE are usually typed under the word Memorandum or centred at the top; if the memo is URGENT this would be typed in the top right-hand corner to ensure it was delivered quickly. Routed copies are indicated in the same way as letters, with 'Copy to' at the end of the memo, followed by the names/department of others that should receive a copy. A request for a blind carbon copy means putting the routing information on to the copies but not on to the original so that the person receiving the original is unaware of the other people to whom copies have been routed.

Memo packs are available that are made from NCR paper ('No Carbon Required'), which enables the original to be produced on the NCR paper without the use of carbon paper. Copies may be coloured to indicate circulation, for example original to addressee, pink copy to catering, blue to security, green file copy.

# ■ DIY 13/14/15.2.1

Collect examples of work that you have produced according to house style. You should include examples of letters and memos that have had enclosures included. Also include material that you have had to mark as confidential (you can block out any confidential text). (You may wish to insert a cross-reference sheet here if you already have such examples in Elements 13.1, 14.1 or 15.1.) Explain, in writing, how you would ensure that copies and originals are correctly collated and routed as directed.

128 Long Acre, London WC2E 9AN

Tel: 0171 379 7383  Fax: 0171 240 5771

24 October 19--

Carly-Jo Born
Top Go Salon
224 Lyndsey Road
Branksome
POOLE
BH30 6DB

Dear Carly-Jo

I have been requested by the French authorities
to send you copies of a work placement agreement,
and I am enclosing three copies, one copy to be
retained by you, one copy for the students and
one to be returned to me in the envelope provided.

The document is required in France by all
students carrying out work placement.  Although
the document is not necessary under British law,
the French students are concerned that they will
not fulfil the requirements of their qualification
if this document is not part of their portfolio.

If you wish to delete any part of the document
please do so, or if there are any queries please
contact me.

Thank you for your co-operation.

Yours sincerely

*L Blakemore*

Leila Blakemore
Co-ordinator

Encs

**Fig 13.18 Letter in fully blocked style on letterheaded paper**

---

**MEMORANDUM**

To      Carol Baker

From    Lara Smith

Date    5 October 199–

Ref     LS/EF

MEDICAL CONFERENCE

Would you please arrange with the conference
centre for a slide projector and screen to be
available for Professor James's lecture on
15 October.

This will be required in addition to the OHP
and flipchart.

*LS*

---

**Fig 13.19 Memo in fully blocked style**

## ▶ *Form design*

Forms are usually typed in double line spacing to allow room to type or write on the lines. The lines are created by using the underscore or full stops and to ensure good presentation the right-hand margin is usually justified. When typing on forms the tails of descending letters such as p, q and j should be just above the line. When designing a form it is essential that adequate space is left for insertions to be made. How many forms have you used that do not allow enough space for you to insert your full details?

Forms that are designed using a word processor can be made to look very professional by using the various display functions such as shadowing, tables, boxes, style, font and so on. However, a word processor cannot be used to fill in forms, unless a template has been supplied, as there is not enough control over where the characters will be positioned on the paper when printed – remember they should be just above the line. A template allows the blank form to be set out on screen and inserts to be keyed in by hand.

456

# ■ DIY 13/14/15.2.2

Design a form that can be used by staff to apply for annual holiday. The form should cover a sheet of A4 paper and must be presented as attractively as possible.

Design your own letterhead or use your own organisation's letterheaded stationery on which to design the form.

## *Landscape and portrait presentation*

A4 portrait paper is 210 mm x 297 mm, and has 100 spaces across the top and 70 lines down (assuming you are using elite type which gives 12 characters to the inch).

A5 paper is exactly half this size, and landscape has 100 spaces across the top and 35 lines down. The paper can be used either way: if the smaller side is put into the typewriter or printer first, this is portrait (as you would draw a person's face); if the longer side is put in first, this is landscape (as you would draw a view).

Portrait style is usual for business correspondence and is the style most commonly used in an office. Landscape style is used most often for display material that requires extra width. For example, an organisation chart is more likely to be produced on landscape paper as the chart grows in width each time a level is added.

You may find that although you have produced correspondence, such as a business letter, using portrait style, you may have to switch to landscape in order to display an accompanying enclosure.

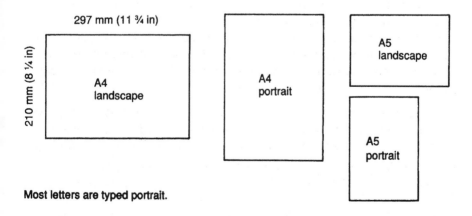

Most letters are typed portrait.

**Fig 13.20 Paper sizes**

## *Tables and tabs*

The terms tabulation and table are used to describe information that has been laid out in rows and columns rather than in written text. Tabs and tables are used because they are easier to understand than written information. Look at the following examples; they both contain the same information, but which is the easier to understand?

**A**

| First name | Surname | Passport? | Languages spoken | Age |
|---|---|---|---|---|
| Amanda | White | Y | German | 19 |
| Sally | Gower | N | French | 20 |
| David | Talbot | N | French | 24 |
| Mark | Harris | Y | Italian | 23 |
| Rachel | Markham | Y | Spanish | 19 |
| Jade | Hamell | Y | German | 28 |
| Perri | Franc | Y | French | 24 |
| Leila | Scott | N | Hindustani | 19 |
| Crystal | Maze | Y | French | 30 |
| John | Patel | N | Hindustani | 23 |
| Lynne | Christanou | Y | Greek | 19 |
| Shervin | Sepanje | N | Spanish | 18 |

**B** The travel department has 12 new couriers. Amanda has a passport and speaks German; she is 19 years old. Sally does not have a passport but does speak French; she is 20 years old. David, Leila, John and Shervin do not have passports but Mark, Rachel, Jade, Perri, Crystal and Lynne do. David also speaks French as do Perri and Crystal. Jade is the only other courier that speaks German. Rachel and Shervin both speak Spanish and Leila and John speak Hindustani. Lynne is the only courier who speaks Greek. Rachel, Leila and Lynne are all 19; Shervin is the youngest and is only 18. The oldest member of the group is Crystal who is 30 years old.

You may be given information written in the style used for example **B**. If this is the case, use your common sense and ask if the person requesting the work would prefer if it was produced in a tabular or table format.

A tabular presentation is achieved by using the 'tab' key on your typewriter or computer keyboard. This key is used to align each column so that comparable information can read across or down. If you wish to prepare a lined tabulation using a typewriter, you will have to insert the horizontal lines as you go along. Some machines allow you to insert the vertical lines using a key on the keyboard, although in some cases you may have to insert vertical lines using a black pen and ruler.

Some word processing packages offer a tables option that will create on screen a table like the one in example **A** above. Boxed-in tables are particularly useful if information needs to be broken down into separate parts. The boxes can be split or joined, shaded, enlarged and/or reduced to produce attractively displayed and easy to understand material, as in Fig 13.21.

| ACE COMPUTER SUPPLIES<br>Catchpole Gardens<br>London SE9 | | VAT No: 423/75894/11 | | |
|---|---|---|---|---|
| Invoice No: 55.2.78.93<br>Order No: C/7658/54 | | Date and<br>Tax Point: 30.2.9- | | |

| Qty | Description | Code | Price | Total |
|---|---|---|---|---|
| 3 | Comp. chairs | 24-m-2309 | 57.69 | 173.07 |
| 6 | Cartridges | 34-n-3425 | 45.90 | 27.54 |
| 3x10 | Diskettes | 38-p-4879 | 8.90 | 26.70 |
| 3 | PC stand | 11-r-5888 | 27.50 | 82.50 |
| 2 | Diskette Cases | 56-o-3099 | 5.99 | 11.98 |
| 1 | Continuous Paper | 45-p-8759 | 9.99 | FREE |

| TOTAL PRICE EXCLUDING VAT | | | | 321.79 |
|---|---|---|---|---|
| VAT @ 17.5% | | | £56.31 | £378.10 |

| Goods delivered to:<br>Bales Paint Supplies<br>144 Knight Lane<br>Kinstone | Terms:<br>5% – 28 days.<br>10% – 14 days<br>E&OE | | | |
|---|---|---|---|---|

**Fig 13.21 Example of a tabular delivery note**

# ◀ DIY 13/14/15.2.3

Display the following material using a tabulated or table display. Use a heading of **TRAINING OFFICE PAPER USAGE**.

1992 – 40 reams in each of the first 2 months of the year, 45 in March, 40 again in April and 37 in each of the last 2 months of the half-year.

1993 – 52 reams used in each of the first 3 months; following 3 months dropped to 48, 45 and 40 respectively.

1994 – first 3 months of the half-year 38, 36 and 34 reams respectively and the last 3 months levelled out at 33 reams each.

1995 – January's usage was down to 30 reams but February saw an increase to 36. The remaining months were all static at 33 reams.

---

## ▶ *Effective display*

Some documents may include items that need to be displayed, such as a letter or memo that requires a table in order to display information effectively. Documents may be required for display on a notice board, such as menus, advertisements, vacancies, programmes etc. There are several ways of producing such material, but typing, word processing or using a desktop publishing package will produce display material of a high quality.

Some spreadsheet programs will allow you to type the information in the form of a table, and by giving different commands the information can be printed in the form of a line graph, bar or pie chart. Special flow chart programs can also be purchased, although it would not be worth buying these unless the package was going to be used frequently. Part of your job could be selecting the most effective method for displaying information.

Word processing packages allow you to change the size and style of the characters, the sizes of which are usually listed in point size (1 point = 0.0138"), the most commonly used being between 11 pt and 13 pt (the low numbers referring to the smaller sizes of print). When you use a typewriter you are likely to use 10, 12 or 15 pitch, where the numbers relate to the number of characters per inch (cpi) – the higher the number, the smaller the type (12 cpi is smaller than 10 cpi).

To display material such as programmes, tickets and posters you would need to select a **size** of print which would be effective for the purpose:

- A3 size posters – 72 pt would be suitable for headings, and 36 pt for other information

- A4 size programmes – 24 pt for headings and 14 pt for information

- A6 (postcard size) – 15 pt for headings and 10 pt for information

Once you have selected an appropriate size of print for your documents, the **style** can be selected to suit your needs. The fonts most commonly used are Courier, Helvetica, Prestige and Roman. Options may also be available for the styles to be in bold, normal, italic, or bold and italic. You will need to experiment with the options obtainable on the software or keyboard available to you.

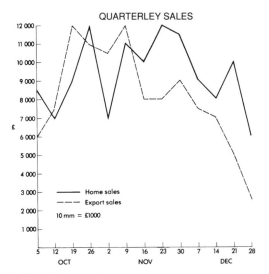

**Fig 13.22 A line graph**

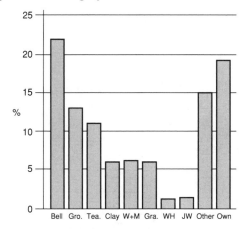

**Fig 13.23 A bar chart**

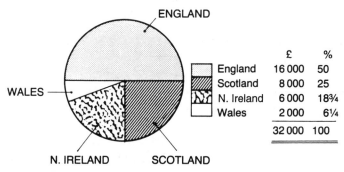

**Fig 13.24 A pie chart showing area sales**

461

If you are unfamiliar with the options, it is useful to keep a copy of all the available fonts and styles as this saves time when selecting attractive display for your documents. It is likely that your word processor or keyboard manual will give details of the fonts and styles available, although when you use a word processor the choice may be restricted by the printer you are using. On a typewriter the style of type can only be changed if you have a variety of different daisy wheels or golf balls.

It may also be possible to shadow or outline your characters; this gives extra effect to displayed material.

The following sizes are Pica (10 cpi) converted to: small, large, very large and extra large.

NVQ LEVEL 3

NVQ LEVEL 3

NVQ LEVEL 3

# NVQ LEVEL 3

The following styles are bold, underline, double underline, italic, outline, shadow, small capital, redline and strikeout.

**BUSINESS OFFICE**

<u>BUSINESS OFFICE</u>

<u>BUSINESS OFFICE</u>

*BUSINESS OFFICE*

BUSINESS OFFICE

**BUSINESS OFFICE**

BUSINESS OFFICE

BUSINESS OFFICE

~~BUSINESS OFFICE~~

These examples have been created using a base font of pica, which is 10 characters per inch (cpi).

The following base fonts are: elite (12 cpi), elite double-wide, pica, pica double-wide.

462

UNIT 13.2

UNIT 13.2

UNIT 13.2

UNIT 13.2

# ■ DIY 13/14/15.2.4

Use a spreadsheet to produce examples of a bar chart, line graph and pie chart. Select appropriate information yourself, that will convert easily into each of the 3 formats required. Remember to label all parts and give your charts and graph a heading. Select a variety of styles, fonts and sizes to make your work as attractive as possible. (Data from DIY activity 13.2.3 can be used for this.)

## ▶ *Special signs*

Mathematical signs and foreign text may also be typed using special signs and some word processors have a secondary keyboard. This means that the normal keys also can be used to type special signs and characters by keying in a special code. You will need to consult your typewriter manual or software manual to find out the facilities available. You will find that some signs may still need to be inserted by hand, using a black pen.

You may be able to find some of the following signs using your word processor or typewriter.

- $\frac{1}{2}$  æ  Σ  ©  ¶  §  ¥  Pt  ®  ●  ☺  ♫

# ■ DIY 13/14/15.2.5

Take this opportunity to find out how to create signs and symbols like the ones above. Prepare an information sheet for other users that explains the options available and how to use them. Include examples of the signs available on your typewriter or word processor.

Electronic machines will usually allow you to change the typeface, embolden and outline characters to make your display material more attractive. Word processors have the best facilities which may include some graphics. What you have available to you will depend on the package you are using, the speed at which your computer operates and the printer you use. Alternatively you may be able to use a desktop publishing package.

Many word processing packages also include graphics in the form of pictures which can be included in the text: these are some of the easiest ones to use. If you become a specialist graphics operator then you will be able to create your own graphics to add to those already available.

The following examples can be found on WordPerfect 5.1.

**Fig 13.25 Examples of graphics**

# ■ DIY 13/14/15.2.6

Display the following notices as attractively as possible. Use A4 landscape paper. Select or draw your own graphics to make the notices as attractive as possible.

**A** Sports Club Members. Badminton Team. Can you play? Would you like to learn? The Sports Club members would like to start a badminton team. Training Monday 7 – 9 pm in the Sports Centre. League games 10 – 11 am at Poole Dolphin Sports Centre. Please contact Maria Morgan for more details on extension 1765.

**B** Notice to all staff. Please note the new internal extension numbers.
P J Adkins – 7689, A R Brown – 2869, T Lowe – 7869, T B Singh 9860,
L Betts – 9906, R Hawkins – 4811, N Petrovsky – 8868, A Groome – 7588,
A R Brown – 2869, Y Yolland – 8113, T Murray – 2759, J P K Patel – 5583,
J J Burns – 6748, M Sears – 7847, L J Scott – 8990, N Vincent – 9911,
L Frazer – 5533, C Vandy – 1761, J G Green – 6551, Vice Principal 7777,
Principal – 7776.

Please display in alphabetical order as attractively as possible. Do you have a
picture of a telephone or something relevant to put on it?

---

## ▶ *Scanners*

Scanners are useful for importing material on to a computer file, but again
it will take specialist training for you to be able to master the techniques
involved. Scanners can be used to copy to memory text and graphics from
an original document so it can be used again and again from the hard disk,
eg a company logo.

The scanner is similar to a photocopier but it copies the document to disk
instead of paper; this saves time as the document does not have to be
keyed in and graphics are transferred automatically. However, it would be
unusual for you to carry out this type of work often; if a company has a
high demand for graphics they are likely to appoint a specialist graphics
designer to deal with all the documents and requests.

## ▶ *Copyright law*

When researching information to be presented in documents you must
ensure that copyright laws are not broken. Graphics, as well as text, are
covered by copyright and you are not able to produce multiple copies of
material under your own name if graphics have been imported from a
software package.

The software itself is also protected by copyright law. You must never take
copies of software to install on other computers. When the software is
bought it usually allows only a designated number of users. Additional
licences have to be bought if more users require the software.

## ▶ *Health and safety laws*

When using any type of equipment health and safety requirements must
be adhered to. The Electricity at Work Regulations and the Display Screen

**Fig 13.26 Check on the safety of your visitors**

Equipment Regulations exist to protect us. Electrical equipment must be checked regularly and maintained in a safe state. Likewise, use of VDU equipment is governed by regulations designed to prevent health risks. Legislation under the Health and Safety at Work Act (HASAWA) ensures that we all work in a safer environment.

The temptation will always be there to cut corners in order to complete tasks quickly. This is quite in order provided the corners being cut will not affect safety in the office. Leaving the filing cabinet drawer open while you answer the telephone, putting boxes on the floor while you find the keys to open the stationery cupboard, or failing to contact the technician to report faulty wiring, are all examples of potential accidents.

It is very easy to lapse when you are under pressure, and if you have the added responsibility of supervising an assistant then that person too has to be kept within the guidelines of company safety policy. Common sense is needed in most cases, together with an awareness that we are all responsible for each other's safety – if we choose to keep an untidy desk, block doors or overload electrical sockets then we not only risk our own safety but that of all other personnel in the office. Using the excuse that you were busy will not be sufficient when trying to explain why one of your colleagues has had an accident because of your unsafe practices!

### ▶ *Data protection legislation*

The rules on data protection exist to protect computerised information on private individuals. If you use a database at work which stores personal information, your company must be registered with the Data Protection Registrar – prosecution and heavy fines can result if it is not.

## ▶ *Unfamiliar vocabulary*

Whichever type of document you are producing it is important to be accurate and consistent in layout, spelling, punctuation and grammar. It is not always possible to rely on others to use the correct spelling. Pay particular attention to words that you are not familiar with, or numerical information: these need to be checked carefully against the original data.

The terminology used by a specialised organisation may be unfamiliar to you and this makes checking your documents more demanding: keep a list of common specialist terms you use or, if you have a computerised spell check, they can be added to the memory.

Special terminology is used for different types of business; medical, legal and computing terms are 3 of many examples. Glossaries are available that list words used in such specialised business, and give an explanation of the word in the same way as a dictionary. If you are new to a particular area of work and unfamiliar with the terminology in use it is very important that you proof-read your work or ask others to check it for you until you are confident with the terms being used.

There are of course specialist training courses available that prepare staff for different types of business; legal and medical secretaries who have followed such a course will have less problems with terminology than an employment agency temporary called in to cover for holiday leave. It is important, however, to make sure that all work is error free and that costly mistakes are not made.

Accuracy is much more important than speed, and when dealing with unfamiliar vocabulary it is vital to ask for clarification if you are unsure and slow down your typing speed so that you can concentrate on each letter of every word. A good, up-to-date glossary and a spell check that has had specialised words and terms added to it will help achieve accurately produced work.

## ◀ DIY 13/14/15.2.7

Copy-type the following letter and articles, paying particular attention to accuracy.

**A**

Anne Schneider
Kopernikusstrasse 10
Berlin
1034

1 April 199–

Personnel Department
Lotus Natural Body Care Products
The Bargates
Christchurch
Dorset
England

Werter Herr/Frau

Hiermit bitte ich um die Zusendung von
Bewerbungsunterlagen, da ich gerne in England
arbeiten wuerde, wenn ich mein Studium an der
Sekretaers Fachhochschule in Deutschland beendet
habe.

Hochachtungsvoll


Anne Schneider

**B**

When choosing a computer you will need to decide on
which assembly language you are going to use. Popular
languages at present include BASIC (Beginner's All-
purpose Symbolic Instruction Code), ALGOL
(Algorithmic Orientated Language), COBOL (Common
Business Orientated Language) and PASCAL (Program
Appliqué à la Sélection).

There are many different types of input device, that
is ways of entering data on to your computer. The
most common is the keyboard, but you may also wish to
investigate the uses of others such as a bootstrap,
card reader, light pen, optical character recognition
or scanner. Data may be dumped from archive to
computer output microfilm or microfiche, magnetic disk,
laser disk, paper and magnetic tape, or hard copy; a
modulator may be considered necessary. Whichever
peripherals are used ensure that they are protected
against corruption of data or crashing, as downtime
can be expensive to the business.

**C**

> Any investment whether it be in alpha securities or
> equities may be subject to backwardation. A bear
> market is unlikely to deal in many gamma securities
> but active trading may exist in beta securities.
> Bulldog bonds are becoming more popular and call
> options are permissible.
>
> OTC has increased since SEAQ, as has roundtripping
> and straddling, although bed and breakfast may be
> initiated as an alternative in some situations. All
> operations are still controlled by Committee.

## ▶ *Security and confidentiality*

Information passing through an office will fall into one of the
following categories:

**1** General or open – can be seen by anyone.
**2** Restricted – limited access to a certain department or group.
**3** Confidential – seen only by the authorised person.

You will be expected to carry out the day's duties with the minimum of
fuss, in an organised fashion that rises above the pressures of the day. In
reality this is not always possible and there are bound to be some days
when the office resembles organised chaos rather than a smoothly running
operation. The telephone continually ringing, other members of the
company in and out of the office asking questions and making demands,
the boss having a 'bad day', together with a host of other distractions – all
of these will ultimately affect the smooth running of the office and your
own strength of character.

The ability to cope with pressure comes with practice but, more
importantly, the ability to ensure security and confidentiality are
maintained at all times will take precedence. It is essential that you stay
calm and keep control in order to ensure the tasks of the day are
completed in accordance with deadlines and with no error. You must be
able to rise to the occasion and 'step up a gear' if the workload of the day
demands it. However, you should not allow aspects of security and
confidentiality to lapse so that tasks can be completed quickly.

Whatever pressure you are under, confidential files, mail or information
should still be kept under lock and key, even if the temptation is there to
leave this material on the desk to come back to. Outgoing mail still has to
be checked for enclosures and the correct letters put into their respective
envelopes, without additional paperwork that has been attached to the
paperclip by mistake! Customers and colleagues will be passing through

**Fig 13.27 Beware of giving visitors confidential information**

the office at all times, therefore you will be required to keep all confidential matter from unauthorised eyes and you and any assistants will have to be especially careful to maintain security procedures during busy periods.

When you use a computer it is normal practice to use passwords to access confidential information. Passwords should be changed regularly and the words chosen should be ones that are easy to remember and that do not have to be written down. You must keep a separate file for all confidential material that should not be seen by any unauthorised person, including any assistants. There must also be separate files for restricted information that may be accessed by a limited number of personnel and by your assistant with discretion.

All back-up copies of confidential or restricted information should be kept under lock and key.

## ■ DIY 13/14/15.2.8

Look at the following list detailing the documents that might pass through your office. Rewrite the list in order of importance and indicate next to each document whether it should be treated in confidence.

**a** Job application form
**b** Memo regarding intended pay increases
**c** Newsletter
**d** Written warning
**e** Company sales brochure

**f** Memo regarding security passes
**g** Authorisation for staff luncheon vouchers
**h** Annual profit and loss sheet
**i** Memo regarding company takeover
**j** Financial forecast for next year

How would you ensure that confidential documents are seen only by authorised personnel?

## Knowledge and understanding question bank

**1** How do you ensure you use keyboarding equipment safely and effectively?
**2** What is meant by 'variable quality sources of information'?
**3** What different business and technical vocabulary have you used?
**4** What are your organisation's presentational styles and formats for documents?
**5** How and when would you use dictionaries, reference materials and glossaries?
**6** What different paper sizes do you use?
**7** What different typefaces and character sizes do you use?
**8** What are your organisation's procedures for security and confidentiality of information?
**9** What is copyright law and data protection legislation?
**10** What conventional presentational styles and formats of documents are there?

## Claiming credit

For Elements 13.2, 14.2 and 15.2 you must provide evidence that proves you can produce error-free documents of approximately 1,500 words in 2.5 hours.
The documents must consist of text, graphics and tables and contain unfamiliar vocabulary, complex grammatical structures and numerical information.
The evidence must show that you are familiar with the use of different typefaces and character sizes, page sizes and page layouts. Again, you must also prove that you have taken into account statutory and non-statutory legal and regulatory requirements such as health and safety, equal opportunities, copyright and data protection requirements. The following work products are potential sources of evidence:

- Documents produced
- Copies of source material
- Records of routing of documents

Once you have completed your final assessment, you will need to write in your record book or folder how, when and what you have done to prove that you are competent.

The following statement is an example of how one trainee completed this claim:

*As the administration assistant at Coopers & Co I use WordPerfect 5.1 to produce tables and graphics. I produce multi-page documents, some with enclosures, that* have to be collated, stapled and routed correctly. I produced a 20-page report for one of the partners that contained pie charts and tabulated material (I used Microsoft Works to do this). The report was printed on portrait paper, but 2 pages which contained organisation charts had to be printed using landscape paper. I always work to deadlines, but if there is a problem I report this to the relevant partner immediately. I choose the most appropriate method of presentation myself unless otherwise instructed and always proof-read the work prior to handing it to the partner. I use the language, style and tone most appropriate and ensure that finished documents are presented to the best of my ability and routed correctly. I have produced reports, synopses, statistical information and correspondence containing foreign language, technical terms, mathematical formulae, footnotes and continuation pages. I have been assessed completing error-free documents of approximately 1,500 words under workplace conditions in 2.5 hours.

# UNIT 14

# Prepare, produce and present documents from own notes

## Element 14.1
## TAKE NOTES AND PREPARE INFORMATION

### Performance criteria

**1** Accurate notes are taken, at an average speed of 100 wpm, under workplace conditions
**2** Uncertainties, arising in taking notes, are identified and clarified
**3** Instructions are interpreted correctly and actioned appropriately
**4** Additional information, when required, is located, selected and incorporated into the integrated material
**5** Work practices are in accordance with legal and regulatory requirements and organisational procedures
**6** Security and confidentiality of information are maintained

### Element introduction

Shorthand is used to take down verbal information and transcribe it back at a later time. The shorthand is usually transcribed using a typewriter or word processor and allows the boss to get on with work while you prepare documents such as reports, letters, minutes and memoranda. Shorthand is also used to note down instructions and messages – anything that needs to be written down quickly and accurately.

Most people speak at a speed of about 80 – 200 words per minute, but we are able to write longhand at only 20 – 50 words per minute. Therefore, we must use some form of shorthand to record the words of even a slow speaker. Quick thinking and controlled penmanship are necessary if acceptable speeds are to be achieved. It is no use taking down dictation that cannot be accurately read back later.

473

There are several forms of shorthand system available. It does not matter which system you use; it is only important that you are able to take down dictation and transcribe it accurately. You must also be familiar with house styles used by the organisation and transcribe documents using the correct form of layout and presentation. You will also have to judge the length of the document when typing it back to make sure you choose the correct size of paper. A sheet of A4 paper will hold approximately 200 typed words in double line spacing.

## ▶ Punctuation, spelling and grammar

You must be good at spelling and grammar if you are to transcribe the dictation error free, with correct sentence construction and punctuation; the person dictating is unlikely to tell you where to insert commas and full stops. You must always check your spelling with a dictionary or the spell check if you are using a word processing package. However, the spell check will not identify words that are used out of context or that are grammatically incorrect.

**Fig 14.1 Taking dictation**

Some shorthand systems are based on phonetics, ie the sound of the word, but when transcribed the word must be as it would be spelt and not as it is spoken. Remember there are many words that sound the same but are spelt differently, depending on their meaning – it is important that you have a good vocabulary and understand the meaning of words.

# DIY 14.1.1

Read through the following text; insert punctuation and correct spelling prior to retyping.

> The Principle though the coarse was a good idea cause the
> student's were so conscious He did fell however that his secretary
> wood need to be discreet about correspondence for this as their
> were arguments in the training censer He has asked four a
> independent report in privet to precede during the students
> summer absente, the stationary required for this would need to be
> chosen and an questionaire exercise designed too ascertain who
> students felt about this.

## ▶ Using apostrophes

Apostrophes can easily be misused. The rules state that they should be used to form possessive nouns, ie to show something belongs to someone. For example:

The Manager's desk

Sari's register

The doctor's prescription

If the noun ends in 's' the apostrophe is placed after the 's' and another 's' is added. For example:

Chris's bike

If the noun is a plural (more than one), the apostrophe would still be after the 's'. For example:

The doctors' parking

This means more than one doctor; if it was 'the doctor's parking', then it would mean only one doctor.

Some nouns are changed slightly when they become plural. Words such as child and woman become children and women. In these cases the 's' is added and the apostrophe appears before it. For example:

The children's socks

The women's handbags

An apostrophe is also used when a letter or letters are missed from a word, for example don't (do not), you're (you are), aren't (are not), can't (cannot), haven't (have not), we've (we have) and I've (I have).

It's is used to mean 'it is'; the apostrophe takes the place of the letter 'i'. Do not use 'it's' to indicate a possessive noun.

## ■ DIY 14.1.2

Copy out the following sentences and put the apostrophes in the correct place.

**a** The childs dog lay on its bed.
**b** The childrens race started at 1.00 but I dont know who won.
**c** Weve got to rush or well be too late for tea.
**d** If youve not got a good report, Ill tell your father.
**e** Perris pocket was full of rubbish and sweets.
**f** Its too late now, so well have to go again in 3 weeks time.
**g** The 2 sisters said theyd be 4 hours late.
**h** The students books havent been seen for days.
**i** Lyndas looking for her bottle.
**j** The cats are in the kitchen eating fishes.
**k** The boys cat lay on its tail.
**l** The dogs are in the kitchen eating the cats dinner.
**m** Susans looking for her son.
**n** Weve got to run or well be late for Sams speech.
**o** I dont think youve got it.
**p** Its too early now – well go later.
**q** The trainees folders havent been seen yet.
**r** Peters trousers were covered in Pauls drink.
**s** The 2 boys said theyd be 2 hours late.
**t** The childrens party began at 2 but I dont know who went.

## ▶ *Improving your speed*

All shorthand systems use short forms or common words. When a phrase is used often it can be written down as an abbreviation of the shorthand outline. Your shorthand book will give you details of all short forms, and you are likely to design some of your own once you are familiar with your work. Most certainly phrases such as 'Thank you for your letter of', 'Dear Sir/Madam' and complimentary closes such as 'Yours sincerely' and 'Yours faithfully' will be written as short forms.

You must practise every day to improve your speed. Always try to take down at a higher speed than normal to quicken your pace. Use shorthand tapes or take dictation from the radio or television and always use a proper shorthand notebook – it is designed for the purpose of taking shorthand notes and will help you to improve your speed. You can use a pen or pencil depending on the system of shorthand being used, although notes in pen are easier to read back for transcription purposes. Special shorthand pens can also be bought.

Always number and date the pages of your book and draw a wide margin down one side to insert alterations. If dictation stops momentarily, use the margin to write in any difficult or unusual words used that may cause you problems later. Make sure your pencil is sharp and always have another in reserve just in case the first pencil breaks in the middle of dictation.

It is useful to put an elastic band round your book so it can be opened at the relevant page easily. If your notebook is nearly finished, make sure you have another readily at hand. As you transcribe each page draw a line through it to show the page is finished with. However, do not destroy the shorthand notebook as it may be needed to check a query. Keep used notebooks for as long as it is company policy to do so, and if you have confidential material in your notebook make sure it is destroyed either in a shredder or an incinerator.

If the dictation is too quick for you say something. Do not sit quietly hoping to catch up later. It is likely that you will fall so far behind that the whole document will need to be dictated again – this will waste not only your time but also the valuable time of others. It is far better to ask the person to stop, and explain that the dictation is too fast. They will be happier going over a sentence or paragraph rather than repeating all the dictation.

## ■ DIY 14.1.3

Make a list of at least 10 short forms and phrases, and next to each write the correct shorthand outline. Practise these each day by writing each one out at least 10 times. If you learn a new short form or phrase add this to your list.

### ▶ *Reading difficult outlines*

The first thing to do is read through the whole passage and look for clues. The outline may be repeated somewhere else in your shorthand and may be clearer to understand. The outline can also be broken down into letters or sets of letters; try to put these together with different vowels filling the spaces. Look for alternatives; could the outline or stroke indicate another meaning or letter? Try to work through as many combinations as possible to give you clues as to the correct word.

If you are still unsure of an outline ask other shorthand users if they can decipher the outline. A different person may recognise the outline straight away. If all else fails ask the person who gave the dictation for help. If this is not possible and you are familiar with the content of the text you may be able to put a suitable word in yourself, but only do this if you are sure the meaning of the sentence has not been changed.

When you first start a job it is a good idea to read back your shorthand notes to check on your transcription. This is particularly important if using unfamiliar vocabulary. This will help you to clarify difficult words and check on spelling. It may be the case that different terminology, such as medical or legal, is being used and you may need a little help learning this.

# ■ DIY 14.1.4

Copy the list of commonly misspelled words below. Next to each word on your list fill in the correct outline. When you come across other words that cause you problems with spelling add these to your list. This list will build into your own personal reference. Keep it close at hand when transcribing dictation.

| | | |
|---|---|---|
| accommodation | accessible | achieved |
| acknowledge | aggravate | all right |
| among | appearance | arrangement |
| beginning | believed | benefited |
| business | colleagues | coming |
| committee | completely | conscientious |
| correspondence | decision | definite |
| disappointed | especially | essential |
| excellent | expenses | extremely |
| February | friend | fulfilled |
| government | height | immediately |
| independent | instalment | knowledge |
| maintenance | minutes | necessary |
| noticeable | occasionally | occurrence |
| permanent | possesses | privilege |
| procedure | professional | quiet |
| recommend | referred | sentence |
| separate | similar | sincerely |
| successfully | surprise | transferred |
| twelfth | unnecessary | usually |
| view | Wednesday | withhold |

## ▶ *Routing copies*

If copies of the finished transcription are to be routed to other personnel or departments or to file, indicate this at the bottom of the document.

The usual style would be:

Copy to:  Mr P Jordan
          Mr K Asad
          File

The original copy is sent to the person named at the top of the document. The copies would be routed by ticking or highlighting Mr Jordan on the first copy, Mr Asad on the second copy and File on the third copy. In this way all copies are clearly marked and their destination known.

## DIY 14.1.5

Your boss, Mrs D Gerrard, is unhappy with the quality of work produced by the new shorthand-typist and has asked you to proof-read and retype each memo shown in Figs 14.2 and 14.3. A copy of each memo is to go on file, with another copy to Mr Jenson, Managing Director. Please indicate this on the memos and route them correctly. Mrs Gerrard has also asked you to note the following and to amend the memo appropriately:

- She has now received 7 applications.
- Deadline date will have to move to next Thursday.
- Carol Barker is off sick – send the memo to her Deputy.
- We now expect 250 to attend the ceremony.
- The Kroy machine is broken; tell the Deputy to make enquiries as to how much it will cost to have the badges made by an outside firm.

```
        M E M O R A N D U M

        FROM

        TO      John Ball, Personnel Director

        DATE

        REF     Applications for junior Clerk typist post

        To date i have received 5 applications for the
cletk typist post

advertised in last weeks evening Echo. I have suggested
a       dealine date of tues. next, with interview to be
arranged for the       following weds. (date please).

        Can I suggest that you drawer up a list list of
your requirements     to aid us in to select a shortlist
and so that we can base our  interview questions around
what you want.

        We need to discus salary as details will need to
be given to the       applicants at inteview - it is it
possible to meet with you    tomorrow\ and weather
accom. can be arranged for the interview    panel.
```

**Fig 14.2 Memo 1 for use with DIY 14.1.5**

```
 .  M E M O R A N D U M

            FROM

            TO      Carol Barker, Head Receptionist

            DATE

            REF     Annual Sales Award Ceremony

            Regarding the above ceremony , would it be
    possible for you to

    ask your stff to prepare sep. name badges on the Kroy
    lettering      machine req'd for all staff attending the
    eveing ?

            The ceremony will be held on the 14th of next
    month and Mr Ball     would like all staff to were name
    badges so that they can      recognise colleagues who
    operate in different regions. I will           sent you a
    list of names once we receive all the tear-off
    portions detailing the how many tickets are required
    and the          names of members of staff attending.
    Their should be about 200.

            You may find yourself receiving telephone
    enquiries regarding the       ceremoney, and to help you
    answer these, |I have attached a draft      copy of the
    memo and notice soon to be sent out to all staff.

            Yours faithfully
```

**Fig 14.3 Memo 2 for use with DIY 14.1.5**

481

## ▶ *Types of letter and memo layout*

As well as making sure the content is correct, part of your job will be to make sure the correct layout is used. Most companies use a 'house style', that is, a particular style the company (the house) has approved and wishes all staff to use. An approved house style is used so that customers receive the same style of documentation, regardless of which department sends it. Some companies are extremely fussy about the house style, even stating what size print and style to use.

The most commonly used layout is the fully blocked style (see Fig 14.4) without punctuation (except in the paragraphs of the letter). In this style everything starts at the left-hand side. This is the quickest style to type, as you do not need to work out spacing or spend time inserting unnecessary punctuation marks.

**Fig 14.4 Letter in fully blocked style**

The date should always be written in the same way whether it is typed at the top of the letter or in one of the paragraphs, eg 25 May 1996 (without punctuation).

The layout for blocked memos is as shown in Fig 14.5.

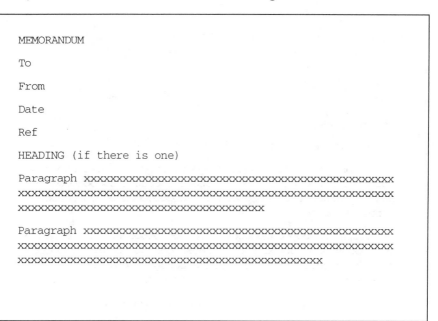

**Fig 14.5 Memo in fully blocked style**

The other style frequently used is semi-blocked (see Fig 14.6). In this style the date is placed on the right-hand side and the signature block is centred. The rest of the letter remains at the left-hand side.

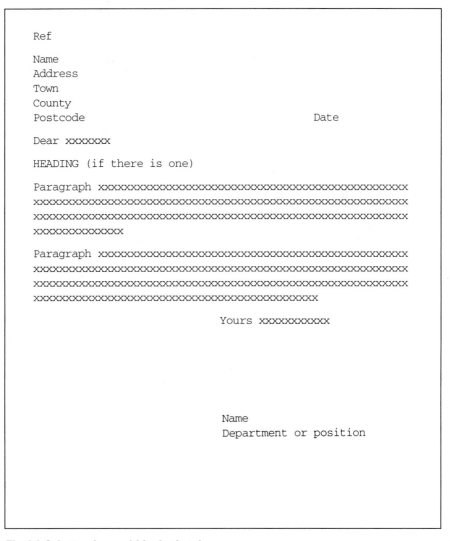

```
Ref

Name
Address
Town
County
Postcode                                    Date

Dear xxxxxxx

HEADING (if there is one)

Paragraph xxxxxxxxxxxxxxxxxxxxxxxxxxxxxxxxxxxxxxxxxxxxxxxxx
xxxxxxxxxxxxxxxxxxxxxxxxxxxxxxxxxxxxxxxxxxxxxxxxxxxxxxxxxxxx
xxxxxxxxxxxxxxxxxxxxxxxxxxxxxxxxxxxxxxxxxxxxxxxxxxxxxxxxxxxx
xxxxxxxxxxxxxx

Paragraph xxxxxxxxxxxxxxxxxxxxxxxxxxxxxxxxxxxxxxxxxxxxxxxxx
xxxxxxxxxxxxxxxxxxxxxxxxxxxxxxxxxxxxxxxxxxxxxxxxxxxxxxxxxxxx
xxxxxxxxxxxxxxxxxxxxxxxxxxxxxxxxxxxxxxxxxxxxxxxxxxxxxxxxxxxx
xxxxxxxxxxxxxxxxxxxxxxxxxxxxxxxxxxxxxxxxxxx

                          Yours xxxxxxxxxxx




                          Name
                          Department or position
```

**Fig 14.6 Letter in semi-blocked style**

For memos typed in a semi-blocked layout the word 'Memorandum' would be moved to the centre and the date and reference to the left-hand side (see Fig 14.7).

```
                         MEMORANDUM

  To                                      Date

  From                                    Ref

  HEADING (if there is one)

  Paragraph xxxxxxxxxxxxxxxxxxxxxxxxxxxxxxxxxxxxxxxxxxxxxxxxxxxx
  xxxxxxxxxxxxxxxxxxxxxxxxxxxxxxxxxxxxxxxxxxxxxxxxxxxxxxxxxxxxxxxx
  xxxxxxxxxxxxxxxxxxxxxxxxxxxxxxxxxxxxxxxxxxxxxxxxxx

  Paragraph xxxxxxxxxxxxxxxxxxxxxxxxxxxxxxxxxxxxxxxxxxxxxxxxxxxx
  xxxxxxxxxxxxxxxxxxxxxxxxxxxxxxxxxxxxxxxxxxxxxxxxxxxxxxxxxxxxxxxx
  xxxxxxxxxxxxxxxxxxxxxxxxxxxxxxx
```

**Fig 14.7 Memo in semi-blocked style**

## ▶ Enclosures

If there is an enclosure mentioned in the letter or memorandum the letters Enc or Encs (if there is more than one) should be placed at the bottom of the page. It is normal practice not to sign memoranda, although some people do prefer to put their initials at the bottom of the page to confirm the contents.

## ▶ Collating documents

Collating means putting the documents you have typed into the correct page order. If you prepare a multi-page document it is wise to number each page so that you do not become confused when the document has to be put together. If you are using a word processor you can instruct it to automatically insert a header or footer that includes the page number of each sheet in the document. It is important that all pages are collated in the correct order before they are stapled or fastened together, otherwise the text may not make sense.

When preparing a multi-page letter it is important to follow the correct house style. When typing letters it is normal practice to insert the page number, date and name of addressee at the top of each consecutive page. For example, a multi-page letter typed in block style is likely to have the following typed at the top of page 2:

> 2
> 20 February 1996
> Mrs J D Carpenter

If the pages become separated, the information at the top of each page will identify where each page belongs. If typing a report, you may have to include the name of the report at the top or bottom of each page rather than a person's name; this would normally be set up as a footer or header.

If you have to prepare copies of the document, these must also be placed in the correct page order. If you are able to send documents to a reprographic service to be copied, make sure that you tell them to collate and fasten the documents for you as this will save you time and help to meet deadlines.

Collating by hand can take a long time, depending on how many pages and copies of the document you have to put together. If you are lucky, your company may have a photocopier that can be programmed to collate the pages as it is copying them, or you may have the use of a collating machine.

If, for example, you have 25 copies of a 30-page report to collate by hand, it will take some time to put the pages in the correct order. You will need to have a work area where the 30 pages can be placed in separate heaps. Alternatively, you will have to sort the first 10 pages (or however many you have space to lay out) followed by the second set of 10 pages and then the third. These three heaps would then have to be collated into the final sets. You will need to lay out the documents in a logical sequence, either in page number order, or to speed up the process, an order where both hands can work at the same time. For example, a 10-page document could be laid out as shown in Fig 14.8:

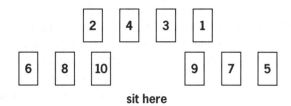

**sit here**

**Fig 14.8 Collating a 10-page document**

The left hand will take one copy of page 10 and place it in the space in front, and then the right hand will take one copy of page 9 and place it on top of page 10. Both hands can move at the same time and the document is collated back to front. Complete sets can be stacked away from the work area.

## ▶ Types of business stationery

Letters are normally typed on A4 headed paper, although some companies do use A5 letterhead. Memos, on the other hand, are commonly available in A4 and A5. A4 portrait paper is 210 mm x 297 mm, has 100 spaces across the top and 70 lines down (assuming you are using elite type which is 12 characters to 25 mm). A5 landscape paper is half this size, and has 100 spaces across the top and 35 lines down. The paper can be used in either the portrait position, with the short side put in to the machine first, or landscape position, with the long side put in first.

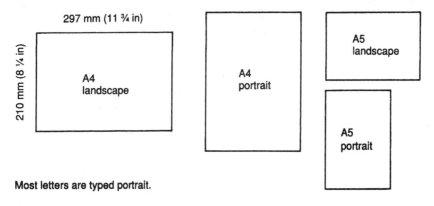

Most letters are typed portrait.

**Fig 14.9 Paper sizes**

The quality of stationery used will depend upon its purpose. Paper and envelopes used for business correspondence will be of good quality as the company will want to convey a good impression to its customers and clients. The quality of paper can be measured by its weight, or gsm (grammes per square metre). Bond, copier and letterheaded paper is fairly thick (80 gsm) and therefore heavier than paper such as bank, which would be cheaper and used for carbon copies.

## ▶ Carrying out instructions

Usually you will be given written documents, corrected typed documents to copy from, dictation or notes. Occasionally someone may add a verbal instruction when they are handing you the work. Make sure that you write down the instructions, either on your note pad or on the document itself. You should not forget to include the instruction, when you carry out the work. An example may be 'Oh, could you do that in double line spacing for me – thanks' or 'Would you do 3 copies when you type this please'.

Verbal instructions are just as important as written instructions, but are easier to forget or to overlook if you are not organised and you do not write them down. Instructions may be given before, during or after dictation and must be followed if time is not to be wasted. Dictation may not have to be taken verbatim but in note form and then you condense or expand the material.

On some occasions you will take notes that have to be expanded into a required document. All you need are the relevant facts and information; the remaining text you will enter yourself. Many documents have a standard content, eg letters of apology, invitation to an interview, requests for information. Your instructions may be a simple 'reply to this and accept the invitation' – all you need is the invitation which contains all the information necessary to produce the reply.

When you are in attendance at meetings it is unlikely that you will take down everything that is said verbatim. Important facts, decisions made and points discussed are all that is needed to enable you to expand the information you have into the minutes of the meeting. The minutes should however always be thoroughly checked before being signed and distributed.

## ▶ *Planning and organising your work*

It is important for you to get into the habit of sorting through your work first thing in the morning to put all your tasks into order of priority. As the day goes by other work will be given to you and you will be expected to fit this in if it takes higher priority than the work you already have. Keep an eye on your intray and rearrange tasks into order each time you are given more work to do.

**Fig 14.10 Mr Disorganised**

**Fig 14.11 Mr Organised**

You must schedule your work so that important tasks are not left to the last minute or forgotten completely. You will not be given one piece of work at a time; it is likely that you will receive a number of tasks at the same time, followed by more tasks as the day progresses. These tasks must be continually prioritised so that urgent work is completed quickly, less urgent work goes to the bottom of the pile and easier tasks are delegated.

Always sort your work into priority order, taking into account the time needed to complete each task. After you have prioritised your work you can set about delegating tasks, giving a completion deadline, to others. When delegating make sure the person understands your instructions or time will be wasted. Monitor the progress of others to check whether deadlines will be met or if more help is needed.

## ▶ *Security and confidentiality*

Never under any circumstances allow yourself to forget security and confidentiality even if you are under pressure to get a task finished.

If you are responsible for processing confidential documents make sure you keep them in a folder marked CONFIDENTIAL, and lock them away when not required. Text on a VDU can easily be read if the screen is left on and poor printouts thrown into the bin can be read at a later date. If you take carbon copies remember the carbon paper can be read after use, thus revealing the full details of the document typed. Do not allow anyone to look over your shoulder when typing, and put all documents out of the way if you have to leave the office for any reason. Remember to use passwords to protect documents held on disks.

## ▶ *Health and safety in the workplace*

Switch off all machinery at the end of the day. (The only exceptions may be the answer machine, which will take telephone calls in your absence, and the fax machine which may send and receive messages during the night.) Make sure that any connecting wires are not trailing across the floor; they should be taped under the desk or placed along the outside of the room. Do not overload sockets. Multi-extension leads should be used when several items need to be plugged in at the same time, or extra sockets should be installed.

Check the leads regularly for fraying or broken connections. New regulations under the Health and Safety at Work Act (HASAWA) and the Electricity at Work Act state that all electrical equipment must be regularly checked to confirm it is safe to use. (See Fig 13.10 on page 441 for examples of safety hazards.) Consult your manager or health and safety representative if you are not sure about the state of any of the equipment you use.

## ■ DIY 14.1.6

Produce a summary of the following:

- Health and Safety at Work Act 1974
- Office, Shops and Railway Premises Act 1963
- Electricity at Work Act

How do these Acts affect your working conditions?

## ▶ *VDU legislation*

The Health and Safety (Display Screen Equipment) Regulations 1992 affect workers who habitually use VDUs for a significant part of their normal work. Employers still have general obligations under health and safety legislation to protect other workers who use VDUs, but to whom this description does not apply. The regulations do not contain detailed technical information, but instead set more general objectives.

Employers have to:

- Analyse workstations of employees covered by the regulations and assess and reduce risks.

- Ensure workstations meet minimum requirements.
- Plan work so there are breaks or changes of activity.
- On request arrange eye and eyesight tests, and provide spectacles if special ones are needed.
- Provide health and safety training.
- Provide information.

In order to reduce any possible negative effects on health through the use of VDU-based equipment for lengthy periods of time, the Health and Safety Executive has recommended a series of guidelines for ensuring that the office environment is compatible with the introduction of new technology. Leaflet IND(G) 36(L) *Working with VDUs* is published by the Health and Safety Executive and provides useful information regarding the use of VDUs in an office environment.

The guidelines recommend that the VDU's adjustable brightness and contrast controls are used to improve the displayed image. Together with screen filters these will reduce eye strain. VDU keyboards should be detached from the screen so that the distance between the screen and operator can be adjusted according to personal preference, and the keys themselves should have a matt surround to minimise glare and have concave tops with adjustable slope to maximise operator comfort.

VDUs generate heat and this will have to be taken into account when heating an office environment to an acceptable temperature. Adequate ventilation and humidity also need to be maintained. Lighting has to be adequate for the operator to read documents but not too bright or directed so that it glares on the screen and makes it difficult to read. Undue noise is also disruptive and therefore printers and other noisy office machinery should be sited away from operators, or provided with acoustic covers.

**Fig 14.12 Computer hardware**

The length of time spent at a VDU will depend upon the nature of the work being performed. Lengthy periods of keying in text may require rapid keyboarding but will not involve extensive concentration on the screen itself. However, if the work involves composition of text, work with spreadsheets, databases or desktop publishing this may require shorter work periods as far greater concentration on the screen is necessary.

If you are do not already have the leaflet *Working with VDUs* contact: HSE Information Centre, Broad Lane, Sheffield, S3 7HQ, or contact their free leaflet line on (Tel) 0114 289 2345 (Fax) 0114 289 2333, and ask for a copy.

## ▶ *Posture*

To make certain you do not suffer from strain and injury, you should sit in the most comfortable position for typing (see Fig 13.12 on page 445). Strain can occur to the neck, back, arms and legs and on occasions can lead to serious complaints. To reduce the risk of injury, or RSI (Repetitive Strain Injury), you should use a chair which can be adjusted to suit you. It should allow you to sit with your feet flat on the floor (use a footrest if necessary), and have an adjustable back rest to support your lower back. Desks for typing are generally lower than normal desks to allow for the keyboard to sit at the correct height.

Your head should be upright, otherwise you will find your neck will ache from constantly looking down at the desk. The document you are copying should be placed on a document holder, either to the right or left of your keyboard, whichever you find most comfortable.

## ■ DIY 14.1.7

The office manager has just employed 2 new junior members of staff and has asked you to show them round the office. He is particularly concerned about safety in the office and the correct maintenance of computing equipment. He has asked you to put together a list of do's and don'ts with regard to looking after the computers in your office. Prepare this list on a piece of A4 paper ready to hand to the new juniors.

You are unhappy about the quality of your assistant's work. He says that he keeps getting a bad back when he types for too long, and that this affects his accuracy. You decide that he needs information regarding posture, seating and the ergonomics of his office environment. Type an information sheet (with illustrations) that will help him.

▶ *Data Protection Act*

If you set up or use a database which contains personal information on individuals then it must be registered with the Data Protection Registrar. The records should not be kept longer than is necessary and proper security procedures should be introduced to make sure only authorised staff have access to the information stored. The information should also be kept up to date and accurate and never be passed to anyone who may use it for other purposes, eg a list of hospital patients being passed to a medical supplies distributor to allow them to send sales material on treatments for their condition. Further information regarding registration can be obtained from the Post Office or direct from the Data Protection Registry who can supply you with an information pack (Telephone 0162 553 5777).

▶ *Copyright law*

Copyright is designed to protect the livelihood of the creators and producers of literary, dramatic, artistic and musical works. Following an EC Directive copyright now in most cases lasts for 70 years from the death of an author and this covers photographs and other illustrations in a book.

Single copies of copyright material may be made for private study, provided no more than a 'reasonable proportion' is copied.

All copyright material is denoted by the symbol © followed by the date, and this can be found on videos, tapes, magazines, computer programs, etc, as well as on books. Multiple copies of this material may not be made without prior permission and payment may have to be made to the publishers for a licence to copy their material. It is normal practice for officers representing the British Copyright Council to visit organisations and ensure that the copyright law is not being broken.

▶ *Sources of information – internal/external to the organisation*

There will be times both at home and at work when you will need to find out information such as the arrival time of a train, what number bus to catch, the address and telephone number of the local college and so on. Nobody would expect you to know the answers to these questions immediately, but when at work you will be expected to know how to go about getting the answers.

There are obvious sources of information like the telephone directory, dictionaries and timetables. You should also be familiar with standard reference books, publicity material and when to contact official organisations to gain more information.

To ensure your success and save you wasting valuable time and effort you must know exactly what is expected of you before you begin your search. You must also be aware of the timescale within which you are working and keep others informed of your progress, or lack of it as the case may be.

## ▶ *Useful sources of information*

You must have a dictionary if you want to transcribe shorthand competently. If you are ever unsure of a word – look it up. Do not rely upon others to spot and correct errors. It is your job to proof-read, correct and check information. Time will have already been spent dictating material which should be typed and presented ready for signing, approval or dispatch. Always check work that you have delegated to others to ensure your standards are maintained and that researched information is correct.

Apart from a dictionary, other useful reference books are:

- **Thesaurus** – This gives alternative words with the same meaning, and can help widen your written and spoken vocabulary.
- **Glossary** – A specialised list of words and their meanings for your particular business, for example legal, medical and computing glossaries.
- General office **reference books** such as *Chambers Office Oracle* or *The Secretary's Handbook*.

On a day-to-day basis you may need to refer to:

- BT's Directory Enquiries
- Railway timetables
- *Yellow Pages*
- *Thomson's Directory*
- *Financial Times*
- Ceefax or Teletext
- Road maps/A–Z street guides
- Travel agents
- Internal telephone directory
- Company organisation chart

A great number of both general and specialist reference books exist, but those which would be of use in your own office would depend on the nature of the company's business. All reference books can be found in your local library, but those which may be of use on a regular basis are:

- *Whitaker's Almanack*
- *Who's Who*
- *Kelly's Business Directory*
- *Good Food Guide/Hotels and Restaurants in Great Britain*
- *Roget's Thesaurus*
- *The Stock Exchange Official Year Book*

Most organisations will provide you with information provided it is not confidential or sensitive. Organisations that you may wish to contact in order to gain information are:

- AA or RAC
- Local Authority
- Chamber of Commerce
- Citizens Advice Bureau
- British Telecommunications plc
- Post Office
- English Tourist Board
- Inland Revenue
- The Department of Trade and Industry
- The Consumers' Association

If you have been asked to locate and abstract information you will find a variety of sources that may be of help to you. When you discover the information needed you will be required to present your findings using one of a variety of methods, but if at any time you are tempted to merely copy the relevant information you must be sure that you are within the copyright laws or you will be committing an unlawful offence.

The following activities can be used separately or as a complete assessment of approximately 1,500 words. All tasks must be error free and completed within 2.5 hours. Extra time must be given for gathering and researching information.

# ◾ DIY 14.1.8

*125 words at 100 wpm*

Memo to Miss Youseff from the International Operations Manager, Mr Peter Kent. Date for today. One copy on file and one copy to Mrs P Gibson.

*Dictation starts*

I have been told by Mrs Gibson that you speak and read Arabic very well, and that you have several times been able to use / **(15)** your knowledge of the language to assist business associates when dealing with firms and government agencies in the Middle East. An opportunity arises now of / **(30)** a 3-week job in Oman starting next month. I should very much like to discuss this with you as soon as possible. Would you / **(45)** please contact me on any day from Tuesday next as I should like to invite you to dinner with your husband where we could talk / **(1)** about the subject? Your services would be required in about a week's time with all travel and expenses covered by the Institute's Manager, Mr Asad. /**(1.15)** (**125 words**)

*Dictation ends*

---

# ■ DIY 14.1.9

*175 words at 100 wpm*

Letter to Mr J Armstrong, 14 Knights Lane, Cleethorpes (please find out what county). Use yesterday's date. One copy for file.

*Dictation starts*

Dear Sir, We have now made arrangements for the removal of all your household effects from 1 Station Road, Crayford, Kent to South Cottage, Clayford, / **(15)** Cumbria, on Friday 16th August.

In accordance with your specific instructions, we shall arrive in Station Road to start packing and loading at 8 am / **(30)** on that morning. We estimate that the loading will take about two hours, and that we ought to arrive at your new address at some / **(45)** time between 2 pm and 3 pm. Please study the leaflets we left with you very carefully and follow them when you pack all small / **(1)** items in the chests that we have supplied.

We have left you some foam bubble wrap packing, but if you find that you need more, /**(1.15)** please call in at our depot at any time between 8 am and 5 pm and we shall be glad to supply you. Copies of / **(1.30)** the removal agreement and of the insurance policy are enclosed. Please sign and return these as soon as possible to the above address.

Yours faithfully / **(1.45)** (**175 words**)

*Dictation ends*

---

# ■ DIY 14.1.10

*200 words at 100 wpm*

Notes regarding today's priorities (transcription does not have to be verbatim).

*Dictation starts*

Today we have to write up schedules for the sale of Holly Bush Farm. When they are ready Anita can type them and she may / **(15)** take them to the sale room tomorrow. We think the farm should sell for about £450,000, it will probably sell / **(30)** to the Yellow 3 Property Developers. The holiday rota will also have to be completed today as the office manager is shouting for it. You / **(45)** will need to find Jenny and ask her to telephone the travel agency to confirm the dates of her flights as we cannot wait any / **(1)** longer. I have a meeting with Jim Clemments tomorrow and must have the AGM report for last year, better get me a copy of this / **(1.15)** in case Jim forgets his. Can you also remind me on the 10th that I have a dentist's appointment, and remember to cancel the other / **(1.30)** appointment that I had with Jim as I will be seeing him tomorrow. Contact Mary Farmer to confirm our meeting next Friday, she's a little / **(1.45)** upset at the moment so make sure you are more than polite. I heard that her dog had died unexpectedly and she was very upset. / **(2.00)** **(200 words)**

*Dictation ends*

# DIY 14.1.11

*200 words at 100 wpm*

Letter to Mr Jameson, 17 Manfred Drive, Windsor, Bucks. Take 2 copies, one for file and the other for claims department.

*Dictation starts*

Dear Mr Jameson, Thank you for your telephone call to my assistant in which you requested us to look at your household insurance policy to / **(15)** make sure you have enough cover now that you have increased the value of your furnishings with some new purchases and have received a present / **(30)** of several items of porcelain to add to your collection.

As the figures you gave did not specify the items in detail, could I ask / **(45)** you to let us have, as soon as possible, a full list of the new items and their value. It would be beneficial to us / **(1)** both if you could provide photographs of each piece so they can be kept on file. If at some future date you were to be / **(1.15)** burgled, the police would find the photographs of immense help in their enquiries.

I believe you told my assistant that you were having the porcelain / **(1.30)** valued and that you will let us have full details when you receive these from the valuer. I hope to hear from you shortly with / **(1.45)** the up-to-date valuation. If you require any further assistance in the meantime please do not hesitate to contact me.

Yours sincerely, Terry Turner. **(2)** **(200 words)**

*Dictation ends*

**Instruction:** Can you please find out the names of 3 different antiques valuers in the local area (*Yellow Pages* should have these). Type the information on a piece of paper for me to keep on file just in case Mr Jameson has problems with his own valuer. Can you staple this to the back of the file copy please.

# ■ DIY 14.1.12

*250 words at 100 wpm*

Report from Sales Manager, Andy Crickshank to Jason Harvey, Sales Director. The report has been requested in response to enquiries made by the Managing Director and is required by Friday of next week.

*Dictation starts*

The company has a high international reputation and we are renowned for our engineering and project management teams which are involved in serving the energy / **(15)** and processing industries.

We are currently being asked to do more and more business in the Middle and Far East, and our Business Development Executives / **(30)** are fully extended in both these areas.

We are meeting with much success in gaining new contracts, particularly in the Middle East. I can report / **(45)** that if all goes well in the final stages of negotiations, we shall shortly be starting a management operation based in Oman. I envisage that / **(1)** this will take 3 to 4 years to complete.

I trust you will agree that this is a most satisfactory state of affairs, especially when / **(1.15)** considering the general state of business development throughout the world. Further marketing of our products and services, I am sure, will create future business in / **(1.30)** Dubai and as far afield as Singapore.

Our Business Development Executives are however fully extended at present and I therefore believe that further appointments must / **(1.45)** be made if we are to capture these markets.

I recommend that there be 3 new appointments in the next 3 months to allow time / **(2)** for training to take place. This would enable us to saturate the market and compete with some very heavy competition.

The International Engineering Show taking / **(2.15)** place in Dubai in April provides an ideal opportunity for us to display our new products. A fully trained sales team is needed for this. **(2.30)** **(250 words)**

*Dictation ends*

**Instruction:** I think the Managing Director's knowledge of the Middle and Far East is fairly little. Can you photocopy a map and highlight the Far East in one colour and the

Middle East in another. You had better indicate Dubai and Oman using arrows. Also can you please use correct report layout, and make sure you number each paragraph.

# ■ DIY 14.1.13

*200 words at 100 wpm*

Memo

To: M A Arnold, Head of Catering
From: P B Bishop, Staff Liaison Officer

Today's date

A memorandum about the staff restaurant containing a list of 5 complaints received from staff.

One copy for file, and one to be sent to Claire Richards in Personnel.

*Dictation starts*

Several members of the staff have recently complained to me about the condition of the restaurant. I am sure you will understand that it is / (**15**) very important indeed that this facility should, without exception, be kept clean at all times. I am told that at present this is far from / (**30**) being the case.

I list the following complaints that have been received by my office:
1  Staff who go into the canteen at 12 o'clock / (**45**) for an early lunch often find that dirty breakfast plates are still on the tables.
2  Bins have not been emptied.
3  The floor is / (**1**) littered with cigarette ends.
4  The whole appearance of the room is unhealthy.
5  The food is often badly cooked and lukewarm.

In my opinion / (**1.15**) adequate staff are provided for the cleaning of the room, and there can be no excuse for this dirty condition. The purpose of this restaurant / (**1.30**) is to provide good food at reasonable prices, and I rely on the members of the catering staff to ensure that a good standard is / (**1.45**) achieved at all times.

In view of these complaints, I must ask you to hold a meeting to discuss these complaints as an urgent matter. / (**2**)

*Dictation ends*

# ◄ DIY 14.1.14

*200 words at 100 wpm*

A letter to Mr J Hope, 89 Frederick Drive, Skelmersdale, Lancs.

From: GHP Estate Agency, 19 High Street, Edinburgh.

One copy for file.

Today's date

A letter from an estate agent about houses in the Edinburgh area.

*Dictation starts*

Dear Mr Hope, We notice from your letter that you are interested in houses in the Edinburgh area. We have a good selection of properties / **(15)** which we would be pleased to show you around. Enclosed are photographs of 3 of them.

'Timberlands' cottage is set in a large garden on / **(30)** a very pretty estate, 2 miles out of town. It has 4 bedrooms and 2 reception rooms together with a recently modernised kitchen. There are / **(45)** 2 en-suite bathrooms and an attractive ground floor toilet and shower room.

The smaller property is called 'Hillview' and has 2 bedrooms. The conservatory / **(1)** has an open view across woodland to the hills. This is a very pleasant property which we are sure you would like to view.

The / **(1.15)** third property is a terraced house with a small garden to the rear. If you want to live near to the town centre, this house / **(1.30)** is ideally situated. The 2 reception rooms and the 2 large bedrooms have recently been refurbished with modern decor and fittings.

These 3 properties cost / **(1.45)** around £105,000 each. If you would care to view please contact me to arrange a day and time.

Yours sincerely / **(2)**

*Dictation ends*

**Instruction:** Please find out the train times from the local station to Edinburgh (Monday – Friday). Also the cost would help. Can you leave a space large enough for a photograph to be inserted after each property description. Can you also include in the letter somewhere details of our charges (8 per cent on sale of the property) just in case he wants to sell through us.

---

# ■ DIY 14.1.15

---

*150 words at 100 wpm*

This is a short report on converting imperial and metric measures. You do not have to take dictation verbatim, but must make sure that you do not omit any conversions. Present the information in a table but first check that the conversions are correct.

*Dictation starts*

Conversions for length are: one inch is equal to 2.5 centimetres and one centimetre is equal to 0.4 inches. One foot / **(15)** equals 0.3 metres and one metre is equal to 1.1 yard. One yard is equal to 0.9 metres and / **(30)** one kilometre is equal to 1.6 miles.

Conversions for weight are: one ounce equals 28 grammes and one gramme is equal to / **(45)** 0.03 ounces. One pound equals 0.4 kilograms and one kilogram is equal to 2.2 pounds. One stone is / **(1)** equal to 6.3 kilograms.

Conversions for capacity are: one pint is equal to 0.57 litres and one litre is equal / **(1.15)** to 1.75 pints, but one gallon equals 24.5 litres.

These conversions are approximate only, they are not exact measurements. / **(1.30)**

*Dictation ends*

## Knowledge and understanding question bank

1 What do you understand by the terms shorthand vocabulary, shortforms and phrases?
2 How do you transcribe the above?
3 What business and/or technical vocabulary do you use?
4 What are grammatical structures? Give 3 examples.
5 What sources of information would you use that are external to your organisation?
6 What sources of information would you use that are internal to your organisation?
7 What dictionaries, reference materials and glossaries do you use?
8 What is the Data Protection Registrar?
9 What is copyright law?
10 How would you deal with unfamiliar vocabulary, complex grammatical structures and numerical information when taking notes in a meeting?

## Claiming credit

For Element 14.1 you must prove that you are able to deal with unfamiliar vocabulary, complex grammatical structures and numerical information. Notes must either be transcribed verbatim or expanded into required documents as per instructions. You must also prove that you have taken into account statutory and non-statutory legal and regulatory requirements such as health and safety, equal opportunities, copyright and data protection requirements. The following work products are potential sources of evidence:

- notes of meetings
- summaries

Once you have completed your final assessment, you will need to write in your record book or folder how, when and what you have done to prove that you are competent.

The following statement is an example of how one trainee completed this claim:

*As the administration assistant at Coopers & Co it is my responsibility to take the minutes at the partners' weekly meetings. Notes are taken at an average speed of 100 words per minute during verbatim dictation, while notes taken at meetings are expanded into minutes (refer to evidence for timed tests). When taking minutes I will ask for clarification if unsure of anything and always follow and action instructions as per the request. During dictation or a meeting I am often asked to insert additional information, such as account details or clients' details. Dictation and minute taking often include unfamiliar vocabulary, complex grammatical structures and numerical information; I always clarify that I have taken this down correctly and produce a draft, to be checked by the partners, so that abbreviations, amendments and alterations can be made. All notebooks are kept secure, even when full, and copies of minutes kept on file in a confidential folder. All work produced on the computer is protected by a password.*

# ■ Element 14.2
# PRODUCE AND PRESENT DOCUMENTS USING A KEYBOARD

## Performance criteria

1 Error-free documents of approximately 1,500 words are produced, under workplace conditions, from selected material, in 2.5 hours

2 Selected presentation conveys the information effectively, appropriately and in accordance with house style

3 Spelling, grammar and punctuation are consistent and correct

4 The language, style and tone of the finished document are suited to its purpose

5 Work practices are in accordance with legal and regulatory requirements and organisation's procedures

6 Security and confidentiality of information are maintained

7 Work is achieved within agreed deadlines

8 Documents are finished for presentation and appropriate routes determined

**The performance criteria for Elements 13.2, 14.2 and 15.2 are exactly the same. Complete Element 13.2 to complete Unit 13, 14 or 15.**

# UNIT 15

# Prepare, produce and present documents from recorded speech

## Element 15.1
## PREPARE INFORMATION FROM VARIABLE QUALITY RECORDED SPEECH

### Performance criteria

1 Instructions and text are taken from variable quality speech, recorded at variable speeds, up to 150 wpm, under workplace conditions
2 Uncertainties arising during transcription of recorded speech are identified and clarified
3 Instructions are interpreted correctly and actioned appropriately
4 Salient points are organised, expanded and integrated into comprehensive summaries
5 Additional information, when required, is located, selected and incorporated into the integrated material
6 Work practices are in accordance with legal and regulatory requirements and organisational procedures
7 Security and confidentiality of information are maintained

### Element introduction

Apart from giving you manuscript documents your manager may also use audio. Audio is quite often preferred to shorthand as the manager is able to record material away from the office, although the quality of such tapes can sometimes be poor, especially when dictation is carried out while travelling. You may find yourself trying to distinguish dictation from your manager's conversation with a taxi driver, or have the background noise of an airport, railway station or underground tube.

The tapes given to trainees in a training centre are usually first class, the dictation is steady, no interruptions occur, some punctuation is usually given, and unusual words are spelt out.

In reality it would be most uncommon to receive such a tape when working. Most managers do not receive training in dictating material on to tapes, although most would benefit from it!

A common mistake made by managers is to give figures followed by the word pounds. A manager who understands the way in which an audio typist works would know to say the word 'pounds' followed by the figures – in the same order that you would type the dictation.

Another error may be the way in which your manager gives you instructions on the tape. Quite often an instruction is an afterthought – at the end of a letter you may hear, 'Oh I forgot, I can't go on that date, delete the second paragraph and just leave the first and last' – not much help once you have typed the letter. However, the problems are not so severe if a word processor is used as documents can easily be altered before printing.

When you work continually for the same person you will get to know their habits and the way in which they dictate. With experience you will be able to anticipate their requirements. You may be responsible for transcribing audio material for a number of people, quite possibly from different departments. In this situation it is important that tapes are recorded with clear instructions. If you find one particular person's dictation always causes you problems, mention this to them.

## ▶ *Audio equipment*

The manager will require a dictation machine and tapes. The most commonly used machines are small pocket machines, which are easily carried and stored. The tapes for these machines can store 15 minutes of dictation on each side and are easily posted back to the office to be typed.

Nevertheless, traditional machines are still in use and the standard C60, C90 and C120 cassettes operate on these. C60 is generally preferred as damage to a longer tape could result in a large amount of work being lost. The C60 tape is also the smallest and can be passed to the typist to start transcription while another tape can be used to carry on with dictation.

Desktop machines are available and may be preferred by managers who do not travel frequently. Some of the desktop machines have special facilities such as telephone connection sockets used to record telephone conversations such as calls containing measurements and numbers and calls in a foreign language.

**Fig 15.1 Dictating machine for audio transcription**

Transcription can be made by either playing the tape back and listening either through the loudspeaker (although this would disturb colleagues) or through a set of headphones. The tape can be controlled by hand, using buttons on the machine, or by foot using a foot pedal. Foot pedals can have a play, reverse and a fast forward facility: when pressure is removed from the pedal the tape stops.

Most transcription machines have an index which can be used to mark the starting point of each separate document on the tape. This facility is not available on hand-held dictation machines. A slip of paper is inserted into the indicator on the desktop machine, and at the beginning of each document a mark is made on the paper, either by hand or by pressing a button on the machine.

If the manager requires a particular document urgently, it would be a simple procedure to run the tape forward to the required point ready for transcription. Alternatively, a tape counter may be used and the number recorded manually at the beginning of each piece of dictation to identify the position of each separate document.

**Fig 15.2 Audio transcription equipment**

Some of the more advanced machines have the same facility but the marks are made electronically and indexing is automatically shown by bleeps or flashing lights.

▶ *Corporate use of audio*

Large companies may use a centralised dictation system which would allow access by all staff to audio facilities. Generally this system would be available through a centralised typing or secretarial service. A centralised system may also be connected to a networked computer system. This would enable documents to be sent via the electronic mail system for approval by the writer. There are 3 main methods used.

1 **Multi-bank** – Several machines are located in the typing centre and are connected to users via wires and the telephone system. Those wishing to use the system will dial the operator who will connect them to a free machine. Once the dictation is complete a supervisor will remove the tape and allocate the work to one of the audio typists.

2 **Tandem** – This is a similar system to the multi-bank, except that each audio typist has 2 machines on the desk, one for dictation and one for transcription. Connection to the system is still via the switchboard, but departments can be allocated particular audio typists. This system relieves the supervisor of allocating work and a typist can become familiar with a particular department's work or personal requirements and terminology.

3 **Continuous** or **loop technique** – dictation is received on a continuous tape via the switchboard or a private line. Typists access the tape to transcribe. On some systems urgent items can be indicated for priority treatment but normally transcription is carried out in the same order as the dictation was made. Some current systems include a visual display unit (VDU) which lists the documents waiting for transcription. Such systems can also monitor the typists' productivity levels and will allow allocation of a department's work to a particular typist.

The cost of these systems can be enormous and careful research should be carried out before recommending a particular system for installation within a business. Central systems may also break down, which could result in business halting for a period of time. The effect of a central system on the audio typists should also be taken into consideration. Would you like to sit in front of a typewriter or word processor all day doing nothing but transcribing audio tapes?

## ▶ *Maintenance of equipment*

All equipment, whether it is centralised or individual should be regularly maintained. It is possible to keep the machine in good order by covering it with a dust cover and using a cleaning tape – how often will depend on machine usage. Connecting wires should not be allowed to trail around the desk and if a machine is not used on a regular basis it should be kept in a cupboard along with the attachments.

## ▶ *Using headphones and earpieces*

Earphones should be cleaned regularly and never lent to other people. Using another person's earphones can result in ear infections. It is wise to use a mild disinfectant to clean ear pieces and when not in use your earphones should be kept in a container or plastic pocket where they cannot be damaged.

Some people find that they can suffer from earache if constantly using headphones for transcription. There are several styles of headphone available on the market today, and one should be selected to suit your preferences. Most of the headphones supplied by the manufacturers have plastic tips which are placed just inside the ear and may have foam surrounds for increased comfort. The headphones used for personal stereos are suitable for audio typing and may be preferred.

If part of your job is to answer the telephone, it can be inconvenient to constantly take off headphones to deal with telephone calls. There is a special adaptor available which is shaped to sit around the ear. With this the audio microphone is held in place on the ear, leaving one ear free for the telephone. However, the user can be easily distracted by surrounding noise and it is of course harder to listen with only one ear.

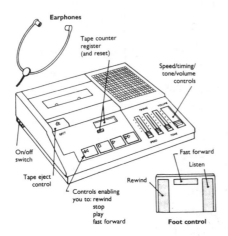

**Fig 15.3 Typical features of an audio-typing machine**

## DIY 15.1.1

Prepare an instruction sheet for your audio machine, referring to its manual if necessary. Explain how to use the machine and include a diagram of the machine with indicators pointing to important parts. Also give details of how to maintain the machine, including information on hygiene and safety.

## ▶ *Audio skills*

Good English is a essential for audio typists. A common error made by trainee audio typists is the typing of incorrect words, especially when they are pronounced the same but are spelt differently. These are called homonyms. These errors are not identified by a computerised spell check, so the text must be proof-read for sense as well as spelling, grammar and punctuation. Ensure that your office has a good dictionary and thesaurus, even if your computer has these facilities.

## ■ DIY 15.1.2

Type a copy of the following list. Below each word write down its meaning. Do not use a dictionary to help you. You will notice that although the words sound similar, they have very different meanings.

| | |
|---|---|
| 1 Accept | 2 Except |
| 3 Check | 4 Cheque |
| 5 Advise | 6 Advice |
| 7 Compliment | 8 Complement |
| 9 Ensure | 10 Insure |
| 11 Quiet | 12 Quite |
| 13 Stationary | 14 Stationery |
| 15 Principle | 16 Principal |
| 17 Insurance | 18 Assurance |
| 19 Affect | 20 Effect |
| 21 Reed | 22 Read |
| 23 Its | 24 It's |
| 25 Course | 26 Coarse |
| 27 Their | 28 There |
| 29 Discreet | 30 Discrete |
| 31 Wood | 32 Would |
| 33 For | 34 Four |
| 35 To | 36 Too |

Now check your answers with a good dictionary and correct any mistakes you have made.

## ▶ *Punctuation, spelling and grammar*

You must be good at spelling and grammar if you are to transcribe the dictation error free, with correct sentence construction and punctuation. (The person dictating is unlikely to tell you where to insert commas and full stops.) You must always check your spelling with a dictionary or the spell check facility if using a word processing package. However, the spell check will not identify words that are used out of context or that are grammatically incorrect.

Remember there are many words that sound the same but are spelt differently with different meanings. It is important that you have a good vocabulary and understand the meaning of words as even your spell check facility will not identify these errors.

## ◼ DIY 15.1.3

Read through the following text; insert punctuation and correct spelling prior to retyping.

```
The Principle though the coarse was a good idea cause
the student's were so conscious He did fell however
that his secretary wood need to be discreet about
correspondence for this as their were arguments in the
training censer He has asked four a independent report
in privet to precede during the students summer
absente, the stationary required for this would need to
be chosen and an questionaire exercise designed too
ascertain who students felt about this.
```

## ▶ *Using apostrophes*

Apostrophes can easily be misused. The rules state that they should be used to form possessive nouns, that is to show something belongs to someone. For example:

The Manager's desk

Sari's register

The doctor's prescription

If the noun ends in 's' the apostrophe is placed after the 's' and another 's' is added. For example:

Chris's bike

If the noun is a plural (more than one), the apostrophe would still be after the 's'. For example:

The doctors' parking

This would mean more than one doctor; if it was 'The doctor's parking', then it would mean only one doctor.

Some nouns are changed slightly when they become plural. Words such as child and woman become children and women. In these cases the 's' is added and the apostrophe would appear before it. For example:

The children's socks

The women's handbags

An apostrophe is also used when a letter or letters are missed from a word, for example don't (do not), you're (you are), aren't (are not), can't (cannot), haven't (have not), we've (we have) and I've (I have).

It's is used to mean 'it is'; the apostrophe takes the place of the letter 'i'. Do not use 'it's' to indicate a possessive noun.

# ■ DIY 15.1.4

Copy out the following sentences and put the apostrophes in the correct place.

**a** The childs dog lay on its bed.
**b** The childrens race started at 1.00 but I dont know who won.
**c** Weve got to rush or well be too late for tea.
**d** If youve not got a good report, Ill tell your father.
**e** Perris pocket was full of rubbish and sweets.
**f** Its too late now, so well have to go again in 3 weeks time.
**g** The 2 sisters said theyd be 4 hours late.
**h** The students books havent been seen for days.
**i** Lyndas looking for her bottle.
**j** The cats are in the kitchen eating fishes.
**k** The boys cat lay on its tail.
**l** The dogs are in the kitchen eating the cats dinner.
**m** Susans looking for her son.
**n** Weve got to run or well be late for Sams speech.
**o** I dont think youve got it.
**p** Its too early now – well go later.
**q** The trainees folders havent been seen yet.
**r** Peters trousers were covered in Pauls drink.
**s** The 2 boys said theyd be 2 hours late.
**t** The childrens party began at 2 but I dont know who went.

510

## ▶ *Dealing with interruptions*

Interruptions can also create errors. In a busy office it is unlikely that you will be able to carry out any job for a long period without some kind of interruption. It could be the telephone, a visitor, a colleague's or manager's request, an emergency, a change of priority, or it could be the end of the day. Your organisational skills are very important, to enable you to cope with routine transcription and deal with everyday interruptions at the same time.

After an interruption make sure you read through the last few sentences of text to familiarise yourself with the content. You will then be able to restart the tape and carry on where you left off. If you are using a word processor it is important for you to save text as you go along. If you are interrupted, save the work you have done and then deal with the interruption. Beware, work left on screen while you deal with another task can be read by anyone and may be deleted in error.

**Fig 15.4 Typing using audio equipment**

## ▶ *Routing documents*

When a document has to be seen by a number of people or departments, or a copy has to be put on file, it is usual practice to route each copy of the document. This is done by listing the names of people and/or departments at the bottom of the document. The word 'File' may also be included to show that one copy has to go on file. The usual style to use is:

```
Copy to: Nigel Parker - Accounts
         Henry Spratt - Purchasing
         File
```

The original copy of the document is sent to the person named at the top of the document. The correct number of copies are then routed by ticking a different name on each copy. In the example above the first copy would have the name Nigel Parker ticked, the second copy Henry Spratt, and the last copy File. In this way all copies are clearly marked and their destination known. The first 2 copies could be placed in the internal postal system for delivery and the last copy would go into the filing cabinet.

## ▶ *Collating documents*

Collating means putting the documents you have typed into the correct page order. If you prepare a multi-page document it is wise to number each page so that you do not become confused when the document has to be put together. If you are using a word processor you can instruct it to automatically insert a header or footer that includes the page number of each sheet in the document. It is important that all pages are collated in the correct order before they are stapled or fastened together, otherwise the text may not make sense.

When preparing a multi-page letter it is important to follow the correct house style. When typing letters it is normal practice to insert the page number, date and name of addressee at the top of each consecutive page. For example, a multi-page letter typed in block style is likely to have the following typed at the top of page 2:

```
2
20 February 1996
Mrs J D Carpenter
```

If the pages become separated, the information at the top of each page will identify where each page belongs. If you are typing a report, you may have to include the name of the report at the top or bottom of each page rather than a person's name. This would normally be set up as a footer or header.

If you have to prepare copies of the document, these must also be placed in the correct page order. If you are able to send documents to a reprographic service to be copied, make sure that you tell them to collate and fasten the documents for you as this will save you time and help to meet deadlines.

Collating by hand can take a long time, depending on how many pages and copies of the document you have to put together. If you are lucky, your company may have a photocopier that can be programmed to collate the pages as it is copying them, or you may have the use of a collating machine.

If you have, for example, 25 copies of a 30-page report to collate by hand, it will take some time to put the pages in the correct order. You will need to have a work area where the 30 pages can be placed in separate heaps. Alternatively, you will have to sort the first 10 pages (or however many you have space to lay out), followed by the second set of 10 pages and then the third. These three heaps would then have to be collated into the final sets.

You will need to lay out the documents in a logical sequence, either in page number order or, to speed up the process, an order where both hands can work at the same time. For example, a 10 page document could be laid out as follows:

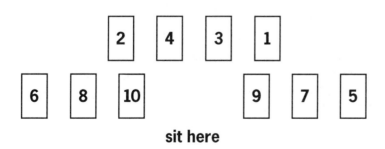

**sit here**

**Fig 15.5 Collating a 10-page document**

The left hand will take one copy of page 10 and place it in the space in front, and then the right hand will take one copy of page 9 and place it on top of page 10. Both hands can move at the same time and the document is collated back to front. Complete sets can be stacked away from the work area.

# ■ DIY 15.1.5

Your boss, Mrs D Gerrard, is unhappy with the quality of work produced by the new audio-typist and has asked you to proof-read and retype each memo shown in Figs 15.6 and 15.7. A copy of each memo is to go on file, with another copy to Mr Jenson, Managing Director. Please indicate this on the memos and route them correctly. Mrs Gerrard has also asked you to note the following, and to amend the memo appropriately:

- She has now received 7 applications.
- Deadline date will have to move to next Thursday.
- Carol Barker is off sick – send the memo to her Deputy.
- We now expect 250 to attend the ceremony.
- The Kroy machine is broken; tell the Deputy to make enquiries as to how much it will cost to have the badges made by an outside firm.

---

```
        M E M O R A N D U M

    FROM

    TO      John Ball, Personnel Director

    DATE

    REF     Applications for junior Clerk typist post

        To date i have received 5 applications for the
cletk typist post

advertised in last weeks evening Echo. I have suggested
a        dealine date of tues. next, with interview to be
arranged for the      following weds. (date please).

        Can I suggest that you drawer up a list list of
your requirements     to aid us in to select a shortlist
and so that we can base our  interview questions around
what you want.

        We need to discus salary as details will need to
be given to the       applicants at inteview – it is it
possible to meet with you     tomorrow\ and weather
accom. can be arranged for the interview    panel.
```

**Fig 15.6 Memo 1 for use with DIY 15.1.5**

MEMORANDUM

    FROM

    TO      Carol Barker, Head Receptionist

    DATE

    REF     Annual Sales Award Ceremony

    Regarding the above ceremony , would it be possible for you to

ask your stff to prepare sep. name badges on the Kroy lettering    machine req'd for all staff attending the eveing ?

    The ceremony will be held on the 14th of next month and Mr Ball    would like all staff to were name badges so that they can    recognise colleagues who operate in different regions. I will    sent you a list of names once we receive all the tear-off portions detailing the how many tickets are required and the    names of members of staff attending. Their should be about 200.

    You may find yourself receiving telephone enquiries regarding the    ceremoney, and to help you answer these, |I have attached a draft    copy of the memo and notice soon to be sent out to all staff.

    Yours faithfully

**Fig 15.7 Memo 2 for use with DIY 15.1.5**

## ▶ *Keyboarding skills*

Your keyboarding skills are vital if you want to be competent at transcribing audio dictation. You must be able to touch type to be able to produce an acceptable quantity of work in one day. Your presentation must be good and your proof-reading excellent. If you make an error this must be corrected so it cannot be noticed. If you are working on a word processor errors are easy to correct, but if you use a typewriter, correcting errors is time consuming and not always to the standard required. It is important to remember that if you are an accurate typist time will be saved if you do not have to continually stop to correct errors.

# ■ DIY 15.1.6

Copy type the list of commonly misspelled words. When you come across other words that cause you problems with spelling add these to your list. This list will build into your own personal reference – keep it close at hand when transcribing dictation.

| | | |
|---|---|---|
| accommodation | accessible | achieved |
| acknowledge | aggravate | all right |
| among | appearance | arrangement |
| beginning | believed | benefited |
| business | colleagues | coming |
| committee | completely | conscientious |
| correspondence | decision | definite |
| disappointed | especially | essential |
| excellent | expenses | extremely |
| February | friend | fulfilled |
| government | height | immediately |
| independent | instalment | knowledge |
| maintenance | minutes | necessary |
| noticeable | occasionally | occurrence |
| permanent | possesses | privilege |
| procedure | professional | quiet |
| recommend | referred | sentence |
| separate | similar | sincerely |
| successfully | surprise | transferred |
| twelfth | unnecessary | usually |
| view | Wednesday | withhold |

## *Types of letter and memo layout*

As well as making sure the content is correct, part of your job will be to make sure the correct layout is used. Most companies use a 'house style,' ie a particular style the company (the house) has approved and wishes all staff to use. An approved house style is used so that customers receive the same style of documentation, regardless of which department sends it. Some companies are extremely fussy about the house style, even stating what size print and style to use.

The most commonly used layout is the fully blocked style without punctuation except in the paragraphs of the letter (see Fig 15.8). In this style everything starts at the left-hand side. This is the quickest style to type, as you do not need to work out spacing or spend time inserting unnecessary punctuation marks.

**Fig 15.8 Letter in fully blocked style**

The date should always be written in the same way whether it is typed at the top of the letter or in one of the paragraphs, eg 25 May 1996 (without punctuation).

The layout for blocked memos is as shown in Fig 15.9:

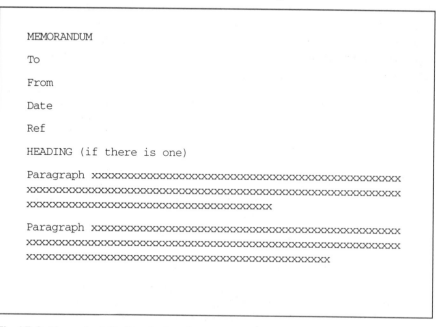

**Fig 15.9 Memo in fully blocked style**

The other style frequently used is semi-blocked (see Fig 15.10). In this style the date is placed on the right-hand side and the signature block is centred. The rest of the letter remains at the left-hand side.

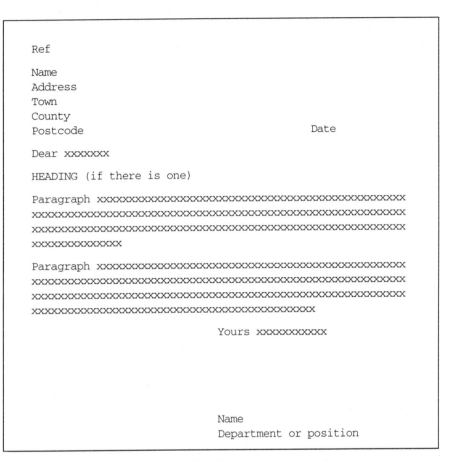

```
Ref

Name
Address
Town
County
Postcode                              Date

Dear xxxxxxx

HEADING (if there is one)

Paragraph xxxxxxxxxxxxxxxxxxxxxxxxxxxxxxxxxxxxxxxxxxxxxxxxxxx
xxxxxxxxxxxxxxxxxxxxxxxxxxxxxxxxxxxxxxxxxxxxxxxxxxxxxxxxxxxxxx
xxxxxxxxxxxxxxxxxxxxxxxxxxxxxxxxxxxxxxxxxxxxxxxxxxxxxxxxxxxxxx
xxxxxxxxxxxxxxx

Paragraph xxxxxxxxxxxxxxxxxxxxxxxxxxxxxxxxxxxxxxxxxxxxxxxxxxx
xxxxxxxxxxxxxxxxxxxxxxxxxxxxxxxxxxxxxxxxxxxxxxxxxxxxxxxxxxxxxx
xxxxxxxxxxxxxxxxxxxxxxxxxxxxxxxxxxxxxxxxxxxxxxxxxxxxxxxxxxxxxx
xxxxxxxxxxxxxxxxxxxxxxxxxxxxxxxxxxxxxxxxxxxxx

                         Yours xxxxxxxxxxx




                         Name
                         Department or position
```

**Fig 15.10 Letter in semi-blocked style**

For memos typed in a semi-blocked layout the word 'Memorandum' would be moved to the centre and the date and reference to the left-hand side (see Fig 15.11).

```
                         MEMORANDUM

   To                                        Date

   From                                      Ref

   HEADING (if there is one)

   Paragraph xxxxxxxxxxxxxxxxxxxxxxxxxxxxxxxxxxxxxxxxxxxxxxxxxxx
   xxxxxxxxxxxxxxxxxxxxxxxxxxxxxxxxxxxxxxxxxxxxxxxxxxxxxxxxxxxxx
   xxxxxxxxxxxxxxxxxxxxxxxxxxxxxxxxxxxxxxxxxxxxxxxxxxxxxxxxxxx

   Paragraph xxxxxxxxxxxxxxxxxxxxxxxxxxxxxxxxxxxxxxxxxxxxxxxxxxx
   xxxxxxxxxxxxxxxxxxxxxxxxxxxxxxxxxxxxxxxxxxxxxxxxxxxxxxxxxxxxx
   xxxxxxxxxxxxxxxxxxxxxxxxxxxxxxxxxxx
```

**Fig 15.11 Memo in semi-blocked style**

## ▶ *Enclosures*

If there is an enclosure mentioned in the letter or memorandum the letters Enc or Encs (if there is more than one) should be placed at the bottom of the page. It is normal practice not to sign memoranda, although some people do prefer to put their initials at the bottom of the page to confirm the contents.

## ▶ *Selecting the correct stationery*

Letters are normally typed on A4 headed paper, although some companies do use A5 letterhead. Memos, on the other hand, are commonly available in A4 and A5. A4 portrait paper is 210 mm x 297 mm, has 100 spaces across the top and 70 lines down (assuming you are using elite type which is 12 characters to 25 mm). A5 landscape paper is half this size, and has 100 spaces across the top and 35 lines down. The paper can be used in either the portrait position, with the short side put in to the machine first, or landscape position, with the long side put in first.

The quality of stationery used will depend upon its purpose. Paper and envelopes used for business correspondence will be of good quality as the company will want to convey a good impression to its customers and clients. The quality of paper can be measured by its weight, or gsm (grammes per square metre). Bond, copier and letterheaded paper is fairly thick (80 gsm) and therefore heavier (usually by about 25 gsm) than paper such as bank, which would be cheaper and used for carbon copies.

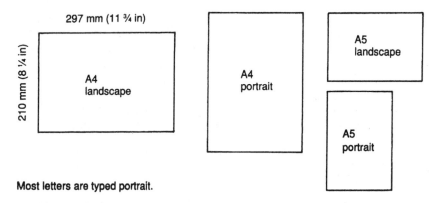

Most letters are typed portrait.

**Fig 15.12 Paper sizes**

## ▶ *Security and confidentiality*

If you are responsible for processing confidential documents make sure you keep them in a folder marked CONFIDENTIAL, and lock them away when not required. Text on a VDU can easily be read if the screen is left on, and poor printouts thrown into the bin can be read at a later date. If you take carbon copies remember the carbon paper can be read after use, giving full details of the document typed. Do not allow anyone to look over your shoulder when typing and put all documents out of the way if you have to leave the office for any reason. Remember to use passwords to protect documents held on disks and keep your cassette tapes locked away so that they cannot be played by unauthorised personnel.

## ▶ *Planning and organising your work*

It is important for you to get into the habit of sorting through your work first thing in the morning to put all your tasks into order of priority. As the day goes by other work will be given to you and you will be expected to fit this in if it takes higher priority than the work you already have. Keep an eye on your in-tray and rearrange tasks into order each time you are given more work to do.

You must schedule your work so that important tasks are not left to the last minute or forgotten completely. You will not be given one piece of work at a time. It is likely that you will receive a number of tasks at the same time, followed by more tasks as the day progresses. These tasks must be continually prioritised so that urgent work is completed quickly, less urgent work goes to the bottom of the pile and easier tasks are delegated.

Always sort your work into priority order, taking into account the time needed to complete each task. After you have prioritised your work you can set about delegating tasks, giving a completion deadline, to others. When delegating make sure the person understands your instructions or time will be wasted. Monitor the progress of others to check whether deadlines will be met or if more help is needed.

Never under any circumstances allow yourself to forget security and confidentiality even if you are under pressure to get a task finished.

### ▶ *Health and safety in the workplace*

Switch off all machinery at the end of the day. (The only exceptions may be the answer machine, which will take telephone calls in your absence, and the fax machine which may send and receive messages during the night.) Make sure that any connecting wires are not trailing across the floor. They should be taped under the desk or placed along the outside of the room. Do not overload sockets. Multi-extension leads should be used when several items need to be plugged in at the same time, or extra sockets should be installed.

Check the leads regularly for fraying or broken connections. Regulations under the Health and Safety at Work Act (HASAWA) and the Electricity at Work Act state that all electrical equipment must be regularly checked to confirm it is safe to use (see Fig 13.10 on page 441 for examples of safety hazards). Consult your manager or health and safety representative if you are not sure about the state of any of the equipment you use.

## ■ DIY 15.1.7

Produce a summary of the following:

- Health and Safety at Work Act 1974
- Offices, Shops and Railway Premises Act 1963
- Electricity at Work Act

How do these Acts affect your working conditions?

Produce a summary sheet of how security and confidentiality can be maintained in a busy workplace. How would you recommend paper-based and computer-based records should be kept secure?

**Fig 15.13 A VDU screen**

## ▶ *VDU legislation*

The Health and Safety (Display Screen Equipment) Regulations 1992 affect workers who habitually use VDUs for a significant part of their normal work. Employers still have general obligations under health and safety legislation to protect other workers who use VDUs, but to whom this description does not apply. The regulations do not contain detailed technical information, but instead set more general objectives.

Employers have to:

- Analyse workstations of employees covered by the Regulations and assess and reduce risks.
- Ensure workstations meet minimum requirements.
- Plan work so there are breaks or changes of activity.
- On request arrange eye and eyesight tests, and provide spectacles if special ones are needed.
- Provide health and safety training.
- Provide information.

In order to reduce any possible negative effects on health through the use of VDU-based equipment for lengthy periods of time, the Health and Safety Executive has recommended a series of guidelines for ensuring that the office environment is compatible with the introduction of new technology. Leaflet IND(G) 36(L) *Working with VDUs* is published by the Health and Safety Executive and provides useful information regarding the use of VDUs in an office environment.

The guidelines recommend that the VDU's adjustable brightness and contrast controls are used to improve the displayed image. Together with screen filters these will reduce eye strain. VDU keyboards should be detached from the screen so that the distance between the screen and operator can be adjusted according to personal preference, and the keys themselves should have a matt surround to minimise glare and have concave tops with adjustable slope to maximise operator comfort.

VDUs generate heat and this will have to be taken into account when heating an office environment to an acceptable temperature. Adequate ventilation and humidity also need to be maintained. Lighting has to be adequate for the operator to read documents but not too bright or directed so that it glares on the screen and makes it difficult to read. Undue noise is also disruptive and therefore printers and other noisy office machinery should be sited away from operators, or provided with acoustic covers.

The time spent at a VDU will depend upon the nature of the work being performed. Lengthy periods of keying in text may require rapid keyboarding but will not involve extensive concentration on the screen itself. However, if the work involves composition of text, work with spreadsheets, databases or desktop publishing this may require shorter work periods as far greater concentration on the screen is necessary.

If you do not already have a copy of the leaflet *Working with VDUs* contact: HSE Information Centre, Broad Lane, Sheffield, S3 7HQ, or contact their free leaflet line on (Tel) 0114 289 2345, (Fax) 0114 289 2333 and ask for a copy.

## ▶ *Posture*

To make certain you do not suffer from strain and injury, you should sit in the most comfortable position for typing (see Fig 13.12 on page 445). Strain can occur to the neck, back, arms and legs and on occasions can lead to serious complaints. To reduce the risk of injury, or RSI (Repetitive Strain Injury), you should use a chair which can be adjusted to suit you. It should allow you to sit with your feet flat on the floor (use a footrest if necessary), and have an adjustable back rest to support your lower back. Desks for typing are generally lower than normal desks to allow for the keyboard to sit at the correct height.

Your head should be upright, otherwise you will find your neck will ache from constantly looking down at the desk. The document you are copying should be placed on a document holder, either to the right or left of your keyboard, whichever you find more comfortable.

# ■ DIY 15.1.8

The office manager has just employed 2 new junior members of staff and has asked you to show them round the office. He is particularly concerned about safety in the office and the correct maintenance of computing equipment. He has asked you to put together a list of do's and don'ts with regard to looking after the computers in your office. Prepare this list on a piece of A4 paper ready to hand to the new juniors.

You are unhappy about the quality of your assistant's work. He says that he keeps getting a bad back when he types for too long, and that this affects his accuracy. You decide that he needs information regarding posture, seating and the ergonomics of his office environment. Type an information sheet (with illustrations) that will help him.

## ▶ *Data Protection Act*

If you set up or use a database which contains personal information on individuals then it must be registered with the Data Protection Registrar. The records should not be kept longer than is necessary and proper security procedures should be introduced to make sure only authorised staff have access to the information stored. The information should also be kept up to date, be accurate and never be passed to anyone who may use it for other purposes, eg a list of hospital patients being passed to a medical supplies distributor to allow them to send sales material on treatments for their condition. Further information regarding registration can be obtained from the Post Office or direct from the Data Protection Registry who can supply you with an information pack (Telephone 0162 553 5777).

## ▶ *Copyright law*

Copyright is designed to protect the livelihood of the creators and producers of literary, dramatic, artistic and musical works. Following an EC Directive, copyright now in most cases lasts for 70 years from the death of an author and this covers photographs and other illustrations in a book.

Single copies of copyright material may be made for private study, provided no more than a 'reasonable proportion' is copied.

All copyright material is denoted by the symbol © followed by the date, and can be found on videos, tapes, magazines, computer programs, etc, as well as on books. Multiple copies of this material may not be made without prior permission and payment may have to be made to the publishers for a licence to copy their material. It is normal practice for officers representing the British Copyright Council to visit organisations and ensure that the copyright law is not being broken.

## ▶ Sources of information – internal/external to organisation

There will be times both at home and at work when you will need to find out information such as the arrival time of a train, what number bus to catch, the address and telephone number of the local college and so on. Nobody would expect you to know the answers to these questions immediately, but when at work you will be expected to know how to go about getting the answers.

There are obvious sources of information like the telephone directory, dictionaries and timetables. You should also be familiar with standard reference books, publicity material and when to contact official organisations to gain more information.

To ensure your success and save you wasting valuable time and effort you must know exactly what is expected of you before you begin your search. You must also be aware of the timescale within which you are working and keep others informed of your progress, or lack of it as the case may be.

### Useful sources of information

You must have a dictionary if you want to transcribe audio tapes competently. If you are ever unsure of a word – look it up. Do not rely upon others to spot and correct errors. It is your job to proof-read, correct and check information. Time will have already been spent dictating material which should be typed and presented ready for signing, approval or dispatch. Always check work that you have delegated to others to ensure your standards are maintained and that researched information is correct.

Apart from a dictionary, other useful reference books are:

- **Thesaurus** – This gives alternative words with the same meaning, and can help widen your written and spoken vocabulary.
- **Glossary** – A specialised list of words and their meanings for your

particular business, for example legal, medical and computing glossaries.
- General office reference books such as *Chambers Office Oracle* or *The Secretary's Handbook*.

On a day-to-day basis you may need to refer to:

- BT's Directory Enquiries
- Railway timetables
- *Yellow Pages*
- *Thomson's Directory*
- *Financial Times*
- Ceefax or Teletext
- Road maps/A–Z street guides
- Travel agents
- Internal telephone directory
- Company organisation chart

A great number of both general and specialist reference books exist, but those which would be of use in your own office would depend on the nature of the company's business. All reference books can be found in your local library, but those which may be of use on a regular basis are:

- *Whitaker's Almanack*
- *Who's Who*
- *Kelly's Business Directory*
- *Good Food Guide/Hotels and Restaurants in Great Britain*
- *Roget's Thesaurus*
- *The Stock Exchange Official Year Book*

Most organisations will provide you with information, provided it is not confidential or sensitive. Organisations that you may wish to contact in order to gain information are:

- AA or RAC
- Local Authority
- Chamber of Commerce
- Citizens Advice Bureau
- British Telecommunications plc
- Post Office
- English Tourist Board
- Inland Revenue
- The Department of Trade and Industry
- The Consumers' Association

If you have been asked to locate and abstract information you will find a variety of sources that may be of help to you. When you discover the information needed you will be required to present your findings using one of a variety of methods, but if at any time you are tempted to merely copy the relevant information you must be sure that you are within the copyright laws or you will be committing an unlawful offence.

# ■ DIY 15.1.9

Produce work from a pre-recorded tape. This must be completed within 2.5 hours and should be error free. If you are unsure of an instruction you are allowed to ask for clarification. Your evidence must include material from tapes that have been dictated under normal working conditions by different speakers, at different speeds and with varying recording qualities. Evidence that you have been provided with salient points that needed organising and expanding into comprehensive summaries and integration of research material must also be provided.

## Knowledge and understanding question bank

1 How do you go about interpreting instructions?
2 When and how would you use manuals?
3 What aspects of safety and hygiene should you consider when using audio equipment?
4 What are your organisation's house rules for the use of audio?
5 What information sources would you use that are internal and external to your organisation?
6 Explain what business and technical vocabulary you use.
7 What do you understand by the term 'grammatical structures'?
8 Explain the use of dictionaries, reference materials and glossaries.
9 What is the Data Protection Registrar?
10 What is copyright law?

## Claiming credit

For Element 15.1 you must prove that instructions and text are taken from variable speech, speeds and quality, up to 150 wpm, under workplace conditions. Recordings must include those that are reproduced verbatim and those which require expanding into required documents. You must also prove that you can deal with unfamiliar vocabulary, complex grammatical structures and numerical information competently. Statutory and non-statutory legal and regulatory requirements such as health and safety, equal opportunities, copyright and data protection requirements must also be taken into account.

The following work products are potential sources of evidence:

- documents produced
- copies of source material

Once you have completed your final assessment, you will need to write in your record book or folder how, when and what you have done to prove that you are competent.

The following statement is an example of how one trainee completed this claim:

*As the administration assistant for Coopers & Co I am responsible for typing up the audio tapes for 3 partners. On some occasions I pass the tapes to one of the juniors but always make sure the work is proof-read before passing to the partners for signature. I process letters, reports, memos, notices, articles and lists using the audio equipment and my personal computer. All work is protected with a password. The tapes contain dictation from 3 different partners with variable quality speech and speed, working under different workplace conditions. Uncertainties are clarified with the relevant partner and instructions interpreted and actioned properly. On some occasions additional information, such as account numbers or clients' details, have to be located and integrated into the material. One of the partners prefers to give brief notes and details for me to expand into the finished document or correspondence. When unfamiliar vocabulary, complex grammatical structures and numerical information are used I always produce a draft copy so that the partner can check it and make amendments if necessary.*

# Element 15.2
# PRODUCE AND PRESENT DOCUMENTS USING A KEYBOARD

## Performance criteria

1 Error-free documents of approximately 1,500 words are produced, under workplace conditions, from selected material, in 2.5 hours

2 Selected presentation conveys the information effectively, appropriately and in accordance with house style

3 Spelling, grammar and punctuation are consistent and correct

4 The language, style and tone of the finished document are suited to its purpose

5 Work practices are in accordance with legal and regulatory requirements and organisation's procedures

6 Security and confidentiality of information are maintained

**7** Work is achieved within agreed deadlines

**8** Documents are finished for presentation and appropriate routes determined

**The performance criteria for Elements 13.2, 14.2 and 15.2 are exactly the same. Complete Element 13.2 to complete Unit 13, 14 or 15.**

# INDEX